A TRANSLATOR'S GUIDE
TO SELECTIONS
FROM THE FIRST FIVE BOOKS
OF THE OLD TESTAMENT

Helps for Translators Series

Technical Helps:

Old Testament Quotations in the
New Testament
Short Bible Reference System
New Testament Index
The Theory and Practice of
Translation
Bible Index

Fauna and Flora of the Bible
Marginal Notes for the Old
Testament
Marginal Notes for the New
Testament
The Practice of Translating

Handbooks:

A Translator's Handbook on . . .

Leviticus
the Book of Joshua
the Book of Ruth
the Book of Psalms
the Book of Amos
the Books of Obadiah and Micah
the Book of Jonah
the Books of Nahum, Habakkuk,
and Zephaniah
the Gospel of Matthew
the Gospel of Mark
the Gospel of Luke
the Gospel of John

the Acts of the Apostles
Paul's Letter to the Romans
Paul's First Letter to the
Corinthians
Paul's Letter to the Galatians
Paul's Letter to the Ephesians
Paul's Letter to the Philippians
Paul's Letters to the Colossians
and to Philemon
Paul's Letters to the Thessalonians
the Letter to the Hebrews
the First Letter from Peter
the Letters of John

Guides:

A Translator's Guide to . . .

Selections from the First Five
Books of the Old Testament
Selected Psalms
the Gospel of Mark
the Gospel of Luke
Paul's Second Letter to the
Corinthians

Paul's Letters to Timothy and to
Titus
the Letters to James, Peter, and
Jude
the Revelation to John

HELPS FOR TRANSLATORS

A TRANSLATOR'S GUIDE
to
SELECTIONS
from the
FIRST FIVE BOOKS
of the
OLD TESTAMENT

by
HEBER F. PEACOCK

UNITED BIBLE SOCIETIES
London, New York,
Stuttgart

Books in the series of **Helps for Translators** may be ordered from a
national Bible Society, or from either of the following centers:

United Bible Societies
European Production Fund
D-7000 Stuttgart 80
Postfach 81 03 40
West Germany

United Bible Societies
1865 Broadway
New York, New York 10023
U.S.A.

L.C. Catalog Card Number: 82-130980

ISBN 0-8267-0298-8

ABS-1992-200-2,450-CM-5-102764

Contents

Preface

This volume, *A Translator's Guide to Selections from the First Five Books of the Old Testament*, represents another in the series of *Helps for Translators* published by the United Bible Societies. Other volumes in the series are listed on the page facing the title page of this book.

A *Guide* is intended to give the kind of concise information that will directly aid the translator in making a satisfactory rendering of difficult passages. It also provides suggestions as to possible and appropriate translations. The discussion is organized according to the order of the TEV text. *Handbooks*, on the other hand, are far more extensive in that they explain the background of the text, textual difficulties, interpretation, vocabulary analysis, and discourse structure. They also include more analyses of translation problems and provide more numerous suggestions as to how these matters may be dealt with. Both the *Guides* and the *Handbooks* are designed to provide the translator with the basic information needed to prepare a translation that is faithful to the meaning of the original and has a style that is appropriate for conveying the message to the reader in his own language.

This *Guide*, however, has a special function. Many language communities have never had a complete Old Testament translation, and to engage in such a project usually requires much time and dedicated effort. Therefore national Bible Societies may wish to publish in these languages a series of selections from the Old Testament. In this way, speakers of the language will have some basic material in their hands while waiting for the completion of the entire Old Testament. This *Guide* discusses passages from the Pentateuch which may be included in such a series. For those communities that prefer to work immediately on complete books of the Old Testament, this *Guide* may also be of some value, for it will help the translator through typical problems that occur in each book of the Pentateuch, and the solutions may then be applied to similar contexts elsewhere in the same book.

Other *Guides* and *Handbooks* are in preparation, covering material from both the Old and the New Testaments. The UBS Subcommittee on Translations will welcome any suggestions for making these *Helps for Translators* more useful and effective.

Abbreviations Used in This Volume

Books of the Bible:

2 Chr	2 Chronicles
Deut	Deuteronomy
Exo	Exodus
Ezek	Ezekiel
Gen	Genesis
Isa	Isaiah
Lev	Leviticus
Num	Numbers

Other Abbreviations:

NEB	New English Bible
RSV	Revised Standard Bible
TEV	Today's English Version
UBS	United Bible Societies

Translating the Pentateuch

This Translator's Guide to Selections from the First Five Books of the Old Testament is essentially a brief commentary on selected passages from Genesis, Exodus, Leviticus, Numbers, and Deuteronomy. These five books are commonly called the "Pentateuch." The Guide is designed to give translators the information they need for preparing translations on these books. The passages themselves have been selected on the basis of what would be most suitable for translation and inclusion in the publication of a shorter Old Testament that would be about one-third the length of the entire Old Testament. The choice of passages to be included grew out of several years of discussion among translation consultants and committees of the United Bible Societies; decisions were based in part on the examination of a number of published shorter Old Testaments. The passages were selected on the basis of what would be most important and useful for an understanding of the Old Testament.

In many language situations around the world, particularly where the number of potential readers is small, practical considerations make it impossible to consider the publication of a complete Old Testament in the near future. The translation and publication of a series of Old Testament selections will provide the community with the opportunity of reading and studying the most important parts of the Old Testament. The publication of such a shorter Old Testament should not, however, be seen as a means of denying access to the full range of Scriptures. Rather, it must be understood as a step toward the publication of a complete Bible as soon as practical considerations make it possible.

This Guide comments on the biblical material, section by section. The Good News Bible, known as Today's English Version (TEV), and the Revised Standard Version (RSV) are printed in parallel columns. The reason for this should be well understood. RSV is printed as a rather literal and formal translation of the original Hebrew. This makes it possible for the translator to gain some insights into the form, structure, and message of the Hebrew text, which in the final analysis must serve as the basis for any translation. TEV, on the other hand, is presented as a dynamic translation of the original Hebrew. This enables the translator to understand the meaning more clearly and to gain some insights into the kind of restructuring that may be required in any good translation. To say this briefly, although the Hebrew text is the final authority, RSV will serve the translator as a base and TEV will serve him as a model as he struggles to find the right way to express the biblical message in his language.

Neither RSV nor TEV should be translated directly. The translator should study both, interpret the real meaning of the text, understand why changes in form may be necessary, and present the message in the most suitable and meaningful form. The translator should begin each section by reading carefully through the RSV text and the TEV text, noting the differences and trying to understand the essential meaning. He should then read the comments on each verse, noting that these have been made on the basis of the TEV text. He may find it helpful to make his own notes on difficult problems of interpretation and translation. He should then be able to start translating the first verse of the section, making use of the comments as he faces interpretive or translational problems.

In addition to the RSV and TEV texts, the translator should have before him copies of other Bibles that may be available. He will also want to make use of commentaries, Bible dictionaries, and other helps for translators. His UBS translations consultant can advise him about the kinds of helps that would be most useful.

In order to indicate to the reader of a set of selections the general content of portions that have been omitted, explanatory sentences have been provided. These also serve as a bridge from one section to the next. Introductions have also been added as examples of the kind that may be used to introduce each book in a shorter Bible. Both the introductions and the bridge sentences are given in italics in this Guide.

Translation is hard work, but it has great rewards. As the translator deepens his own understanding of the Word of God, he can rejoice that he has a part in freeing the Word to speak its message clearly to his people. He will want to thank God and ask for further guidance as he struggles with translation problems in his effort to make the Word so clear that everyone who reads will understand.

GENESIS

THE NAME OF THE BOOK

Book titles often present problems to translators. This is particularly true in new language situations in which there is no established tradition in regard to the names of the biblical books. In
Hebrew the name of this book is simply the first word, which can be
translated "in the beginning." The name "Genesis" comes from the Greek
translation, and it has the meaning "origin" or "beginning" (of the
world). In some traditions the book is called "The First Book of
Moses," but the translator is advised to use an expression that will
be more descriptive if this is possible. Suggestions would include "The
Book of Beginnings," "The Beginning of the World," or "The Book of
Early History."

INTRODUCTION

The name Genesis *means "origin." The book tells about the creation
of the universe, the origin of mankind, the beginning of sin and suffering in the world, and about God's way of dealing with mankind.*
*While this book tells about people, it is first and foremost an
account of what God has done. It begins with the affirmation that God
created the universe, and it ends with a promise that God will continue
to show his concern for his people. Throughout the book the main character is God, who judges and punishes those who do wrong, leads and
helps his people, and shapes their history. This ancient book was written
to record the story of a people's faith and to help keep that faith
alive.*

CHAPTER 1

SECTION HEADING

The Story of Creation (1.1—2.4a): "How the World Was Created,"
"How God Made the World."

1.1	TEV	RSV
	In the beginning, when God created the universe,^{a}	In the beginning God created^a the heavens and the earth.

^aIn the beginning...the universe;   ^aOr *When God began to create*
or In the beginning God created
the universe; *or* When God began
to create the universe.

In the beginning: it is important that the word chosen to translate "beginning" be understood by the reader as referring to the time
when the universe came into existence. In some languages it may be
necessary to use "Before the world (or, the universe) existed," "When
all things began," or "In the beginning of this world."
when God created: created may have to be translated with "made"
or "put together," although the Hebrew word is used only of the creative
act of God.
the universe: in Hebrew, literally "the heavens and the earth"
(RSV), but this is the Hebrew way of describing everything that has
been made, the total orderly universe that God created, and not just
the sky and the earth. In some languages, "the earth, the sky, and
everything else there is."
As you will note, there are different interpretations of this
verse. It may be taken as a kind of title for what follows, but more
than likely it is an introduction to verse 3 in the sense that verses
1 and 2 describe the chaotic situation that existed before God acted
in creation. If this interpretation is accepted, one would translate
When God began to create the universe, as in the TEV note.

1.2	TEV	RSV

TEV	RSV
the earth was formless and deso-late. The raging ocean that cov-ered everything was engulfed in total darkness, and the power of God^b was moving over the water.	The earth was without form and void, and darkness was upon the face of the deep; and the Spirit^b of God was moving over the face of the waters.
^bthe power of God; *or* the spirit of God; *or* a wind from God; *or* an awesome wind.	^bOr *wind*

the earth: a word should be used that refers to the whole created
world and not just to the dry ground. Water and land are still mixed in
a chaotic state, as is seen in what follows.
was formless: "had not yet been given any shape or form," "had
not yet been put in order," "was still unformed."
desolate: "empty," "not inhabited," but the sense may well be parallel to "formless," in which case the two words would have the meaning
"totally unformed," "without shape or form."
The raging ocean: literally "the deep" (RSV). The Hebrew word emphasizes the underlying idea that the mighty ocean (for the Hebrews the
water in the oceans and the water under the land) is always threatening
to destroy mankind and the world in which he lives. The ocean (or the
water) should be described as "storming" or "threatening." In some
languages it may be possible to speak of "the angry ocean."
that covered everything: the literal "the face of the deep" (RSV)

refers particularly to the surface of the water, but water was everywhere and there was nothing that was not covered.

was engulfed in: "was covered by." The literal "darkness was upon"
(RSV) expresses the message in an active form. However, it may be wise
to use as strong a statement as possible to indicate that the water
which covered everything was itself covered by total darkness.

total darkness: every effort should be made to find a way to express the totality of darkness. A word like "shadow" or even "night"
may not be adequate. Perhaps it will be necessary to say "there was
absolutely no light anywhere."

the power of God: the Hebrew word translated "power" may mean
"wind," "spirit," or "power." Even the Hebrew word translated "of God"
may have the meaning "from God," "of God," or "awesome, mighty, powerful." This leads to various interpretations, but the translator is advised to choose between the alternatives presented in the text and in
the note of TEV. If verses 1 and 2 are seen as introductory to the
creative act in verse 3, the most likely meaning would be "a mighty
wind."

was moving: the meaning of the Hebrew verb is not certain. It is
traditionally translated "hover," but the reference may be to any kind
of motion. The choice will depend upon the word used to translate "wind/
spirit."

water: the Hebrew word is a plural form, but there is no reason
to retain the plural in translation as RSV does.

1.3	TEV	RSV
Then God commanded, "Let there be light"—and light appeared.	And God said, "Let there be light"; and there was light.	

God commanded: "God spoke this command," "God said and commanded."
Note that in English the construction with "Let" is a command and not
permission.

"Let there be light": it would be possible to use indirect discourse: "God commanded that the light appear." But in this context it
is probably much wiser to retain direct address, since there is a heavy
emphasis upon the spoken word of God as creating.

light appeared: "was there," "came into being," or even "began to
shine." What is needed here is not a word for the sun but a general
word for light. If such a word does not exist in the language, perhaps
some way can be found to describe daylight, the light of day, or even
the day. This command may be expressed in several ways: "There is to be
light," "Light is to appear," "Light must now shine," "Light, shine."

1.4	TEV	RSV
God was pleased with what he saw. Then he separated the light from the darkness,	And God saw that the light was good; and God separated the light from the darkness.	

was pleased with what he saw: literally "saw that the light was
good" (RSV), but the sense is not that the light had a certain quality,

but that it was good as God viewed it, "he thought it was good," "he was pleased with it." In some languages it may be necessary to say "God saw the light and was pleased with it."

separated the light from the darkness: this may be a difficult idea to express. The thought is that even when light came into being it was at first mixed with darkness, and God put the light in one place and the darkness in another. Perhaps this may be expressed by "God caused the light to shine at one time and the darkness to appear at another time," or "God made a difference between the light and the darkness, and he set a time for the light to shine."

1.5 TEV	RSV
and he named the light "Day" and the darkness "Night." Evening passed and morning came—that was the first day.	God called the light Day, and the darkness he called Night. And there was evening and there was morning, one day.

named: "gave a name to," "called by the name."

Evening passed and morning: the order should be preserved if possible, because the Hebrews considered the full day to begin at sundown one evening and extend to sundown the following evening. In most translations a footnote should indicate that the Hebrews held this view.

1.6-7 TEV	RSV
Then God commanded, "Let there be a dome to divide the water and to keep it in two separate places"—and it was done. So God made a dome, and it separated the water under it from the water above it.	And God said, "Let there be a firmament in the midst of the waters, and let it separate the waters from the waters." 7 And God made the firmament and separated the waters which were under the firmament from the waters which were above the firmament. And it was so.

Let there be: this command may be expressed in several ways. See verse 3.

dome: it may be difficult to find a word to translate this term. The Hebrews thought of the sky as a kind of inverted bowl made out of hard material. It was thought of as strong enough to keep the waters above it—that is, the waters in the sky—from coming down upon the earth to flood it. It may be necessary to use some such word as "skin" or "plate" to describe this dome or vault. If necessary, perhaps some word can be used which would describe the bowl-like shape of the sky. The English word "firmament" (RSV) expresses the idea that the sky is a solid structure.

keep it in two separate places: this is what is meant by the literal "separate the waters from the waters" (RSV); the dome prevents the water above the sky from coming down and flooding the earth.

and it was done: the Hebrew text places these words at the end of verse 7, but the Greek translation and the usage of the same word in verses 9,11,15,20,24, and 30 make it likely that it should be placed at this point. (That is why TEV has combined verses 6 and 7.) Verse 7 then becomes a kind of summary of the creative act described in verse 6, and So means "In this way."

1.8 TEV	RSV
He named the dome "Sky." Evening passed and morning came—that was the second day.	And God called the firmament Heaven. And there was evening and there was morning, a second day.

named: see verse 5.
Evening passed and morning: see verse 5.

1.9 TEV	RSV
Then God commanded, "Let the water below the sky come together in one place, so that the land will appear"—and it was done.	And God said, "Let the waters under the heavens be gathered together into one place, and let the dry land appear." And it was so.

Let the water: see verse 3.
water below the sky: keep in mind that up to this point nothing but two bodies of water can be "seen," the one above the sky and the one below. The next event describes the creative act for the water-covered mass below the sky. In many languages it may be necessary to describe the water below the sky as "the water over the earth," "the water covering the earth."
so that the land will appear: the point is that once the water is pushed back into the sea, it would no longer cover the land.
land: the Hebrew word is sometimes translated "dry land" (RSV), but this may convey the idea of land which has absolutely no water. The point is that the continents (with their rivers and lakes) are separated from the great body of water, the sea.
and it was done: see verses 6-7.

1.10 TEV	RSV
He named the land "Earth," and the water which had come together he named "Sea." And God was pleased with what he saw.	God called the dry land Earth, and the waters that were gathered together he called Seas. And God saw that it was good.

named: see verse 5.
Sea: if no word for Sea is known, a descriptive phrase may be used such as "the large body of water covering most of the earth's surface." The Hebrew word is plural in form, but it does not necessarily have a plural meaning; it may be used to include all the water.
was pleased: see verse 4.

[7]

1.11   TEV   RSV
Then he commanded, "Let the earth   And God said, "Let the earth put
produce all kinds of plants,   forth vegetation, plants yielding
those that bear grain and those   seed, and fruit trees bearing
that bear fruit"—and it was done.   fruit in which is their seed,
                                       each according to its kind, upon
                                       the earth." And it was so.

    Let the earth produce: "The earth is to bring forth," "The earth
is to cause to grow," "The ground must make things grow," "Plants must
grow from the ground."
    all kinds of plants: this is intended to include all plant life,
which the Hebrews divided into two categories: plants that bear grain
(RSV "seed"), that is, the grasses, and those that bear fruit, that is,
trees and bushes. A literal translation of "their own kinds" and "its
kind" hides this fact.
    those that bear fruit: a literal translation of the word "trees"
obscures the fact that all fruit-bearing plants, including bushes and
trees, are being described.
    and it was done: as in verses 3,6, and 9, the emphasis falls on
the fact that God's command is immediately carried out. When he spoke,
it happened.

1.12   TEV   RSV
So the earth produced all kinds   The earth brought forth vegetation,
of plants, and God was pleased   plants yielding seed according to
with what he saw.   their own kinds, and trees bearing
                                       fruit in which is their seed, each
                                       according to its kind. And God saw
                                       that it was good.

    So: the verse is seen as a summary of the preceding command and
fulfillment (see verse 6).
    God was pleased: see verse 4.

1.13   TEV   RSV
Evening passed and morning came—   And there was evening and there
that was the third day.   was morning, a third day.

    Evening passed and morning came: see verse 5.

1.14   TEV   RSV
    Then God commanded, "Let   And God said, "Let there be
lights appear in the sky to   lights in the firmament of the
separate day from night and to   heavens to separate the day from
show the time when days, years,   the night; and let them be for
and religious festivals^c begin;   signs and for seasons and for days
                                       and years,

^creligious festivals; or seasons.

[8]

lights: a word is needed here for "objects that produce light." The word could refer to a lamp but here must include the sun, the moon, and the stars. If no general word can be found, it may be necessary to use some descriptive phrase.

in the sky: literally "in the dome of the sky" (see verses 6 and 7). In some languages it may be necessary to use "above the earth" or something similar.

to separate: the same Hebrew word is used here as in verse 4, and it may be necessary in some languages to use a different formula, since day and night are separated in verses 4-5. One possibility would be to translate "to shine during the day and to shine during the night."

and to show the time when days, years, and religious festivals begin: literally "and they shall be signs," but "to show" or "to indicate" is what is intended.

religious festivals: although it is quite probable that this is the meaning of the Hebrew word, some people interpret it as meaning "seasons" (RSV), as in the TEV footnote. "Religious festivals" might be translated "special days on which to worship God," "special days for worship."

1.15   TEV   RSV
they will shine in the sky to give   and let them be lights in the
light to the earth"—and it was   firmament of the heavens to
done.   give light upon the earth." And
                                          it was so.

they will shine in the sky: literally "and let them be lights in the dome of the sky" (see RSV), but the words must be translated in such a way as to indicate that the lights are placed in the sky to shine upon the earth.

1.16   TEV   RSV
So God made the two larger lights,   And God made the two great lights,
the sun to rule over the day and   the greater light to rule the day,
the moon to rule over the night;   and the lesser light to rule the
he also made the stars.   night; he made the stars also.

the two larger lights: the Hebrew has "the two great lights, the greater light to rule the day, and the lesser light to rule the night" (RSV). Although the word "great" may have other components, it may be necessary to use the word which refers to size or to strength. If it is not possible to say something like "the two big lights...the larger (or the stronger)...the smaller (or the weaker)," it may be necessary to do what TEV has done and identify the larger light as the sun and the smaller light as the moon, which is the intended meaning.

to rule over: "rule over," "control," "govern"—it may be difficult to find a word which can convey the idea that the sun rules during the day; in this case it may be necessary to speak of the sun "being the power" during the day. It may even be necessary to reduce the terminology to "shine during the day...shine during the night."

[9]

Since, however, this would repeat verses 14-15, it might be better to find some way of speaking of the sun being in control during the day and the moon being in control during the night. One might speak of "being important" or "being like a chief, a king."

1.17 TEV	RSV
He placed the lights in the sky to shine on the earth,	And God set them in the firmament of the heavens to give light upon the earth,

He placed: if possible, in verse 16 the distinction should be maintained that God made the sun, the moon, and the stars; in verse 17 the emphasis should be that he placed them in the sky.

the sky: literally "the dome of the sky" (see RSV).

1.18 TEV	RSV
to rule over the day and the night, and to separate light from darkness. And God was pleased with what he saw.	to rule over the day and over the night, and to separate the light from the darkness. And God saw that it was good.

This verse includes elements of verses 14 and 16 and should present no particular difficulties to the translator.

1.19 TEV	RSV
Evening passed and morning came— that was the fourth day.	And there was evening and there was morning, a fourth day.

Evening passed and morning came—that was the fourth day: see verse 5.

1.20 TEV	RSV
Then God commanded, "Let the water be filled with many kinds of living beings, and let the air be filled with birds."	And God said, "Let the waters bring forth swarms of living creatures, and let birds fly above the earth across the firmament of the heavens."

Let: once again, as in verse 3, this should be formulated as a command and not as permission: "The waters are to be (must be) filled with." In some languages it may be necessary to translate "Then God said, 'I command the water to be filled with,'" "...'The water must be filled with.'"

be filled: this obviously does not mean that the waters are to be so full of living beings that there is no space left. The point is that there are to be many of these creatures in the waters.

many kinds of living beings: The Hebrew uses an expression which emphasizes the large number of creatures. "Living beings" is one way of

expressing what is needed here: a general reference to all kinds of
creatures which live in water. This obviously includes the fish, but
also such creatures as whales, seals, squids, octopuses, clams, etc.

let the air be filled with birds: literally "let birds fly above
the earth across the dome of the heavens" (see RSV). The point is that
the birds are created so that they might fly in the space between the
earth and the dome.

1.21 TEV	RSV
So God created the great sea monsters, all kinds of creatures that live in the water, and all kinds of birds. And God was pleased with what he saw.	So God created the great sea monsters and every living creature that moves, with which the waters swarm, according to their kinds, and every winged bird according to its kind. And God saw that it was good.

So God created: this is a summary of verse 20. God created three
kinds of animals: sea monsters, other water creatures, and birds.

the great sea monsters: this refers not only to the large sea
creatures like whales, but also to certain dragon-like creatures. If
possible a general expression should be used which could include all of
these, for example, "the big water creatures that live in the sea." The
Hebrew word may also mean "serpent," "snake," and some have assumed
that the word may refer to crocodiles or alligators, but this is less
likely.

all kinds of creatures that live in the water: this represents
more directly the literal "every living creature that moves, with which
the waters swarm, according to their kinds" (RSV).

1.22 TEV	RSV
He blessed them all and told the creatures that live in the water to reproduce and to fill the sea, and he told the birds to increase in number.	And God blessed them, saying, "Be fruitful and multiply and fill the waters in the seas, and let birds multiply on the earth."

He blessed them: this is always a difficult idea to convey. The
point being made here is that God spoke words to encourage and to help
the things he had created. The actual blessing is probably found in the
words that are used to tell the creatures to reproduce and fill the sea.
In some languages it may be necessary to use "caused good things to
happen to them because of what he said," or even "spoke words that did
them good," "said, 'I want all to go well for you.'"

reproduce: literally "Be fruitful and multiply" (RSV), but with
the sense of "have many young."

fill the sea: once again, the meaning is that there will be many
water creatures in the sea, not that it will be completely full.

to increase in number: literally "multiply on the earth" (RSV).
But the term "earth" is used to distinguish the birds from the water
creatures; so in most languages "earth" should not be translated, since

birds are not thought of as living primarily on the earth. The sense is once again that the birds should reproduce and have many young, have large families.

1.23   TEV   RSV
Evening passed and morning came—   And there was evening and there
that was the fifth day.   was morning, a fifth day.

Evening passed and morning came—that was the fifth day: see verse 5.

1.24   TEV   RSV
Then God commanded, "Let the   And God said, "Let the earth
earth produce all kinds of animal   bring forth living creatures
life: domestic and wild, large and   according to their kinds: cattle
small"—and it was done.   and creeping things and beasts
                                       of the earth according to their
                                       kinds." And it was so.

Let the earth produce: "Let the earth cause animals to appear." In some languages it may be necessary to reverse the emphasis. For example, "Let living animals be born upon the earth."
all kinds of animal life: this is what is intended by the more literal "living beings," "living creatures" (RSV). It should be kept in mind that the verse intends to cover the totality of animal life. Choices of vocabulary should be made in line with this idea.
domestic: "domesticated animals," "animals tamed by man," "animals that people take care of," "animals that live with people."
wild: literally "animals of the earth" (see RSV), but the word is intended to cover all kinds of animals that have not been domesticated, and not just the fierce animals like lions and tigers.
large and small: the Hebrew word here translated "small" is sometimes translated "creeping things" (RSV), but the reference is not only to snakes and lizards, but to insects, small rodents, and all other kinds of small animals, in contrast to the larger animals. All animal life is divided into three categories: domestic animals, large wild animals, and small wild animals.

1.25   TEV   RSV
So God made them all, and he was   And God made the beasts of the
pleased with what he saw.   earth according to their kinds
                                          and the cattle according to
                                          their kinds, and everything
                                          that creeps upon the ground
                                          according to its kind. And God
                                          saw that it was good.

made them all: the TEV has chosen to summarize in this way rather than repeat what is found in verse 24, all kinds of animal life:

domestic and wild, large and small. Whether the translator chooses to repeat or not will depend upon the function of repetition in his language.

1.26   TEV

Then God said, "And now we will make human beings; they will be like us and resemble us. They will have power over the fish, the birds, and all animals, domestic and wild,^{d} large and small."

^{d}*One ancient translation* animals, domestic and wild; *Hebrew* domestic animals and all the earth.

       RSV

Then God said, "Let us make man in our image, after our likeness; and let them have dominion over the fish of the sea, and over the birds of the air, and over the cattle, and over all the earth, and over every creeping thing that creeps upon the earth."

we will make human beings; they will be like us and resemble us: the first person plurals used in this verse present certain problems of interpretation and of translation. The plural may indicate that God is conferring with his heavenly court (that is, his angels); but since the word for "God" in Hebrew is a plural form, the plural pronoun forms may also mean that God is, so to speak, conferring with himself. If the target language allows it, it is probably best simply to use an undefined plural, as TEV and most English translations do. But some translations take the plurals as referring only to God and translate "I will make...be like me and resemble me."

human beings: although the Hebrew word "man" is singular, it is often used in a collective sense; it is quite clear that "man" is collective here, since the pronoun following it is a plural. At this point the reference is not to the first man, Adam, but to mankind in general—human beings, people.

they will be like us and resemble us: literally "in our image, after our likeness" (RSV). The exact nature of the likeness is not stated, and although two words are used in Hebrew, it is not easy to make a sharp distinction between them. In many languages it may be necessary to use something like "they will be like us and look like us," or even to compress into one comparison, for example, "they will be like us."

have power over: "rule," "have control over."

domestic and wild: although the standard Hebrew text has literally "over all the earth" (RSV), there is good reason to believe that the original form is preserved in one ancient translation, which reads "all the animals of the earth," as in verse 24. As we have seen, this means the wild animals.

1.27   TEV

So God created human beings, making them to be like himself. He created them male and female,

       RSV

So God created man in his own image, in the image of God he created him; male and female he created them.

    human beings: once again, the singular word "man" refers to human beings in general, as is seen in what follows.

    like himself: the Hebrew literally has "in his own image, in the image of God" (RSV).

    He created them male and female: that is, God created some human beings who were male and some who were female.

1.28 TEV	RSV
blessed them, and said, "Have many children, so that your descend- ants will live all over the earth and bring it under their control. I am putting you in charge of the fish, the birds, and all the wild animals.	And God blessed them, and God said to them, "Be fruitful and multiply, and fill the earth and subdue it; and have dominion over the fish of the sea and over the birds of the air and over every living thing that moves upon the earth."

    blessed them: see verse 22.

    Have many children: literally "Be fruitful and multiply" (RSV).

    your descendants: "your children and your children's children."

    live all over the earth: literally "fill the earth" (RSV), but as in verse 22, this is not understood literally but in the sense of living everywhere.

    bring it under their control: although the original is a command, literally "subdue it" (RSV), the clear intention of the Hebrew is to state that, by having many children, it will be possible for human beings to bring the things on earth under their control; the control refers particularly to plant and animal life rather than the forces of nature such as wind or lightning.

    I am putting you in charge of: the you is a plural referring to the created human beings and their descendants. "Put in charge of" has the sense of "take control of," "rule over," "manage," "be master over." In some languages one may have to say more directly "I am telling you to give orders to."

    all the wild animals: although there are some textual problems in the verse, this is the probable meaning. Note, however, that some translations interpret this to mean "all the living things that move upon the earth" (see RSV), meaning all animal life (see verse 24).

1.29 TEV	RSV
I have provided all kinds of grain and all kinds of fruit for you to eat;	And God said, "Behold, I have given you every plant yielding seed which is upon the face of all the earth, and every tree with seed in its fruit; you shall have them for food.

    provided: "given you," "made available for you."

    all kinds of grain: this is the meaning of the literal "every plant yielding seed which is upon the face of all the earth" (RSV). Grain refers to seeds that can be eaten and which are harvested from grasses.

all kinds of fruit: literally "every tree with seed in its fruit"
(RSV), but it is very obvious that the focus is upon the edible fruit
which is made available for the use of human beings.

1.30 TEV	RSV
but for all the wild animals and for all the birds I have provided grass and leafy plants for food"— and it was done.	And to every beast of the earth, and to every bird of the air, and to everything that creeps on the earth, everything that has the breath of life, I have given every green plant for food." And it was so.

wild animals: the Hebrew includes wild animals, both large and
small, and in some languages it may be wise to indicate this. For example, "the large animals and the small animals."
    grass and leafy plants: literally "all green plants" (see RSV),
but in focus is the kind of plants that animals eat, in contrast to the
kind of food human beings can eat, as mentioned in verse 29.

1.31 TEV	RSV
God looked at everything he had made, and he was very pleased. Evening passed and morning came— that was the sixth day.	And God saw everything that he had made, and behold, it was very good. And there was evening and there was morning, a sixth day.

very pleased: the verse parallels the statements made earlier in
the chapter, but there is a strong emphasis in this verse that God was
very pleased indeed.

CHAPTER   2

2.1 TEV	RSV
And so the whole universe was completed.	Thus the heavens and the earth were finished, and all the host of them.

And so: the Hebrew has only "and," but the connecting link used
to carry on the story will have to be chosen to fit the pattern of the
receptor language. The Hebrew "and" will often need to be translated
as "when," "after a while," or "therefore," according to the way stories
are told in the receptor language. Here the "and" introduces a summary.
    the whole universe: literally "the heaven and the earth and all
the multitude of them" (see RSV). As in chapter 1.1, the reference is
to the total universe, including sky, earth, sea, animals, and mankind.

2.2   TEV   RSV
By the seventh day God finished   And on the seventh day God
what he had been doing and stopped   finished his work which he had
working.   done, and he rested on the
                                         seventh day from all his work
                                         which he had done.

          By the seventh day: literally "on the seventh day" (RSV), and it
is possible to translate in this way. But in some languages it may be
necessary to translate "on the sixth day," as some early translations
do, to prevent the possibility of understanding the text to mean that
some work was done on the seventh day.
          finished: "completed," "did all his work," "brought his work to
an end."
          stopped working: the literal Hebrew is a bit redundant: "stopped
working on the seventh day from all his work which he had done" (see
RSV). Although the Hebrew verb for "stopped working" is sometimes
translated "rested," the idea should be avoided that God was tired and
therefore had to stop to rest. The point is the cessation of activity,
not the recovery of strength.

2.3   TEV   RSV
He blessed the seventh day and   So God blessed the seventh day
set it apart as a special day,   and hallowed it, because on it
because by that day he had com-   God rested from all his work
pleted his creation^e and stopped   which he had done in creation.
working.

^{e}by that day he had completed his
 creation; or on that day he completed his creation.

          blessed: this word, as always, is difficult to translate. Perhaps
something like "said that it would have his favor" would fit here, or
even "made it important," "spoke well of." See 1.22.
          set it apart as a special day: literally "made it holy" (see RSV),
but the idea of "holy" is primarily that of setting something apart for
special use, and in particular for God's use, or in this case, "for
man's use in worshiping God." One might translate "set it apart as a
special day of worship."
          by that day: as is indicated in the note, the more literal form
would be "on that day." See verse 2.
          his creation: this refers to God's act of creating and not just to
the universe that he had created; that is, this is an event, "his creating."

2.4a   TEV   RSV
And that is how the universe was   These are the generations of
created.   the heavens and the earth when
                                         they were created.

And that is how the universe was created: this is a summary of the creative activity and brings the story that begins in 1.1 to a close.

that is how: "this is the story" of the creation. The Hebrew word "story" is sometimes translated "generations" (RSV). It seems also to have the sense of "a history," and that is how TEV has understood it.

universe: see 1.1.

SECTION HEADING

The Garden of Eden (2.4b-25): in many languages it may be necessary to say "God Plants a Garden in Eden" or something similar. Care should be taken to choose a word for "garden" that will suit the situation in verses 8-9. In other words, we are not dealing with a vegetable garden but with what might be called a park, an area planted with trees. It would also be possible to use a different type of section heading, for example, "God Creates Man and Woman."

2.4b   TEV   RSV
      When the LORD^x God made the   In the day that the LORD God
universe,   made the earth and the heavens,

^{x}THE LORD: *Where the Hebrew text has Yahweh, traditionally transliterated as Jehovah, this translation employs LORD with capital letters, following a usage which is widespread in English versions.*

When: literally "In the day that" (RSV), but the Hebrew frequently uses the term "day" in a very general sense to refer to any period of time. The time reference here is to the beginning of creation, before there were plants, as can be seen from verse 5. Most interpreters recognize that a new paragraph and a new section begin at 2.4b. It should be remembered that verse divisions are a very late addition to the Hebrew text.

the LORD God: note that the word LORD is in small capital letters. This is significant in that up to this point in the story only the word "God" has been used for God. The word LORD in small capital letters is an attempt to indicate that at this point we are dealing with the personal name of God—Yahweh God (sometimes referred to as Jehovah). Although a few translations retain the name Yahweh for God, most translations follow the early Greek translation in using a word for "Lord" or "Master" to replace the personal name, in line with the Jewish tendency to avoid use of the divine name. This is probably a wise choice for most translations, since a word like Yahweh may not easily be understood as a personal name. This will be particularly true if the dominant language tradition uses LORD. For the word "Lord," a word should be chosen that can represent the idea of master, ruler, chief.

[17]

In many languages it will not be possible to combine the two words as in English—"the Lord God"—and it may be necessary to find some way of speaking of "the Master who is God" or something similar. In any case, great care should be taken in the choice of this term, and the New Testament use of the word "Lord" for Christ should be kept in mind as the choice is made.

<u>universe</u>: see 1.1.

2.5	TEV	RSV
	there were no plants on the earth and no seeds had sprouted, because he had not sent any rain, and there was no one to cultivate the land;	when no plant of the field was yet in the earth and no herb of the field had yet sprung up—for the LORD God had not caused it to rain upon the earth, and there was no man to till the ground;

<u>there were no plants on the earth</u>: "no plants grew on the earth."
<u>no seeds had sprouted</u>: nothing had begun to grow from the earth.
<u>because</u>: it may be necessary to restructure this fairly long sentence. In some cases it might be possible to break the sentence at this point and begin a new sentence: "Nothing was growing on the earth because God had not sent any rain."
<u>sent any rain</u>: "caused it to rain" (RSV).
<u>cultivate</u>: the primary focus may well be upon digging up the ground and turning it over so the plants could grow. But "preparing the land" or "working the land" probably includes not only the plowing but also planting and caring for the crops.

2.6	TEV	RSV
	but water would come up from beneath the surface and water the ground.	but a mist^c went up from the earth and watered the whole face of the ground—

^cOr flood

<u>water</u>: the meaning of the Hebrew word is uncertain. It probably refers to a flood of water, but others understand it to mean "a mist" (RSV).
<u>would come up</u>: this formulation attempts to express the idea that this is a habitual thing. From time to time the water came up. In some languages it may be necessary to break the sentence after verse 5 and begin verse 6 with "At that time..." or "During that time water came up."
<u>and water the ground</u>: "and make the ground wet."

2.7	TEV	RSV
	Then the LORD God took some soil from the ground^f and formed a man^f out of it; he breathed	then the LORD God formed man of dust from the ground, and breathed into his nostrils the breath of

life-giving breath into his nos-   life; and man became a living
trils and the man began to live.   being.

f GROUND...MAN: *The Hebrew words for "man" and "ground" have similar sounds.*

soil: although the Hebrew word is often translated "dust" (RSV), it here has the sense of soil, earth, clay, and not that of a finely powdered dry soil.

formed: shaped, fashioned, worked, molded, as one shapes clay.

ground and formed a man: in Hebrew there is frequently a play on word sounds. Here the word for man ("adam") sounds very much like the word for ground ("adamah"). If the reader is to understand this word-play, it will be necessary to provide a note explaining this, as TEV has done, but it is not necessary to indicate the Hebrew sounds or words.

life-giving breath: this is what the literal "breath of life" (RSV) means. "Breath that gives life," "breath that causes man to live."

began to live: literally "became a living being" (RSV). This is sometimes translated quite literally as "man became a living soul." But the Hebrew word for "living soul" is used in the sense of "a person," as it frequently is in the Old Testament; man as a whole is given life; he becomes a living being. The Hebrew word "living (thing)" is used of animals in verse 19.

2.8	TEV	RSV
	Then the LORD God planted a garden in Eden, in the East, and there he put the man he had formed.	And the LORD God planted a garden in Eden, in the east; and there he put the man whom he had formed.

planted a garden: as noted above, the word chosen must refer to a space large enough to include a park-like area where trees are planted.

in Eden: although Eden is obviously a place name, as is clearly indicated here, the term "Garden of Eden" is frequently used (see verse 15). The location of Eden is unknown.

in the East: "the lands of the East." It may be that the receptor language requires more specification than this, in which case one could translate "in the lands east of Judah," "east of the Promised Land," or "east of Israel."

2.9	TEV	RSV
	He made all kinds of beautiful trees grow there and produce good fruit. In the middle of the garden stood the tree that gives life and the tree that gives knowledge of what is good and what is bad.*g*	And out of the ground the LORD God made to grow every tree that is pleasant to the sight and good for food, the tree of life also in the midst of the garden, and the tree of the knowledge of good and evil.

⁹knowledge of what is good and
what is bad; *or* knowledge of
everything.

He made all kinds of beautiful trees grow there and produce good
fruit: literally "The LORD God made to grow out of the ground every
tree that is pleasant to the sight and good for food" (see RSV). In
English "all kinds of beautiful trees" expresses the meaning more accurately than a literal translation. It is clear that the literal
"good for food" refers to the fruit which the trees produce and not to
the trees themselves. It is possible to say "made beautiful trees grow
and made them produce good fruit" or "made beautiful trees grow which
brought forth good fruit."

In the middle: the word does not necessarily mean "in the exact
geographical center" but rather "in the central area" of the garden.

stood: it is also possible to interpret "God placed."

the tree that gives life: literally "the tree of life" (RSV). The
point is that by eating fruit from this tree, unending life might be
obtained (see 3.23). One might translate "the tree that causes people
to live."

tree that gives knowledge of what is good and what is bad: here
again it is the eating of the fruit of the tree, as is seen in chapter
3, that gives knowledge of what is good and what is bad. In Hebrew
the words translated "good and bad" are sometimes used in an idiomatic
way to express "everything," and this may be the meaning here, as is
seen in the note. If this interpretation is followed, one might translate "the tree that makes everyone who eats its fruit know everything."

2.10   TEV   RSV
    A stream flowed in Eden and   A river flowed out of Eden to
watered the garden; beyond Eden   water the garden, and there it
it divided into four rivers.   divided and became four rivers.

stream: the same word may be used as at the end of the verse—
"river...rivers."

in Eden: although the Hebrew is somewhat compressed, it is quite
clear that the thought of the writer is that a stream flowed out of
the ground within the Garden of Eden, watered it, and then divided
into four rivers.

beyond Eden: literally "from there," but it is quite clear that
the writer intends to say that as the single river left the Garden of
Eden it divided into four rivers.

2.11   TEV   RSV
The first river is the Pishon;   The name of the first is Pishon;
it flows around the country of   it is the one which flows around
Havilah.   the whole land of Havilah, where
                                      there is gold;

The first river: "first" is only a matter of order, and not of
importance.

Pishon: the location of this river is not known. The point of the author is to show that the four large bodies of water thought to surround the four parts of the ancient world have their origin in the Garden of Eden. It is not possible to reconstruct the geographical view.

2.12 TEV	RSV
(Pure gold is found there and also rare perfume and precious stones.)	and the gold of that land is good; bdellium and onyx stone are there.

Pure gold: literally a part of verses 11 and 12—"11...where there is gold; 12 and the gold of that land is good." "Good" gold will refer to its purity, and one might translate "Gold of high (or good) quality is found there..."

rare perfume: literally "bdellium" (RSV). The meaning of the Hebrew word is not certain. It probably means a type of gum from a tree, a sort of aromatic resin used in perfume. Rather than transliterate a meaningless word, TEV has chosen to generalize with rare perfume.

precious stones: the Hebrew word is a clear reference to a type of precious stone, probably carnelian (RSV "onyx"), but since this is not generally known, it seems better to generalize and use the term "precious stones," "jewels." Parentheses or round brackets are used to show that this statement interrupts the description of the four rivers. It is a kind of explanation added by the writer.

2.13 TEV	RSV
The second river is the Gihon; it flows around the country of Cush.*h*	The name of the second river is Gihon; it is the one which flows around the whole land of Cush.

*h*Cush (of Mesopotamia); *or* Sudan.

Gihon: the location of this river is unknown.

the country of Cush: Cush is used elsewhere in the Bible to refer to the territory now known as Sudan. It is possible that the name is also applied to another Cush, possibly in the area of Mesopotamia. In any case, there is considerable uncertainty about the exact location of the territory named in this verse.

2.14 TEV	RSV
The third river is the Tigris, which flows east of Assyria, and the fourth river is the Euphrates.	And the name of the third river is Tigris, which flows east of Assyria. And the fourth river is the Euphrates.

the Tigris, which flows east of Assyria, and the fourth river is the Euphrates: these are the well-known rivers of Mesopotamia.

[21]

2.15	TEV	RSV
	Then the LORD God placed the man in the Garden of Eden to cultivate it and guard it.	The LORD God took the man and put him in the garden of Eden to till it and keep it.

to cultivate it: the Hebrew word is a general word that may apply to any kind of work in connection with taking care of a garden, including plowing the ground and caring for the plants and trees.

guard it: although the Hebrew has the idea of guard or protect, there is no indication as to what the garden is to be protected from. If it is not possible to use such a word without specifying the source of danger, it may be necessary to follow the pattern of some translations in interpreting the word as having the general idea of "to take care of," which gives an idea parallel to the word for cultivate.

2.16	TEV	RSV
	He told him, "You may eat the fruit of any tree in the garden,	And the LORD God commanded the man, saying, "You may freely eat of every tree of the garden;

He told him: literally "And the LORD God commanded the man, saying" (RSV). In many languages the use of pronouns is more acceptable, but the nouns should be used if there is any problem with meaning.

2.17	TEV	RSV
	except the tree that gives knowledge of what is good and what is bad.*g* You must not eat the fruit of that tree; if you do, you will die the same day."	but of the tree of the knowledge of good and evil you shall not eat, for in the day that you eat of it you shall die."

*g*knowledge of what is good and what is bad; *or* knowledge of everything.

the tree that gives knowledge: see verse 9.
die the same day: "die on the day that you eat it." The Hebrew "die" is an emphatic form that means "certainly, surely die."

2.18	TEV	RSV
	Then the LORD God said, "It is not good for the man to live alone. I will make a suitable companion to help him."	Then the LORD God said, "It is not good that the man should be alone; I will make him a helper fit for him."

said: from the context it is clear that God "said to himself." In some languages it may be necessary to translate this as "he thought."

a suitable companion to help him: literally "a helper fit for him/like him" (see RSV). It should be kept in mind that at this point a general word is needed for "someone who helps." See verse 20. It is also important to state that this someone who helps is to be suitable for him, or even "like him." The Hebrew word "helper" has the meaning of "someone who provides support," "someone who can aid," but it does not have the sense of inferiority that a word like "assistant" would convey.

2.19 TEV	RSV
So he took some soil from the ground and formed all the animals and all the birds. Then he brought them to the man to see what he would name them; and that is how they all got their names.	So out of the ground the LORD God formed every beast of the field and every bird of the air, and brought them to the man to see what he would call them; and whatever the man called every living creature, that was its name.

soil: see verse 7.

formed: see verse 7. It is important that the animals and the birds are formed in the same way that man is.

brought them: literally "caused them to go." The idea that God carried them to the man should be avoided. The sense is that God led them to man, or caused them to walk in front of man, or caused them to fly in front of man.

to see what he would name them: this is the intention of bringing the various animals to the man. In some languages it may be necessary to use such a formulation as "he brought them to the man and asked him what name he would give them," or "asked the man to name them."

that is how they all got their names: literally "whatever the man called every living being, that was its name" (RSV). The point is that the animals and birds continued to bear the name that man gave to each of them. It may be necessary to translate "and they all had the names that the man gave them."

2.20 TEV	RSV
So the man named all the birds and all the animals; but not one of them was a suitable companion to help him.	The man gave names to all cattle, and to the birds of the air, and to every beast of the field; but for the man there was not found a helper fit for him.

all the birds and all the animals: literally "domesticated animals, birds, and wild animals" (see RSV). This is intended to include all animal life.

a suitable companion to help him: the phrase is identical in Hebrew with that in verse 18.

2.21 TEV	RSV
Then the LORD God made the man fall into a deep sleep, and	So the LORD God caused a deep sleep to fall upon the man, and

while he was sleeping, he took out one of the man's ribs and closed up the flesh.	while he slept took one of his ribs and closed up its place with flesh;

made the man fall into a deep sleep: literally "caused a deep sleep to fall upon the man" (RSV). Languages will differ in the way of expressing this idea, but the point is that by the activity of God the man is caused to sleep very soundly.

while he was sleeping: the Hebrew uses a different verb from that found in the first part of the verse, but no sharp distinction can be maintained. Perhaps the first word implies somewhat more strongly than the second that it was a very deep sleep, that he was sleeping very soundly. No effort need be made to find two distinct words in the receptor language.

took out: the Hebrew word is a very general word with no indication of how this process was carried out.

closed up: this, too, is a general word which does not indicate the method. Something like "put back the flesh where the rib was" may be used.

2.22 TEV	RSV
He formed a woman out of the rib and brought her to him.	and the rib which the LORD God had taken from the man he made into a woman and brought her to the man.

formed a woman out of the rib: the Hebrew verb has the basic idea of build—"build a rib into a woman"; but in most languages it will be necessary to use something like "made the rib into a woman" or "transformed the rib into a woman" or "caused the rib to become a woman."

brought: this is the same Hebrew verb as in verse 19.

2.23 TEV	RSV

Then the man said,
    "At last, here is one of my
        own kind—
Bone taken from my bone, and
        flesh from my flesh.
'Woman' is her name, because
        she was taken out of
        man."*i*
	Then the man said,
	    "This at last is bone of my
	        bones
	    and flesh of my flesh;
	    she shall be called Woman,*d*
	        because she was taken out
	            of Man."*e*

*i*WOMAN...MAN: *The Hebrew words for "woman" and "man" have rather similar sounds.*

*d*Heb *ishshah*
*e*Heb *ish*

the man said: the person addressed is not named, but the form of the statement seems to indicate that the man is speaking to himself.

The quoted words are in poetic form in Hebrew and are printed in poetry lines in many translations. It should be noted, however, that a

translation into poetry will need to conform to the poetic norms of
the receptor language. In many cases it is wiser to use prose.

At last: the original Hebrew means something like "this time,"
but it is clear that the word intends to emphasize that at last, after
all the other animals have been brought to man, the LORD God has
brought to him one that is suitable.

here is one of my own kind: although these words do not actually
occur in the Hebrew text, they are added to make clear what is intended
by the Hebrew construction. The point is not the origin of woman, but
her suitability as a companion for man. It would be possible, of
course, even to pick up the terms used in verses 18 and 20, although
a more general term as used in TEV is a better choice.

Bone taken from my bone, and flesh from my flesh: these words must
be seen as a kind of idiomatic expression rather than as a mere statement of origin. The point is one of likeness—the woman is like the
man so much that bone and flesh are seen as identical.

'Woman' is her name: literally "she shall be called Woman" (RSV).
It should be clearly understood that the man is giving her the name
"Woman." In some languages it may be necessary to translate "I will
name her 'Woman'" in order to make this clear.

because: this statement explains why the name "Woman" is given to
her, but it will be clear to the reader only if some explanation is
given by note or in some other way.

'Woman'...man: the two nouns have somewhat similar sounds in Hebrew: ishshah ("woman") and ish ("man"). A footnote will not need to
indicate the Hebrew sounds but will need to indicate that the names
are similar in sound.

taken out: this is the same verb used in verse 21.

2.24	TEV	RSV
	That is why a man leaves his father and mother and is united with his wife, and they become one.	Therefore a man leaves his father and his mother and cleaves to his wife, and they become one flesh.

That is why: this explanation refers not only to the immediately
preceding statement that she was taken out of man, but also to the
whole story of her creation, beginning with verse 18. It is because
woman was formed from man to be a suitable companion to help him that
a man leaves his parents to be with his wife. It should be made clear
that verse 24 has general application and is no longer speaking simply
of the first man and the first woman.

leaves: although the Hebrew uses a general word for "leave," the
sense is not that he simply goes away from his father and mother, but
that he leaves home. A man leaves one family to form a new union with
his wife. The emphasis is on the new home and not on the rejection or
abandonment of father and mother.

is united with: the Hebrew verb has the general sense of be joined,
stay close to, cling to. In this context the sense must be that of being joined to, united with. Although the sexual act may be implicit in
the choice of the term, the primary focus seems to be in the new family
unit that is formed.

his wife: in Hebrew the same word is used for woman and wife. The addition of the possessive pronoun makes it clear that the Hebrew writer intends the idea of wife at this point.

and they become one: literally "and they become one flesh" (RSV), but it should be remembered that "flesh" in Hebrew has a very broad meaning and here may have the sense of "become one family unit." The man leaves one family unit to create a new family unit with his wife. In many languages it will not be possible to say "they become one" without indicating what kind of unity is intended. In such cases it may be wise to use some formulation such as "they become one family," "they become a new family."

2.25	TEV	RSV
	The man and the woman were both naked, but they were not embarrassed.	And the man and his wife were both naked, and were not ashamed.

naked: "undressed," "not wearing any clothes." The meaning is that they were totally naked, and a term is needed that includes the idea that the genitals were uncovered, but this need not be stated explicitly.

were not embarrassed: the Hebrew word means "to feel embarrassment" or "feel shame." The fact that they were naked did not make them feel ashamed.

C H A P T E R   3

SECTION HEADING

The Disobedience of Man (3.1-13): in this section heading the word Man refers to "mankind" or "human beings." Other forms of the heading are possible: "The First Sin," "Human Beings Disobey God."

3.1	TEV	RSV
	Now the snake was the most cunning animal that the LORD God had made. The snake asked the woman, "Did God really tell you not to eat fruit from any tree in the garden?"	Now the serpent was more subtle than any other wild creature that the LORD God had made. He said to the woman, "Did God say, 'You shall not eat of any tree of the garden'?"

Now: "now" is not time oriented, but is an expression in English that introduces an explanatory statement and often occurs at the beginning of a section of discourse. In many languages it will be omitted, or some other introductory formula to this new paragraph will be used.

the snake: although at a later stage, partly as a result of this

[26]

story, the snake assumes symbolic character, here it is best to use a normal word for "snake" without any of the later implications.

the most cunning: "crafty," "sly," "wise." If possible, a word should be chosen which conveys the idea of wisdom, knowledge, with a certain evil intent. The Hebrew word sounds like the word "naked" in 2.25.

animal: in Hebrew, literally "living beings of the field," in other words, wild animals.

asked: "inquired," "said."

really: in Hebrew the question is introduced by an intensive particle. This needs to be conveyed in some way, perhaps even "Is it true that...?"

fruit from: "fruit that grows on any tree in the garden."

3.2	TEV	RSV
	"We may eat the fruit of any tree in the garden," the woman answered,	And the woman said to the serpent, "We may eat of the fruit of the trees of the garden;

the woman answered: literally "the woman said to the serpent" (RSV). The repetition of the noun is stylistically difficult in English. Each translator will need to make decisions about pronoun or noun choices in the light of their usage in the receptor language.

3.3	TEV	RSV
	"except the tree in the middle of it. God told us not to eat the fruit of that tree or even touch it; if we do, we will die."	but God said, 'You shall not eat of the fruit of the tree which is in the midst of the garden, neither shall you touch it, lest you die.'"

God told us not to eat: in the Hebrew this is expressed by direct discourse: "God said, 'Do not eat'" (see RSV). The choice of direct or indirect discourse will depend once again on stylistic factors. If indirect discourse is chosen there is some adjustment to be made in verb and subject.

if we do, we will die: the Hebrew uses a particle with the sense "lest," "otherwise," meaning "so that we will not die," "in order that we will not die." If this construction cannot be used, perhaps the conditional sentence will carry the right meaning (as in TEV).

3.4	TEV	RSV
	The snake replied, "That's not true; you will not die.	But the serpent said to the woman, "You will not die.

The snake replied: literally "said to the woman" (RSV).

That's not true: the Hebrew uses an emphatic verb form to indicate absolute denial of the statement that we will die. It will be necessary in many languages to use a statement of denial such as "That is not the truth," or even "That is a lie."

[27]

3.5   TEV

God said that because he knows
that when you eat it, you will
be like God^j and know what is
good and what is bad."^{k}

RSV

For God knows that when you eat
of it your eyes will be opened,
and you will be like God, knowing
good and evil."

^{j}God; *or* the gods.
^{k}know what is good and what is
bad; *or* know everything.

God said that because: the Hebrew just has the single word which
means "For" or "Because." However, it is very clear that the causal
connection is not between what has just been said and verse 5, but
rather with the prohibition that God has given about eating the fruit.
     when: literally "in the day when," but this is a general Hebrew
way of expressing time. The idea is that "as soon as you eat it."
     be like God: this is a simple comparison, and the Hebrew does not
use either of the technical words found in 1.26. From the Hebrew it
seems clear that the comparison relates to knowledge: "like God in
knowing." The word for God is a plural form in Hebrew and may mean
here gods, thus "You will be like gods."
     and know: literally "your eyes will be opened...and you will know"
(see RSV). Of course, the opening of the eyes is not understood literally but in the sense of increased insight and knowledge. TEV has combined this clause with the verb "know," but in some languages it may
be simpler to retain the idea with a translation such as "you will be
given understanding and become like God, knowing what is good and what
is bad."
     what is good and what is bad: see 2.9.

3.6   TEV

     The woman saw how beautiful
the tree was and how good its
fruit would be to eat, and she
thought how wonderful it would
be to become wise. So she took
some of the fruit and ate it.
Then she gave some to her husband, and he also ate it.

RSV

So when the woman saw that the
tree was good for food, and that
it was a delight to the eyes,
and that the tree was to be desired to make one wise, she took
of its fruit and ate; and she
also gave some to her husband,
and he ate.

how beautiful the tree was: TEV has reversed the order of the Hebrew to better fit English style. Literally "pleasing to the eye" (see
RSV), with the sense "attractive to look at," "lovely."
     how good its fruit would be to eat: literally "the tree was good
for food" (RSV). It is the fruit of the tree and not the tree itself
which is here in focus. The woman saw that the fruit of the tree would
taste good.
     and she thought how wonderful it would be to become wise: liter-
ally "that the tree was to be desired to make one wise" (RSV). It is
clear that the seeing also involves thinking about what eating fruit
from the tree would accomplish. The woman was not able to "see" that

the tree would make one wise, but she thought about this in the light of the prohibition of God (2.16,17) and the snake's statement (3.5). She realized that eating the fruit would make her wise.

wise: the Hebrew word, not the same word as "know," has the sense of understanding, insight, comprehension; this idea of wisdom is to be distinguished from the more general thought of having knowledge or information.

3.7	TEV	RSV
	As soon as they had eaten it, they were given understanding and realized that they were naked; so they sewed fig leaves together and covered themselves.	Then the eyes of both were opened, and they knew that they were naked; and they sewed fig leaves together and made themselves aprons.

As soon as they had eaten it: although this represents a simple connective in the Hebrew, "And" or "Then," the abruptness would indicate that what follows comes immediately.

they were given understanding: literally "their eyes were opened" (see RSV). See verse 5. It may be necessary to translate "they became wise," "they understood."

realized: "saw," "knew," "came to understand."

sewed: the Hebrew word would normally mean "fastened together with needle and thread," but the exact nature of this operation is not more closely specified. Something like "fastened," "fastened together" might be used.

fig leaves: fig trees have large, broad leaves.

covered themselves: literally "made for themselves skirts (or loin cloths or aprons)" (see RSV). The exact meaning of the Hebrew word is not certain, although it must refer to some kind of garment that can be tied around the waist. Skirt, loin cloth, apron, and the like are suggested. However, rather than to try to determine the exact nature of the garment, it may be sufficient (as in TEV) to indicate that they sewed the fig leaves together in order to cover themselves or to make a garment to cover themselves or to cover their nakedness.

3.8	TEV	RSV
	That evening they heard the LORD God walking in the garden, and they hid from him among the trees.	And they heard the sound of the LORD God walking in the garden in the cool of the day, and the man and his wife hid themselves from the presence of the LORD God among the trees of the garden.

evening: literally "wind of the day," but in that part of the world a cooling breeze often blows in the evening (see RSV).

heard the LORD: literally "heard the sound (voice) of the LORD" (see RSV). That is, heard the LORD moving about or walking.

[29]

3.9   **TEV**

But the LORD God called out to
the man, "Where are you?"

RSV

But the LORD God called to the
man, and said to him, "Where
are you?"

called out: literally "called and said."

3.10   **TEV**

He answered, "I heard you
in the garden; I was afraid and
hid from you, because I was
naked."

RSV

And he said, "I heard the sound
of thee in the garden, and I was
afraid, because I was naked; and
I hid myself."

I heard you: literally "I heard the sound (voice) of you" (see
RSV).

I was naked: that is, "I was naked when I heard you and I still
am." In many languages this will be expressed by "I am naked."

3.11   **TEV**

"Who told you that you were
naked?" God asked. "Did you eat
the fruit that I told you not to
eat?"

RSV

He said, "Who told you that you
were naked? Have you eaten of
the tree of which I commanded
you not to eat?"

fruit: literally "from the tree" (see RSV), but the sense is
clear: "some of the fruit from the tree."

3.12   **TEV**

The man answered, "The
woman you put here with me gave
me the fruit, and I ate it."

RSV

The man said, "The woman whom
thou gavest to be with me, she
gave me fruit of the tree, and
I ate."

you put here with me: literally "you gave with me" (see RSV), with
the clear sense of "put here with me," "put here by me."

the fruit: see verse 11.

3.13   **TEV**

The LORD God asked the
woman, "Why did you do this?"
She replied, "The snake
tricked me into eating it."

RSV

Then the LORD God said to the
woman, "What is this that you
have done?" The woman said,
"The serpent beguiled me, and
I ate."

"Why did you do this?": more literally "What is this that you
have done?" (RSV). But in context the question clearly does not ask
for facts but asks for motives: "What do you mean by doing this?"

tricked me: the Hebrew word has the sense of trick, deceive,
cheat, fool, lead astray.

into eating it: literally "and I ate" (RSV), but the clear sense is "the snake deceived me in such a way that I ate the fruit."

SECTION HEADING

God Pronounces Judgment (3.14-21): in many languages it will be necessary to add the indirect objects: "God Pronounces Judgment on the Snake, the Woman, and the Man." Pronounces Judgment: this refers to what follows in the curse upon the snake and in the promise of trouble for the woman and for the man. Languages will vary in the way they refer to this type of pronouncement: "God Speaks about Punishment," "God Speaks His Threats."

3.14 TEV	RSV
Then the LORD God said to the snake, "You will be punished for this; you alone of all the animals must bear this curse: From now on you will crawl on your belly, and you will have to eat dust as long as you live.	The LORD God said to the serpent, "Because you have done this, cursed are you above all cattle, and above all wild animals; upon your belly you shall go, and dust you shall eat all the days of your life.

You will be punished: in many languages it will be preferable to change the passive into an active form: "I will punish you." The word "punish" expresses the meaning of the Hebrew word for "curse" (see RSV).

for this: literally "because you did this" (see RSV), which refers to the whole act of deceiving the woman and the man into disobeying God.

you alone of all the animals: literally "from all the animals from all the living creatures of the field" (see RSV). This will include all wild and domestic animals, and TEV has chosen to use the term all the animals as including both domesticated and wild animals.

must bear this curse: literally "you are cursed more than all the animals" (see RSV). The idea of a curse is difficult to translate in many languages. Where a specific word for a curse is available, there is little problem, although often the idea will have to be expressed by an active verb: "I place upon you a curse." It should be kept in mind that the Hebrew does not intend to say that all the animals are cursed and that the snake is cursed more than the rest. Rather, the idea is that the snake, set apart from all other animals, is placed under a curse. In many cases it may be necessary to use something like "I pronounce that the following evil will come upon you, in contrast to all other animals." In some languages it may be easier to restructure the verse, "I will punish you for what you have done, and this is how I will do it. I will place this curse on you: from now on you alone...."

From now on...as long as you live: these two expressions translate the literal Hebrew, "all the days of your life" (RSV). It is often necessary to indicate that a radical change is now to begin, as TEV has done with From now on.

you will crawl on your belly: this and the following statements are the content of the curse. The curse is this: you will crawl on your belly, etc. Nothing is indicated as to how the snake moved prior to the beginning of the curse.

you will have to eat dust: literally "you will eat dust" (see RSV), but the sense is not that this is by choice; it is a part of the curse. That is why TEV has chosen the more emphatic form, you will have to eat dust.

3.15 TEV	RSV
I will make you and the woman hate each other; her offspring and yours will always be enemies. Her offsrping will crush your head, and you will bite their*x* heel."	I will put enmity between you and the woman, and between your seed and her seed; he shall bruise your head, and you shall bruise his heel."

*x*their; or his.

I will make you and the woman hate each other: literally "I will put enmity between you and the woman" (RSV). The Hebrew word has the idea of enmity, hostility, hatred.

her offspring and yours: literally "between your seed and her seed" (RSV), but the Hebrew word is frequently used in the sense of "descendants." The descendants of the woman and the descendants of the snake will be enemies.

will always be enemies: literally "and (enmity) between your seed and her seed" (RSV). The point being made is that not only will the first woman and the snake be enemies, but the descendants of both will continue to be enemies.

her offspring: although the Hebrew uses a singular pronoun, the reference is clearly to the "seed" of the woman, which refers to the descendants of the woman. The various attempts to relate the seed of the woman to Mary or Jesus rest upon a misunderstanding of the meaning of the Hebrew text, aided by early translations.

crush...bite: in the Hebrew the same word is used for both of these verbs, although it is not certain that it has identical meanings in each case. The verb seems to have the sense of "trample upon," "bruise," "strike," "bite." In any case, the receptor language will have to determine what verbs will suit the objects "head" and "heel." Human beings can "crush, trample on, bruise, strike at" the head of a snake, and a snake can "bite, strike at" the heel of a human.

3.16 TEV	RSV
And he said to the woman, "I will increase your trouble in pregnancy and your pain in giving birth. In spite of this, you	To the woman he said, "I will greatly multiply your pain in childbearing; in pain you shall bring

[32]

will still have desire for your husband, yet you will be subject to him."

forth children, yet your desire shall be for your husband, and he shall rule over you."

I will increase your trouble: the Hebrew uses an intensive construction: "I will very much increase (make worse, enlarge) your trouble" (see RSV). The Hebrew word "trouble" means pain, work, difficulty, labor.

pain: the Hebrew word is the same as that translated "trouble" in the line above. It is clear that trouble and pain refer to difficulties of pregnancy and childbearing, but in particular to birth pains at the time of giving birth.

in giving birth: literally "in pain you will give birth to children" (see RSV). The thought is that birth pangs (birth pains) will accompany the birth of children.

In spite of this: although the Hebrew has a simple connective, there seems to be a very sharp contrast with what precedes.

you will still have desire: the word "still" emphasizes the continuing of that desire: "You will continue to have desire."

desire: the literal translation would be "your desire will be toward your husband" (see RSV), and the word "desire" emphasizes "attraction," "longing for," "eagerness for," and may refer to sexual attraction.

yet: here again, although the Hebrew has a simple connective, a contrast is probably intended.

you will be subject to him: literally "he will rule over you" (see RSV). The thought is parallel to that expressed elsewhere in the Bible, that the man is the head of the house and rules over, controls, has responsibility for the woman. In many languages it will be more satisfactory to place the focus on the woman (as TEV has done) by stating "you will be subject," "you will have to obey," "you will be controlled by," "you will be responsible to" your husband. In other languages it may be more satisfactory to keep the original focus and make a statement that "your husband will rule over you, control you, be your master."

3.17 TEV	RSV
And he said to the man, "You listened to your wife and ate the fruit which I told you not to eat. Because of what you have done, the ground will be under a curse. You will have to work hard all your life to make it produce enough food for you.	And to Adam he said, "Because you have listened to the voice of your wife, and have eaten of the tree of which I commanded you, 'You shall not eat of it,' cursed is the ground because of you; in toil you shall eat of it all the days of your life;

to the man: some translations introduce the proper name "Adam" at this point. "Adam" in Hebrew is the same as the word for "man." But

[33]

it seems more natural to introduce the proper name "Adam" in 3.20 at
the time Eve is given her name. It should be noted, however, that there
is considerable variety among the translations as to where "man" becomes
"Adam."

You listened to your wife: literally "listened to the voice of
your wife" (RSV), but the meaning is that the man listened to what his
wife had to say when she gave him the fruit. "You obeyed your wife."
"You did what she told you to do."

ate the fruit: literally "ate from the tree" (see RSV), but as we
have seen, this is a traditional way of speaking about the fruit of the
tree.

which I told you not to eat: "which I commanded you, 'You shall
not eat of it'" (RSV). It is possible to retain direct discourse if
this is stylistically suitable in the receptor language. In English
it is more natural to summarize by the use of indirect discourse rather than repeat the direct command, but this will depend upon the receptor language usage.

Because of what you have done: this refers to the statement in
the first part of the verse—listened to your wife and ate the fruit.
The form is used in order to break the very long Hebrew sentence and
put the elements in proper logical order.

the ground will be under a curse: literally "cursed" (RSV). "A
curse will be placed on the ground." It is often difficult to translate this word, and in some languages it may be necessary to move to
an active form—"I will place a curse on the ground." The meaning is
that Yahweh will make something evil happen to the ground. Here the
sense seems to be that by the pronouncement the LORD causes the ground
to be less productive. In some languages it may be necessary to state
the meaning quite directly: "I will make the ground no longer grow as
much food as it did." The word "ground" refers, of course, to the
land, the fields.

You will have to work hard all your life to make it produce
enough food for you: literally "in toil you shall eat of it" (RSV).
The Hebrew is compressed and the clear sense is "You will have to work
hard in tilling, plowing, working the ground in order to have enough
to eat." "You will have to work hard to grow enough food from the
ground." The point is that in contrast to the previous situation,
hard work in cultivating the ground will now be required to grow food.

all your life: literally "all the days of your life" (RSV), but
this Hebrew idiomatic use need not be reproduced.

3.18	TEV	RSV
	It will produce weeds and thorns, and you will have to eat wild plants.	thorns and thistles it shall bring forth to you; and you shall eat the plants of the field.

weeds and thorns: literally "thorn bushes and thistle plants."
What is needed in translation is a normal expression for the kind of
plants that choke out and prevent the growth of food-bearing plants;
it is not necessary to find a word to translate exactly the kind of

plant referred to by the Hebrew. The emphasis is upon any kind of plant that hinders the growth of food plants, and the meaning of "thorn" or "thistle" is secondary.

wild plants: literally "plants of the field" (RSV). The Hebrew word used here for "plants" is a general term that includes weeds, grass, vegetables, cereal, grains, but here the emphasis falls on the edible plants. TEV leaves the impression that food is simply to be gathered from wild plants, but it is more likely that cultivated plants are included. Perhaps "food from plants growing in the fields." Previously in this section human beings have eaten fruit from trees (see 2.16; 3.20).

3.19 TEV	RSV
You will have to work hard and sweat to make the soil produce anything, until you go back to the soil from which you were formed. You were made from soil, and you will become soil again."	In the sweat of your face you shall eat bread till you return to the ground, for out of it you were taken; you are dust, and to dust you shall return."

You will have to work hard and sweat: literally "By the sweat of your face (nose)" (see RSV), but this is used in an extended sense to refer to the whole person. It is a compressed Hebrew expression. The meaning is that hard work and sweat will be required to make the ground produce food. In most languages it is not possible to use the literal translation, and it will be more satisfactory to translate with something like "You will have to toil and sweat," "You will have to work hard."

to make the soil produce anything: literally "you shall eat bread" (RSV), but the Hebrew word for bread is frequently used in the general sense for any kind of food, and that is clearly the meaning here. In this context it is also clear that the word "eat" is a compressed expression for "make the soil produce enough food for you to eat." In most languages it will be necessary to make this meaning quite explicit rather than depending upon an interpretation of the compressed expression.

until you go back to the soil: the reference is to the death and burial of the body and its return to the ground. Human beings are made from soil (see 2.7), and at death they are buried in the ground and through decay once again become soil. In some languages it may be necessary to translate "until you die and become soil again."

from which you were formed: this refers back to 2.7.

3.20 TEV	RSV
Adam[l] named his wife Eve,[m] because she was the mother of all human beings.	The man called his wife's name Eve,[f] because she was the mother of all living.

[l]ADAM: *This name in Hebrew means "mankind."*

[f]The name in Hebrew resembles the word for *living*

[35]

*m*EVE: *This name sounds similar to
the Hebrew word for "living,"
which is rendered in this context
as "human beings."*

Adam: as noted above, "Adam" and "man" are the same. The Hebrew
text here has "The man" (RSV), but it seems logical to introduce the
proper name "Adam" at this point when the man gives his wife her name.

named: literally "called the name of" in the sense of "gave the
name Eve to."

Eve: in Hebrew the sound of the name "Eve" is similar to the Hebrew word for "living," which here is a reference to human beings, that
is, all the descendants of Adam and Eve. The play on words is intentional in Hebrew and will need to be explained in a footnote, as TEV has
done.

mother of all human beings: literally "mother of all living" (RSV),
but it is very clear in context that the reference is to all the descendants of Adam and Eve, that is, all human beings. The Hebrew word
is used elsewhere for animals as well as human beings, but in this
context it is clear that only human beings are in focus.

3.21 TEV	RSV
And the LORD God made clothes out of animal skins for Adam and his wife, and he clothed them.	And the LORD God made for Adam and for his wife garments of skins, and clothed them.

clothes out of animal skins: the Hebrew word "skin" refers to the
actual hide of the animal or to leather made from the hide, and not to
cloth woven from hair or wool. Here the clothes are not made of cloth,
but of the hides of animals. The kind of animals or the nature of the
clothes is not indicated.

he clothed them: he put on them the clothes he had made.

SECTION HEADING

Adam and Eve Are Sent Out of the Garden (3.22-24): "God Sends Adam
and Eve Out of the Garden."

3.22 TEV	RSV
Then the LORD God said, "Now the man has become like one of us and has knowledge of what is good and what is bad.*n* He must not be allowed to take fruit from the tree that gives life, eat it, and live forever."	Then the LORD God said, "Be-hold, the man has become like one of us, knowing good and evil; and now, lest he put forth his hand and take also of the tree of life, and eat, and live for ever"—

*n*knowledge of what is good and

what is bad; *or* knowledge of
everything.

Now: the Hebrew word is often translated "Behold" (RSV), but it
has a broad meaning and usually emphasizes what follows. It is simply
an emphatic sentence opening. The translator will need to find an appropriate form or particle in his language—perhaps "look" or "listen"
—or it may be more appropriate in his language to use no introductory
formula. The English Now here means that the present situation is a
new one that did not exist before.

the man: it is quite clear that at this point the word "man" refers to all of mankind, all human beings, including male and female.

has become like one of us: see 3.5 and note that there "like God"
may be interpreted "like gods." See also 1.26 and note the possible interpretations of the plural "us." The Hebrew is not identical with the
words in 1.26 but is rather a simple comparison, "like one among us."
The point of the comparison here is, of course, what follows: mankind
now has knowledge. In some languages it may be necessary to use a
plural and "they" for the following pronouns.

has knowledge of what is good and what is bad: see 2.9 and the
note there.

He must not be allowed to: the Hebrew construction is fairly complicated in that the idea carries on into verse 23: "so that he will
not eat...the LORD God sent him out of the garden." Since this is
quite complicated and will be misunderstood in many languages, it seems
wiser to break the sentence, as TEV has done. The meaning may also be
expressed actively: "he must not eat," "we must prevent him from eating."

to take: in Hebrew, literally "lest he put out his hand and take
...and eat...and live." The Hebrew word translated "lest" (RSV) has
the sense "in order that not."

fruit from the tree that gives life: literally "from the tree of
life" (see RSV), but obviously the sense is the fruit that is produced by
the tree.

the tree that gives life: literally "the tree of life." See 2.9.

and live forever: this simply underlines what is meant by the
"tree that gives life," "everlasting life."

3.23 TEV	RSV
So the LORD God sent him out of the Garden of Eden and made him cultivate the soil from which he had been formed.	therefore the LORD God sent him forth from the garden of Eden, to till the ground from which he was taken.

sent him out: the Hebrew word for "sent" is a general word that
does not indicate the method. One may assume that the sense is "commanded that he leave." TEV has not repeated a word with the same meaning which occurs at the beginning of verse 24. That word also means
"send away," "banish."

3.24 TEV	RSV
Then at the east side of the garden he put living creatures^o and a flaming sword which turned in all directions. This was to keep anyone from coming near the tree that gives life.	He drove out the man; and at the east of the garden of Eden he placed the cherubim, and a flaming sword which turned every way, to guard the way to the tree of life.

^oLIVING CREATURES: *See Word List.*

east side of the garden: that is, outside the garden on the east side.

put: the Hebrew word means "cause to settle, dwell, live" but here seems to be used in a general way.

living creatures: the Hebrew word is plural, transliterated as "cherubim," but the English word "cherub" has come to mean an angelic being, a winged child with a chubby, rosy face. The Hebrew word refers to fierce animals with wings, the body of a lion or a bull, and the face of a man. They are the living creatures, classed among the angels, who serve God and do his bidding. (See Ezek 1.5-12; 10.21.)

a flaming sword which turned in all directions: the picture is not perfectly clear in Hebrew, and one may translate "a sword made of fire" or "a sword that looked like fire." The Hebrew does not indicate that the sword was held by the living creatures; it seems to be thought of as a separate method of guarding the entrance to the Garden of Eden.

C H A P T E R   4

SECTION HEADING

Cain and Abel (4.1-16): "The Story of Cain and Abel," "Cain Kills His Brother Abel."

4.1 TEV	RSV
Then Adam had intercourse with his wife, and she became pregnant. She bore a son and said, "By the LORD's help I have gotten a son." So she named him Cain.^p	Now Adam knew Eve his wife, and she conceived and bore Cain, saying, "I have gotten^g a man with the help of the LORD." ^gHeb *qanah*, get

^pCAIN: *This name sounds like the Hebrew for "gotten."*

had intercourse with: this is the meaning of the Hebrew word often translated "know," and some way should be found in the receptor language to speak of this in polite terms that could be used in public reading of the Scriptures. In some languages it may be necessary to drop the details and translate "Then Adam and Eve had a son" or "Then a son was born to Adam and Eve."

bore: "gave birth to."

By the LORD's help: "The LORD has helped me and...."

Cain: although the exact meaning of the Hebrew word is not known, it is clear that because of similarity of sound, the name is here equated with "gotten," "acquired," "gained." A footnote will be needed if the reader is to understand the reason the name is given.

4.2	TEV	RSV
	Later she gave birth to another son, Abel. Abel became a shepherd, but Cain was a farmer.	And again, she bore his brother Abel. Now Abel was a keeper of sheep, and Cain a tiller of the ground.

shepherd: "one who takes care of (or, raises) sheep and goats."

farmer: "one who cultivates the soil to produce food."

4.3	TEV	RSV
	After some time Cain brought some of his harvest and gave it as an offering to the LORD.	In the course of time Cain brought to the LORD an offering of the fruit of the ground,

After some time: literally "And it happened at the end of days." The starting point for this time measurement is not indicated, and some adjustment will need to be made in the translation, such as "After awhile" or "After they had been working for some time."

some of his harvest: "a part of the crops that his land had produced," "some of the food that he had grown."

an offering to the LORD: the Hebrew word for "offering" is later used in the specific sense of a "grain offering," but here it has its more general sense of a gift, something given to honor someone. The text does not say how the gift was offered, but we may assume that it was burned on an altar. In some languages it may be necessary to say "he brought some grain and burned it on the altar as a gift to the LORD."

4.4	TEV	RSV
	Then Abel brought the first lamb born to one of his sheep, killed it, and gave the best parts of it as an offering. The LORD was pleased with Abel and his offering,	and Abel brought of the firstlings of his flock and of their fat portions. And the LORD had regard for Abel and his offering,

first lamb born to one of his sheep: this may also be translated "first kid from one of his goats," as the Hebrew "flock" does not distinguish between sheep and goats.

best parts: literally "the fat parts" (see RSV), but in Hebrew

[39]

the word is sometimes used in a figurative way for "best." In most
languages it is more meaningful to speak of the best parts than of
the "fat parts."

was pleased with: the word in Hebrew has the meaning of "look at,"
but the sense is "look with favor on," "have regard for" (see RSV).

	TEV	RSV
4.5	but he rejected Cain and his of-fering. Cain became furious, and he scowled in anger.	but for Cain and his offering he had no regard. So Cain was very angry, and his countenance fell.

rejected: literally "was not pleased with," which is the negative
of the verb in verse 9. No reason is given as to why one offering was
accepted and the other rejected.

Cain became furious: "was very angry." The Hebrew expression is
quite strong; note how TEV has emphasized this by adding in anger to
scowled.

he scowled: literally "his face (countenance) fell" (see RSV).
Perhaps "looked angry," "showed his anger in his face."

	TEV	RSV
4.6	Then the LORD said to Cain, "Why are you angry? Why that scowl on your face?	The LORD said to Cain, "Why are you angry, and why has your countenance fallen?

Why are you angry?: the same Hebrew words are used for "anger"
and "scowl" as in verse 5.

	TEV	RSV
4.7	If you had done the right thing, you would be smiling;^{q} but be-cause you have done evil, sin is crouching at your door. It wants to rule you, but you must overcome it."	If you do well, will you not be accepted? And if you do not do well, sin is couching at the door; its desire is for you, but you must master it."

^{q}you would be smiling; or I would
have accepted your offering.

This is an extremely difficult verse to translate, largely because
of the disagreement about what the Hebrew text means. This can be seen
in the many differences found in modern and ancient translations. The
explanations given here will follow the interpretation of the Hebrew
reflected in the TEV, but the translator should be cautioned that
there can be no certainty about the translation.

If you had done the right thing: this is taken as referring to the
offering that has been made: "If you had acted in the right way," "If
you had made the right offering." RSV "If you do well" could refer to

future action but is probably to be understood as a timeless, general statement.

you would be smiling: the footnote in TEV, I would have accepted your offering, is certainly possible. The reason for the difficulty is that the Hebrew "lifting up" can be understood as Cain's "lifting the face in a smile" or as God's "lifting up a gift to accept it." RSV translates "will you not be accepted?"

you have done evil: literally "have not done the right thing," "have not done well" (see RSV), the same verb as in the first part of the verse.

sin is crouching at your door: sin is presented as if it were an animal ready to spring on the person coming out of the door of a house. It may be necessary in some languages to translate "sin is like an animal lying at your door ready to attack you."

It wants to rule you: the Hebrew is the same word used in 3.16 for "desire." Literally "its desire is for you" (RSV). Sin is still seen as a vicious animal wanting to attack and overcome Cain.

but you must overcome it: literally "you must rule over it," with the sense "you must not let sin rule over you, but you must rule over it" (see RSV).

4.8	TEV	RSV
	Then Cain said to his brother Abel, "Let's go out in the fields."*r* When they were out in the fields, Cain turned on his brother and killed him.	Cain said to Abel his brother, "Let us go out to the field."*h* And when they were in the field, Cain rose up against his brother Abel, and killed him.

rSome ancient translations Let's go out in the fields; *Hebrew does not have these words.*

hSam Gk Syr Compare Vg: Heb lacks Let us go out to the field

"Let's go out in the fields": several ancient translations have these words, but the Hebrew does not have them; it seems clear that some quotation such as this has fallen out of the Hebrew.

in the fields: may be translated simply as "outside," "out of the house," but the situation is clearer if we understand that the brothers have walked into the fields or the countryside where they are no longer visible from the home.

turned on: literally "rose up against" (RSV), with the sense of "attacked."

killed him: how the murder was committed is not stated. If in the translation the method has to be stated, one might use "killed him with a stone."

4.9	TEV	RSV
	The LORD asked Cain, "Where is your brother Abel?" He answered, "I don't know. Am I supposed to take care of my brother?"	Then the LORD said to Cain, "Where is Abel your brother?" He said, "I do not know; am I my brother's keeper?"

Am I supposed to take care of my brother?: literally "Am I my brother's keeper?" (RSV). The verb has the meaning "take care of," "guard," "protect." Perhaps one might translate "Have I been appointed to protect my brother?" or "Is it my duty to guard my brother?" The rhetorical question expects the answer "No!" and in some languages one may have to make a statement, "I am not supposed to take care of my brother."

4.10   TEV

Then the LORD said, "Why have you done this terrible thing? Your brother's blood is crying out to me from the ground, like a voice calling for revenge.

      RSV

And the LORD said, "What have you done? The voice of your brother's blood is crying to me from the ground.

Why have you done this terrible thing?: literally "What have you done?" (RSV). But this is not a request for information. Rather it is a rhetorical question that emphasizes the terrible nature of the murder, and some way should be found to express this idea in translation, as TEV has done. If a statement is needed, one might suggest "You should not have done such a terrible thing."

Your brother's blood is crying out to me from the ground, like a voice calling for revenge: the blood of Abel is seen as if it were a person crying out for vengeance. One needs to keep in mind that for the Hebrew the blood represented the life of the individual. In some languages it may be necessary to restructure along the following lines: "You have killed your brother and spilled his blood on the ground; that blood is a witness against you; it is like the voice of a person asking that you be punished for what you have done."

4.11   TEV

You are placed under a curse and can no longer farm the soil. It has soaked up your brother's blood as if it had opened its mouth to receive it when you killed him.

And now you are cursed from the ground, which has opened its mouth to receive your brother's blood from your hand.

You are placed under a curse: "A curse is now placed upon you." For "curse" see 3.17, and note that here also the curse is related to the ground but is placed directly on Cain.

and can no longer farm the soil: this probably expresses what is meant by the literal "from the soil (ground)" (RSV). It is possible, but less likely, that the meaning is "You are placed under a curse that is greater than the curse placed on the ground."

It has soaked up your brother's blood: see verse 10.

as if it had opened its mouth: the ground is pictured as if it were a hungry animal opening its mouth to drink the blood of Abel. It may be necessary to restructure: "it was like a hungry animal that opened its mouth to drink his blood."

[42]

when you killed him: literally "from your hand" (RSV), but this is a way of speaking about the murder.

4.12 TEV	RSV
If you try to grow crops, the soil will not produce anything; you will be a homeless wanderer on the earth."	When you till the ground, it shall no longer yield to you its strength; you shall be a fugitive and a wanderer on the earth."

homeless wanderer: literally "a fugitive and a wanderer" (RSV), but the Hebrew often uses this construction of two nouns to indicate a single basic idea. Cain is condemned to a life of homeless wandering as a nomad of the desert.

4.13 TEV	RSV
And Cain said to the LORD, "This punishment is too hard for me to bear.	Cain said to the LORD, "My punishment is greater than I can bear.

too hard for me to bear: "more than I can endure."

4.14 TEV	RSV
You are driving me off the land and away from your presence. I will be a homeless wanderer on the earth, and anyone who finds me will kill me."	Behold, thou hast driven me this day away from the ground; and from thy face I shall be hidden; and I shall be a fugitive and a wanderer on the earth, and whoever finds me will slay me."

You are driving me off the land: the sentence in Hebrew begins with the attention-getter "Behold" (see 3.22), which has not been retained in TEV. Here land refers to cultivated land; Cain is banished to the desert, which is noncultivated land.
and away from your presence: literally "and I shall be hidden from (kept away from) your face" (see RSV). The Hebrew word for "face" is often used to express the idea of the presence of God. Cain here reflects the early view that God manifests his presence only in his own land. The desert is often thought of as the place where only demons dwell.
homeless wanderer: see verse 12.
finds: the Hebrew word may mean "happen to meet," "meet by chance," which is the meaning here, or "find after looking for."

4.15 TEV	RSV
But the LORD answered, "No. If anyone kills you, seven lives will be taken in revenge." So the LORD put a mark on Cain to	Then the LORD said to him, "Not so!^{i} If any one slays Cain, vengeance shall be taken on him sevenfold." And the LORD put a

warn anyone who met him not to kill him.

mark on Cain, lest any who came upon him should kill him.

[i]Gk Syr Vg: Heb *Therefore*

No: "This is not so," "That is not the way it will be." The standard Hebrew text has "Therefore" (see RSV note), which is interpreted by early translations as "Not so." In any case a strong contrast with verses 13 and 14 is involved.

seven lives will be taken in revenge: if the receptor language requires an active verb with a subject, one may translate "I will kill (cause to kill) seven other people in revenge."

a mark: "a sign" to protect Cain from being killed. There is no indication of what the sign was, but one may assume some kind of tattoo mark placed on the forehead. (See Ezek 9.4,6.)

met: the Hebrew verb is the same as that translated "find" in verse 14.

4.16   TEV
And Cain went away from the LORD's presence and lived in a land called "Wandering," which is east of Eden.

RSV
Then Cain went away from the presence of the LORD, and dwelt in the land of Nod,[j] east of Eden.

[j]That is *Wandering*

the LORD's presence: see verse 14.

a land called "Wandering": the Hebrew word transliterated "Nod" (RSV) means "wandering" and is the same root word as that translated "wanderer" in verses 12 and 14. In English "the land of Nod" can mean "sleep," and TEV avoids this by translating the word rather than transliterating it. If one retains "Nod," a note should explain the meaning. The location of the land is not known, apart from the fact that it is east of Eden.

4.17—5.32: This section includes stories about the descendants of Cain, the birth of Seth and Enoch, and a list of the descendants of Adam.

C H A P T E R   6

SECTION HEADING

The Wickedness of Mankind (6.1-8): "Man's Sinfulness," "The Sinfulness of Human Beings."

6.1   TEV
When mankind had spread all

When men began to multiply on

over the world, and girls were   the face of the ground, and
being born,   daughters were born to them,

When: this introduces a sentence that runs through verse 2. It
may be better to make a new beginning at verse 2 and drop the conjunc-
tion here.
    mankind: the Hebrew word is the familiar word for "man," with the
meaning "mankind," "human beings," and includes all the people living
at that time.
    had spread all over the world: literally "began to increase on
the face (surface) of the ground" (see RSV). That is, human beings
were having children, and the families were moving into all parts of
the world.
    girls were being born: that is, human beings were having daughters
as well as sons.

6.2   TEV   RSV
some of the heavenly beings[v] saw   the sons of God saw that the
that these girls were beautiful,   daughters of men were fair; and
so they took the ones they liked.   they took to wife such of them
                                           as they chose.
[v]heavenly beings; or sons of the
gods; or sons of God.

    some: if "when" has been dropped in verse 1, the sentence may be-
gin "at that time...."
    heavenly beings: literally "sons of the gods" or "sons of God"
(RSV), but this is one of the ways Hebrew refers to the divine beings
around God (see 1.26) who make up his heavenly court or who are his
servants (angels). In Hebrew "sons of God" would mean "beings who belong to the god-class of beings" and would say nothing about their
origin from God as their father. The translator may be wise to avoid
the use of the word "son" and use something like "supernatural
beings," heavenly beings, "divine creatures," or even "angels."
    these girls: "the daughters of human beings."
    they took: literally "took to themselves as wives" (see RSV). The
words refer to sexual intercourse between the supernatural beings and
the daughters of men, but some polite way must be found of speaking
of this.
    the ones they liked: "the ones they chose," "the ones they se-
lected."

6.3   TEV   RSV
Then the LORD said, "I will not   Then the LORD said, "My spirit
allow people to live forever;   shall not abide in man for ever,
they are mortal. From now on   for he is flesh, but his days
they will live no longer than   shall be a hundred and twenty
120 years."   years."

    I will not allow people to live forever: literally "my spirit will not *dun* in man forever" (see RSV), but the meaning of *dun* is unknown and has to be guessed from this context. TEV has chosen to follow many translations, ancient and modern, which understand the word as meaning "remain, stay, dwell," and has understood "my spirit" to refer to the life-giving spirit of God, and "man" to mean human beings. If this is correct, although there are several other possibilities of interpretation, the sense will be "I will not let human beings go on living forever."

they are mortal: the Hebrew introduces this statement with a word that probably means "since," "because," "for," which ties the statement closely with what goes before. The word mortal translates the literal "flesh" (RSV), which is used for that which is passing or temporary in contrast to the eternal character of God.

they will live no longer than 120 years: literally "his days shall be 120 years" (RSV), but the "his" refers to mankind, they; the sense is "they will die by the time they are 120 years old."

6.4	TEV	RSV
	In those days, and even later, there were giants on the earth who were descendants of human women and the heavenly beings. They were the great heroes and famous men of long ago.	The Nephilim were on the earth in those days, and also afterward, when the sons of God came in to the daughters of men, and they bore children to them. These were the mighty men that were of old, the men of renown.

In those days, and even later: this order of words makes it clear that giants were descended from the union between the heavenly beings and human women.

giants: the Hebrew word is transliterated "Nephilim" (RSV), a plural, but there is no point in retaining this Hebrew word for giants.

great heroes and famous men of long ago: the reference is to the ancient heroes such as Nimrod (see 10.8). They are here identified with the giants.

6.5	TEV	RSV
	When the LORD saw how wicked everyone on earth was and how evil their thoughts were all the time,	The LORD saw that the wickedness of man was great in the earth, and that every imagination of the thoughts of his heart was only evil continually.

how wicked everyone on earth was: literally "that the wickedness of man on earth was great" (see RSV). Wicked and evil translate the same Hebrew word, "bad."

their thoughts: literally "the tendency of the thoughts of their hearts" (see RSV), but in Hebrew the heart is thought of as the part of the body that does the deciding and willing, and is what we might call "the mind."

6.6   TEV
he was sorry that he had ever
made them and put them on the
earth. He was so filled with regret

RSV
And the LORD was sorry that he
had made man on the earth, and
it grieved him to his heart.

was sorry: "regretted," "wished that he had not."
He was so filled with regret: literally "he was hurt (or, grieved)
to his heart" (see RSV), a strong way of expressing sorrow. The so
connects with the that at the beginning of verse 7. In some languages
it may be easier to make this a simple statement, "He was filled with
regret," and begin a new sentence with verse 7.

6.7   TEV
that he said, "I will wipe out
these people I have created, and
also the animals and the birds,
because I am sorry that I made
any of them."

RSV
So the LORD said, "I will blot
out man whom I have created from
the face of the ground, man and
beast and creeping things and
birds of the air, for I am sorry
that I have made them."

I will wipe out: "I will destroy," "I will remove from the earth."
Note that the literal form is "I will wipe out man (mankind) that I
created from upon the face (surface) of the earth" (see RSV).
animals: literally "animals and small animals." The word here
translated "small animals" is often translated "creeping things," but
the word is used for all kinds of small animals (see 1.23). All animal
life is included here.
birds: literally "birds of the heavens" (see RSV), but this is a
standard formula in Hebrew to mean "birds that fly," and in most languages it is redundant to add a qualifier to "birds."
I am sorry: the same Hebrew verb is used in verse 5.

6.8   TEV
But the LORD was pleased with
Noah.

RSV
But Noah found favor in the
eyes of the LORD.

The Hebrew is literally "But Noah found favor in the eyes of the
LORD" (RSV), but the meaning is "The LORD looked with favor on Noah,"
"The LORD was pleased with Noah," or "Noah pleased the LORD."

SECTION HEADING

Noah (6.9-22): "The Story of Noah," "Noah Prepares for the Flood."

6.9-10   TEV
    This is the story of Noah.
He had three sons, Shem, Ham, and

RSV
    These are the generations of
Noah. Noah was a righteous man,

[47]

Japheth. Noah had no faults and was the only good man of his time. He lived in fellowship with God,

blameless in his generation; Noah walked with God. 10 And Noah had three sons, Shem, Ham, and Japheth.

TEV has reversed the order to provide better English style and to make the connection with verse 11 clearer.

the story: the Hebrew word has the meaning of "generation," "line of descendants," but it is also used in the sense of "history," "story," and that seems to be the sense here: a sort of title to what follows (see 2.4a).

had: "begat," "became the father of."

had no faults: the Hebrew word means "perfect," "blameless."

the only good man of his time: "the only righteous man in his generation."

He lived in fellowship with God: literally "walked with God" (RSV), but the verb "walk" in Hebrew is frequently used for manner of life, conduct, and "to live with God" means to conduct one's life in fellowship with God, doing what God wants. See 5.22.

6.11   TEV   RSV
but everyone else was evil in God's sight, and violence had spread everywhere.

Now the earth was corrupt in God's sight, and the earth was filled with violence.

everyone else: literally "the world" (see RSV), but the word here refers to people in the world.

was evil: the Hebrew uses a word that means "had become corrupt, spoiled, ruined" (see RSV).

evil in God's sight: literally "evil before God," but the sense is "they refused to do what God wanted," "they disobeyed the will of God," "they did not obey God." One might translate "everyone else was evil and refused to obey God."

violence: the word in Hebrew has the sense of "lawlessness," "injustice," "wrong."

had spread everywhere: literally "the earth was filled with" (RSV), in the sense that everywhere people were involved in lawlessness and violence.

6.12   TEV   RSV
God looked at the world and saw that it was evil, for the people were all living evil lives.

And God saw the earth, and behold, it was corrupt; for all flesh had corrupted their way upon the earth.

evil: the same Hebrew verb as in verse 11 is used twice in this verse.

the people were all living evil lives: literally "all flesh had corrupted its way upon the earth" (see RSV); but "all flesh" is a Hebrew form of speaking of all people, and the Hebrew "way" has the sense of manner of life (see verses 9-10).

6.13   TEV
God said to Noah, "I have
decided to put an end to all
mankind. I will destroy them
completely, because the world
is full of their violent deeds.

          RSV
And God said to Noah, "I have
determined to make an end of all
flesh; for the earth is filled
with violence through them; behold, I will destroy them with
the earth.

I have decided: literally "The end...has come before me," with
the sense "has come to my mind," that is, "I have decided to bring an
end to," "I have decided to destroy."

all mankind: literally "all flesh" (RSV), but with the sense of
all people, as in verse 12.

destroy them completely: the same Hebrew verb translated "wipe
out" in verse 7. There is a minor textual-interpretive problem here.
The Hebrew may mean "destroy them with the earth," and the Greek and
some modern translations interpret "destroy them and the earth." But
it is also possible to interpret the text in the sense of "earth" referring to all living things (see verse 11), and this is the basis for
TEV completely. Others read "destroy them from the earth."

the world is full of their violent deeds: see verse 11.

6.14   TEV
Build a boat for yourself out of
good timber; make rooms in it and
cover it with tar inside and out.

          RSV
Make yourself an ark of gopher
wood; make rooms in the ark,
and cover it inside and out
with pitch.

boat: the Hebrew word, often translated "ark," can mean a chest
or box or, as here, a ship or boat. The Hebrew word "box" is probably
used to indicate that Noah does not control or sail a boat, but is in
a "box" controlled by God.

good timber: literally "gopher wood" (RSV). But no one knows just
what kind of wood this is.

rooms: this seems to be the meaning of the Hebrew word, but others
translate differently. See, for example, New English Bible (NEB)
"reeds."

tar: "pitch," "bitumen," "mineral pitch," or "asphalt."

6.15   TEV
Make it 450 feet long, 75 feet
wide, and 45 feet high.

          RSV
This is how you are to make it:
the length of the ark three hundred cubits, its breadth fifty
cubits, and its height thirty
cubits.

Although the dimensions in Hebrew are given in cubits, the translator is advised to convert to the linear terms for measurement common
in his language, for example, 133 meters long, 22 meters wide, and 13
meters high.

[49]

6.16   TEV

Make a roof^w for the boat and
leave a space of 18 inches between the roof^w and the sides.
Build it with three decks and
put a door in the side.

^{w}roof; *or* window.

RSV

Make a roof^k for the ark, and
finish it to a cubit above; and
set the door of the ark in its
side; make it with lower, second,
and third decks.

^{k}Or *window*

    roof: this is the probable meaning, but others take the Hebrew
word to mean "window."
    leave a space of 18 inches between the roof and the sides: it is
not certain that this is the meaning of the Hebrew, which is not clear.
The literal "cubit" was approximately 44 centimeters or 18 inches long.
    three decks: "three different levels," "three floors."

6.17   TEV

I am going to send a flood on the
earth to destroy every living being. Everything on the earth will
die,

RSV

For behold, I will bring a flood
of waters upon the earth, to destroy all flesh in which is the
breath of life from under heaven;
everything that is on the earth
shall die.

    I am going to send a flood: literally "And I, behold I, am bring-
ing the flood of water upon the earth" (see RSV). The introductory
formula is a Hebrew way of emphasizing the intensity of the statement.
Each language will have its own way of making this emphasis; note that
TEV has done this simply with I am going to.
    every living being: literally "all flesh in which is the breath
of life" (RSV), which has the meaning of "all animal life," including
man and animals. The Hebrew word "flesh" is used in verses 12 and 13
to refer to human beings.
    Everything on the earth: "All animal life."

6.18   TEV

but I will make a covenant with
you. Go into the boat with your
wife, your sons, and their wives.

RSV

But I will establish my covenant
with you; and you shall come into
the ark, you, your sons, your
wife, and your sons' wives with
you.

    I will make a covenant with you: the word "covenant" is frequently
used in the Old Testament. It has the meaning of an agreement between
two parties, with mutual promises in regard to duties and responsibil-
ities. The covenant with Noah will be found in 8.21-22 and 9.8-17.

6.19-20   TEV

Take into the boat with you a

RSV

And of every living thing of all

male and a female of every kind
of animal and of every kind of
bird, in order to keep them
alive.

flesh, you shall bring two of
every sort into the ark, to keep
them alive with you; they shall
be male and female. 20 Of the
birds according to their kinds,
and of the animals according to
their kinds, of every creeping
thing of the ground according to
its kind, two of every sort shall
come in to you, to keep them
alive.

of every kind of animal and of every kind of bird: this is the
meaning of the expressions in Hebrew, "of every living thing of all
flesh" and "of the birds according to their kinds, and of the animals
according to their kinds, of every small animal (creeping thing) of
the earth, according to its kind" (see RSV). In most languages it is
not possible to retain the literal form, which may be good style in
Hebrew but is considered extremely redundant when translated literally
into most languages.

6.21	TEV	RSV
Take along all kinds of food for you and for them."	Also take with you every sort of food that is eaten, and store it up; and it shall serve as food for you and for them."

Take along all kinds of food for you and for them: literally "Also
take with you some of all the foods that are eaten and gather it to
you, and it shall be for you and for them for food," but in most languages there is no point in including all the redundancies in translation.

6.22	TEV	RSV
Noah did everything that God com-manded.	Noah did this; he did all that God commanded him.

In the Hebrew there is a repetition of "he did this" (see RSV),
but it need not be retained in translation.

C H A P T E R   7

*7.1-10: These verses give another account of the LORD's command
to take animals into the boat.*

SECTION HEADING

The Flood (7.11-24): "The Flood of Water on the Earth."

7.11 TEV	RSV
When Noah was six hundred years old, on the seventeenth day of the second month all the outlets of the vast body of water beneath the earth burst open, all the floodgates of the sky were opened,	In the six hundredth year of Noah's life, in the second month, on the seventeenth day of the month, on that day all the fountains of the great deep burst forth, and the windows of the heavens were opened.

the second month: it is not clear whether this means the second month after Noah's birthday, or more probably, the second month of the calendar year. Since we are not sure which calendar was followed, some have supposed that the second month would mean our November, while others have assumed our May. If a choice has to be made, November is possibly to be preferred.

outlets: "fountains," "springs," "openings."

vast body of water beneath the earth: the Hebrew word refers to the great ocean upon which the flat world was placed. The flood is seen in the first place as coming from this great underground body of water, which was tamed at the time of creation (see 1.2; 6.9) but was always threatening to break out.

burst open: literally "were split open, broken open." The small openings of normal springs are seen as broken open to let the flood waters come on the earth.

floodgates of the sky: the Hebrew word means "windows," "openings." It is through these openings that the water held above the dome (see 1.6-7) is let down upon the earth in the form of rain.

7.12 TEV	RSV
and rain fell on the earth for forty days and nights.	And rain fell upon the earth forty days and forty nights.

forty days and nights: the rain is continuous.

7.13 TEV	RSV
On that same day Noah and his wife went into the boat with their three sons, Shem, Ham, and Japheth, and their wives.	On the very same day Noah and his sons, Shem and Ham and Japheth, and Noah's wife and the three wives of his sons with them entered the ark,

On that same day: this refers to verse 11.

7.14 TEV	RSV
With them went every kind of animal, domestic and wild, large and small, and every kind of bird.	they and every beast according to its kind, and all the cattle according to their kinds, and every creeping thing that creeps on the earth according to its kind, and every bird according to its kind, every bird of every sort.

The verse includes all animal life, with the exception of water animals.

7.15 TEV	RSV
A male and a female of each kind of living being went into the boat with Noah,	They went into the ark with Noah, two and two of all flesh in which there was the breath of life.

of each kind of living being: literally "of all flesh in which is the breath of life" (see RSV), that is, all animals. See 6.17.

7.16 TEV	RSV
as God has commanded. Then the LORD shut the door behind Noah.	And they that entered, male and female of all flesh, went in as God had commanded him; and the LORD shut him in.

Note that TEV has not retained the repetition found in Hebrew in the first part of the verse and reflected in RSV.

7.17 TEV	RSV
The flood contined for forty days, and the water became deep enough for the boat to float.	The flood continued forty days upon the earth; and the waters increased, and bore up the ark, and it rose high above the earth.

forty days: it is assumed that this also includes forty nights, but the words are not included in the Hebrew text.

deep enough for the boat to float: this is what is meant by the literal "the water increased (deepened) and lifted up the boat, and it went high above the earth" (see RSV).

7.18 TEV	RSV
The water became deeper, and the boat drifted on the surface.	The waters prevailed and increased greatly upon the earth; and the ark floated on the face of the waters.

became deeper: the Hebrew uses two words, "rose and increased" (see RSV). The verse is little more than a repetition of the last part of verse 17 with different words, but in the story it intensifies the idea of the increasing flood.

drifted on the surface: "floated freely on the water," "floated without touching the ground."

7.19	TEV	RSV
It became so deep that it covered the highest mountains;	And the waters prevailed so mightily upon the earth that all the high mountains under the whole heaven were covered;

the highest mountains: literally "all the highest mountains which are underneath all the heavens" (see RSV), but the Hebrew expression "under the heavens" means "everywhere." One might translate "covered all the highest mountains everywhere on earth."

7.20	TEV	RSV
it went on rising until it was about twenty-five feet above the tops of the mountains.	the waters prevailed above the mountains, covering them fifteen cubits deep.

about twenty-five feet: the literal "fifteen cubits" should be converted to the normal terms in the language, for example, "seven meters."

the mountains: one may assume that this refers to the highest mountains, as some ancient translations indicate.

7.21	TEV	RSV
Every living being on the earth died—every bird, every animal, and every person.	And all flesh died that moved upon the earth, birds, cattle, beasts, all swarming creatures that swarm upon the earth, and every man;

every animal: the Hebrew includes "large animals and small animals (creeping things)," but the classification is intended to include all animal life, with the exception of the water animals.

7.22	TEV	RSV
Everything on earth that breathed died.	everything on the dry land in whose nostrils was the breath of life died.

breathed: this is the meaning of "in whose nostrils was the breath of life" (RSV).

7.23 TEV	RSV
The LORD destroyed all living beings on the earth—human beings, animals, and birds. The only ones left were Noah and those who were with him in the boat.	He blotted out every living thing that was upon the face of the ground, man and animals and creeping things and birds of the air; they were blotted out from the earth. Only Noah was left, and those that were with him in the ark.

destroyed: "wiped out." See 6.7.
left: "still alive."

7.24 TEV	RSV
The water did not start going down for a hundred and fifty days.	And the waters prevailed upon the earth a hundred and fifty days.

did not start going down: the Hebrew verb may mean "rose," "increased," "kept rising" (see verse 18), but the word may mean that the water stayed at the same level, and TEV expresses this interpretation negatively, did not start going down. RSV "prevailed" translates the same Hebrew word used in verse 18.

CHAPTER 8

SECTION HEADING

The End of the Flood (8.1-19): "The Flood Comes to an End."

8.1 TEV	RSV
God had not forgotten Noah and all the animals with him in the boat; he caused a wind to blow, and the water started going down.	But God remembered Noah and all the beasts and all the cattle that were with him in the ark. And God made a wind blow over the earth, and the waters subsided;

had not forgotten: literally "remembered" (RSV), but in Hebrew the word has the sense of "be mindful of" rather than that of suddenly recalling something that has been forgotten. There is an underlying idea of "concern," and it would not be incorrect to translate "God was concerned for."
caused a wind to blow: with the purpose of drying up the water.
started going down: not in the sense of "draining off," "going down through holes," but of the water level being reduced as the water evaporated.

8.2   TEV

The outlets of the water beneath
the earth and the floodgates of
the sky were closed. The rain
stopped,

RSV

the fountains of the deep and
the windows of the heavens were
closed, the rain from the heavens
was restrained,

The outlets of the water...rain stopped: see 7.11.

8.3   TEV

and the water gradually went down
for 150 days.

RSV

and the waters receded from the
earth continually. At the end
of a hundred and fifty days the
waters had abated;

and the water...150 days: the Hebrew verse uses several terms to
indicate that the water gradually subsided during the 150 days.

8.4   TEV

On the seventeenth day of the
seventh month the boat came to
rest on a mountain in the Ararat
range.

RSV

and in the seventh month, on the
seventeenth day of the month,
the ark came to rest upon the
mountains of Ararat.

seventh month: see 7.11.
came to rest: the bottom of the boat stuck fast, and the boat was
no longer floating.
a mountain in the Ararat range: this seems to be the meaning of
the literal "the mountains of Ararat" (RSV). Ararat is the name of a
region in Armenia.

8.5   TEV

The water kept going down, and on
the first day of the tenth month
the tops of the mountains appeared.

RSV

And the waters continued to abate
until the tenth month; in the
tenth month, on the first day of
the month, the tops of the mountains were seen.

tops of the mountains: "peaks of the surrounding mountains."

8.6   TEV

After forty days Noah opened
a window

RSV

At the end of forty days Noah
opened the window of the ark which
he had made,

After forty days: in the present context this means "forty days
after the tops of the mountains appeared."

8.7	TEV	RSV

and sent out a raven. It did not come back, but kept flying around until the water was completely gone.

and sent forth a raven; and it went to and fro until the waters were dried up from the earth.

raven: or "crow," a large bird with black plumage and a croaking cry.

was completely gone: literally "were dried up from the ground" (see RSV).

8.8	TEV	RSV

Meanwhile, Noah sent out a dove to see if the water had gone down,

Then he sent forth a dove from him, to see if the waters had subsided from the face of the ground;

Meanwhile: that is, during the period between the sending out of the raven and the drying up of the ground, but the Hebrew simply has "and" or "then." The translator should introduce this new event in accordance with his language usage.

dove: a bird that is related to the pigeon and smaller than the raven.

8.9	TEV	RSV

but since the water still covered all the land, the dove did not find a place to light. It flew back to the boat, and Noah reached out and took it in.

but the dove found no place to set her foot, and she returned to him to the ark, for the waters were still on the face of the whole earth. So he put forth his hand and took her and brought her into the ark with him.

Note how TEV's rearrangement of elements in the verse (see RSV) makes the picture clearer.

a place to light: literally "a resting place for the sole of her foot." For the writer this means that there was no tree for the dove to settle on. Apparently he does not think of the top of the mountains (verse 5) as a proper place for a dove to light. But we must remember that he was not concerned with logical details in the way we may be.

reached out and took it in: literally "reached out his hand (arm), took hold of it, and brought it to him into the boat" (see RSV).

8.10	TEV	RSV

He waited another seven days and sent out the dove again.

He waited another seven days, and again he sent forth the dove out of the ark;

another seven days: after sending out the dove the first time (see verse 8).

[57]

8.11 TEV	RSV
It returned to him in the evening with a fresh olive leaf in its beak. So Noah knew that the water had gone down.	and the dove came back to him in the evening, and lo, in her mouth a freshly plucked olive leaf; so Noah knew that the waters had subsided from the earth.

fresh olive leaf: "an olive leaf that had been freshly picked," that is, a green leaf from an olive tree.

8.12 TEV	RSV
Then he waited another seven days and sent out the dove once more; this time it did not come back.	Then he waited another seven days, and sent forth the dove; and she did not return to him any more.

Then he waited...come back: the verse should present no difficulties.

8.13 TEV	RSV
When Noah was 601 years old, on the first day of the first month, the water was gone. Noah removed the covering of the boat, looked around, and saw that the ground was getting dry.	In the six hundred and first year, in the first month, the first day of the month, the waters were dried from off the earth; and Noah removed the covering of the ark, and looked, and behold, the face of the ground was dry.

first month: see verse 7.11.
was gone: literally "was dried up from the ground."
covering: this is the first time the word has been used. It may be understood as identical with, or a part of, the roof (6.16) or some other covering not previously mentioned. In any case, by removing the cover, Noah could look around.

8.14 TEV	RSV
By the twenty-seventh day of the second month the earth was completely dry.	In the second month, on the twenty-seventh day of the month, the earth was dry.

completely dry: see verse 13.

8.15-17 TEV	RSV
God said to Noah, 16 "Go out of the boat with your wife, your sons, and their wives. 17 Take all the birds and animals out with you, so that they may reproduce and spread over all the earth."	Then God said to Noah, 16 "Go forth from the ark, you and your wife, and your sons and your sons' wives with you. 17 Bring forth with you every living thing that is with you of all

flesh—birds and animals and every
creeping thing that creeps on the
earth—that they may breed abun-
dantly on the earth, and be fruitful and multiply upon the earth."

birds and animals: see 6.20.
reproduce and spread over all the earth: literally "become many
on earth and be fruitful (have many offspring, young) and increase on
earth" (see RSV). See 1.22,28.

8.18-19 TEV	RSV
So Noah went out of the boat with his wife, his sons, and their wives. 19 All the animals and birds went out of the boat in groups of their own kind.	So Noah went forth, and his sons and his wife and his sons' wives with him. 19 And every beast, every creeping thing, and every bird, everything that moves upon the earth, went forth by families out of the ark.

All the animals: see 6.20.
in groups of their own kind: literally "by families (clans)," but
a word will be needed that can apply to all types of animals.

SECTION HEADING

Noah Offers a Sacrifice (8.20-22): "Noah Burns a Sacrifice as an
Offering to God," "Noah Burns Animals as a Gift to God."

8.20 TEV	RSV
Noah built an altar to the LORD; he took one of each kind of ritually clean animal and bird, and burned them whole as a sacrifice on the altar.	Then Noah built an altar to the LORD, and took of every clean animal and of every clean bird, and offered burnt offerings on the altar.

altar: probably constructed of stones. If no word exists one might
consider: "a table built of stones on which animals may be burned as
an offering," or perhaps "a platform (or, pile) of stones."
to the LORD: "dedicated to the LORD," "to honor the LORD."
ritually clean: this is a difficult idea to translate, but read
Leviticus 11.1-47. Instead of using "clean" or "pure," many translators
will find it more meaningful to speak of animals or birds that may be
eaten or offered in sacrifice to God. For example, "Noah took one of
each kind of animal that is acceptable for sacrifice or that can be
eaten."
burned them whole as a sacrifice: the point here is that after
the animals are killed, cleaned, and skinned, the whole animal carcass
is burned up on the altar; none of the meat is kept for people to eat,

[59]

as in some other types of sacrifice (see Lev 1.1-17). If there is no adequate word for sacrifice, something like "a gift to God" might be considered.

8.21   TEV   RSV

The odor of the sacrifice pleased   And when the LORD smelled the
the LORD, and he said to himself,   pleasing odor, the LORD said in
"Never again will I put the earth   his heart, "I will never again
under a curse because of what man   curse the ground because of man,
does; I know that from the time   for the imagination of man's heart
he is young his thoughts are evil.   is evil from his youth; neither
Never again will I destroy all   will I ever again destroy every
living beings, as I have done this   living creature as I have done.
time.

The odor of the sacrifice pleased the LORD: literally "and the LORD smelled the smell of the sacrifice." A word should be chosen for "smell" which means a pleasant smell and not an unpleasant smell.

said to himself: literally "said in his heart" (RSV). See 6.5 for "heart."

put the earth under a curse: literally "place a curse on the earth." For curse, see 3.14,17; the word has not been used in the flood narrative, but the word refers to the destruction of all animal life on earth.

man: the meaning is "mankind," "human beings."

thoughts: see 6.5.

8.22   TEV   RSV

As long as the world exists,   While the earth remains, seed-
there will be a time for plant-   time and harvest, cold and heat,
ing and a time for harvest.   summer and winter, day and night,
There will always be cold and   shall not cease."
heat, summer and winter, day
and night."

The verse is in poetic form in Hebrew, but this cannot be retained in most languages.

As long as the world exists: literally "Until all the days of the world," that is, "Until the world ends."

a time for planting and a time for harvest: this is what is meant by the literal "seed and harvest," referring to the time for planting grain and the time for cutting it when it is ripe.

CHAPTER 9

SECTION HEADING

God's Covenant with Noah (9.1-17): "God Makes a Covenant with Noah."

9.1 TEV	RSV
God blessed Noah and his sons and said, "Have many children, so that your descendants will live all over the earth.	And God blessed Noah and his sons, and said to them, "Be fruitful and multiply, and fill the earth.

blessed: see 1.22,28.
Have many children: see 1.28.

9.2 TEV	RSV
All the animals, birds, and fish will live in fear of you. They are all placed under your power.	The fear of you and the dread of you shall be upon every beast of the earth, and upon every bird of the air, upon everything that creeps on the ground and all the fish of the sea; into your hand they are delivered.

All the animals, birds, and fish: the literal form (see RSV) is a summary in Hebrew categories of all animal life (see 1.26).
will live in fear of you: literally "fear of you and terror of you will be upon them" (see RSV), but in English it is more natural to speak of "living in fear" or "being afraid" rather than of fear being on someone.
placed under your power: this is the meaning of the literal "they are given into your hand" (see RSV), that is, "you will control them, have power over them."

9.3 TEV	RSV
Now you can eat them, as well as green plants; I give them all to you for food.	Every moving thing that lives shall be food for you; and as I gave you the green plants, I give you everything.

you can eat: literally "will be food for you" (RSV), but the active form is natural in English.
them: that is, "all the animals, birds, and fish." The literal "Every moving thing that lives" (RSV) is a Hebrew way of referring to all animal life.
green plants: see 1.29.

[61]

9.4 TEV	RSV
The one thing you must not eat is meat with blood still in it; I forbid this because the life is in the blood.	Only you shall not eat flesh with its life, that is, its blood.

meat with blood still in it...the life is in the blood: the Hebrew is very compressed "meat with its life, its blood," but in most languages it will be necessary to translate the meaning more fully. It is clear that "blood" is identified with "life," and this needs to be explained to the reader. See particularly Leviticus 17.10-14. The blood is a symbol that represents life.

9.5 TEV	RSV
If anyone takes human life, he will be punished. I will punish with death any animal that takes a human life.	For your lifeblood I will surely require a reckoning; of every beast I will require it and of man; of every man's brother I will require the life of man.

anyone: literally "of mankind, of a man's brother" (see RSV), but this is a Hebrew way of speaking of everyone or anyone.

takes human life: literally "your blood for your life," but what is meant is that for human beings (as well as for animals) blood represents life, and "to shed blood" means "to kill." Here the clear meaning is "kill another human being."

will be punished: literally "I will seek from his hand," which is a Hebrew figure meaning "I will hold him responsible and punish him for doing it," that is, for taking human life, for killing a fellow human being.

punish with death: that is, "must be put to death in accordance with my Law."

any animal that takes a human life: although the Hebrew is compressed, this is clearly what is meant.

9.6 TEV	RSV
Man was made like God, so whoever murders a man will himself be killed by his fellow-man.	Whoever sheds the blood of man, by man shall his blood be shed; for God made man in his own image.

like God: see 1.27.

murders: literally "sheds blood" (see RSV), but this is a figure for causing death, and since accidental death is not in focus, the reference is to a deliberate act of killing someone, that is, "murder" as distinct from legal execution or accidental killing.

be killed: literally "his blood will be shed" (see RSV), which here refers to putting to death in punishment for a crime. The man who murders is to be put to death by his fellow-men in obedience to the laws of God.

9.7	TEV	RSV
	"You must have many children, so that your descendants will live all over the earth."	And you, be fruitful and multiply, bring forth abundantly on the earth and multiply in it."

many children...earth: see 1.28.

9.8	TEV	RSV
	God said to Noah and his sons,	Then God said to Noah and to his sons with him,

his sons: literally "his sons with him" (RSV), but in context it is clear that his sons are with him, and in English it sounds strange to state it.

9.9	TEV	RSV
	"I am now making my covenant with you and with your descendants,	"Behold, I establish my covenant with you and your descendants after you,

I am now making a covenant: this is the sense of the literal "and I, behold I, am establishing my covenant" (see RSV). There is a strong emphasis in the Hebrew, and some of this is felt in the TEV now.

your descendants: literally "your seed after you." The word "seed" means descendants, and in English it is redundant to state that descendants come after the forefather.

9.10	TEV	RSV
	and with all living beings—all birds and all animals—everything that came out of the boat with you.	and with every living creature that is with you, the birds, the cattle, and every beast of the earth with you, as many as came out of the ark.[l]

[l]GK: Heb repeats *every beast of the earth*

all living beings...animals: there is some repetition in the Hebrew, but this is clearly the meaning. See RSV footnote.

9.11	TEV	RSV
	With these words I make my covenant with you: I promise that never again will all living beings be destroyed by a flood; never again will a flood destroy the earth.	I establish my covenant with you, that never again shall all flesh be cut off by the waters of a flood, and never again shall there be a flood to destroy the earth."

[63]

With these words: although these words are not present in Hebrew, something like this is needed to make clear that the repetition of the literal "I establish my covenant" (verse 9, and see RSV) is understood to refer to what follows.

I promise: these words are not present in the Hebrew, but by using them the English can make clear the meaning of the Hebrew, with its clear indication of promise found in the Hebrew form that is used.

all living beings: literally "all flesh" (RSV), but the Hebrew word has a wide range of meaning and here means "all animal life," including mankind.

be destroyed: literally "be cut off" (RSV), but in Hebrew this often has the meaning of "be put to death," "be destroyed."

9.12 TEV	RSV
As a sign of this everlasting covenant which I am making with you and with all living beings,	And God said, "This is the sign of the covenant which I make between me and you and every living creature that is with you, for all future generations:

sign: that is, something that has meaning apart from its own existence. The rainbow will be a sign (that is, an indication, a statement) that has a meaning: God will not again destroy.

everlasting covenant: literally "a covenant for all future generations" (see RSV), that is, that will last forever.

9.13 TEV	RSV
I am putting my bow in the clouds. It will be the sign of my covenant with the world.	I set my bow in the cloud, and it shall be a sign of the covenant between me and the earth.

bow: "the rainbow."

in the clouds: it is clear that a rainbow is produced when the sun is reflected and refracted from rain drops, and usually clouds are present. It may be necessary, however, in some languages to say simply "in the sky."

the world: that is, "the world of human and animal life," as in verse 12.

9.14 TEV	RSV
Whenever I cover the sky with clouds and the rainbow appears,	When I bring clouds over the earth and the bow is seen in the clouds,

cover the sky with clouds: "cause clouds to appear in the sky."

9.15 TEV	RSV
I will remember my promise to you and to all the animals that a	I will remember my covenant which is between me and you and every

| flood will never again destroy
all living beings. | living creature of all flesh; and
the waters shall never again be-
come a flood to destroy all flesh. |

my promise: literally "my covenant, between me and you" (see RSV),
but the entire emphasis is on God's promise in the agreement.

9.16-17 TEV	RSV
When the rainbow appears in the clouds, I will see it and remem- ber the everlasting covenant be- tween me and all living beings on earth. 17 That is the sign of the promise which I am making to all living beings."	When the bow is in the clouds, I will look upon it and remember the everlasting covenant between God and every living creature of all flesh that is upon the earth." 17 God said to Noah, "This is the sign of the covenant which I have established between me and all flesh that is upon the earth."

These verses present no particular problems that have not been
dealt with in the preceding verses.

*9.18—10.32: These verses contain a story about Noah and his sons,
and a list of the descendants of Noah.*

C H A P T E R   11

SECTION HEADING

The Tower of Babylon (11.1-9): "People Build the Tower of Babylon,"
"The LORD Mixes Up Man's Language." For the word Babylon see verse 19.

11.1 TEV	RSV
At first, the people of the whole world had only one language and used the same words.	Now the whole earth had one language and few words.

At first: this introductory English formula, like the literal
"And it was that," is simply an attempt to set the stage for the following story. The translator will need to find an appropriate form in
his own language. Note that RSV uses "Now" as an introductory word.
used the same words: this is the probable meaning of the Hebrew,
although some translate "used few words" (see RSV).

11.2 TEV	RSV
As they wandered about in the East, they came to a plain in Babylonia and settled there.	And as men migrated from the east, they found a plain in the land of Shinar and settled there.

[65]

wandered about: the Hebrew word means "pull up stakes," "break camp," "start out," which is probably to be understood in the sense of TEV, "move about," although some understand it in the sense of "migrate" (see RSV).

in the East: the Hebrew expression is often taken as "from the east," but the expression is vague and can be understood as "eastward." TEV has assumed the sense "in an eastern land."

they came to: the Hebrew word can mean "found" (RSV), but here the sense is "came upon," "chanced upon." See 4.14.

a plain in Babylonia: the Hebrew has "the land of Shinar" (RSV), but this name refers to the land more widely known as Babylonia, and in most languages it is better to use the more familiar name rather than using two names to refer to the same place.

settled there: "stayed there," "made their home there."

11.3	TEV	RSV
They said to one another, "Come on! Let's make bricks and bake them hard." So they had bricks to build with and tar to hold them together.	And they said to one another, "Come, let us make bricks, and burn them thoroughly." And they had brick for stone, and bitumen for mortar.

to one another: literally "a man to his neighbor," but this is a frequently used Hebrew expression for "to one another."

Come on!: the Hebrew word is an interjection used to get attention, and each language will have its own way of saying this. If nothing in the language is appropriate, the expression may be dropped. It is also possible to restructure in a form of indirect discourse, for example, "They talked with one another and agreed that they would make bricks and bake them."

bricks: these were molded from clay and hardened by baking them in a kiln.

tar: "bitumen," "asphalt." In 6.14 a different Hebrew word is used, but the same substance is referred to.

to hold them together: literally "for mortar" (RSV), the material used to bind the bricks together.

11.4	TEV	RSV
They said, "Now let's build a city with a tower that reaches the sky, so that we can make a name for ourselves and not be scattered all over the earth."	Then they said, "Come, let us build ourselves a city, and a tower with its top in the heavens, and let us make a name for ourselves, lest we be scattered abroad upon the face of the whole earth."

Now: the Hebrew has the same word translated Come on in verse 3.

tower: the Hebrew word is used for any kind of tower, but here it refers to a kind of pyramid or temple tower, technically known as a ziggurat.

[66]

that reaches the sky: literally "and its head (top) in the heavens (sky)" (see RSV). Here possibly the thought is not only that the tower will reach as high as the dome of the sky, but that it would reach the dwelling place of God or the gods.

make a name for ourselves: "become renowned, famous."

scattered: "dispersed," "separated," "spread out."

11.5	TEV	RSV
	Then the LORD came down to see the city and the tower which those men had built,	And the LORD came down to see the city and the tower, which the sons of men had built.

came down: that is, "descended from heaven."

those men: literally "the sons of men" (RSV) in the sense of "human beings," but the formulation emphasizes the contrast with God. One might translate "men destined to die," "people who can live only a short time," but the expression chosen should apply to human beings in general and not just to these particular men.

11.6	TEV	RSV
	and he said, "Now then, these are all one people and they speak one language; this is just the beginning of what they are going to do. Soon they will be able to do anything they want!	And the LORD said, "Behold, they are one people, and they have all one language; and this is only the beginning of what they will do; and nothing that they propose to do will now be impossible for them.

Now then: this translates the literal "Behold" (RSV).

one people: "one race of people," "one nation."

just the beginning of what they are going to do: "there is no telling what they will do," "what will they do next?"

Soon: literally "now" (RSV), but in the sense "if they can finish this tower, then they will be able to...."

they will be able to do anything: "nothing will be impossible for them."

11.7	TEV	RSV
	Let us go down and mix up their language so that they will not understand each other."	Come, let us go down, and there confuse their language, that they may not understand one another's speech."

Let us go down: see 1.26. "We will go down," "I will go down." The same verb is used as in verse 5. The verse begins with the same interjection translated Come on in verse 3 and Now in verse 4. TEV has omitted it on stylistic grounds.

mix up: "confuse," "confound."

11.8 TEV	RSV
So the LORD scattered them all over the earth, and they stopped building the city.	So the LORD scattered them abroad from there over the face of all the earth, and they left off building the city.

scattered: the Hebrew has the same verb as in verse 4.

the city: the Hebrew does not have here "with (and) the tower," as in verses 4 and 5, but it would be included in the city. Some ancient translations add "and the tower" to make it perfectly clear, but the translator is advised to follow the Hebrew text.

11.9 TEV	RSV
The city was called Babylon,^{a} because there the LORD mixed up the language of all the people, and from there he scattered them all over the earth.	Therefore its name was called Babel, because there the LORD confused^p the language of all the earth; and from there the LORD scattered them abroad over the face of all the earth.
^{a}BABYLON: *This name sounds like the Hebrew for "mixed up."*	^{p}Compare Heb *balal*, confuse

Babylon: the name for the city sounds somewhat like the Hebrew verb for "mixed up," and a note needs to be provided so that the reader may understand this intended play on words. Traditionally the tower is called "the tower of Babel," but the Hebrew name is the same as the name for the city of Babylon, and TEV has chosen to make this clear.

11.10-32: This includes a list of the descendants of Shem and Terah.

C H A P T E R   12

SECTION HEADING

God's Call to Abram (12.1-9): "God Calls Abram to Obey Him."

12.1 TEV	RSV
The LORD said to Abram, "Leave your country, your relatives, and your father's home, and go to a land that I am going to show you.	Now the LORD said to Abram, "Go from your country and your kindred and your father's house to the land that I will show you.

Abram: note the form of the name and see 17.5. Your choice of a transliterated form of the name should keep the change of name in mind. In a number of languages, however, where the use of two names has proved to be difficult, translators have preferred to use a

well-known form of the name throughout the text, and they deal with
17.5 by the use of an explanatory note; but 17.5 has not been included
in the current series for a condensed Bible. In other cases translators
have preferred to use a shortened form of the name in the text here
with the full name Abraham in the section headings, with a note or
bracket to indicate that two names are being used for the same person.

country...land: in Hebrew the same word is used, but the context
of the word first used shows that it means "home country," "native
land," while the second refers to an "unknown land."

father's home: literally "father's house" (RSV), but this does
not refer to a building. The word here means "home," "family," "close
relatives of your father."

show you: "take you to see."

12.2 TEV	RSV
I will give you many descendants, and they will become a great nation. I will bless you and make your name famous, so that you will be a blessing.	And I will make of you a great nation, and I will bless you, and make your name great, so that you will be a blessing.

I will give you many descendants, and they will become a great
nation: literally "I will make you into a great nation" (see RSV), but
what is meant is that Abram will have many children, grandchildren,
and descendants until his descendants are like a nation in number.

I will bless you: see 1.22,28. The meaning is "cause you to prosper," but not only in the number of possessions. The blessing of God
will make Abram an important person, and this element is included in
the next expression.

make your name famous: literally "make your name great" (RSV).
This has the sense of "make your name known and recognized by everyone," but the Hebrew also has the underlying idea that the name really
represents the person. So one might translate here quite correctly,
"I will make of you a great person, a famous person."

so that you will be a blessing: the Hebrew "be a blessing" is difficult to translate, but it may have the sense of "be a symbol for
what God's blessing really means," or it may be an idiomatic expression
for "be richly blessed." It is more probable, however, that the original subject of the verb was "your name," and that the meaning is
"your name will be a blessing," that is, "People will use your name
when they pronounce blessings." See the footnote to verse 3 in TEV,
which expresses a similar idea.

12.3 TEV	RSV
I will bless those who bless you, But I will curse those who curse you. And through you I will bless all the nations."[b]	I will bless those who bless you, and him who curses you I will curse; and by you all the families of the earth shall bless themselves."[q]

^bAnd through...nations; *or* All
the nations will ask me to
bless them as I have blessed
you.

^qOr *in you all the families of
the earth shall be blessed*

    you: the Hebrew is singular, but it is clear that the reference
is to "Abram and his descendants."
    through you I will bless all the nations: in this form the sense
is clearly that God will work through Abram to extend the blessing
given to him and his family (nation) to all other families (nations).
It is possible, and in the light of 22.18 and 26.4 probable, that the
intended meaning of the Hebrew is expressed by "All the nations will
ask me to bless them as I have blessed you."

12.4   TEV   RSV

    When Abram was seventy-five
years old, he started out from
Haran, as the LORD had told him
to do; and Lot went with him.

    So Abram went, as the LORD had
told him; and Lot went with him.
Abram was seventy-five years old
when he departed from Haran.

    Haran: a city in northern Mesopotamia, where Abram lived.
    Lot: Abram's nephew. In a condensed Bible which has not introduced
his name earlier, the translation in this verse should read "and Lot,
Abram's nephew," rather than in verse 5.

12.5   TEV   RSV

Abram took his wife Sarai, his
nephew Lot, and all the wealth
and all the slaves they had
acquired in Haran, and they
started out for the land of
Canaan.
    When they arrived in Canaan,

And Abram took Sarai his wife,
and Lot his brother's son, and
all their possessions which they
had gathered, and the persons
that they had gotten in Haran;
and they set forth to go to the
land of Canaan. When they had
come to the land of Canaan,

    wealth: literally "all the possessions which they had acquired,"
referring to silver and gold, clothing, and the like, but also to the
herds of animals they owned.
    slaves: this is the meaning of "souls" (RSV "persons") in this
context.
    the land of Canaan: identical with Palestine west of the Jordan
River and part of Syria (modern Lebanon).

12.6   TEV   RSV

Abram traveled through the land
until he came to the sacred tree
of Moreh, the holy place at
Shechem. (At that time the Canaanites were still living in
the land.)

Abram passed through the land to
the place at Shechem, to the oak^r
of Moreh. At that time the Canaanites were in the land.

^rOr *terebinth*

the sacred tree of Moreh: the Hebrew word is often translated "terebinth tree" or "oak tree" (see RSV) of Moreh, but there is strong evidence that the reference is to "a sacred tree," "a tree dedicated to the gods."

the holy place: the Hebrew word "place" has the meaning of "holy place," "a place where God is worshiped (or the gods are worshiped)." Here the sacred tree of Moreh is also called the holy place at Shechem.

Shechem: a town about 65 kilometers (40 miles) north of Jerusalem, but Abram is at the sacred site outside the town.

(At that time...land.): this parenthetical statement reminds the reader that although the Canaanites had been driven out by the time Genesis was written (see The Book of Joshua), when Abram was there he was passing through a country still owned and controlled by the Canaanites.

12.7 TEV	RSV
The LORD appeared to Abram and said to him, "This is the country that I am going to give to your descendants." Then Abram built an altar there to the LORD, who had appeared to him.	Then the LORD appeared to Abram, and said, "To your descendants I will give this land." So he built there an altar to the LORD, who had appeared to him.

appeared: it is not explicitly stated how God revealed himself to Abram (dream, vision, angel, etc.) as is sometimes done, but the Hebrew word does include the basic idea of God becoming visible to Abram in some way.

altar: see 8.20.

to the LORD: "dedicated to the LORD," "to honor the LORD."

12.8 TEV	RSV
After that, he moved on south to the hill country east of the city of Bethel and set up his camp between Bethel on the west and Ai on the east. There also he built an altar and worshiped the LORD.	Thence he removed to the mountain on the east of Bethel, and pitched his tent, with Bethel on the west and Ai on the east; and there he built an altar to the LORD and called on the name of the LORD.

hill country: the Hebrew has "the mountain," but the word is used not for a particular mountain but for "mountainous, hilly country."

east of the city of Bethel: about 50 kilometers (30 miles) south of Shechem.

Bethel...Ai: the two towns were close to each other, about 15 kilometers (10 miles) north of Jerusalem.

12.9 TEV	RSV
Then he moved on from place to place, going toward the southern part of Canaan.	And Abram journeyed on, still going toward the Negeb.

[71]

moved on from place to place: "moved his camp from place to place." As a nomad with his herds and flocks he gradually moves south, camping for a few days here and a few days there.

southern part of Canaan: that is, the Negev, the area south of the Dead Sea.

12.10-20: Abram in Egypt tells the king that Sarai (Sarah) is his sister.

13.1-18: Abram and Lot separate because there is not enough pasture for all their animals; Lot moves to the Jordan Valley, while Abram moves to Hebron.

14.1-24: Abram rescues Lot during a period of war, and Melchizedek blesses Abram.

C H A P T E R   15

SECTION HEADING

God's Covenant with Abram (15.1-6): "God Makes a Covenant (or, an Agreement) with Abram."

15.1 TEV	RSV
After this, Abram had a vision and heard the LORD say to him, "Do not be afraid, Abram. I will shield you from danger and give you a great reward."	After these things the word of the LORD came to Abram in a vision, "Fear not, Abram, I am your shield; your reward shall be very great."

After this: apparently after Abram had rescued Lot, but it is a rather vague time reference. In a set of selections one might use "One time," "On one occasion."

had a vision: the Hebrew word (not the same as in 12.7) emphasizes the subjective character of the event. But the word does not tell us exactly how Abram "saw" or just what he saw, because the emphasis falls on what he heard. If no way can be found to speak about a vision, it may be necessary to translate "saw something (something unusual?) and heard...."

heard the LORD say to him: literally "the word (message) of the LORD came to him" (see RSV), but this is a Hebrew way of speaking of hearing the voice of the LORD, particularly in appearances or visions. The translator is advised to use the normal expression in the language for "heard the LORD speak to him and say."

Do not be afraid: this is not in reference to chapter 14 but to the future: "Do not be afraid, worried, about what will happen."

I will shield you from danger: literally "I am a shield for you" (see RSV), but this is a figure of speech: "Just as a shield protects the soldier from the arrows of the enemy, I will protect you from any dangers that might come."

and give you a great reward: literally "and your reward very great" (see RSV). The word for "reward" should not convey the idea of money paid for work that Abram has done for God. Rather, the idea is "I will give you (as a gift) many good things," "I will do many good things for you."

15.2 TEV	RSV
But Abram answered, "Sovereign LORD, what good will your reward do me, since I have no children? My only heir is Eliezer of Damascus.^{d}	But Abram said, "O Lord GOD, what wilt thou give me, for I continue childless, and the heir of my house is Eliezer of Damascus?"

^{d}My...Damascus; *Hebrew unclear.*

Sovereign LORD: "Lord GOD," that is "the Lord (Master, Ruler) who is GOD (Yahweh)." The Hebrew combines the word "Lord" with the personal name of God (Yahweh). The translator might use "Lord, my GOD," "GOD, my Master."

what good will your reward do me: literally "what can you give me?" That is, "there is nothing you can give me as a blessing, because I am going to die childless." In Hebrew thought the greatest tragedy was to die without children to carry on the name and the memory of the departed. Here, of course, the reference is to the gift mentioned in verse 1 and to the promise of many descendants in 12.2.

heir: "the one who will inherit my property after I die." The Hebrew is not clear, but this seems to be the meaning.

Damascus: a city north of Lake Galilee, the capitol of modern Syria.

15.3 TEV	RSV
You have given me no children, and one of my slaves will inherit my property."	And Abram said, "Behold, thou hast given me no offspring; and a slave born in my house will be my heir."

The verse repeats the last part of verse 2, and in some translations it would be wise to combine the two verses.

children: literally "seed," which is a standard Hebrew way of referring to children and descendants.

one of my slaves: this seems to be the meaning of the literal "a son of my house."

15.4 TEV	RSV
Then he heard the LORD speaking to him again: "This slave Eliezer will not inherit your property; your own son will be your heir."	And behold, the word of the LORD came to him, "This man shall not be your heir; your own son shall be your heir."

[73]

he heard: see verse 1.

This slave Eliezer: literally "This man" (RSV), and the translator should use what seems best stylistically, "This man," "This person," or "Eliezer."

your own son: that is the meaning of the literal "the one that will come out of your own body."

15.5	TEV	RSV
The LORD took him outside and said, "Look at the sky and try to count the stars; you will have as many descendants as that."		And he brought him outside and said, "Look toward heaven, and number the stars, if you are able to number them." Then he said to him, "So shall your descendants be."

took him outside: "led him outside the tent."
try to count: "count the stars if you can."
as that: "as there are stars in the sky."

15.6	TEV	RSV
	Abram put his trust in the LORD, and because of this the LORD was pleased with him and accepted him.	And he believed the LORD; and he reckoned it to him as righteousness.

put his trust in: the Hebrew word is sometimes translated "believed," (RSV), but the word has a stronger force: "rely upon," "have faith in," "rest oneself firmly upon."

was pleased with him and accepted him: the Hebrew is difficult to translate. Perhaps "considered his faith to be righteousness" or "counted his faith as righteousness," but such an expression is in abstract terms and makes little sense in most languages. It will be much more satisfactory to analyze the meaning and translate with language that is not abstract. In Hebrew the word "righteousness" and its related forms contain the element of "one who is right with God, in right relation to God." TEV has broken the whole expression into two parts: 1) the LORD was pleased with Abram, with Abram's trusting himself to him, and 2) the LORD accepted Abram, put his approval upon him, considered him to be in right relationship with himself.

15.7-21: The covenant with Abram is sealed after Abram cuts animals in half.

16.1-16: These verses tell the story of Hagar and the birth of Abram's son, Ishmael.

C H A P T E R   17

17.1-14: Circumcision is given as the sign of God's covenant with Abram, and his name is changed to Abraham.

SECTION HEADING

The Birth of Isaac Is Promised (17.15-27): "God Promises that
Abraham and Sarah Will Have a Son and Will Name Him Isaac."

17.15 TEV	RSV
God said to Abraham, "You must no longer call your wife Sarai; from now on her name is Sarah.^{x}	And God said to Abraham, "As for Sarai your wife, you shall not call her name Sarai, but Sarah shall be her name.

^{x}SARAH: *This name in Hebrew means "princess."*

Sarai: see 12.1. Just as Abram is given a new name, Abraham, so
his wife Sarai is given a new name, Sarah.

17.16 TEV	RSV
I will bless her, and I will give you a son by her. I will bless her, and she will become the mother of nations, and there will be kings among her descendants."	I will bless her, and moreover I will give you a son by her; I will bless her, and she shall be a mother of nations; kings of peoples shall come from her."

bless: the use of the vow twice in the same verse is unusual,
and many have assumed that the early translations have preserved the
correct text in reading the second vow as "I will bless him (the son)."
But the repetition is not impossible and may be understood as marking
a new stage in the blessing, although both blessings are possible only
through the birth of a son.
the mother of nations: that is, through this son, who will have
many descendants, Sarah will be considered the mother (or the grand-
mother) of nations that will some day look back to her as the female
ancestor from whom the nations descended.
kings among her descendants: the Hebrew may be translated "kings
of peoples shall come from her" (RSV). But the point is that in later
years, when her descendants have become nations, some of her descendants
will be kings of those nations; the point is not that she is going to
have other sons besides Isaac who will become kings.

17.17 TEV	RSV
Abraham bowed down with his face touching the ground, but he began to laugh when he thought, "Can a man have a child when he is a hundred years old? Can Sarah have a child at ninety?"	Then Abraham fell on his face and laughed, and said to himself, "Shall a child be born to a man who is a hundred years old? Shall Sarah, who is ninety years old, bear a child?"

bowed down with his face touching the ground: literally "he fell
on his face" (see RSV), but this should be translated in such a way as
to indicate that he bowed down in reverence, for example, "kneeled

[75]

down and put his face to the ground in reverence." The meaning is not that he stumbled and fell down on his face.

began to laugh: although the Hebrew has "and he laughed" (see RSV), it is clear that this follows his bowing down and relates to his view of the impossibility of his having children.

he thought: literally "he said in his heart," with the sense of "he said to himself" (see RSV), or he thought.

Can a man have a child...old?: it should be understood that Abraham is not asking whether this is possible, but is saying by his question that it is not possible. If the translator's language does not use such rhetorical questions, he may have to translate an answer, for example, "Can a man have a child when he is a hundred years old? No, of course not." Or it may be easier to drop the question form and translate "It is totally impossible for a man to have a child when he is a hundred years old."

Can Sarah have a child at ninety?: this is also a rhetorical question that should be handled by the translator in the same way. It is also possible to combine the questions, for example, "I am a hundred years old and Sarah is ninety; how can we ever have a child? (we can never have a child.)"

17.18   TEV   RSV
He asked God, "Why not let Ishmael   And Abraham said to God, "Oh that
be my heir?"   Ishmael might live in thy sight!"

asked: or "said" (RSV).

Why not: in many languages it will be best to avoid the question and translate "I wish that Ishmael might be..." or "It would be better if you would make Ishmael...."

Ishmael: in a condensed Bible, which omits chapter 16, it will be necessary to identify Ishmael, either in the text ("Ishmael, the son my slave Hagar bore me," for example) or in a footnote explaining that Ishmael was the son of Abraham and of Hagar, the slave of Sarah.

be my heir: the Hebrew has literally "shall live before you" in the sense of "live under your special care," but this refers to 15.4 and 17.2,4-8, and could best be translated as TEV has done or with something like "receive the promises you have made to me." The whole point is that Abraham rejects the promise that Sarah will have a son. Essentially he tells God that if he is to bless Abraham as he has promised, he should carry out the promise through Ishmael.

17.19   TEV   RSV
        But God said, "No. Your wife   God said, "No, but Sarah your
Sarah will bear you a son and you   wife shall bear you a son, and
will name him Isaac.^{i} I will keep   you shall call his name Isaac.^{z}
my covenant with him and with his   I will establish my covenant
descendants forever. It is an   with him as an everlasting cov-
everlasting covenant.   enant for his descendants after
                                       him.

^{i}ISAAC: *This name in Hebrew means* ^{z}*That is he laughs*
"he laughs."

No: this is the negative response to the suggestion that the promise be carried out through Ishmael. It may be necessary to translate "It will not be Ishmael," "I will not do it through Ishmael."

you will name: the father names the child.

Isaac: the name has the meaning "he laughs" and connects directly with he began to laugh in verse 17. A footnote will be needed to explain to the reader this intentional play on words.

I will keep my covenant: it is not that a new covenant will be made with Isaac, but that the covenant made with Abraham will be extended to Isaac and his descendants.

an everlasting covenant: "a covenant that will continue forever."

17.20 TEV	RSV
I have heard your request about Ishmael, so I will bless him and give him many children and many descendants. He will be the father of twelve princes, and I will make a great nation of his descendants.	As for Ishmael, I have heard you; behold, I will bless him and make him fruitful and multiply him exceedingly; he shall be the father of twelve princes, and I will make him a great nation.

I have heard your request: literally "I have heard you," in the sense "I have heard what you have asked me to do (and I will do something about it)."

twelve princes: see 25.12-18 for the names of the twelve sons of Ishmael and the twelve Ishmaelite tribes.

17.21 TEV	RSV
But I will keep my covenant with your son Isaac, who will be born to Sarah about this time next year."	But I will establish my covenant with Isaac, whom Sarah shall bear to you at this season next year."

about this time: this is probably the meaning of the Hebrew word for "fixed time, appointed time," although some translate it as "this season" (RSV).

17.22 TEV	RSV
When God finished speaking to Abraham, he left him.	When he had finished talking with him, God went up from Abraham.

he left him: literally "God went up from Abraham" (RSV). This could possibly have the meaning "went up into heaven" (see 11.5), but it is more likely that it simply means "went away from."

17.23 TEV	RSV
On that same day Abraham	Then Abraham took Ishmael his son

TEV	RSV
obeyed God and circumcised his son Ishmael and all the other males in his household, including the slaves born in his home and those he had bought.	and all the slaves born in his house or bought with his money, every male among the men of Abraham's house, and he circumcised the flesh of their foreskins that very day, as God had said to him.

obeyed God: literally "did as God had told him to do." The command is found in verses 10-14, but in sets of selections which do not include these words, the translation of obeyed God will need to be expressed in general terms. It would also be possible to translate "obeyed God's command to circumcise all the males."

circumcised: literally "circumcise (cut around) the flesh (skin) of the penis." If circumcision is not known in the language, some way will need to be found to speak of the cutting of the foreskin that will not be considered improper in public reading of the Scriptures.

17.24-27 TEV	RSV
Abraham was ninety-nine years old when he was circumcised, 25 and his son Ishmael was thirteen. 26 They were both circumcised on the same day, 27 together with all of Abraham's slaves.	Abraham was ninety-nine years old when he was circumcised in the flesh of his foreskin. 25 And Ishmael his son was thirteen years old when he was circumcised in the flesh of his foreskin. 26 That very day Abraham and his son Ishmael were circumcised; 27 and all the men of his house, those born in the house and those bought with money from a foreigner, were circumcised with him.

the same day: the Hebrew emphasizes that this happened on the same day.

18.1-15: The LORD appears to Abraham, and three men promise that Sarah will have a child.

18.16—19.29: This section describes the sinfulness of Sodom, Abraham's plea to God that Sodom be spared, the escape of Lot, and the destruction of Sodom and Gomorrah.

19.30—20.18: This section describes the origin of the Moabites and Ammonites and tells of Abraham's lying to King Abimelech about Sarah his wife.

CHAPTER 21

SECTION HEADING

The Birth of Isaac (21.1-8): "A Son Is Born to Abraham and Sarah," "Abraham's Son, Isaac, Is Born."

21.1   TEV   RSV
   The LORD blessed Sarah, as   The LORD visited Sarah as he
he had promised,   had said, and the LORD did to
                                     Sarah as he had promised.

   blessed: the Hebrew word is often translated "visited" (RSV), but
it has the sense of "come to help," "take care of," "cause to prosper."
The statements are necessarily vague, but here, as in many cases, the
nature of the "blessing" is quite clear: God made it possible for Sarah
to become pregnant. Hebrew belief assumes that all life, including the
birth of children, is the direct result of God's free gift. A literal
translation of "visited" might be misleading in that it might leave
open the possibility of understanding the verb in a sexual way, which
is certainly not intended by the Hebrew.
   as he had promised: see 18.10 and particularly in a condensed
Bible, 17.15-22.

21.2   TEV   RSV
and she became pregnant and bore   And Sarah conceived, and bore
a son to Abraham when he was old.   Abraham a son in his old age
The boy was born at the time God   at the time of which God had
had said he would be born.   spoken to him.

   at the time God had said he would be born: see 17.21.

21.3   TEV   RSV
Abraham named him Isaac,   Abraham called the name of his
                                     son who was born to him, whom
                                     Sarah bore him, Isaac.

   Isaac: see 17.19.

21.4   TEV   RSV
and when Isaac was eight days   And Abraham circumcised his son
old, Abraham circumcised him, as   Isaac when he was eight days old,
God had commanded.   as God had commanded him.

   circumcised: see 17.23.
   as God had commanded: see 17.23.

21.5   TEV   RSV
Abraham was a hundred years old   Abraham was a hundred years old
when Isaac was born.   when his son Isaac was born to
                                     him.

   a hundred years old: see 17.24.

[79]

21.6 TEV	RSV
Sarah said, "God has brought me joy and laughter.P Everyone who hears about it will laugh with me."	And Sarah said, "God has made laughter for me; every one who hears will laugh over me."

PLAUGHTER: *The name Isaac in Hebrew means "he laughs" (see also 17.17-19).*

laughter: see 17.17-19. There is here also an intended play on the name Isaac, which should be explained in a footnote, as TEV has done.

21.7 TEV	RSV
Then she added, "Who would have said to Abraham that Sarah would nurse children? Yet I have borne him a son in his old age."	And she said, "Who would have said to Abraham that Sarah would suckle children? Yet I have borne him a son in his old age."

Who would have said...?: this rhetorical question may need to be changed into a statement: "No one would have said...," "It is not possible that anyone would have said...."

I have borne him a son: "I have given birth to his son."

in his old age: "even though Abraham is an old man." The translator must take care that the reference is clear; Abraham, not the newborn baby, is in his old age.

21.8 TEV	RSV
The child grew, and on the day that he was weaned, Abraham gave a great feast.	And the child grew, and was weaned; and Abraham made a great feast on the day that Isaac was weaned.

was weaned: that is, when Sarah stopped breast-feeding him. The child would have been three or four years old, as breast-feeding normally continued that long.

feast: "banquet." The Hebrew word has the basic meaning of "drinking" and refers to a joyful celebration at which wine was drunk.

21.9-21: Abraham sends away Hagar and Ishmael.
21.22-34: Abraham agrees with King Abimelech about a well.

C H A P T E R   22

SECTION HEADING

God Commands Abraham to Offer Isaac (22.1-19): "God Tells Abraham to Kill Isaac as a Sacrifice."

22.1   TEV
Some time later God tested
Abraham; he called to him, "Abraham!" And Abraham answered, "Yes,
here I am!"

RSV
After these things God tested
Abraham, and said to him, "Abra-
ham!" And he said, "Here am I."

Some time later: literally "After these matters" (see RSV), but
the time reference is indefinite and should cause no problem in a
series of Old Testament selections.
tested: "put to the test." The Hebrew word has the meaning of "try
out," "put to the test," but it should be kept in mind that the intention here is positive, in contrast to "temptation," where the intention
is to cause one to fail. If a word is not readily available, one may
use something like "wanted to find out if Abraham was faithful to him
(or, would obey him)."
called to: literally "said to" (RSV), but the translator should
feel free to use a word that indicates a form of speech that is appropriate to the situation. This is because the Hebrew word for "said" in
different contexts may have such meanings as "called to," "cried out,"
"shouted," etc.
Yes, here I am!: here also the kind of language that would be
appropriate to answering a call should be used, for example, "Yes, I
hear you," "I am listening," since the Hebrew has that general meaning.

22.2   TEV
"Take your son," God said,
"your only son, Isaac, whom you
love so much, and go to the land
of Moriah. There on a mountain
that I will show you, offer him
as a sacrifice to me."

RSV
He said, "Take your son, your
only son Isaac, whom you love,
and go to the land of Moriah, and
offer him there as a burnt offering upon one of the mountains of
which I shall tell you."

your only son: this is emphatic, "the only one you have." It is
true that Ishmael is his son, but not in the same sense. Isaac is the
son of promise and in that sense the only son, particularly now that
Ishmael has been sent away.
the land of Moriah: the location is unknown, although later tradition identifies it in some way with "Mount Moriah" in Jerusalem (2 Chr
3.1).
offer him as a sacrifice: the Hebrew uses "an offering that is
burned whole," that is, totally burned up on the altar (see 8.20). In
some languages it may be necessary to use something like "kill him and
burn his body as a gift to me."

22.3   TEV
Early the next morning Abra-
ham cut some wood for the sacri-
fice, loaded his donkey, and took
Isaac and two servants with him.
They started out for the place

RSV
So Abraham rose early in the morning, saddled his ass, and took two
of his young men with him, and his
son Isaac; and he cut the wood for
the burnt offering, and arose and

that God had told him about.   went to the place of which God
                                  had told him.

cut some wood: the original order has been changed in TEV (see
RSV), but the order that seems logical in the receptor language should
be used. The Hebrew word is literally "split," but it refers to cutting
wood and splitting it so that it will burn well.

wood for the sacrifice: "wood to be burned in offering the sacrifice," "wood to be used in making the fire to burn the sacrifice."

donkey: "ass," the normal beast of burden at that time, a small
horse-like animal used to carry burdens.

servants: the Hebrew describes them as young men, and they were
Abraham's slaves; but it may be better to avoid the word "slave,"
particularly if the word has a strong negative meaning. A word that
might be understood to mean servants that have been hired should be
avoided.

22.4	TEV	RSV
	On the third day Abraham saw the place in the distance.	On the third day Abraham lifted up his eyes and saw the place afar off.

on the third day: that is, after they had traveled two days, some-
time on the third day of travel.

22.5	TEV	RSV
	Then he said to the servants, "Stay here with the donkey. The boy and I will go over there and worship, and then we will come back to you."	Then Abraham said to his young men, "Stay here with the ass; I and the lad will go yonder and worship, and come again to you."

The boy: "The young man"; an expression will be needed that a
father could use in speaking of his son. If nothing suitable is found,
it is possible to use "my son" or even "Isaac."

over there: "to that place," pointing to the mountain in the distance.

worship: literally "bow down," but the Hebrew word, used frequently in "bow down before God," means to worship God. If worship
presents a problem in translation, one may use a more descriptive
phrase: "offer a sacrifice to God."

22.6	TEV	RSV
	Abraham made Isaac carry the wood for the sacrifice, and he himself carried a knife and live coals for starting the fire. As they walked along together,	And Abraham took the wood of the burnt offering, and laid it on Isaac his son; and he took in his hand the fire and the knife. So they went both of them together.

made Isaac carry: literally "took the wood for the sacrifice and put it on Isaac, his son."

a knife: "a sharp knife," "a butcher knife."

and live coals for starting the fire: literally "the fire," but it is probable that the Hebrew word is used either for the live coals from the previous night's fire carried in a container, or even for the firestone or flint used in starting a fire.

22.7	TEV	RSV
	Isaac spoke up, "Father!"	And Isaac said to his father
	He answered, "Yes, my son?"	Abraham, "My father!" And he
	Isaac asked, "I see that you	said, "Here am I, my son." He
	have the coals and the wood, but	said, "Behold, the fire and the
	where is the lamb for the sacri-	wood; but where is the lamb for
	fice?"	a burnt offering?"

I see that you have: literally "Look," "Behold," but in Hebrew this is an idiomatic way of saying "I see" or "Here is."

coals: "the fire." See verse 6.

lamb: a young animal, either a lamb (young of sheep) or a kid (young of goat). The Hebrew does not distinguish, as both are used for sacrifice. See 4.4, where "flock" includes sheep and goats.

for the sacrifice: "to be killed and burned in sacrifice," "...as a gift to God."

22.8	TEV	RSV
	Abraham answered, "God him-	Abraham said, "God will provide
	self will provide one." And the	himself the lamb for a burnt
	two of them walked on together.	offering, my son." So they went
		both of them together.

will provide one: literally "will see for himself the lamb for the sacrifice," but "see" here has the sense of "choose," "look out for," "take care of," "provide." See verse 14 and the play on this word that develops there.

22.9	TEV	RSV
	When they came to the place	When they came to the place of
	which God had told him about,	which God had told him, Abraham
	Abraham built an altar and ar-	built an altar there, and laid the
	ranged the wood on it. He tied	wood in order, and bound Isaac his
	up his son and placed him on	son, and laid him on the altar,
	the altar, on top of the wood.	upon the wood.

the place which God had told him about: that is, "the mountain."

built an altar: see 8.20.

arranged: "laid," "stacked," that is, put the wood on the altar in such a way that he could start the fire.

tied up his son: "tied the feet and the hands of his son."

[83]

on top of the wood: the wood has been arranged for burning, but the fire has not yet been lit.

22.10 TEV	RSV
Then he picked up the knife to kill him.	Then Abraham put forth his hand, and took the knife to slay his son.

picked up the knife to kill him: literally "put out his hand and took the knife to kill his son" (see RSV), that is, he picked up the knife and was just ready to use it to kill his son. The choice between "kill him," "kill his son," or "kill Isaac" will need to be made with the whole story in mind in the light of receptor language usage.

22.11 TEV	RSV
But the angel of the LORD called to him from heaven, "Abraham, Abraham!" He answered, "Yes, here I am."	But the angel of the LORD called to him from heaven, and said, "Abraham, Abraham!" And he said, "Here am I."

the angel of the LORD: in this part of the Old Testament the angel of the LORD is a kind of personification of the LORD. Note how in verse 12 and in verse 16 the voice of the angel becomes the voice of the LORD. For that reason it is probably best to translate "the angel of the LORD' or "the LORD's angel" rather than "an angel of the LORD," although that would be possible here. Note that in 16.7-10 the same shift occurs from "the angel of the LORD" to the LORD himself.
    called: "spoke in a loud voice."
Yes, here I am: see verse 1.

22.12 TEV	RSV
"Don't hurt the boy or do anything to him," he said. "Now I know that you honor and obey God, because you have not kept back your only son from him."	He said, "Do not lay your hand on the lad or do anything to him; for now I know that you fear God, seeing you have not withheld your son, your only son, from me."

hurt: literally "don't put out your hand upon the boy." The Hebrew verb is the same as in verse 10, but here it is clear that "put the hand upon" has the sense of "hurt," "harm," "kill." One might translate "Stop! Do not do anything to hurt your son."
    do anything to him: 'harm him in any way."
Now: the sense is 'Now that you have been willing to obey my command to kill your son," "Now that you have obedient reverence for God."
    you honor and obey God: literally "you fear God" (RSV), but the Hebrew word for "fear" does not here have the sense of "be in fear of," 'be terrified of." Rather, the word has the sense of "obey, worship, have reverence for, hold in awe," and TEV has attempted to express

this with honor and obey. One might use "obey and worship," "obey and follow," or something like that to convey the meaning. Or the meaning may be expressed, "Now I know that you are obedient to God."

God: although the angel is speaking, it is really God who is speaking through his angel. For that reason, in some languages it is more correct to translate "for me," using the first person pronoun as the Hebrew does at the end of the verse. Hebrew can easily shift between third and first person, but most languages cannot, and it may be necessary to make adjustments in the translation. For example, one might find it necessary also here to use the device that the Hebrew uses in verse 16. One would then translate this verse "I speak for God. Don't hurt the boy...I know that you have obedient reverence for me...you have not kept back your only son from me."

you have not kept back...from him: the Hebrew word has the meaning "hold back," "withhold," "spare." Here the sense is "you have not refused to let him have," "you have not held as your own, but you have given to him." This may be expressed in a positive way: "you have proved that you are willing to sacrifice your only son to him."

your only son: see verse 2.

22.13	TEV	RSV

TEV	RSV
Abraham looked around and saw a ram caught in a bush by its horns. He went and got it and offered it as a burnt offering instead of his son.	And Abraham lifted up his eyes and looked, and behold, behind him was a ram, caught in a thicket by his horns; and Abraham went and took the ram, and offered it up as a burnt offering instead of his son.

looked around: literally "lifted up his eyes" (RSV), but the meaning is "looked up," "looked around him."

a ram: "a male goat." There is a small textual problem here. Many Hebrew manuscripts have "a ram," "one ram," but some manuscripts have "a ram after," which really makes no sense in Hebrew. It is this text, nevertheless, that has been followed in translating "behind him" (as RSV, for example), which cannot be correct.

caught: "held fast," "entangled in." The animal's horns are entangled in the bush and it cannot escape.

bush: the Hebrew word means "a thicket," "a patch of underbrush," that is, an area where many bushes have grown together and twisted together. If this idea is not easy to express, it is satisfactory to speak of a single bush, as TEV has done, but the word chosen must represent a bush that is large enough for a ram to get his horns caught in.

offered it: "killed it and gave it to God as a gift."

22.14	TEV	RSV

TEV	RSV
Abraham named that place "The LORD Provides."[u] And even today	So Abraham called the name of that place The LORD will provide;[k]

people say, "On the LORD's mountain he provides."*v*

*u*Provides; *or* Sees.

*v*provides; *or* is seen.

as it is said to this day, "On the mount of the LORD it shall be provided."*l*

*k*Or *see*

*l*Or *he will be seen*

named: "called the name of."

The LORD Provides: the Hebrew verb is "see," used in the same way as in verse 8. The name used here should correspond to the verb used in verse 8, and a note may be needed to help the reader see the connection between the name that Abraham gives to the place and the statement in verse 8. Some translations simply transliterate the Hebrew, "Yahweh-Yireh," but it is usually better to translate, as the name is not known and will have to be translated in a footnote in any case.

even today: that is, at the time the book of Genesis was written.

he provides: this is probably what the last word of the Hebrew originally meant, but in the present form of the Hebrew text the vowels that are given (added long after the book was written) make the meaning "is seen," "appears." It is recommended that one of the meanings be chosen for the text of the translation and the other given in a note, as TEV has done.

22.15	TEV	RSV
	The angel of the LORD called to Abraham from heaven a second time,	And the angel of the LORD called to Abraham a second time from heaven,

called: see verse 11.

22.16	TEV	RSV
	"I make a vow by my own name—the LORD is speaking—that I will richly bless you. Because you did this and did not keep back your only son from me,	and said, "By myself I have sworn, says the LORD, because you have done this, and have not withheld your son, your only son,

I make a vow by my own name : literally "by me I take an oath." A vow is a solemn promise to do something, and the "by me," "by my own name" means that God makes a promise such as this: "I make a solemn promise—and may I no longer be recognized as God, may my name no longer be honored, if I do not keep my promise."

the LORD is speaking: literally "(this is) the declaration, statement, of the LORD" (see RSV), and it serves not only to indicate that it is really the LORD who is speaking (see verse 12), but it also serves to make the promise more solemn and sure. In some languages one may say "I, the LORD, am speaking."

that I will richly bless you: this is the solemn promise that God makes. In Hebrew these words do not come until verse 17, but in many languages (as in English) it is not possible to separate the expression of a vow or promise from the statement of the promise, and it is wise to move the statement forward to verse 16. In Hebrew <u>richly bless</u> is a very emphatic statement. Here <u>bless</u> has its concrete expression in verse 17 with its promise of many descendants.

<u>did this</u>: "acted this way," "obeyed me and were willing to offer your son."

<u>did not keep back</u>: see verse 12. One might restructure the verse: [...and said to Abraham,] "I, the Lord, vow in my own name that I will richly bless you. I make this vow because you obeyed me and were willing to offer your only son to me." Or perhaps "Just as surely as I am the Lord, I will bless you...."

22.17 TEV	RSV
I promise that I will give you as many descendants as there are stars in the sky or grains of sand along the seashore. Your descendants will conquer their enemies.	I will indeed bless you, and I will multiply your descendants as the stars of heaven and as the sand which is on the seashore. And your descendants shall possess the gate of their enemies,

<u>I promise</u>: if one breaks up the very long Hebrew structure into shorter sentences, it will be necessary to indicate the vow again by a repetition of "I promise," "I vow," "I solemnly promise."

<u>stars</u>: see 15.5.

<u>conquer their enemies</u>: literally "take possession of the gate of their enemies" (see RSV); but "to take over the gate" of a city means to conquer it, and the image here is that the descendants of Abraham will break down the defenses (the gate) of their enemies and conquer them. In many languages it is not possible to retain the figure of a gate, and one must translate as TEV has done: "conquer," "overthrow," "defeat."

22.18 TEV	RSV
All the nations will ask me to bless them as I have blessed your descendants—all because you obeyed my command."	and by your descendants shall all the nations of the earth bless themselves, because you have obeyed my voice."

<u>ask me to bless them...your descendants</u>: see 12.2-3, but here the only meaning the Hebrew can have relates to the use of the name in blessing. Literally "they will bless themselves by your descendants" (see RSV), but this means "when they ask God's blessings upon themselves, they will cite the descendants of Abraham as the example," "they will ask God to bless them as he has blessed the descendants of Abraham."

<u>all because</u>: "all this will happen because you obeyed...."

[87]

22.19 TEV	RSV
Abraham went back to his servants, and they went together to Beersheba, where Abraham settled.	So Abraham returned to his young men, and they arose and went together to Beer-sheba; and Abraham dwelt at Beer-sheba.

Abraham: it is assumed that Isaac went back also, but Abraham is named as the principal figure. In some languages it may be necessary to translate "Abraham with his son Isaac," "Abraham and Isaac."

Beersheba: later a city of the Negev, located about 70 kilometers (45 miles) southwest of Jerusalem. See 22.31; 26.33.

settled: "lived," but in the sense of having a more permanent home than he did when he was moving about (see 12.9).

22.20-24: These verses give a list of the descendants of Abraham's brother Nahor.

23.1-20: Sarah dies and Abraham purchases a field with a cave in which to bury her.

24.1-67: Abraham sends a slave to his relatives in northern Mesopotamia to get a wife for Isaac, and Rebecca is chosen and brought to marry Isaac.

C H A P T E R   25

25.1-18: These verses give a list of the other descendants of Abraham, tell of his death and burial, and give a list of the descendants of Ishmael.

SECTION HEADING

The Birth of Esau and Jacob (25.19-26): "Twin Sons Are Born to Isaac and Rebecca," "Esau and Jacob Are Born."

25.19 TEV	RSV
This is the story of Abraham's son Isaac.	These are the descendants of Isaac, Abraham's son: Abraham was the father of Isaac,

story: the Hebrew word means "list of descendants," "generations," but it is also used for "history," "story." See 6.9.

Abraham's son Isaac: in addition to this, the Hebrew has "Abraham became the father of Isaac" (see RSV), which sounds like the beginning of a list of descendants. But since the list is not continued, there is no reason to retain the words, which only repeat the first part of the verse.

25.20 TEV	RSV
Isaac was forty years old when he married Rebecca, the daughter of Bethuel (an Aramean from Mesopotamia) and sister of Laban.	and Isaac was forty years old when he took to wife Rebekah, the daughter of Bethuel the Aramean of Paddan-aram, the sister of Laban the Aramean.

Rebecca: see 24.10-60.

Aramean: the Arameans were a nomadic people, wandering from place to place.

Mesopotamia: literally "Paddan-aram" (RSV), but this is another name for the northern part of Mesopotamia, the land between the Euphrates and Tigris rivers. It is the early home of Abraham and the Arameans. See 12.4.

25.21 TEV	RSV
Because Rebecca had no children, Isaac prayed to the LORD for her. The LORD answered his prayer, and Rebecca became pregnant.	And Isaac prayed to the LORD for his wife, because she was barren; and the LORD granted his prayer, and Rebekah his wife conceived.

had no children: the possibility of having children is seen as a gift of God (see 15.2-3; 21.1-2). For a woman to have no children was considered a great tragedy.

prayed...for her: "entreated," "asked the LORD to give her children."

answered his prayer: "heard his prayer and decided to give him what he had asked."

became pregnant: care should be taken in choosing a word that will be acceptable in polite circles. In some languages it may be necessary to drop any specific reference to conception or pregnancy.

25.22 TEV	RSV
She was going to have twins, and before they were born, they struggled against each other in her womb. She said, "Why should something like this happen to me?" So she went to ask the LORD for an answer.	The children struggled together within her; and she said, "If it is thus, why do I live?"q So she went to inquire of the LORD. qSyr: Heb obscure

She was going to have twins: these words as such are not in the Hebrew text, but the idea is clearly there, and in many languages it is necessary to make such a statement if the reader is to understand what follows.

before they were born: literally "in her body (womb)," but the idea needs to be expressed in terms that will be acceptable in public reading of the Scriptures.

struggled against each other: "pushed against each other," "wrestled with one another," "pushed each other around."

Why should something like this happen to me?: the Hebrew is not
very clear; literally "If it is that way, why this, I?" This is often
interpreted according to more ancient translations, "If it is this
way, why do I live?" (see RSV). Others take the meaning to be "If it
is going to be like this, what good is it to become pregnant?" In any
case, the Hebrew for "be like this" refers to the fighting of the
twins before they are born, which continues throughout their lives.
It is clear that their fighting is deeply disturbing to Rebecca, and
what she says should be understood as a bitter complaint. It need not
be translated as a question. The translator might consider "How terrible
it is going to be for me if these twins are fighting now and will continue to fight after they are born!" And this would convey rather
closely what the Hebrew is saying.

went to ask the LORD for an answer: the Hebrew is a technical
phrase for seeking a revelation from the LORD. The phrase indicates
that the person goes to a sacred place, a place of worship, and asks
for a revelation. One might translate "went to a sacred place, a holy
place (see 12.6), to ask for a message from the LORD."

25.23	TEV	RSV
	The LORD said to her,	And the LORD said to her,
	"Two nations are within you;	"Two nations are in your womb, and two peoples, born of you,
	You will give birth to two rival peoples.	shall be divided;
	One will be stronger than the other;	the one shall be stronger than the other,
	The older will serve the younger."	the elder shall serve the younger."

Two nations are within you: the meaning is "After the twins
within you have grown up and had children, they will have many descendants, and their descendants will become two nations."

You will give birth to two rival peoples: note that in accordance
with Hebrew poetry (Hebrew parallelism), this line uses different words
to say the same thing as the first line does. In many languages the
repetition is not stylistically pleasing and should be avoided. In that
case the ideas of the two lines could be combined into one statement;
for example, "The twins within you will be born and grow up to be the
fathers of two nations that will continue to oppose (fight with) one
another." The word "peoples" is another way of speaking of a nation
or a tribe with a common ancestor.

rival: the Hebrew verb means "be divided," "be separated," but
this is a way of speaking of the fact that the two nations will "oppose one another," "be enemies of one another," and the translation
should make this clear.

One will be stronger: the "one" means "one of the nations" (which
the twins will become), and not "one of the twins." "Stronger" means
"more powerful," "larger."

The older will serve the younger: this refers to the twins and
also to the nations that will be descended from them, but the emphasis

falls on the nations. It may be necessary to translate "The nation that descends from the older son will serve (be slaves to, be a slave to, have to serve) the nation that descends from the younger son." The thought is not only that Esau will be subject to Jacob, but that the Edomites (descended from Esau) will be subject to the Israelites (descended from Jacob). See 27.29.

25.24 TEV	RSV
The time came for her to give birth, and she had twin sons.	When her days to be delivered were fulfilled, behold, there were twins in her womb.

The time came for her to give birth: literally "her days to give birth were fulfilled" (see RSV), but one should use a normal expression, such as "when the day came for her to have her babies."

she had twin sons: "she gave birth to twins." Literally "there were twins in her womb" (RSV), but this is used in the sense "the twins in her womb were born," and this is quite clear in Hebrew, but not in a literal translation.

25.25 TEV	RSV
The first one was reddish, and his skin was like a hairy robe, so he was named Esau.ʸ	The first came forth red, all his body like a hairy mantle; so they called his name Esau.

ʸESAU: *This name is taken to refer to Seir, the territory later inhabited by Esau's descendants; Seir sounds like the Hebrew for "hairy."*

The first one: "The first to be born." Literally "The first one came out" (and it was).

reddish: "his skin was a red color." A word for "red," "reddish" (somewhat red, a shade of red) should be chosen that could normally be used for the color of skin. The Hebrew word sounds somewhat like Edom (Edomites) and is a wordplay on the name of Esau's descendants. But since this wordplay is not involved in the naming of the child at this point, a footnote to explain the wordplay is not required.

his skin: literally "all of him," but this clearly refers to his skin. One could translate "his whole body" in some languages.

was like a hairy robe: "was covered with hair so thickly that it was like a garment made of animal fur."

Esau: see the footnote in TEV. The descendants of Esau, the Edomites, later lived in Seir, a territory south of the Dead Sea, and the name "Seir" is sometimes used for the nation of the Edomites. A footnote will be needed to explain to the reader the play on words intended. If the footnote in TEV seems too complicated, one might use a footnote such as this: "Esau was given this name because in Hebrew there is a connection between his name and the word hairy (or hair)."

25.26   TEV

The second one was born holding on tightly to the heel of Esau, so he was named Jacob.*z* Isaac was sixty years old when they were born.

*z*JACOB: *This name sounds like the Hebrew for "heel."*

        RSV

Afterward his brother came forth, and his hand had taken hold of Esau's heel; so his name was called Jacob.*r* Isaac was sixty years old when she bore them.

*r*That is *He takes by the heel* or *He supplants*

The second one was born: literally "After this his brother came forth" (see RSV).

holding on tightly: "his hand held tightly to the heel of Esau" or "with his hand he held...."

Jacob: a note will be needed to explain that in Hebrew Jacob sounds like the word for "heel." The name also sounds like other words (see 27.36), but that information is not needed here.

SECTION HEADING

Esau Sells His Rights as the First-born Son (25.27-34)" "Esau Sells Jacob the Right to Be the First-born Son."

25.27   TEV

The boys grew up, and Esau became a skilled hunter, a man who loved the outdoors, but Jacob was a quiet man who stayed at home.

        RSV

When the boys grew up, Esau was a skilful hunter, a man of the field, while Jacob was a quiet man, dwelling in tents.

grew up: "became adults," "grew to be men."

a skilled hunter: "a man who knew how to hunt animals."

loved the outdoors: "liked to stay away from home, in the field," "lived away from home while he hunted."

a quiet man: "a man who lived quietly, peacefully," "a man who did not go out hunting."

stayed at home: literally "lived in tents" (see RSV), but the meaning is that instead of going hunting he stayed at home, taking care of the sheep and goats, and sleeping in his tent each night. One might translate "Jacob became a shepherd and lived in his tent at home."

25.28   TEV

Isaac preferred Esau, because he enjoyed eating the animals Esau killed, but Rebecca preferred Jacob.

        RSV

Isaac loved Esau, because he ate of his game; but Rebekah loved Jacob.

Isaac preferred: "loved Esau more than Jacob," "liked Esau better than Jacob."

enjoyed eating: "liked to eat," "liked the taste of."
the animals Esau killed: that is, when he went hunting.
Rebecca preferred: "loved Jacob more than Esau," "liked Jacob better than Esau."

25.29	TEV	RSV
	One day while Jacob was cooking some bean soup, Esau came in from hunting. He was hungry	Once when Jacob was boiling pottage, Esau came in from the field, and he was famished.

cooking some bean soup: "cooking beans," "boiling some lentils (kind of beans)," "cooking a stew of beans (or lentils)." In the light of verse 30, it would be helpful to speak of some type of bean (or other seed) that has a reddish or brownish color when it is cooked.
    came in from hunting: "came back home after he had been out hunting for animals, trying to kill animals." In the context it is clear that he had not killed any animals on this hunt.

25.30	TEV	RSV
	and said to Jacob, "I'm starving; give me some of that red stuff." (That is why he was named Edom.)^a	And Esau said to Jacob, "Let me eat some of that red pottage, for I am famished!" (Therefore his name was called Edom.^{8})
	^{a}EDOM: *This name sounds like the Hebrew for "red."*	^{8}That is *Red*

starving: not to be understood literally; rather, "I am very hungry," "I feel so hungry that I think I will starve to death."
    give me: "let me eat," "let me gulp down," "I want."
    that red stuff: this refers to the bean soup that was cooking and to which Esau would have pointed. The word for "red," "brown," that is used should be one that could readily be applied to the color of food. If "red stuff," "red food," is too indefinite, the translator may use "red soup, stew," as in verse 29.
    he was named Edom: "his name was Edom," "he had been named Edom." This is another name for Esau, and the meaning should be explained in a footnote. In the text, round brackets (parentheses) or dashes should be used to indicate that the statement about the name is not part of the story but an explanation added by the writer.

25.31	TEV	RSV
	Jacob answered, "I will give it to you if you give me your rights as the first-born son."	Jacob said, "First sell me your birthright."

I will give it to you if you give me: this is really what the literal "First give me" (see RSV) means.
    give: "hand over," "give in trade," "sell," "turn over to," "exchange."

[93]

your rights as the first-born son: this may be difficult to translate. Perhaps "the right to inherit property from our father (receive
from our father after his death) as if I were the first-born son," "the
privilege of being considered the first-born son." In Hebrew culture
the first-born son was entitled to receive a larger share of the in-
heritance at the death of the father, and he also had the right of
carrying on the family line of descendants.

25.32	TEV	RSV
	Esau said, "All right! I am about to die; what good will my rights do me?"	Esau said, "I am about to die; of what use is a birthright to me?"

All right!: "I agree," "I will give it to you." These words are
not actually in the Hebrew text but are clearly understood. In most
languages it will be necessary to indicate specifically that Esau
accepts Jacob's proposal.

I am about to die: "I am so hungry I am going to die." See verse
30.

what good will my rights do me?: in many languages this rhetorical
question (see 17.17), which assumes the answer "nothing, none," has to
be translated as a statement: "When I am dead my rights as the first-
born son will do me absolutely no good."

25.33	TEV	RSV
	Jacob answered, "First make a vow that you will give me your rights."	Jacob said, "Swear to me first."*t*
	Esau made the vow and gave his rights to Jacob.	So he swore to him, and sold his birthright to Jacob.
		*t*Heb *today*

First: "I will not give it to you until."
make a vow: "make a solemn promise." See 22.16,17.

25.34	TEV	RSV
	Then Jacob gave him some bread and some of the soup. He ate and drank and then got up and left. That was all Esau cared about his rights as the first-born son.	Then Jacob gave Esau bread and pottage of lentils, and he ate and drank, and rose and went his way. Thus Esau despised his birthright.

bread: if in the culture bread is not a normal food or is a luxury item, perhaps some other food suitable for eating with soup or
stew might be used.

soup: "bean soup," "lentil soup." See verse 29.

He ate...left: the Hebrew, literally "and he ate and he drank and
he stood up and he left" (see RSV), with its short compressed statements, shows Esau to be ill-mannered and only concerned for himself.
It would not be wrong to translate "He gulped down the food and drank

[94]

some wine, and then without a further word stood up and left."

That was all Esau cared about: the Hebrew word means "despise," "think lightly of," "not care about." The translator might consider "Esau cared so little for his rights as the first-born son that he could walk away like that and leave it." The point is that for Esau a belly full of food at the moment was more important than any future benefit from his rights as the first-born.

26.1-33: Isaac visits Abimelech at Gerar, he lies about his wife, and he makes an agreement with Abimelech at Beersheba.
26.34-35: Esau marries foreign wives.

CHAPTER 27

SECTION HEADING

Isaac Blesses Jacob (27.1-29): "Isaac Gives His Blessing to Jacob," "Jacob Deceives Isaac and Receives His Blessing."

27.1 TEV	RSV
Isaac was now old and had become blind. He sent for his older son Esau and said to him, "Son!" "Yes," he answered.	When Isaac was old and his eyes were dim so that he could not see, he called Esau his older son, and said to him, "My son"; and he answered, "Here I am."

Isaac was now old: "When Isaac grew old."

had become blind: literally "his eyes had become dim" (see RSV), but this means that he had lost the use of his eyes and could not see. A literal translation might sound as if he couldn't see as well as earlier, but he is blind, and this should be said.

sent for: "called," "sent word that he should come."

older: "first-born."

Yes: "Here I am," "What is it, sir?" The translation should use a form that would be a suitable response for a man speaking to his elderly father. See 22.1, where the same Hebrew word is used.

27.2 TEV	RSV
Isaac said, "You see that I am old and may die soon.	He said, "Behold, I am old; I do not know the day of my death.

may die soon: literally "I do not know the day of my death," but the meaning here is that he knows his death is near but does not know the day, although it may be very soon.

27.3 TEV	RSV
Take your bow and arrows, go out	Now then, take your weapons, your

[95]

into the country, and kill an
animal for me.

quiver and your bow, and go out
to the field, and hunt game for
me,

bow and arrows: literally "your equipment (weapons), your quiver
(holder for arrows), and your bow" (see RSV), but the weapons are
really bow and arrows, and it is a quiver full of arrows, not an empty
quiver.

27.4	TEV	RSV
Cook me some of that tasty food that I like, and bring it to me. After I have eaten it, I will give you my final blessing before I die."		and prepare for me savory food, such as I love, and bring it to me that I may eat; that I may bless you before I die."

tasty food: the Hebrew word probably means "delicacy," "food that
is especially good," "gourmet food," probably a specific dish, but we
cannot identify it (see verse 9).

I will give you my final blessing: the Hebrew has literally "my
soul will bless you," but "my soul" is a frequent Hebrew idiom used for
the person. To translate literally would leave the impression that
Isaac's soul was something different from Isaac, but this is not what
the Hebrew means; it is merely Isaac's way of referring to himself.
The word "blessing" will once again be difficult to translate, particularly since the blessing of a dying person is considered especially
powerful and binding. It should be noted that man's pronouncing a
blessing is different from God's (see 1.22), in that man's blessing is
really a prayer to God that he will bless (see verse 28). It may be
necessary to translate "I will ask God's blessing upon you," "I will
pray to God for him to bless you."

27.5	TEV	RSV
While Isaac was talking to Esau, Rebecca was listening. So when Esau went out to hunt,		Now Rebekah was listening when Isaac spoke to his son Esau. So when Esau went to the field to hunt for game and bring it,

was listening: "heard what was said."

27.6	TEV	RSV
she said to Jacob, "I have just heard your father say to Esau,		Rebekah said to her son Jacob, "I heard your father speak to your brother Esau,

to Jacob...to Esau: whether the full form of the Hebrew ("to her
son Jacob...to your brother Esau") is retained as in RSV will depend
on how repetitions are handled in the receptor language.

27.7   TEV

'Bring me an animal and cook it
for me. After I have eaten it, I
will give you my blessing in the
presence of the LORD before I
die.'

          RSV

'Bring me game, and prepare for me
savory food, that I may eat it,
and bless you before the LORD before I die.'

Bring me: in some languages it will be simpler to shift this
report to indirect discourse, "I heard your father tell Esau to bring
him.... He said that after he had eaten he would bless him...."
     in the presence of the LORD: this expression (RSV "before the
LORD") is sometimes used to mean "at the sanctuary" (see 25.22), but
here it is more likely to have the meaning "(blessing) which the LORD
approves," or even "(the blessing) of (from) the LORD." The translator
might even consider "my blessing according to the LORD's will," "I will
give you the LORD's blessing," or "I will tell you what the LORD's
blessing will be."

27.8   TEV

Now, son," Rebecca continued,
"listen to me and do what I say.

          RSV

Now therefore, my son, obey my
word as I command you.

Rebecca continued: this is not in the Hebrew text, but it is important to help the reader, and particularly the listener, to recognize that the quotation of Isaac has ended and Rebecca is once again
speaking.
     listen to me: literally "hear my word," but in the sense of "obey
me," "pay attention to what I am saying." In Hebrew the word "hear"
often has the meaning of obey.

27.9   TEV

Go to the flock and pick out two
fat young goats, so that I can
cook them and make some of that
food your father likes so much.

          RSV

Go to the flock, and fetch me two
good kids, that I may prepare
from them savory food for your
father, such as he loves;

     fat: literally "good" (RSV), but in the sense of "fat," "tender,"
"ready to be eaten."
     young goats: the Hebrew word means "young goat," "kid," and not
"lamb," "young sheep," although often no distinction is made. If the
distinction is not made or if such an animal is not known in the receptor language, there would be no great loss in using "young sheep."
     some of that food your father likes so much: in Hebrew the same
words as in verse 4, "tasty food that I like." Rebecca plans to use
goat meat instead of a wild animal to prepare the gourmet dish that
Isaac has mentioned.

27.10   TEV

You can take it to him to eat,

          RSV

and you shall bring to your father

and he will give you his blessing before he dies."

to eat, so that he may bless you
before he dies."

You can...dies: see verse 4.

27.11   TEV   RSV
     But Jacob said to his mother,   But Jacob said to Rebekah his
"You know that Esau is a hairy   mother, "Behold, my brother Esau
man, but I have smooth skin.   is a hairy man, and I am a smooth
                                 man.

hairy: see 25.25.
     smooth skin: this is the meaning of the Hebrew, but in contrast to
"hairy." Perhaps "I have no hair on my arms."

27.12   TEV   RSV
Perhaps my father will touch me   Perhaps my father will feel me,
and find out that I am deceiving   and I shall seem to be mocking
him; in this way, I will bring a   him, and bring a curse upon my-
curse on myself instead of a   self and not a blessing."
blessing."

Perhaps: "It may happen that," "It could be that."
     touch: "feel," "put his hand on."
     and find out that: literally "I will be in his eyes." But remember
that Isaac is blind and the idiom "in his eyes" has the meaning "he
will consider me to be," "think me to be," "know that I am," "see me
as."
     deceiving him: "lying," "cheating," but the Hebrew word is even
stronger, "one who profanes something solemn," "one who makes fun of
something sacred." But it is usually difficult to find a way of stating
this in translation, and the translator may have to be satisfied with
"trying to deceive him."
     in this way: "when he finds out," "if I do this."
     bring a curse on myself: "cause myself to be cursed," "cause my
father to pronounce a curse on me." The word "curse" is the opposite
of "bless," and to curse or bring a curse on someone is to "say things
that will cause harm to a person" or "ask God to harm a person." See
4.11, where God puts a curse on Cain. The translator might consider
"...and instead of blessing me, he will place a curse on me (or, ask
God to place a curse on me)."

27.13   TEV   RSV
     His mother answered, "Let   His mother said to him, "Upon me
any curse against you fall on me,   be your curse, my son; only obey
my son; just do as I say, and go   my word, and go, fetch them to
and get the goats for me."   me."

curse against you: literally "your curse" (RSV), but this is the

Hebrew way of saying "curse that has been pronounced against you."

    Let...fall on me: "May it come to me." It is possible to translate "I will receive any curse against me," "If your father pronounces a curse upon you, it will come on me instead of you."

27.14	TEV	RSV
	So he went to get them and brought them to her, and she cooked the kind of food that his father liked.	So he went and took them and brought them to his mother; and his mother prepared savory food, such as his father loved.

    So he went...liked: see verses 4 and 9.

27.15	TEV	RSV
	Then she took Esau's best clothes, which she kept in the house, and put them on Jacob.	Then Rebekah took the best garments of Esau her older son, which were with her in the house, and put them on Jacob her younger son;

    best clothes: the reference will be to robe, sandals, etc., that Esau wore for dress-up occasions, his best suit of clothes.

27.16	TEV	RSV
	She put the skins of the goats on his arms and on the hairless part of his neck.	and the skins of the kids she put upon his hands and upon the smooth part of his neck;

    put...on his arms: the Hebrew word is the one used for putting on clothes, "clothed his arms with," but nothing is said about how this was done. One may assume, if necessary, that the skins were tied on his arms.

    skins of the goats: "skins from the goats that Jacob had killed."

27.17	TEV	RSV
	She handed him the tasty food, along with the bread she had baked.	and she gave the savory food and the bread, which she had prepared, into the hand of her son Jacob.

    handed him: "gave to him," "put in his hands."

27.18	TEV	RSV
	Then Jacob went to his father and said, "Father!" "Yes," he answered. "Which of my sons are you?"	So he went in to his father, and said, "My father"; and he said, "Here I am; who are you, my son?"

    Father: here, and often elsewhere, the Hebrew uses "My father"

(RSV) as the form of address. The translator will need to choose the form of address that would be suitable in similar circumstances in his culture.

Which of my sons are you?: literally "who are you, my son?" (RSV), but it is clear that he recognizes from the voice that it is one of his sons; he does not know which one.

27.19	TEV	RSV
	Jacob answered, "I am your older son Esau; I have done as you told me. Please sit up and eat some of the meat that I have brought you, so that you can give me your blessing."	Jacob said to his father, "I am Esau your first-born. I have done as you told me; now sit up and eat of my game, that you may bless me."

sit up and eat: the Hebrew has "arise, sit down and eat," and is simply an invitation to come and eat. The sit up and eat (TEV, RSV) leaves the impression that Isaac has been lying down. This is not impossible, but the Hebrew does not state this.

meat: the Hebrew is more specific, "meat that I have killed, caught (in the hunt)," but this becomes evident in the context.

27.20	TEV	RSV
	Isaac said, "How did you find it so quickly, son?" Jacob answered, "The LORD your God helped me find it."	But Isaac said to his son, "How is it that you have found it so quickly, my son?" He answered, "Because the LORD your God granted me success."

your God: not "my God."

helped me find it: this is the meaning of the literal "caused it to happen before me," that is, "gave me success." (See 24.12.)

27.21	TEV	RSV
	Isaac said to Jacob, "Please come closer so that I can touch you. Are you really Esau?"	Then Isaac said to Jacob, "Come near, that I may feel you, my son, to know whether you are really my son Esau or not."

Isaac said...touch you: see verse 12.

Are you really Esau?: "Are you telling me the truth when you say that you are Esau?"

27.22	TEV	RSV
	Jacob moved closer to his father, who felt him and said, "Your voice sounds like Jacob's voice, but your arms feel like Esau's arms."	So Jacob went near to Isaac his father, who felt him and said, "The voice is Jacob's voice, but the hands are the hands of Esau."

Your voice sounds like Jacob's voice: this is the meaning of the
literal "The voice is the voice of Jacob" (see RSV).

27.23	TEV	RSV
	He did not recognize Jacob, be-	And he did not recognize him, be-
	cause his arms were hairy like	cause his hands were hairy like
	Esau's. He was about to give	his brother Esau's hands; so he
	him his blessing,	blessed him.

did not recognize: "did not know that it was Jacob."
was about to give him his blessing: "started to bless him." The
Hebrew form of the verb "blessed" has this meaning, and must have it
here, since the actual blessing does not come until verse 27. RSV has
"blessed him" here and in verse 27, but there is only one blessing,
and verses 24-27a are an interlude which comes between the beginning
of the blessing and the action.

27.24	TEV	RSV
	but asked again, "Are you really	He said, "Are you really my son
	Esau?"	Esau?" He answered, "I am."
	"I am," he answered.	

Are you really Esau?: see verse 21.

27.25	TEV	RSV
	Isaac said, "Bring me some	Then he said, "Bring it to me,
	of the meat. After I eat it, I	that I may eat of my son's game
	will give you my blessing." Jacob	and bless you." So he brought it
	brought it to him, and he also	to him, and he ate; and he brought
	brought him some wine to drink.	him wine, and he drank.

meat: see verse 19.

27.26	TEV	RSV
	Then his father said to him,	Then his father Isaac said to
	"Come closer and kiss me, son."	him, "Come near and kiss me, my
		son."

kiss me: the word "kiss" presents problems of translation is some
cultures. The Hebrew word means "touch the lips to" (here probably to
the cheek, rather than to the lips of Isaac), but one may find it necessary to use "embrace," "hug," "throw the arms around," or even a more
general term such as "greet." If the word for "kiss" ("suck lips" or
whatever) is understood as having sexual connotations, it must be
avoided.

[101]

27.27   TEV   RSV

As he came up to kiss him, Isaac smelled his clothes—so he gave him his blessing. He said, "The pleasant smell of my son is like the smell of a field which the LORD has blessed.

So he came near and kissed him; and he smelled the smell of his garments, and blessed him, and said,
"See, the smell of my son
    is as the smell of a field
        which the LORD has blessed!

smelled his clothes: although it is not said, it is evident that the meaning is "he smelled his clothes and recognized that they were Esau's."

blessing: the actual words of blessing are contained in what is said.

The pleasant smell: the Hebrew word simply means "smell," but it is obvious from the context that it is a smell that is agreeable, pleasant, and not disagreeable.

field: this probably does not refer to a plowed and planted field, but to a part of the open country, the fields in which Esau hunted (see 25.27,29). This is not certain, however, as what follows seems to refer to fertile farming land.

which the LORD has blessed: if "field" means "open country," this will refer to a field well wooded and well supplied with animals to be hunted and food to be gathered. If "field" refers to "planted field" (see verse 28), the reference will be to a fertile field, one that had rich soil in which to grow good crops. If a choice is required, it may be preferable to translate "which the LORD has blessed by putting many animals there" and assume that a shift to farmland begins with verse 28.

27.28   TEV   RSV

May God give you dew from heaven and make your fields fertile! May he give you plenty of grain and wine!

May God give you of the dew
    of heaven,
and of the fatness of the
    earth,
and plenty of grain and
    wine.

May God give you: "I pray (I ask) that God will give to you," "that God will cause the dew to fall on your field." The thought is certainly not that Esau himself would be wet with dew.

dew from heaven: it is known that dew is made up of droplets of water that condense from the air on cool surfaces, but the Hebrews thought it fell from heaven without being seen.

make your fields fertile: literally "(give you) some of the fatness of the earth," but the Hebrew word for "fatness" is used first of all to refer to "olive oil," and then generally to all kinds of crops. A literal translation is meaningless in most languages. It is better to use something like "I pray that God will cause your fields to produce good crops, plenty of food."

May he give you: "I pray that God will cause your fields to produce."

plenty of: "much."

grain: particularly "wheat," and then other grains (grass seeds that are eaten) such as barley.

wine: "grapes that can be made into wine."

27.29	TEV	RSV
May nations be your servants, and may peoples bow down before you. May you rule over all your relatives, and may your mother's descendants bow down before you. May those who curse you be cursed, and may those who bless you be blessed."	Let peoples serve you, and nations bow down to you. Be lord over your brothers, and may your mother's sons bow down to you. Cursed be every one who curses you, and blessed be every one who blesses you!"

May nations be your servants: "I pray that other nations will serve you and your descendants." The Hebrew word translated "nations" is used for "people," "tribe." The "you" means first of all Jacob, but it also means "the nation that is going to develop from his descendants," that is, "the people of Israel."

peoples: another Hebrew word for "tribe," "nations."

bow down before: the meaning is "bow down to show reverence," but the deeper meaning is "obey your commands," "stand ready to serve you." That is, the two parts of this sentence say the same thing in different words (Hebrew parallelism), and in some languages the two lines will need to be combined; much will depend on the use of poetic imagery in the receptor language.

rule over: "be the master over," "be the chief over."

all your relatives: literally "your brothers" (RSV), but in Hebrew the word is frequently used for other relatives also. Here the primary focus is on the descendants of the two brothers, "May you and your descendants be masters over your brother and his descendants."

bow down before: see above. This statement also is parallel to the preceding line and may need to be combined with it.

May those who curse you: "I pray that God will bring a curse on those who pronounce curses against you," "May evil come to all who wish you evil."

and may those who bless: "but may those prosper who wish you well."

SECTION HEADING

Esau Begs for Isaac's Blessing (27.30-45): "Esau Asks Isaac to Bless Him."

27.30	TEV	RSV
	Isaac finished giving his	As soon as Isaac had finished

[103]

blessing, and as soon as Jacob left, his brother Esau came in from hunting.	blessing Jacob, when Jacob had scarcely gone out from the presence of Isaac his father, Esau his brother came in from his hunting.

finished giving his blessing: "stopped speaking the blessing," "came to the end of the blessing."

as soon as: the Hebrew is emphatic: "As soon as Isaac had finished the blessing and immediately after Jacob had left his father, Esau came in." It may be necessary to use two stages, as TEV has done.

27.31 TEV	RSV
He also cooked some tasty food and took it to his father. He said, "Please, father, sit up and eat some of the meat that I have brought you, so that you can give me your blessing."	He also prepared savory food, and brought it to his father. And he said to his father, "Let my father arise, and eat of his son's game, that you may bless me."

He also...blessing: see verse 19.

27.32 TEV	RSV
"Who are you?" Isaac asked. "Your older son Esau," he answered.	His father Isaac said to him, "Who are you?" He answered, "I am your son, your first-born, Esau."

older son Esau: the receptor language will determine how the ideas are expressed. In some languages it may be possible to use the literal "I am your son, your first-born, Esau" (RSV).

27.33 TEV	RSV
Isaac began to tremble and shake all over, and he asked, "Who was it, then, who killed an animal and brought it to me? I ate it just before you came. I gave him my final blessing, and so it is his forever."	Then Isaac trembled violently, and said, "Who was it then that hunted game and brought it to me, and I ate it all^x before you came, and I have blessed him?—yes, and he shall be blessed."

^{x}Cn: Heb *of all*

tremble and shake all over: the Hebrew is very emphatic, "tremble violently all over exceedingly," and the translator will need to find words to paint this picture of Isaac's terror as he begins to recognize what has happened.
Who was it, then: "Who could it have been?"
it is his forever: literally "and indeed he shall be blessed" (see RSV), but the meaning clearly is "I have given the blessing, and there is no way that it can be changed," "...and it will stand

unchanged." In Hebrew thought a blessing once spoken could not be recalled, because the blessing was seen as having a power of its own (see verses 4,7). It is possible to translate "...and I cannot take it back" or "...and there is no way that I can change it."

27.34	TEV	RSV
	When Esau heard this, he cried out loudly and bitterly and said, "Give me your blessing also, father!"	When Esau heard the words of his father, he cried out with an exceedingly great and bitter cry, and said to his father, "Bless me, even me also, O my father!"

cried out loudly and bitterly: the Hebrew is emphatic, "he cried out very loudly with a very bitter cry." The word "bitter" when applied to crying out means that the cry expresses the deep sorrow and anguish within the person. It may be necessary to translate "he cried a loud cry that showed the deep sorrow within him."

Give me your blessing also: in Hebrew this is part of the loud cry and is emphatic: "Bless me, even me, my father" (see RSV).

27.35	TEV	RSV
	Isaac answered, "Your brother came and deceived me. He has taken away your blessing."	But he said, "Your brother came with guile, and he has taken away your blessing."

deceived me: "tricked me," "used fraud and deceit to make me believe that he was Esau."

your blessing: this means "the blessing that should have been given to you."

27.36	TEV	RSV
	Esau said, "This is the second time that he has cheated me. No wonder his name is Jacob.[c] He took my rights as the first-born son, and now he has taken away my blessing. Haven't you saved a blessing for me?"	Esau said, "Is he not rightly named Jacob? For he has supplanted me these two times. He took away my birthright; and behold, now he has taken away my blessing." Then he said, "Have you not reserved a blessing for me?"

[c]JACOB: *This name sounds like the Hebrew for "cheat."*

he has cheated me: the word "cheat" has the sense of "get what is not rightly his by some trick or deception."

No wonder: "He has certainly been given the right name," "His name clearly fits his character."

Jacob: the name sounds like the Hebrew verb for "cheat," and a footnote will be needed to explain this connection for the reader.

saved: "put aside," "reserved," "kept back." Or perhaps "Don't

[105]

you have an additional blessing (not yet spoken) that you can give me?"

27.37   TEV   RSV

TEV	RSV
Isaac answered, "I have already made him master over you, and I have made all his relatives his slaves. I have given him grain and wine. Now there is nothing that I can do for you, son!"	Isaac answered Esau, "Behold, I have made him your lord, and all his brothers I have given to him for servants, and with grain and wine I have sustained him. What then can I do for you, my son?"

  Isaac answered...grain and wine: see verse 28.
  there is nothing: in Hebrew this is a rhetorical question (see RSV) that does not ask for information but is a way of making a strong statement: "I can do nothing."

27.38   TEV   RSV

TEV	RSV
Esau continued to plead with his father: "Do you have only one blessing, father? Bless me too, father!" He began to cry.	Esau said to his father, "Have you but one blessing, my father? Bless me, even me also, O my father." And Esau lifted up his voice and wept.

  continued to plead: "asked again," "begged once more."
  Do you have only one: the question may need to be replaced with a statement, such as "Surely there must be some other blessing you can give me" or "That can't be the only blessing that you have."
  began to cry: literally "lifted up his voice and wept" (RSV), which has the sense of beginning to weep out loud.

27.39   TEV   RSV

TEV	RSV

Then Isaac said to him,
  "No dew from heaven for
    you,
  No fertile fields for you.
	Then Isaac his father answered him:
	    "Behold, away from^y the
	      fatness of the earth
	      shall your dwelling be,
	    and away from^y the dew of
	      heaven on high.

^{y}Or of

  No dew from heaven for you: literally "the place where you live shall be without dew, etc.," but a clear contrast with verse 28 is intended, although some interpret in a different way. It is possible to translate "You will live far from fruitful lands; no dew will fall on your fields."
  dew...fertile fields: see verse 28.

27.40

TEV	RSV
You will live by your sword, But be your brother's slave. Yet when you rebel,^{d} You will break away from his control."	By your sword you shall live, and you shall serve your brother; but when you break loose you shall break his yoke from your neck."

^{d}rebel; *or* grow restless.

live by your sword: "become a brigand, robber, to earn your living." Here, as in verses 28-29, the reference is first of all to Esau, but really also includes the descendants of Esau, that is, the Edomites.

slave: this is the same word translated "servant" in verse 28. The point is that Jacob and Jacob's descendants (the people of Israel) will be masters over Esau and his descendants (the Edomites).

when you rebel: the meaning of the Hebrew word is uncertain; "rebel," "regain control" is possible (as TEV), but "be restless," "roam" is equally possible. The translator is advised to put one of the meanings in the text and the other in a footnote.

break away from his control: literally "break his yoke from your neck" (RSV), but this is a figure; "you will break his control over you just like an ox that has been able to throw off the yoke that the master has used to control him." In some languages it may be possible to retain the figure, but in most it will be far easier to express the meaning by dropping the figure and using general terms—"no longer be under control."

27.41

TEV	RSV
Esau hated Jacob, because his father had given Jacob the blessing. He thought, "The time to mourn my father's death is near; then I will kill Jacob."	Now Esau hated Jacob because of the blessing with which his father had blessed him, and Esau said to himself, "The days of mourning for my father are ap- proaching; then I will kill my brother Jacob."

hated: "held a grudge," "held on to his animosity," "remained an enemy."

thought: literally "said in his heart," that is, to himself.

The time to mourn my father's death is near: the meaning is clear: "My father will soon die, and we will mourn his death; then I will...."

27.42

TEV	RSV
But when Rebecca heard about Esau's plan, she sent for Jacob and said, "Listen, your brother Esau is planning to get even	But the words of Esau her older son were told to Rebekah; so she sent and called Jacob her younger son, and said to him, "Behold,

with you and kill you.   your brother Esau comforts himself
                                                by planning to kill you.

    heard: literally "the words of Esau were told to her" (see RSV),
that is, someone learned of Esau's plan and told Rebecca about it.
    sent for: "sent someone to tell Jacob to come to her."
    Listen: this attention getter should be translated according to
the normal use in the language or be omitted.
    get even with you and kill you: the Hebrew words mean "plans to
take revenge against you by killing you." The Hebrew word is related
to "comfort himself," but that is only a way of speaking of revenge.
The translator should consider "threatens" or "plans to get even,"
"plans to take revenge."

27.43	TEV		RSV

Now, son, do what I say. Go at   Now therefore, my son, obey my
once to my brother Laban in   voice; arise, flee to Laban my
Haran,   brother in Haran,

    do what I say: literally "hear my voice," but the meaning of
"hear" is "obey," and the meaning of "voice" is "what I say."
    my brother Laban: see 12.41.

27.44	TEV		RSV

and stay with him for a while,   and stay with him a while, until
until your brother's anger cools   your brother's fury turns away;
down

    for a while: literally "some days," but this is a way of speaking
of an indefinite period of time.
    anger cools down: literally "anger turns back" (see RSV). It will
be necessary to use an expression that describes quieting of anger in
terms that are common in the language, for example, "to make become
cold again," "anger blows away."

27.45	TEV		RSV

and he forgets what you have done   until your brother's anger turns
to him. Then I will send someone   away, and he forgets what you
to bring you back. Why should I   have done to him; then I will
lose both of my sons on the same   send, and fetch you from there.
day?"   Why should I be bereft of you
                                          both in one day?'

    Note that TEV has not repeated "until his anger cools down" at
the beginning of the verse, as the Hebrew has done (see RSV).
    Why should I: this is another rhetorical question with the mean-
ing "I am sending you away so that I won't lose both sons." That is,
if Jacob stays, Esau will kill him, and then Esau would have to be
punished as a murderer.

SECTION HEADING

Isaac Sends Jacob to Laban (27.46—28.5): "Isaac Sends Jacob to Mesopotamia to Live with Laban."

27.46 TEV	RSV
Rebecca said to Isaac, "I am sick and tired of Esau's foreign wives. If Jacob also marries one of these Hittite girls, I might as well die."	Then Rebekah said to Isaac, "I am weary of my life because of the Hittite women. If Jacob marries one of the Hittite women such as these, one of the women of the land, what good will my life be to me?"

I am sick and tired of: literally "I am disgusted with life because of" (see RSV), with the sense "I am so disgusted that I could die," "I am sick to death," "I cannot stand (them) any longer."

Esau's foreign wives: "the foreign women Esau has married." The literal "daughters of the Hittites" is a Hebrew way of speaking of "Hittite women" or "foreign women" and has clear reference to Esau's wives (see 26.34-35).

these: literally "women of the land" (RSV), but Isaac and Rebecca are living in a foreign land, and the expression means "these women of the people living around us," that is, Canaanite people, including the Hittites, who were considered to be among the original inhabitants of the land of Canaan (see 23.3,7).

girls: "women," "young women." English uses "girls" to refer to "women of marriagable age," but most languages do not, and the proper term should be used here.

I might as well die: the Hebrew has the rhetorical question "what good will life be to me?" (see RSV), but this expects the answer "nothing," and the meaning is "my life will be no good to me at all."

CHAPTER   28

28.1 TEV	RSV
Isaac called Jacob, greeted him, and told him, "Don't marry a Canaanite girl.	Then Isaac called Jacob and blessed him, and charged him, "You shall not marry one of the Canaanite women.

greeted him: literally "blessed him," but this is not a specific blessing as in chapter 27. Rather it is a greeting formula like 'May God be with you." In most languages it is better to use "greeted him" or to use a greeting formula, if there is one in the language; for example, "God bless you," "God be with you."

told him: literally "commanded him and said to him." It might be possible to use "gave him this command."

Canaanite girl: "a woman who lives near us here in Canaan." See 27.46.

28.2 TEV	RSV
Go instead to Mesopotamia, to the home of your grandfather Bethuel, and marry one of the girls there, one of your uncle Laban's daughters.	Arise, go to Paddan-aram to the house of Bethuel your mother's father; and take as wife from there one of the daughters of Laban your mother's brother.

Mesopotamia: literally "Paddan-aram" (RSV). But since this is just another name for northern Mesopotamia, it is wiser to use the more familiar name (see 25.20).

28.3 TEV	RSV
May Almighty God bless your marriage and give you many children, so that you will become the father of many nations!	God Almighty[z] bless you and make you fruitful and multiply you, that you may become a company of peoples.

[z]Heb *El Shaddai*

May Almighty God bless: "I pray that Almighty God will bless." The exact meaning of the Hebrew word translated "Almighty" is not known, but it is better to follow the traditional interpretation of 'most powerful," "who has all power," rather than transliterate or follow one of the more recent guesses as to the meaning of the word.

bless your marriage: literally "bless you" (RSV), but the content of the blessing is to have many children, and it is natural in English to speak of blessing a marriage.

give you many children: the language of the rest of the verse is typical of blessings spoken since the first chapter.

28.4 TEV	RSV
May he bless you and your descendants as he blessed Abraham, and may you take possession of this land, in which you have lived and which God gave to Abraham!"	May he give the blessing of Abraham to you and to your descendants with you, that you may take possession of the land of your sojournings which God gave to Abraham!"

bless you...as he blessed Abraham: this is the meaning of the literal "give you Abraham's blessing" (see 12.3).

28.5 TEV	RSV
Isaac sent Jacob away to Mesopotamia, to Laban, who was the son of Bethuel the Aramean and the	Thus Isaac sent Jacob away; and he went to Paddan-aram to Laban, the son of Bethuel the Aramean,

| brother of Rebecca, the mother | the brother of Rebekah, Jacob's |
| of Jacob and Esau. | and Esau's mother. |

28.6-9: Esau marries another woman.

SECTION HEADING

Jacob's Dream at Bethel (28.10-22): "Jacob Dreams at Bethel."

28.10   TEV

Jacob left Beersheba and started toward Haran.

RSV

Jacob left Beer-sheba, and went toward Haran.

    Beersheba: see 22.19.
    Haran: see 12.4.

28.11   TEV

At sunset he came to a holy place*e* and camped there. He lay down to sleep, resting his head on a stone.

*e*a holy place; *or* a place.

RSV

And he came to a certain place, and stayed there that night, because the sun had set. Taking one of the stones of the place, he put it under his head and lay down in that place to sleep.

    holy place: the same Hebrew word is used in 12.6. RSV translates "a certain place," but the Hebrew probably means "a special place," "a sacred place."
    resting his head on a stone: literally "he took one of the stones and placed it under his head" (see RSV).

28.12   TEV

He dreamed that he saw a stairway reaching from earth to heaven, with angels going up and coming down on it.

RSV

And he dreamed that there was a ladder set up on the earth, and the top of it reached to heaven; and behold, the angels of God were ascending and descending on it!

    stairway: "staircase," "series of steps." This seems to be the meaning of the Hebrew word, rather than the traditional "ladder" (RSV).
    angels: see 22.11. Here, of course, the angels are seen as coming down from heaven to do what God tells them to do. In some languages it may be necessary to translate "some angels were coming down from heaven while others were going back up."

28.13   TEV

And there was the LORD standing

RSV

And behold, the LORD stood above

[111]

beside him.*f* "I am the LORD, the God of Abraham and Isaac," he said. "I will give to you and to your descendants this land on which you are lying.

*f*beside him; *or* on it.

it*a* and said, "I am the LORD, the God of Abraham your father and the God of Isaac; the land on which you lie I will give to you and to your descendants;

*a*Or *beside him*

And there was: the Hebrew uses a word (often translated "behold") that calls special attention to what follows.

beside him: it is not possible to determine whether the Hebrew means "beside Jacob," "on the stairway," or "above the stairway," although the TEV text is the most likely.

the God of Abraham and Isaac: that is, "the God that Abraham and Isaac worshiped."

28.14	TEV	RSV

They will be as numerous as the specks of dust on the earth. They will extend their territory in all directions, and through you and your descendants I will bless all the nations.*g*

*g*through you...nations; *or* all the nations will ask me to bless them as I have blessed you and your descendants.

and your descendants shall be like the dust of the earth, and you shall spread abroad to the west and to the east and to the north and to the south; and by you and your descendants shall all the families of the earth bless themselves.*b*

*b*Or *be blessed*

This verse echoes earlier blessings, beginning with 12.2-3.

extend their territory in all directions: literally "you (your descendants) shall break out to the west, to the east, to the north, and to the south," but the language is that of enlarging national territory, extending the borders of a country.

28.15	TEV	RSV

Remember, I will be with you and protect you wherever you go, and I will bring you back to this land. I will not leave you until I have done all that I have promised you."

Behold, I am with you and will keep you wherever you go, and will bring you back to this land; for I will not leave you until I have done that of which I have spoken to you."

Remember: once again, the Hebrew "Behold" (RSV) is an attention getter.

be with you: in the sense "be your God," "guide and direct you."

protect you: "guard you," "keep you safe."

until: this should not be interpreted to mean that after God has done what he promised he will leave Jacob. It may be simpler to translate "I will not leave you; I will do all that I have promised."

28.16　　　TEV

Jacob woke up and said, "The LORD is here! He is in this place, and I didn't know it!"

RSV

Then Jacob awoke from his sleep and said, "Surely the LORD is in this place; and I did not know it."

woke up: literally "woke up from his sleep."
The LORD is here: the Hebrew introduces this statement with an exclamation that emphasizes that something unexpected has taken place. The English exclamation mark is a substitute for the word, which is not easy to translate, although "Surely" (RSV), "Truly," or "Indeed" are sometimes used.

28.17　　　TEV

He was afraid and said, "What a terrifying place this is! It must be the house of God; it must be the gate that opens into heaven."

RSV

And he was afraid, and said, "How awesome is this place! This is none other than the house of God, and this is the gate of heaven."

afraid...terrifying: the Hebrew uses the same basic word for both of these expressions. A word is needed that will express the idea of the fear of being in the presence of God or in a holy place, for example, "awesome," "fearsome," "awe-inspiring."
house of God: "the place where God appears," "where God dwells."
the gate that opens into heaven: literally "the gate of heaven" (RSV), but this must be understood as the point at which God communicates with humans on earth. The stairway between heaven and earth is in mind.

28.18　　　TEV

Jacob got up early next morning, took the stone that was under his head, and set it up as a memorial. Then he poured olive oil on it to dedicate it to God.

RSV

So Jacob rose early in the morning, and he took the stone which he had put under his head and set it up for a pillar and poured oil on the top of it.

set it up: "stood it upright," "placed it on end."
memorial: the Hebrew word is used for an upright stone pillar, a standing stone, used for religious purposes, here used as a marker to indicate that this was a holy place. It may be helpful to translate "a reminder (or, sign) to show that this was a holy place," "...a place where God appeared."
poured olive oil on it: this is a symbolic action that indicates that sacred objects are set apart for God's use and can no longer be considered as ordinary. To make this symbolic meaning clear, TEV has added to dedicate it to God. If this is not done, a footnote will be needed to explain to the reader the meaning of this action.

[113]

28.19   TEV

He named the place Bethel.*h* (The town there was once known as Luz.)

*h*BETHEL: *This name in Hebrew means "house of God."*

28.19   RSV

He called the name of that place Bethel;*c* but the name of the city was Luz at the first.

*c*That is *The house of God*

    Bethel: see 12.8. The Hebrew name means "house of God," and a footnote will be needed to help the reader understand the meaning of the name and the connection with verse 17.
    once: "at an earlier time," "previously."

28.20   TEV

Then Jacob made a vow to the LORD: "If you will be with me and protect me on the journey I am making and give me food and clothing,

28.20   RSV

Then Jacob made a vow, saying, "If God will be with me, and will keep me in this way that I go, and will give me bread to eat and clothing to wear,

    a vow: "a solemn promise" (see 22.16).
    you: literally "God." The Hebrew often uses a third person form, where English more naturally uses a second person. The vow is clearly spoken to God. This is evident from the fact that in verse 22 the Hebrew uses the second person "you" about God. In most languages it will be necessary to use the form normally used in addressing another person.
    be with me: see verse 15.
    food: literally "bread to eat" (RSV), but the Hebrew word for "bread" often means food in general (see 3.19).
    clothing: literally "clothes to wear" (see RSV).

28.21   TEV

and if I return safely to my father's home, then you will be my God.

28.21   RSV

so that I come again to my father's house in peace, then the LORD shall be my God,

    if I return: the sense is "if you allow me to return," "if you bring me back." It may be wise to translate "and if you bring me safely home."
    safely: the literal "in peace" (RSV) is frequently used in the Old Testament in the sense of "living in safety or security." Here the emphasis is on safety, "without allowing anyone to harm me."
    you will be my God: "I will worship you as my God," "I will acknowledge you alone as my God."

28.22   TEV

This memorial stone which I have set up will be the place where you are worshiped, and I will give you a tenth of everything you give me."

28.22   RSV

and this stone, which I have set up for a pillar, shall be God's house; and of all that thou givest me I will give the tenth to thee."

the place where you are worshiped: literally "the house of God" (see RSV), reflecting verses 17 and 19, but there is a clear promise involved, and it seems better to translate the idea rather than translate literally. It would also be possible to translate "I will recognize this place as the place where God is present, where God appears."

I will give you: in the sense of "offer to you as an offering," "give you as a sacrifice."

C H A P T E R   29

SECTION HEADING

Jacob Arrives at Laban's Home (29.1-14): "Jacob Meets Rachel in Haran."

29.1	TEV	RSV
	Jacob continued on his way and went toward the land of the East.	Then Jacob went on his journey, and came to the land of the people of the east.

continued on his way: literally "lifted up his feet and went," but the meaning of continuing on his journey is clear.

land of the East: literally "land of the sons of the East," that is, the eastern people. The term is an expression for the lands east of Palestine and here refers specifically to Mesopotamia.

29.2	TEV	RSV
	Suddenly he came upon a well out in the fields with three flocks of sheep lying around it. The flocks were watered from this well, which had a large stone over the opening.	As he looked, he saw a well in the field, and lo, three flocks of sheep lying beside it; for out of that well the flocks were watered. The stone on the well's mouth was large,

Suddenly he came upon: the Hebrew combines the word for "see" with the attention getter, and it is possible to translate "he suddenly saw" (while he was traveling). In English it is more natural to speak of "coming upon" or "coming to."

a well: a hole dug to obtain water from underground sources, to be distinguished from a cistern, a hole dug to store water.

out in the fields: "in the country," "away from any town."

were watered: "were given water to drink." The entire verse may be restructured: "One day he came to a well where the shepherds of that region watered their flocks. Three flocks of sheep were lying around the well, but the large stone was still over the opening."

29.3   TEV

Whenever all the flocks came together there, the shepherds
would roll the stone back and
water them. Then they would
put the stone back in place.

          RSV

and when all the flocks were
gathered there, the shepherds
would roll the stone from the
mouth of the well, and water
the sheep, and put the stone
back in its place upon the
mouth of the well.

the shepherds would roll: as the story unfolds it becomes clear
that the stone covering the opening of the well was so large that it
normally took all the shepherds to move the stone (see verses 8,10).

29.4   TEV

     Jacob asked the shepherds,
"My friends, where are you from?"
     "From Haran," they answered.

          RSV

     Jacob said to them, "My broth-
ers, where do you come from?"
They said, "We are from Haran."

My friends: literally "My brothers" (RSV), but the word is used
in a general way and does not refer here to a close relative. Rather,
the address is to strangers.
     Haran: see 12.4.

29.5   TEV

     He asked, "Do you know Laban
son of Nahor?"
     "Yes, we do," they answered.

          RSV

He said to them, "Do you know
Laban the son of Nahor?" They
said, "We know him."

Do you know...?: "Are you acquainted with...?" The exact form of
the question will be determined by practices in the receptor language
culture.

29.6   TEV

     "Is he well?" he asked.
     "He is well," they answered.
"Look, here comes his daughter
Rachel with his flock."

          RSV

He said to them, "Is it well
with him?" They said, "It is
well; and see, Rachel his
daughter is coming with the
sheep!"

Is he well?: the proper receptor language form for inquiring about
the health of a person should be used.

29.7   TEV

     Jacob said, "Since it is
still broad daylight and not
yet time to bring the flocks in,
why don't you water them and
take them back to pasture?"

          RSV

He said, "Behold, it is still
high day, it is not time for
the animals to be gathered together; water the sheep, and go,
pasture them."

broad daylight: "the sun is still high," "it is a long time until dark."

take them back to pasture: "take them back to the fields where they can eat grass."

29.8   TEV
They answered, "We can't do that until all the flocks are here and the stone has been rolled back; then we will water the flocks."

            RSV
But they said, "We cannot until all the flocks are gathered together, and the stone is rolled from the mouth of the well; then we water the sheep."

See verse 3.

29.9   TEV
While Jacob was still talking with them, Rachel arrived with the flock.

            RSV
While he was still speaking with them, Rachel came with her father's sheep; for she kept them.

the flock: literally "her father's sheep" (RSV). But in English it seems more natural to introduce the thought that the sheep belong to her father in verses 6 and 10 rather than here.

29.10   TEV
When Jacob saw Rachel with his uncle Laban's flock, he went to the well, rolled the stone back, and watered the sheep.

            RSV
Now when Jacob saw Rachel the daughter of Laban his mother's brother, and the sheep of Laban his mother's brother, Jacob went up and rolled the stone from the well's mouth, and watered the flock of Laban his mother's brother.

uncle: "mother's brother." The original has repetitions which are not suitable in English (see RSV).

29.11   TEV
Then he kissed her and began to cry for joy.

            RSV
Then Jacob kissed Rachel, and wept aloud.

kissed her: see 27.26.
began to cry for joy: literally "lifted up his voice and wept," but this is idiomatic for "began to weep." It is obvious here that he sheds tears of joy, and TEV has made this clear for the reader.

29.12   TEV
He told her, "I am your father's

            RSV
And Jacob told Rachel that he was

[117]

relative, the son of Rebecca." She ran to tell her father;	her father's kinsman, and that he was Rebekah's son; and she ran and told her father.

relative: literally "brother" (see verse 4), but here the sense is "kinsman" and not "one born of the same parent or parents."

29.13 TEV	RSV
and when he heard the news about his nephew Jacob, he ran to meet him, hugged him and kissed him, and brought him into the house. When Jacob told Laban everything that had happened,	When Laban heard the tidings of Jacob his sister's son, he ran to meet him, and embraced him and kissed him, and brought him to his house. Jacob told Laban all these things,

nephew: "his sister's son" (RSV).
everything that had happened: at his home and on the journey, which is the meaning of the literal "all these things" (RSV).

29.14 TEV	RSV
Laban said, "Yes, indeed, you are my own flesh and blood." Jacob stayed there a whole month.	and Laban said to him, "Surely you are my bone and my flesh!" And he stayed with him a month.

Yes, indeed: the Hebrew uses an emphatic particle "Surely" (RSV). One could translate "certainly," "without doubt," but the emphasis may be expressed in many ways in other languages.
my own flesh and blood: this is the English form of the literal "my bone and my flesh" (RSV). Both of these figures express the idea of close relationship, family membership (see 2.34), but many languages will use quite different figures to express this meaning; for example, "you are part of my family," "we come from the same root."

SECTION HEADING

Jacob Serves Laban for Rachel and Leah (29.15-28): "Jacob Works for Laban in Order to Marry Rachel and Leah," "Jacob Works Fourteen Years to Marry Rachel and Leah."

29.15 TEV	RSV
Laban said to Jacob, "You shouldn't work for me for nothing just because you are my relative. How much pay do you want?"	Then Laban said to Jacob, "Because you are my kinsman, should you therefore serve me for nothing? Tell me, what shall your wages be?"

You shouldn't: the Hebrew uses a question which expects a negative answer (see RSV): "Should you work for me for nothing? No!" It is

[118]

usually simpler to make a statement rather than retain the rhetorical question.

my relative: literally "my brother," but see verse 12.

pay: "What wages do you ask?" "How much shall I pay you?"

29.16	TEV	RSV
	Laban had two daughters; the older was named Leah, and the younger Rachel.	Now Laban had two daughters; the name of the older was Leah, and the name of the younger was Rachel.

older...younger: this is what the literal "larger...smaller" means.

29.17	TEV	RSV
	Leah had lovely^i eyes, but Rachel was shapely and beautiful.	Leah's eyes were weak, but Rachel was beautiful and lovely.

^{i}lovely; or weak.

lovely: the meaning of the Hebrew word is "tender," "delicate," which can be understood in the sense of "beautiful," as TEV text has done, or in the sense of "weak," as TEV margin has done. A footnote may be used in the translation to indicate that the exact meaning is not certain.

shapely and beautiful: literally "beautiful in form (shape) and beautiful in appearance." The translator should choose terms normally used in his culture to describe feminine beauty.

29.18	TEV	RSV
	Jacob was in love with Rachel, so he said, "I will work seven years for you, if you will let me marry Rachel."	Jacob loved Rachel; and he said, "I will serve you seven years for your younger daughter Rachel."

was in love with: "loved."

he said: to Laban.

work...for you: "serve you" (RSV), "do the work you ask me to do."

if you will let me marry: literally "for" (RSV), in the sense of "to get," "to have as my wife."

Rachel: the Hebrew adds "your younger daughter." In some languages this repetition of material from verse 15 is quite appropriate, as it is in Hebrew; but in other languages, such as English, the repetition is stylistically awkward. The translator's desire for good style in his language will determine whether or not the repetition is retained.

29.19   TEV   RSV
     Laban answered, "I would   Laban said, "It is better that
rather give her to you than to   I give her to you than that I
anyone else; stay here with   should give her to any other
me."   man; stay with me."

     I would rather: literally "It is better" (RSV), with the sense of
"better for me," "I would prefer."
     give her to you: that is, "as your wife," "let you marry her,"
"let her become your wife."
     stay here with me: this is Laban's way of saying "I agree to the
bargain, I agree to give you Rachel if you will stay here and work for
me." In some languages it will be helpful to convey this meaning to
the reader.

29.20   TEV   RSV
Jacob worked seven years so   So Jacob served seven years for
that he could have Rachel,   Rachel, and they seemed to him
and the time seemed like only   but a few days because of the
a few days to him, because he   love he had for her.
loved her.

     so that he could have Rachel: "in order to get Rachel as his
wife," which is the meaning of the literal "for" (RSV). See verse 18.
     the time: "the seven years."
     seemed like only a few days: literally "were in his eyes like a
few days." But the meaning is that this is the way he thought about
the time. One could translate "The years passed as quickly as if they
had been days."

29.21   TEV   RSV
     Then Jacob said to Laban,   Then Jacob said to Laban,
"The time is up; let me marry   "Give me my wife that I may go
your daughter."   in to her, for my time is com-
                                    pleted."

     The time is up: "The time I promised to work for you has been
finished," "I have now worked seven years for you, as I promised to
do."
     let me marry: literally "Give me my wife that I may go in to her"
(RSV), which has the sense "let me have Rachel as my wife, so that I
may have sexual relations with her." In English the polite way to
speak of this is to use "marry," "take as a wife."

29.22   TEV   RSV
So Laban gave a wedding feast   So Laban gathered together all
and invited everyone.   the men of the place, and made
                                    a feast.

wedding feast: the Hebrew word, "drinking party," refers to a banquet or feast where wine is served, here in joyful celebration of the wedding.

everyone: the Hebrew word for "man" is used here in the sense of "people," "person," and not just male people.

29.23	TEV	RSV
	But that night, instead of Rachel, he took Leah to Jacob, and Jacob had intercourse with her.	But in the evening he took his daughter Leah and brought her to Jacob; and he went in to her.

instead of Rachel: these words are not actually in the Hebrew text but are clearly implied. Laban had promised to give Rachel to Jacob as his wife, but instead of doing that he broke his promise and took Leah into the bedroom of Jacob. Bringing the bride to the bedroom was part of the marriage ceremony, and the deception was possible because the bride remained veiled until she was brought into the dark room.

had intercourse with her: literally "went in to her" (RSV). See verse 21 for the advisability of speaking of the sexual act in terms that will be acceptable in the culture.

29.24	TEV	RSV
	(Laban gave his slave girl Zilpah to his daughter Leah as her maid.)	(Laban gave his maid Zilpah to his daughter Leah to be her maid.)

This verse is important for the later story (see 30.9), but it interrupts the narrative here. This may be indicated by the use of round brackets (parentheses).

29.25	TEV	RSV
	Not until the next morning did Jacob discover that it was Leah. He went to Laban and said, "Why did you do this to me? I worked to get Rachel. Why have you tricked me?"	And in the morning, behold, it was Leah; and Jacob said to Laban, "What is this you have done to me? Did I not serve with you for Rachel? Why then have you deceived me?"

Not until the next morning: the Hebrew uses emphatic words, which perhaps could be translated "It happened in the morning that Jacob looked and it was Leah" (instead of Rachel).

Why did you do this: literally "What is this you have done to me?" (RSV), but Jacob is not asking what has happened; he is using the rhetorical question to express his surprise and anger that Laban could have done this. If the question Why did you do this...? is not strong enough, one may translate "You have done a terrible thing to me."

I worked: this is also a rhetorical question in Hebrew, "Didn't I work for you to get Rachel?" (see RSV). But the expected answer is

[121]

"Yes," and it is simpler in many languages to translate with a statement.

tricked: "deceived," "told me one thing and did something else,"
"promised to give me Rachel and then gave me Leah."

29.26	TEV	RSV
Laban answered, "It is not the custom here to give the younger daughter in marriage before the older.	Laban said, "It is not so done in our country, to give the younger before the first-born.

It is not the custom here: literally "It is not done in this way
in our place" (see RSV). The clear sense is that "our traditions, the
way we do things, do not permit the younger daughter to marry first."

28.27	TEV	RSV
Wait until the week's marriage celebrations are over, and I will give you Rachel, if you will work for me another seven years."	Complete the week of this one, and we will give you the other also in return for serving me another seven years."

the week's marriage celebrations: that is the meaning of the
literal "the week of this one" (RSV).

29.28	TEV	RSV
Jacob agreed, and when the week of marriage celebrations was over, Laban gave him his daughter Rachel as his wife.	Jacob did so, and completed her week; then Laban gave him his daughter Rachel to wife.

agreed: this is clearly the meaning of the literal "did so," which
has the sense, "Jacob accepted the promise of Laban and agreed to work
for him for seven more years."

29.29—30.24: Jacob's wives bear children to him.
30.25-43: Jacob bargains with Laban about the flocks.
31.1-55: Jacob attempts to escape from Laban, he has a confronta-
tion with Laban, and they make an agreement with one another.
32.1-32: Jacob prepares to meet Esau, and he wrestles at Peniel.
33.1-20: Jacob returns to Palestine and he meets Esau.
34.1-31: Dinah is raped, and her brothers take revenge.
35.1-29: God blesses Jacob at Bethel, and Rachel and Isaac die.
36.1-43: This chapter gives a list of the descendants of Esau.

C H A P T E R   37

SECTION HEADING

Joseph and His Brothers (37.1-4): "Jacob Loves Joseph More Than His Other Sons," "Joseph Is Hated by His Brothers."

37.1 TEV	RSV
Jacob continued to live in the land of Canaan, where his father had lived,	Jacob dwelt in the land of his father's sojournings, in the land of Canaan.

where his father had lived: literally "his father lived as a foreigner." If this emphasis on being a foreigner in the land of Canaan can readily be retained, it would be good to do so. In many languages it will be helpful to translate "where his father Isaac had lived," as this will help the reader recall the circumstances in previous chapters.

37.2 TEV	RSV
and this is the story of Jacob's family. Joseph, a young man of seventeen, took care of the sheep and goats with his brothers, the sons of Bilhah and Zilpah, his father's concubines. He brought bad reports to his father about what his brothers were doing.	This is the history of the family of Jacob. Joseph, being seventeen years old, was shepherding the flock with his brothers; he was a lad with the sons of Bilhah and Zilpah, his father's wives; and Joseph brought an ill report of them to their father.

story: see 6.9.

sheep and goats: literally "flock" (RSV), composed of sheep and goats.

concubines: the Hebrew word used here is "wives," "women," but TEV has recognized that Bilhah and Zilpah are slave women (see 27.24-29) and has used concubines, which translates a Hebrew word that refers specifically to a wife with a secondary status. If no such word is used in the receptor language, it may be possible to translate with "wife" here and use a descriptive phrase in those places where the technical term for "second-status-wife" is used in Hebrew.

brought bad reports: "told bad things about." Some general expression should be found, since one can only guess at what the bad reports actually were.

37.3 TEV	RSV
Jacob loved Joseph more than all his other sons, because he had been born to him when he	Now Israel loved Joseph more than any other of his children, because he was the son of his old

[123]

was old. He made a long robe
with full sleeves^m for him.

age; and he made him a long robe
with sleeves.

^mrobe with full sleeves; or dec-
orated robe.

Jacob: literally "Israel" (RSV). The Hebrew readily shifts between
the two names for this one person, and in most languages it will be
less disturbing to the reader if the translation uses the more familiar
name for the person. This is particularly important at this point, since
the name "Israel" is more frequently used for the tribes of the nation
descended from Jacob.

had been born to him when he was old: literally "was the son of
his old age to him" (see RSV), but it will be necessary to use a normal
expression in the receptor language to indicate that Jacob was an old
man when Joseph was born.

long robe with full sleeves: the exact nature of this garment is
not known, and it is not possible to determine whether it was with
long sleeves, decorated, reached the ankles, or was made of colored
pieces. It is obviously a special garment (robe, coat, shirt) of some
luxury.

37.4   TEV
When his brothers saw that their
father loved Joseph more than
he loved them, they hated their
brother so much that they would
not speak to him in a friendly
manner.

                      RSV
But when his brothers saw that
their father loved him more than
all his brothers, they hated him,
and could not speak peaceably
to him.

would not speak to him in a friendly manner: literally "could not
speak to him for (in) peace," that is, "could not say a kind word to
him," "spoke in an unfriendly way to him."

SECTION HEADING

Joseph's Dreams (37.5-11): "Joseph Tells His Dreams."

37.5   TEV
One time Joseph had a dream,
and when he told his brothers
about it, they hated him even
more.

                      RSV
Now Joseph had a dream, and
when he told it to his brothers
they only hated him the more.

One time: the Hebrew has simply "And," but most languages will
require a different type of introductory formula.

[124]

37.6 TEV	RSV
He said, "Listen to the dream I had.	He said to them, "Hear this dream which I have dreamed:

Listen: a polite form is used in the Hebrew, "Please listen."

37.7 TEV	RSV
We were all in the field tying up sheaves of wheat, when my sheaf got up and stood up straight. Yours formed a circle around mine and bowed down to it."	behold, we were binding sheaves in the field, and lo, my sheaf arose and stood upright; and behold, your sheaves gathered round it, and bowed down to my sheaf."

sheaves of wheat: a sheaf is a bundle of wheat stalks that have been cut and tied together, with the grain at the top.
my sheaf: that is, "the sheaf I had cut and tied up."

37.8 TEV	RSV
"Do you think you are going to be a king and rule over us?" his brothers asked. So they hated him even more because of his dreams and because of what he said about them.	His brothers said to him, "Are you indeed to reign over us? Or are you indeed to have domin-ion over us?" So they hated him yet more for his dreams and for his words.

be a king and rule over us: one Hebrew verb means "rule as king," but it is translated sometimes as "reign" (RSV). Another Hebrew verb is also used, with a more general sense, "govern, control." In English, "be a king and rule" covers both ideas, and in some languages a single word will include both meanings.

37.9 TEV	RSV
Then Joseph had another dream and told his brothers, "I had an-other dream, in which I saw the sun, the moon, and eleven stars bowing down to me."	Then he dreamed another dream, and told it to his brothers, and said, "Behold, I have dreamed another dream; and behold, the sun, the moon, and eleven stars were bowing down to me."

eleven stars: it is clear in the context that Joseph considers himself as a twelfth star. That is, twelve stars represent the twelve brothers.

37.10 TEV	RSV
He also told the dream to his father, and his father scolded him: "What kind of a dream is	But when he told it to his father and to his brothers, his father rebuked him, and said to him,

[125]

that? Do you think that your mother, your brothers, and I are going to come and bow down to you?"	"What is this dream that you have dreamed? Shall I and your mother and your brothers indeed come to bow ourselves to the ground before you?"

scolded: "rebuked," "reprimanded," "told him not to talk that way."

What kind of a dream is that?: literally "What is this dream that you have dreamed?" (RSV). But the question is clearly rhetorical, and in many languages it will need to be changed to a statement, for example, "It's not right to tell dreams like that."

Do you think...?: this rhetorical question expects the answer "No." In many languages the meaning will need to be expressed as a statement: "Your mother and I...will certainly not bow down to you!"

37.11 TEV	RSV
Joseph's brothers were jealous of him, but his father kept thinking about the whole matter.	And his brothers were jealous of him, but his father kept the saying in mind.

jealous: "envious," "resentful." The brothers were angry with him and determined to hurt him.

kept thinking about the whole matter: literally "guarded the matter (word)." But here the sense of "guard" is "to keep in mind," "to continue to think about," and the Hebrew "word" is frequently used in the sense of "thing," "matter," that is, "the whole situation of Joseph's dreams and his brothers' reactions.

SECTION HEADING

Joseph is Sold and Taken to Egypt (37.12-36): "Joseph Is Sold as a Slave and Taken to Egypt."

37.12 TEV	RSV
One day when Joseph's brothers had gone to Shechem to take care of their father's flock,	Now his brothers went to pasture their father's flock near Shechem.

One day when: the Hebrew makes a separate statement, and it would be correct to translate "One time Joseph's brothers went," with a new sentence beginning at verse 13.

Shechem: a city located about 65 kilometers (40 miles) north of Jerusalem.

37.13 TEV	RSV
Jacob said to Joseph, "I want	And Israel said to Joseph, "Are

you to go to Shechem, where your brothers are taking care of the flock."

Joseph answered, "I am ready."

not your brothers pasturing the flock at Shechem? Come, I will send you to them." And he said to him, "Here I am."

Jacob: literally "Israel." See verse 3.

I want you to go: literally "Come, I will send you."

where your brothers are: the Hebrew again uses a rhetorical question: "Are not your brothers...?" But this expects the answer "Yes," and in most languages it will be more natural to use a statement.

flock: that is, "of sheep and goats."

I am ready: this is what is meant by the literal "Behold me," "Here I am."

37.14   TEV   RSV

His father told him, "Go and see if your brothers are safe and if the flock is all right; then come back and tell me." So his father sent him on his way from Hebron Valley.

Joseph arrived at Shechem

So he said to him, "Go now, see if it is well with your brothers, and with the flock; and bring word again." So he sent him from the valley of Hebron, and he came to Shechem.

safe: the Hebrew uses a word that is often translated "peace," but the word has the sense of "safe," "secure," "not in any difficulty."

all right: in Hebrew this is the same word for "peace" as in the line above, and the same word could be used in translation.

So: this sentence is a summary of verses 13 and 14.

Hebron Valley: the town of Hebron is about 32 kilometers (20 miles) south of Jerusalem. The reference is to the valley in which the town was located.

37.15   TEV   RSV

and was wandering around in the country when a man saw him and asked him, "What are you looking for?"

And a man found him wandering in the fields; and the man asked him, "What are you seeking?"

in the country: "out in the fields," that is, in the countryside and not in the city.

37.16   TEV   RSV

"I am looking for my brothers, who are taking care of their flock," he answered. "Can you tell me where they are?"

"I am seeking my brothers," he said, "tell me, I pray you, where they are pasturing the flock."

Can you tell me...?: literally "Please tell me," but one will need to use the polite form for asking such a question in the receptor language.

37.17	TEV	RSV

The man said, "They have already left. I heard them say that they were going to Dothan." So Joseph went after his brothers and found them at Dothan.

And the man said, "They have gone away, for I heard them say, 'Let us go to Dothan.'" So Joseph went after his brothers, and found them at Dothan.

that they were going: this is the form of indirect discourse that would correspond to the literal "Let us go" (RSV).

Dothan: a town about 24 kilometers (15 miles) north of Shechem.

37.18	TEV	RSV

They saw him in the distance, and before he reached them, they plotted against him and decided to kill him.

They saw him afar off, and before he came near to them they conspired against him to kill him.

in the distance: "while he was still some distance from them."

before he reached them: this repeats in other words what has just been said, and in some languages it may be necessary to combine the two statements into one.

plotted against him and decided to kill him: "made up their minds to kill him," "agreed on a secret plan to kill him."

37.19	TEV	RSV

They said to one another, "Here comes that dreamer.

They said to one another, "Here comes this dreamer.

to one another: literally "a man to his brother," but this is the Hebrew way of speaking of a conversation of the whole group with one another.

that dreamer: this is a scornful way of speaking about Joseph that reflects the meaning of the literal "this master of dreams." The reference is to the dreams about his superior position to his brothers (see verses 5-11).

37.20	TEV	RSV

Come on now, let's kill him and throw his body into one of the dry wells. We can say that a wild animal killed him. Then we will see what becomes of his dreams."

Come now, let us kill him and throw him into one of the pits; then we shall say that a wild beast has devoured him, and we shall see what will become of his dreams."

Come on now: literally "And now come," but this is not a reference to time and movement; it is a strong attention getter that emphasizes the importance of what follows. Each language will have its own way and words for this function, and "Come now" need not be translated literally.

one of the dry wells: the Hebrew word refers to a cistern, a pit dug to hold water, but here clearly the cistern is dry (see verse 24).

We can say: "We can tell our father" (see verses 31-33).

37.21   TEV
Reuben heard them and tried to save Joseph. "Let's not kill him," he said.

RSV
But when Reuben heard it, he delivered him out of their hands, saying, "Let us not take his life."

tried to save Joseph: literally "was saving him from their hands," but Hebrew uses "hands" frequently in the sense of "power, control," and it is clear here that the meaning is "save him from being killed." Also the Hebrew verb here probably has the sense of "trying to save."

kill him: literally "strike his life," "take his life" (RSV). The Hebrew word for "life" is often translated "soul," but the word refers to what makes the body live, its "breath." See Genesis 2.7.

37.22   TEV
"Just throw him into this well in the wilderness, but don't hurt him." He said this, planning to save him from them and send him back to his father.

RSV
And Reuben said to them, "Shed no blood; cast him into this pit here in the wilderness, but lay no hand upon him"—that he might rescue him out of their hand, to restore him to his father.

don't hurt him: literally "do not send your hand upon him," which is a Hebrew way of speaking of doing bodily harm. The Hebrew in this verse also repeats "do not kill him" (literally "do not shed blood" [see RSV]), but language use in regard to repetition should determine if it is to be translated.

37.23   TEV
When Joseph came up to his brothers, they ripped off his long robe with full sleeves.[n]

RSV
So when Joseph came to his brothers, they stripped him of his robe, the long robe with sleeves that he wore;

[n]robe with full sleeves; or decorated robe.

long robe with full sleeves: see verse 3.

37.24   TEV   RSV
Then they took him and threw him   and they took him and cast him
into the well, which was dry.   into a pit. The pit was empty,
                                          there was no water in it.

well, which was dry: see verse 20. Here the Hebrew states that the
cistern was empty, with no water in it.

37.25   TEV   RSV
    While they were eating, they   Then they sat down to eat; and
suddenly saw a group of Ishmael-   looking up they saw a caravan
ites traveling from Gilead to   of Ishmaelites coming from
Egypt. Their camels were loaded   Gilead, with their camels bear-
with spices and resins.   ing gum, balm, and myrrh, on
                                          their way to carry it down to
                                          Egypt.

    While they were eating: literally "And they sat down to eat bread
(food)" (see RSV). Whether or not a time clause (While...) is used will
depend on how the receptor language makes connections between statements such as these.
    they suddenly saw: literally "they lifted up their eyes and saw,
and behold," which means "they happened to look up (from their eating)
and saw suddenly."
    a group: literally "a caravan" (RSV), that is, "a company of
travelers journeying together."
    Ishmaelites: the word means "descendants of Ishmael" (see 16.11),
but it is used here primarily in the sense of "traders," "people who
transport goods to other areas for sale." In fact, if the name is retained, it might be wise to translate as "Ishmaelite traders."
    Gilead: a territory east of the Jordan River.
    spices and resins: this is a general description of three specific
substances named in the Hebrew text, probably: (1) a resin, that is, a
substance that comes from the sap of certain bushes or trees; (2) another type of resin from a different type of tree; and (3) a bark from
certain trees. The difficulty is that these substances cannot be
identified exactly, although it is known that they were used for their
smell or taste, particularly in such things as perfumes and incense.
It may be best to use some general expression that will include sweet-
smelling substances.

37.26   TEV   RSV
Judah said to his brothers,   Then Judah said to his brothers,
"What will we gain by killing   "What profit is it if we slay
our brother and covering up   our brother and conceal his
the murder?   blood?

    What will we gain: "What advantage will there be for us?" It is
clear that the question expects the answer "Nothing," and in some
languages it will be best to translate as a statement, "We will gain
absolutely nothing."

covering up the murder: literally "covering his blood" (see RSV), but the Hebrew uses the word "blood" to mean "violent killing," and a literal translation will hide the real meaning of the Hebrew.

37.27	TEV	RSV
	Let's sell him to these Ishmael- ites. Then we won't have to hurt him; after all, he is our brother, our own flesh and blood." His brothers agreed,	Come, let us sell him to the Ishmaelites, and let not our hand be upon him, for he is our brother, our own flesh." And his brothers heeded him.

our own flesh and blood: literally "our own flesh" (RSV). See 29.14.

37.28	TEV	RSV
	and when some Midianite traders came by, the brothers^o pulled Joseph out of the well and sold him for twenty pieces of silver to the Ishmaelites, who took him to Egypt.	Then Midianite traders passed by; and they drew Joseph up and lifted him out of the pit, and sold him to the Ishmaelites for twenty shekels of silver; and they took Joseph to Egypt.

^othe brothers; *Hebrew* they.

Midianite: "people from the land of Midian," a territory in Arabia east of the Gulf of Aqaba.

the brothers: the Hebrew simply has "they pulled Joseph out." It is much more likely that the "they" refers to the Midianites. In that case, while the brothers are still eating and are at a distance from the well, the Midianites pull Joseph out without the brothers knowing it (see verse 29). Then the Midianites sell him to the Ishmaelites, who take him to Egypt. If, on the other hand, the "they" is taken as referring to the brothers (as TEV has done), the mention of the Midian- ites is purely incidental, and the brothers simply carry out the plan developed in verses 26-27. The translator must make a choice and may wish to include a footnote to indicate the other possibility.

twenty pieces of silver: literally "twenty shekels" (RSV). The shekel is a unit of weight equivalent to approximately ten grams or half an ounce, and it should be kept in mind that silver was not at that time minted into coins, but was used in trade by being weighed. However, the actual weight of the shekel cannot be accurately calcu- lated, and it varied much over the centuries. Furthermore, we cannot know the purchasing power of ten grams of silver at that time. There- fore it is usually more satisfactory to use some general expression, as TEV has done.

37.29	TEV	RSV
	When Reuben came back to the well and found that Joseph	When Reuben returned to the pit and saw that Joseph was not

was not there, he tore his   in the pit, he rent his clothes
clothes in sorrow.

     came back to the well: it is clear that Reuben expects to pull
Joseph out of the well (see verse 22).
     tore his clothes in sorrow: literally "tore his clothes" (see
RSV), but this action has the meaning in Hebrew culture of showing
that one is overcome by grief. If the reader is to understand the
meaning of the action, it will need to be explained in the text or in
a note. Reuben tore his clothes deliberately to show that he was
grieving, in sorrow.

37.30	TEV	RSV
He returned to his brothers and said, "The boy is not there! What am I going to do?"	and returned to his brothers, and said, "The lad is gone; and I, where shall I go?"	

     The boy: "The young man." One should use a term that could be
spoken by an older brother about a seventeen-year-old brother (see
verse 2).
     What am I going to do?: literally "Where shall I go?" (RSV), but
this is a way of speaking of the total hopelessness of the situation.
This may be expressed by "What can I do?" or "Where can I turn for
help?" In some languages a statement will be more pointed, for example,
"There is no hope left for me," "There is nothing I can do," "I don't
know what to do."

37.31	TEV	RSV
Then they killed a goat and dipped Joseph's robe in its blood.	Then they took Joseph's robe, and killed a goat, and dipped the robe in the blood;	

     robe: see verse 3.

37.32	TEV	RSV
They took the robe to their father and said, "We found this. Does it belong to your son?"	and they sent the long robe with sleeves and brought it to their father, and said, "This we have found; see now whether it is your son's robe or not."	

     Does it belong to your son?: this is the sense of the literal
"Please see if this is your son's robe or not" (see RSV).

37.33	TEV	RSV
He recognized it and said, "Yes, it is his! Some wild animal has killed him. My son Joseph has	And he recognized it, and said, "It is my son's robe; a wild beast has devoured him; Joseph	

been torn to pieces!"   is without doubt torn to pieces."

has killed him: literally "has eaten him," "has devoured him" (RSV).

has been torn to pieces: the Hebrew uses a verb form that is very strong: "Surely my son must have been torn to pieces."

37.34	TEV	RSV
	Jacob tore his clothes in sorrow and put on sackcloth. He mourned for his son a long time.	Then Jacob rent his garments, and put sackcloth upon his loins, and mourned for his son many days.

tore his clothes in sorrow: see verse 29.

sackcloth: a coarse cloth made of goats' hair, which was worn as a sign of mourning or distress. This will need to be explained to the reader, either in a footnote or in a list of explanations at the end of the publication, as TEV has done.

a long time: literally "for many days," but this is a Hebrew expression which may even mean "for many years."

37.35	TEV	RSV
	All his sons and daughters came to comfort him, but he refused to be comforted and said, "I will go down to the world of the dead still mourning for my son." So he continued to mourn for his son Joseph.	All his sons and all his daughters rose up to comfort him; but he refused to be comforted, and said, "No, I shall go down to Sheol to my son, mourning." Thus his father wept for him.

came: literally "stood up" (see RSV), but the Hebrew word has a much larger sense than "rise," which perhaps can best be translated with "came to him."

comfort him: "act and speak in such a way as to help him forget his sorrow."

refused to be comforted: "could not forget his sorrow," "would not listen to their words of comfort."

go down to the world of the dead: literally "go down to Sheol" (RSV), which in the first place means "I will die," and in some languages will need to be translated that way. The word "Sheol" is the name for the world of the dead, the place where everyone, good and bad, was thought to go at the time of death. The translator is advised to use some such expression as the world of the dead or "the world where dead people go"; but if "Sheol" is retained, a note will be needed to explain the meaning. One should make sure that the word is not understood as "hell," the place of punishment. The meaning here could be expressed with "I will mourn for my son as long as I live," but since the world of the dead is an important idea throughout the Old Testament, it would be wise to employ some expression for it that can be used here and elsewhere.

37.36   TEV
    Meanwhile, in Egypt the
Midianites had sold Joseph to
Potiphar, one of the king's
officers, who was the captain
of the palace guard.

                              RSV
    Meanwhile the Midianites had
sold him in Egypt to Potiphar,
an officer of Pharaoh, the captain of the guard.

    the king's: it should be noted that "Pharaoh" is not the name
of the king of Egypt, but a title which means "the king." TEV uses
this meaning throughout and never uses "Pharaoh."
    one of the king's officers: the Hebrew word for "officer" can
also mean "eunuch," but it is used frequently in the general sense of
an official who serves the king.

    *38.1-30: This chapter tells of Judah's relationship with his
daughter-in-law Tamar.*
    *39.1-23: Joseph is tempted by Potiphar's wife and is then thrown
into prison.*
    40.1-23: Joseph interprets the dreams of fellow prisoners.

                    C H A P T E R   41

SECTION HEADING

    Joseph Interprets the King's Dreams (41.1-16,25-36): "Joseph Tells
the King the Meaning of His Dreams."

41.1   TEV
    After two years had passed,
the king of Egypt dreamed that he
was standing by the Nile River,

                              RSV
    After two whole years, Pharaoh
dreamed that he was standing by
the Nile,

    After two years: the point of reference is the death of the baker
(40.22), but in a series of selections that does not tell of this
event, it may be necessary to say something like "After Joseph had been
in prison more than two years."

41.2   TEV
when seven cows, fat and sleek,
came up out of the river and
began to feed on the grass.

                              RSV
and behold, there came up out
of the Nile seven cows sleek
and fat, and they fed in the
reed grass.

    fat and sleek: literally "handsome in appearance and fat in the
flesh." What is needed in translation is a description of well-fed,
fine-looking cattle in language that would normally be used for
such cattle.

41.3	TEV	RSV

Then seven other cows came up;
they were thin and bony. They
came and stood by the other cows
on the riverbank,

And behold, seven other cows,
gaunt and thin, came up out of
the Nile after them, and stood
by the other cows on the bank
of the Nile.

thin and bony: literally "bad in appearance and thin in flesh."
The translation should express the opposite of what was said about the
cows in verse 2.

41.4	TEV	RSV

and the thin cows ate up the
fat cows. Then the king woke
up.

And the gaunt and thin cows ate
up the seven sleek and fat cows.
And Pharaoh awoke.

ate up: "devoured," "swallowed down."

41.5	TEV	RSV

He fell asleep again and had
another dream. Seven heads of
grain, full and ripe, were
growing on one stalk.

And he fell asleep and dreamed
a second time; and behold, seven
ears of grain, plump and good,
were growing on one stalk.

had another dream: "dreamed again," "dreamed a second dream."
heads of grain: the reference is to a head of grain, such as
wheat, and one should not be misled by KJV "ears of corn" or RSV "ears
of grain" into thinking that the reference is to maize.
full and ripe: literally "fat and good," that is, "full of ripe
grain," "heavy with ripe grain."

41.6	TEV	RSV

Then seven other heads of grain
sprouted, thin and scorched by
the desert wind,

And behold, after them sprouted
seven ears, thin and blighted
by the east wind.

thin: in contrast to the heads of grain in verse 5. Perhaps "not
containing any grain."
scorched by the desert wind: literally "scorched (burned) by the
east wind" (see RSV), but the point is that a wind coming to Palestine
from the east blows across the desert and is so hot and dry that it
quickly causes plants to wither and die.

41.7	TEV	RSV

and the thin heads of grain
swallowed the full ones. The
king woke up and realized that
he had been dreaming.

And the thin ears swallowed up
the seven plump and full ears.
And Pharaoh awoke, and behold,
it was a dream.

realized that he had been dreaming: literally "and behold, it was a dream" (RSV), that is, when he woke up he suddenly discovered that the whole thing had been a dream and not real, as he had imagined while he was dreaming.

41.8 TEV	RSV
In the morning he was worried, so he sent for all the magicians and wise men of Egypt. He told them his dreams, but no one could explain them to him.	So in the morning his spirit was troubled; and he sent and called for all the magicians of Egypt and all its wise men; and Pharaoh told them his dream, but there was none who could interpret^j to Pharaoh.

^{j} Gk: Heb *them*

he was worried: literally "his spirit was disturbed" (see RSV), but the word "spirit" refers to his thoughts; "his mind was troubled," "he was concerned about the meaning of the dream."

sent for: "sent word that they should come."

magicians: probably a class of Egyptian priests credited with the knowledge of such mysteries as dreams.

wise men: probably another class of Egyptian priests, but the words are widely used for people with special knowledge and insight.

explain: "interpret," "give the meaning of."

41.9 TEV	RSV
Then the wine steward said to the king, "I must confess today that I have done wrong.	Then the chief butler said to Pharaoh, "I remember my faults today.

wine steward: literally "the chief of the wine servers" (see 40.1-23).

I must confess today that I have done wrong: literally "I remember my sins today" (see RSV), but the point is that he now wishes to tell the king what he should have told him earlier.

41.10 TEV	RSV
You were angry with the chief baker and me, and you put us in prison in the house of the captain of the guard.	When Pharaoh was angry with his servants, and put me and the chief baker in custody in the house of the captain of the guard,

You: the Hebrew uses the third person in referring to the king, but most languages will need to shift to second person, as TEV has done.

captain of the guard: the same Hebrew words are translated captain of the palace guard in 37.36 and mean "chief of the executioners or body guards." The following account summarizes the story told in chapter 40.

41.11   **TEV**   **RSV**

TEV	RSV
One night each of us had a dream, and the dreams had different meanings.	we dreamed on the same night, he and I, each having a dream with its own meaning.

the dreams had different meanings: "each dream had its own meaning."

41.12   **TEV**   **RSV**

TEV	RSV
A young Hebrew was there with us, a slave of the captain of the guard. We told him our dreams, and he interpreted them for us.	A young Hebrew was there with us, a servant of the captain of the guard; and when we told him, he interpreted our dreams to us, giving an interpretation to each man according to his dream.

he interpreted them for us: the Hebrew adds "he interpreted for each man according to his dream." But since this simply repeats with almost the same Hebrew words the end of verse 11, the dreams had different meanings, many languages will need to drop the repetition, as TEV has done.

41.13   **TEV**   **RSV**

TEV	RSV
Things turned out just as he said: you restored me to my position, but you executed the baker."	And as he interpreted to us, so it came to pass; I was restored to my office, and the baker was hanged."

executed: literally "hanged" (RSV). In light of 40.19, where the same verb is used, the translator should think of the form of execution as beheading the person and hanging the body on a pole.

41.14   **TEV**   **RSV**

TEV	RSV
The king sent for Joseph, and he was immediately brought from the prison. After he had shaved and changed his clothes, he came into the king's presence.	Then Pharaoh sent and called Joseph, and they brought him hastily out of the dungeon; and when he had shaved himself and changed his clothes, he came in before Pharaoh.

sent for: literally "sent and called." That is, "sent someone (a servant) to bring Joseph to him."
changed his clothes: "put on clean clothes."

[137]

41.15   TEV

The king said to him, "I have
had a dream, and no one can
explain it. I have been told
that you can interpret dreams."

RSV

And Pharaoh said to Joseph, "I
have had a dream, and there is
no one who can interpret it; and
I have heard it said of you that
when you hear a dream you can
interpret it."

I have been told: literally "I have heard it said," that is,
"Someone has told me."

41.16   TEV

    Joseph answered, "I cannot,
Your Majesty, but God will give
a favorable interpretation."

RSV

    Joseph answered Pharaoh, "It
is not in me; God will give
Pharaoh a favorable answer."

    I cannot: literally "Not I."
    favorable interpretation: the Hebrew uses the word often trans-
lated "peace," but the word also includes "well-being," "prosperity,"
"success," and here the sense has to be "an interpretation of the
dream that will in some way be good for the king."

    41.17-24: These verses repeat the dream of the king as told in
41.1-8.

41.25   TEV

    Joseph said to the king,
"The two dreams mean the same
thing; God has told you what
he is going to do.

RSV

    Then Joseph said to Pharaoh,
"The dream of Pharaoh is one;
God has revealed to Pharaoh what
he is about to do.

    The two dreams mean the same thing: literally "The dream of the
king is one" (see RSV), with the meaning "The two dreams are really
one dream with a single meaning."
    you: the Hebrew uses third person, but most languages should
shift to second, as TEV has done.

41.26   TEV

The seven fat cows are seven
years, and the seven full heads
of grain are also seven years;
they have the same meaning.

RSV

The seven good cows are seven
years, and the seven good ears
are seven years; the dream is
one.

    are: in the sense of "stand for," "symbolize," "picture," "rep-
resent."
    they have the same meaning: literally "the dream is one" (RSV).

41.27 TEV	RSV
The seven thin cows which came up later and the seven thin heads of grain scorched by the desert wind are seven years of famine.	The seven lean and gaunt cows that came up after them are seven years, and the seven empty ears blighted by the east wind are also seven years of famine.

famine: the Hebrew word means "hunger" and refers to a period of extreme hunger and starvation because there is not enough food.

41.28 TEV	RSV
It is just as I told you—God has shown you what he is going to do.	It is as I told Pharaoh, God has shown to Pharaoh what he is about to do.

God has shown...: see verse 25. A different verb is used but with essentially the same meaning, "show," "reveal."

41.29 TEV	RSV
There will be seven years of great plenty in all the land of Egypt.	There will come seven years of great plenty throughout all the land of Egypt,

great plenty: the Hebrew emphasizes that there is more than enough food for the people to eat.

41.30 TEV	RSV
After that, there will be seven years of famine, and all the good years will be forgotten, because the famine will ruin the country.	but after them there will arise seven years of famine, and all the plenty will be forgotten in the land of Egypt; the famine will consume the land,

good years: literally "the plenty" (RSV), that is, "the years in which there was a great abundance of food."
will ruin: literally "will finish," "destroy," "cause to disappear," but the sense is that the country and its people will be completely ruined.

41.31 TEV	RSV
The time of plenty will be entirely forgotten, because the famine which follows will be so terrible.	and the plenty will be unknown in the land by reason of that famine which will follow, for it will be very grievous.

will be so terrible: the Hebrew has "will be very heavy," but this is a way of describing what is terribly severe, very hard.

41.32   TEV
The repetition of your dream
means that the matter is fixed
by God and that he will make
it happen in the near future.

RSV
And the doubling of Pharaoh's
dream means that the thing is
fixed by God, and God will
shortly bring it to pass.

the matter is fixed by God: "God has firmly established what is
going to happen," "God has definitely decided what will happen."

41.33   TEV
     "Now you should choose some
man with wisdom and insight and
put him in charge of the country.

RSV
Now therefore let Pharaoh select
a man discreet and wise, and set
him over the land of Egypt.

man with wisdom and insight: "a man of understanding (that is,
who sees the needs clearly) and of wisdom (that is, who has the ex-
perience to know what to do)."
     put him in charge: literally "set him over," in the sense of
"make him chief over," "give him the rule or authority over."

41.34   TEV
You must also appoint other officials and take a fifth of the
crops during the seven years of
plenty.

RSV
Let Pharaoh proceed to appoint
overseers over the land, and
take the fifth part of the
produce of the land of Egypt
during the seven plenteous years.

other officials: probably local overseers for the various regions
of the country.
     take a fifth of the crops: this seems to be the meaning of the
Hebrew, "fifth of the land of Egypt."

41.35   TEV
Order them to collect all the
food during the good years that
are coming, and give them authority to store up grain in the
cities and guard it.

RSV
And let them gather all the
food of these good years that
are coming, and lay up grain
under the authority of Pharaoh
for food in the cities, and
let them keep it.

all the food: this must refer to the food taken as one-fifth of
the crop in verse 34.

41.36   TEV
The food will be a reserve supply
for the country during the seven
years of famine which are going
to come on Egypt. In this way

RSV
That food shall be a reserve for
the land against the seven years
of famine which are to befall the
land of Egypt, so that the land

the people will not starve."   may not perish through the
                                                      famine."

    <u>reserve supply</u>: "a supply of food stored in reserve."
    <u>people will not starve</u>: literally "the land will not be destroyed"
(see verse 30), but the ruin of the land would follow the starvation
of the people, which is in focus here.

SECTION HEADING

    <u>Joseph Is Made Governor over Egypt</u> (41.37-41, 46-49, 53-57):
"...<u>Made Ruler over...</u>," "...<u>Put in Charge of...</u>."

41.37   TEV   RSV
    The king and his officials   This proposal seemed good to
approved this plan,   Pharaoh and to all his servants.

    <u>approved</u>: literally "was good in the eyes of," but with the sense
"they thought the plan was good and approved it."

41.38   TEV   RSV
and he said to them, "We will   And Pharaoh said to his servants,
never find a better man than   "Can we find such a man as this,
Joseph, a man who has God's   in whom is the Spirit of God?"
spirit in him."

    <u>has God's spirit in him</u>: the meaning is that God had given Joseph
special gifts of wisdom and insight, as is clear from verse 39.

41.39   TEV   RSV
The king said to Joseph, "God   So Pharaoh said to Joseph,
has shown you all this, so it   "Since God has shown you all
is obvious that you have greater   this, there is none so discreet
wisdom and insight than anyone   and wise as you are;
else.

    <u>wisdom and insight</u>: see verse 33.

41.40   TEV   RSV
I will put you in charge of my   you shall be over my house, and
country, and all my people will   all my people shall order them-
obey your orders. Your authority   selves as you command; only as
will be second only to mine.   regards the throne will I be
                                         greater than you."

    <u>my country</u>: literally "my house" (RSV), but the word "house" is
used in a variety of ways in Hebrew, and here refers to the people who

make up the court of the king. By extension, if Joseph controls the king's court, he controls the country.

obey your orders: there is some uncertainty about the meaning of the Hebrew. It can be translated "kiss you upon the mouth," but it seems far more likely that the verb has the meaning "accept orders," that is, "obey what you say." Or with a slight change of vowels, which were not originally written in Hebrew and only added later, it could be understood as "run at your command," with the sense "obey your command." In any case, the translator is advised to translate with something similar to "obey the commands that you give."

Your authority will be second only to mine: literally "only in the throne will I be greater than you" (see RSV), where "throne" is used to indicate the reigning, the ruling, of the king. The meaning is that Joseph is made "second in command," "the prime minister" to the king.

41.41	TEV	RSV
I now appoint you governor over all Egypt."		And Pharaoh said to Joseph, "Behold, I have set you over all the land of Egypt."

I now appoint: the literal translation, "I have appointed you," should not be taken as referring to some time in the past. It is just at this moment that the king makes the appointment.

41.42-45: These verses give the details of Joseph's appointment and tell of his marriage.

41.46	TEV	RSV
	Joseph was thirty years old when he began to serve the king of Egypt. He left the king's court and traveled all over the land.	Joseph was thirty years old when he entered the service of Pharaoh king of Egypt. And Joseph went out from the presence of Pharaoh, and went through all the land of Egypt.

traveled all over the land: TEV has combined into one statement what is stated in both verse 45 and 46 (see RSV).

41.47	TEV	RSV
During the seven years of plenty the land produced abundant crops,		During the seven plenteous years the earth brought forth abundantly,

See verse 35.

41.48	TEV	RSV
all of which Joseph collected and stored in the cities. In each		and he gathered up all the food of the seven years when there

city he stored the food from the fields around it.	was plenty^l in the land of Egypt, and stored up food in the cities; he stored up in every city the food from the fields around it.

^{l}Sam Gk: Heb *which were*

all: see verse 35.

41.49　　　TEV	RSV
There was so much grain that Joseph stopped measuring it—it was like the sand of the sea.	And Joseph stored up grain in great abundance, like the sand of the sea, until he ceased to measure it, for it could not be measured.

stopped measuring: literally "stopped measuring it because (there was so much that) it could not be measured" (see RSV).

41.50-52: Joseph's sons, Manasseh and Ephraim, are born.

41.53　　　TEV	RSV
The seven years of plenty that the land of Egypt had enjoyed came to an end,	The seven years of plenty that prevailed in the land of Egypt came to an end;

came to an end: "ended," "were finished."

41.54　　　TEV	RSV
and the seven years of famine began, just as Joseph had said. There was famine in every other country, but there was food throughout Egypt.	and the seven years of famine began to come, as Joseph had said. There was famine in all lands; but in all the land of Egypt there was bread.

in every other country: "in all the other countries (of the world)."

41.55　　　TEV	RSV
When the Egyptians began to be hungry, they cried out to the king for food. So he ordered them to go to Joseph and do what he told them.	When all the land of Egypt was famished, the people cried to Pharaoh for bread; and Pharaoh said to all the Egyptians, "Go to Joseph; what he says to you, do."

began to be hungry: that is, at a later time even in Egypt food began to be scarce. In some languages it may be necessary to say "As

[143]

time went on, food became scarce even in Egypt, and the people began to be hungry. They cried out...."

food: literally "bread," but frequently used in the general sense of food.

41.56	TEV	RSV
	The famine grew worse and spread over the whole country, so Joseph opened all the storehouses and sold grain to the Egyptians.	So when the famine had spread over all the land, Joseph opened all the storehouses,^{O} and sold to the Egyptians, for the famine was severe in the land of Egypt.

^{O}Gk Vg Compare Syr: Heb *all that was in them*

whole country: literally "all the surface of the land," but the reference is to the land of Egypt.

storehouses: there is a slight problem with the Hebrew text at this point, as some letters seem to have dropped out, but there can be little doubt that this is the meaning intended.

41.57	TEV	RSV
	People came to Egypt from all over the world to buy grain from Joseph, because the famine was severe everywhere.	Moreover, all the earth came to Egypt to Joseph to buy grain, because the famine was severe over all the earth.

People...from all over the world: literally "All the world" (see RSV), but the reference is to the people.

42.1—45.28: This is the delightful story of how Joseph's brothers went to Egypt to buy grain and finally learned that the prime minister was their brother Joseph.

CHAPTER 46

SECTION HEADING

Jacob and His Family Go to Egypt (46.1-7): "Jacob Takes His Whole Family to Egypt."

46.1	TEV	RSV
	Jacob packed up all he had and went to Beersheba, where he offered sacrifices to the God of his father Isaac.	So Israel took his journey with all that he had, and came to Beersheba, and offered sacrifices to the God of his father Isaac.

all he had: "all his possessions," "all that he owned."

Beersheba: see 22.19. This place is on the way to Egypt from Hebron.

sacrifices: the Hebrew word is a general term for sacrifices, that is, it does not specify the particular type of sacrifice, although it refers to animal sacrifices. Jacob killed animals and offered them to God on the altar, where they were burned in whole or in part.

the God of his father Isaac: "the God his father Isaac worshiped." This should not be translated in such a way as to leave the impression that this was a different God from the Lord God frequently referred to. The point is being made that Jacob is worshiping God as his father did. See particularly 28.13.

46.2 TEV	RSV
God spoke to him in a vision at night and called, "Jacob, Jacob!" "Yes, here I am," he answered.	And God spoke to Israel in visions of the night, and said, "Jacob, Jacob." And he said, "Here am I."

vision at night: the word "vision" refers to something that is seen, and here one may think of a dream-like appearance.

Jacob: the Hebrew uses both names, "Israel" and "Jacob," in this verse, but in most languages it will be far more satisfactory to use only one name for the same person, as TEV has done (see 37.3).

Yes, here I am: see 22.1.

46.3 TEV	RSV
"I am God, the God of your father," he said. "Do not be afraid to go to Egypt; I will make your descendants a great nation there.	Then he said, "I am God, the God of your father; do not be afraid to go down to Egypt; for I will there make of you a great nation.

your descendants: literally "you," but the sense is that his children will have many children and grandchildren until his descendants become a great nation (see 28.13-14).

46.4 TEV	RSV
I will go with you to Egypt, and I will bring your descendants back to this land. Joseph will be with you when you die."	I will go down with you to Egypt, and I will also bring you up again; and Joseph's hand shall close your eyes."

go with you: in the sense that God will continue to be his God and also guide and protect him on the journey into Egypt (see 28.15).

Joseph will be with you when you die: literally "Joseph will put his hand upon your eyes," which has the meaning "Joseph will close your eyes at the time of your death." But the real point is that Jacob will not die alone, and his beloved Joseph will be with him at the time of death.

[145]

46.5   TEV

    Jacob set out from Beersheba. His sons put him, their small children, and their wives in the wagons which the king of Egypt had sent.

RSV

Then Jacob set out from Beer- sheba; and the sons of Israel carried Jacob their father, their little ones, and their wives, in the wagons which Pharaoh had sent to carry him.

    <u>which the king of Egypt had sent</u>: this refers to 45.19, but in a condensed Bible the meaning should be clear at this point from the text itself.

46.6-7   TEV

They took their livestock and the possessions they had acquired in Canaan and went to Egypt. Jacob took all his descendants with him: 7 his sons, his grandsons, his daughters, and his granddaughters.

RSV

They also took their cattle and their goods, which they had gained in the land of Canaan, and came into Egypt, Jacob and all his offsrping with him, 7 his sons, and his sons' sons with him, his daughters, and his sons' daughters; all his offspring he brought with him into Egypt.

    It is clear that the writer wishes to emphasize that in taking all his possessions and his whole family, Jacob is making a major move and not just a temporary visit. This is also clear from verse 4, which assumes that Jacob will die in Egypt.

    46.8—48.22: This section lists the members of Jacob's family, describes the arrival in Egypt, tells of the famine, and recounts Jacob's last request and the blessing of Ephraim and Manasseh.

C H A P T E R   49

    49.1-28: A poem giving the last words of Jacob as he blesses each of his sons.

SECTION HEADING

    <u>The Death and Burial of Jacob</u> (49.29—50.14): "Jacob Dies in Egypt and Is Buried in Canaan."

49.29   TEV

    Then Jacob commanded his sons, "Now that I am going to join my people in death, bury

RSV

Then he charged them, and said to them, "I am to be gathered to my people; bury me with my

me with my fathers in the cave   fathers in the cave that is in
that is in the field of Ephron   the field of Ephron the Hittite,
the Hittite,

    sons: the literal "them" (RSV) refers to the sons named in the
poem (see verse 28).
    I am going to join my people in death: the literal "be gathered
to my family" (see RSV) is a Hebrew figure of speech for death. The
sense essentially is "I am going to die," but this is expressed as
being taken from this world and united with my ancestors in the world
of the dead.
    fathers: that is, his father and his grandfather.
    the cave: the story of Abraham's purchase of this cave is found
in 23.1-19.

49.30   TEV   RSV
at Machpelah east of Mamre in   in the cave that is in the field
the land of Canaan. Abraham   at Machpelah, to the east of
bought this cave and field from   Mamre, in the land of Canaan,
Ephron for a burial ground.   which Abraham bought with the
                                        field from Ephron the Hittite
                                        to possess as a burying place.

    Machpelah east of Mamre: a sacred site near Hebron (see 37.14).

49.31   TEV   RSV
That is where they buried Abraham   There they buried Abraham and
and his wife Sarah; that is where   Sarah his wife; there they
they buried Isaac and his wife   buried Isaac and Rebekah his
Rebecca; and that is where I   wife; and there I buried Leah—
buried Leah.

    See 23.19; 25.29; 35.29. The burials of Rebecca and Leah are not
recorded prior to this.

49.32   TEV   RSV
The field and the cave in it   the field and the cave that is
were bought from the Hittites.   in it were purchased from the
Bury me there."   Hittites."

    The purchase of the property is recorded in 23.1-19.

49.33   TEV   RSV
When Jacob had finished giving   When Jacob finished charging his
instructions to his sons, he   sons, he drew up his feet into
lay back down and died.   the bed, and breathed his last,
                                        and was gathered to his people.

[147]

he lay back down: literally "pulled his feet into the bed" (see RSV), but one may assume that he has been sitting up and now lies down.

died: literally "breathed his last breath and was gathered to his people" (see RSV), but both of these expressions are descriptive ways of speaking about death. See verse 29 for the second. In languages in which death is not named, it will be necessary to use one of the normal figures of speech that are applied to death.

C H A P T E R   50

50.1   TEV   RSV
   Joseph threw himself on his   Then Joseph fell on his fa-
father, crying and kissing his   ther's face, and wept over him,
face.   and kissed him.

threw himself on his father: this translation, as well as the literal "fell on his father's face" (RSV), is open to misunderstanding. The translator will need to describe an action that is characteristic of a manifestation of grief in the receptor culture.

50.2   TEV   RSV
Then Joseph gave orders to em-   And Joseph commanded his servants
balm his father's body.   the physicians to embalm his
                                    father. So the physicians em-
                                    balmed Israel;

gave orders: literally "ordered his servants the physicians" (see RSV), but "his servants" refers to the people who obeyed him as gover- nor, and "physicians" refers to the "embalmers," "morticians." If an object is needed it would be possible to speak of "those who took care of dead bodies."

embalm: "treat the body to preserve it." If embalming is not known, one might consider "prepare the body for burial." At the close of the verse the Hebrew has "and the physicians (embalmers) embalmed Israel (Jacob)," and whether these words are included in translation will depend on receptor language style. In some languages it must be stated specifically that the orders were carried out.

50.3   TEV   RSV
It took forty days, the normal   forty days were required for it,
time for embalming. The Egyptians   for so many are required for
mourned for him seventy days.   embalming. And the Egyptians
                                    wept for him seventy days.

It took: "The process of embalming required forty days."

50.4 TEV	RSV
When the time of mourning was over, Joseph said to the king's officials, "Please take this message to the king:	And when the days of weeping for him were past, Joseph spoke to the household of Pharaoh, saying, "If now I have found favor in your eyes, speak, I pray you, in the ears of Pharaoh, saying,

the king's officials: literally "the house of the king," but see 41.40.

Please: in English this is the way a polite request is introduced, and this word corresponds in function to the literal "If now I have found favor in your eyes, speak, I pray you" (RSV), which is also merely a polite formula used to introduce a request and is found frequently in Hebrew.

take this message to the king: literally "speak in the ears of the king" (see RSV), which is a figurative way of saying "go to the king and say to him."

50.5 TEV	RSV
'When my father was about to die, he made me promise him that I would bury him in the tomb which he had prepared in the land of Canaan. So please let me go and bury my father, and then I will come back.'"	My father made me swear, saying, 'I am about to die: in my tomb which I hewed out for myself in the land of Canaan, there shall you bury me.' Now therefore let me go up, I pray you, and bury my father; then I will return."

made me promise: literally "caused me to make a solemn promise, a vow" (see 22.16). Note that TEV has changed the direct discourse of the original ("I am about to die...bury me") into indirect discourse (that I would bury him). Receptor language usage must determine whether direct or indirect discourse is to be used in translation.

prepared: the Hebrew word may mean "bought" but more probably means "dug," in which case we should probably think of digging a burial place within the cave.

50.6 TEV	RSV
The king answered, "Go and bury your father, as you promised you would."	And Pharaoh answered, "Go up, and bury your father, as he made you swear."

as you promised: "as he made you vow (or, promise)."

50.7 TEV	RSV
So Joseph went to bury his father. All the king's officials, the senior men of his court, and	So Joseph went up to bury his father; and with him went up all the servants of Pharaoh,

[149]

all the leading men of Egypt went with Joseph.	the elders of his household, and all the elders of the land of Egypt,

officials: literally "slaves," "servants" (RSV), but the word refers to government officials who "serve" the king, and not to his household servants.

the senior men of his court: literally "the elders of his house" (see RSV), but the word "elders" refers primarily not to age but to position, and might be translated "leaders." It is clear that "house" refers to the king's court, that is, his advisers (see 41.40).

the leading men of Egypt: literally "the elders of the land of Egypt" (RSV).

50.8 TEV	RSV
His family, his brothers, and the rest of his father's family all went with him. Only their small children and their sheep, goats, and cattle stayed in the region of Goshen.	as well as all the household of Joseph, his brothers, and his father's household; only their children, their flocks, and their herds were left in the land of Goshen.

Goshen: the region of Egypt where the Israelites lived, in part of the Nile delta (see 45.10; 46.28).

50.9-10 TEV	RSV
Men in chariots and men on horseback also went with him; it was a huge group. 10 When they came to the threshing place at Atad east of the Jordan, they mourned loudly for a long time, and Joseph performed mourning ceremonies for seven days.	And there went up with him both chariots and horsemen; it was a very great company. 10 When they came to the threshing floor of Atad, which is beyond the Jordan, they lamented there with a very great and sorrowful lamentation; and he made a mourning for his father seven days.

threshing place: a place where grain is beaten to remove the edible grain from the outside husk.

Atad: the exact location is not known.

mourned loudly for a long time: the Hebrew is quite emphatic, "they mourned a mourning there that was great and heavy exceedingly."

mourning ceremonies: the exact details of these ceremonies in preparation for the funeral are not known, but they probably included wailing, beating oneself, singing funeral dirges, and other ritual acts.

50.11 TEV	RSV
When the citizens of Canaan saw those people mourning at Atad,	When the inhabitants of the land, the Canaanites, saw the mourning

they said, "What a solemn cere- | on the threshing floor of Atad,
mony of mourning the Egyptians | they said, "This is a grievous
are holding!" That is why the | mourning to the Egyptians."
place was named Abel Mizraim.^{c} | Therefore the place was named
| Abel-mizraim;^{d} it is beyond the
^{c}ABEL MIZRAIM: *This name sounds* | Jordan.
like the Hebrew for "mourning of
the Egyptians." | ^{d}That is *meadow (or mourning) of*
| *Egypt*

What a: this is an English device, used to underline the emphatic character of the statement of the Hebrew, "That is a very great mourning."

Egyptians: the Canaanites are portrayed as assuming that the Israelites, dressed like the Egyptians, are also Egyptians.

Abel Mizraim: this name in Hebrew sounds something like the Hebrew for "mourning of the Egyptians," and the text explains the name in this way. A note will be needed to explain to the reader what the connection is between the event and the name. It would also be possible to give the name in translation, "the place was named Egyptian Mourning," but this presents problems elsewhere where the name is well known. It is probably wise to adopt a single pattern of explaining the meaning of names in footnotes when the text requires an explanation.

50.12 TEV

So Jacob's sons did as he had commanded them;

RSV

Thus his sons did for him as he had commanded them;

commanded them: see 49.29.

50.13 TEV

they carried his body to Canaan and buried it in the cave at Machpelah east of Mamre in the field which Abraham had bought from Ephron the Hittite for a burial ground.

RSV

for his sons carried him to the land of Canaan, and buried him in the cave of the field at Machpelah, to the east of Mamre, which Abraham bought with the field from Ephron the Hittite, to possess as a burying place.

See 44.29.

50.14 TEV

After Joseph had buried his father, he returned to Egypt with his brothers and all who had gone with him for the funeral.

RSV

After he had buried his father, Joseph returned to Egypt with his brothers and all who had gone up with him to bury his father.

for the funeral: literally "to bury his father." Language style should determine the vocabulary choice.

[151]

SECTION HEADING

Joseph Reassures His Brothers (50.15-21): "Joseph Tells His Brothers That He Will Not Retaliate," "Joseph Forgives His Brothers."

50.15 TEV	RSV
After the death of their father, Joseph's brothers said, "What if Joseph still hates us and plans to pay us back for all the harm we did to him?"	When Joseph's brothers saw that their father was dead, they said, "It may be that Joseph will hate us and pay us back for all the evil which we did to him."

After the death of their father: literally "And the brothers of Joseph saw that their father was dead" (see RSV), which sounds strange in literal translation. But "saw" is used in a wide sense, and it is probably best to translate with the use of a time phrase, as TEV has done.

What if: the English rhetorical question translates the literal "It may be that" (RSV), "Suppose."

still hates us: "holds a grudge against us."

plans to pay us back: the Hebrew uses an intensive verb construction, "really causes to return to us the evil we did to him." The use of plans to in English helps to convey something of the intensity of the Hebrew.

50.16 TEV	RSV
So they sent a message to Joseph: "Before our father died,	So they sent a message to Joseph, saying, "Your father gave this command before he died,

our father: literally "Your father" (RSV), which is quite acceptable in Hebrew, but which sounds strange in English usage.

50.17 TEV	RSV
he told us to ask you, 'Please forgive the crime your brothers committed when they wronged you.' Now please forgive us the wrong that we, the servants of your father's God, have done." Joseph cried when he received this message.	'Say to Joseph, Forgive, I pray you, the transgression of your brothers and their sin, because they did evil to you.' And now, we pray you, forgive the transgression of the servants of the God of your father." Joseph wept when they spoke to him.

Please: this is once again the English form used to introduce a polite request (see 50.4), although only one part of the Hebrew formula is used here.

crime: literally "transgression and sin."

they wronged you: "they did evil to you."

wrong that we...have done: the Hebrew uses a third person

construction, but most languages will need to shift to first person,
as TEV has done.

servants of your father's God: the word "servants" is here used,
as it frequently is in Hebrew, in the religious sense of "worshipers,"
"those who worship and obey your father's God" (see 46.1).

received this message: often translated literally "when they spoke
to him" (RSV), but it is clear that the brothers have not yet come
personally to Joseph (see verses 16,18), and it is better to translate
in such a way as to make this point clear; the Hebrew can mean "when
they sent this message to him."

50.18	TEV	RSV
	Then his brothers themselves came and bowed down before him. "Here we are before you as your slaves," they said.	His brothers also came and fell down before him, and said, "Behold, we are your servants."

bowed down: literally "fell down" (RSV), but the sense is that
they bowed down with their faces to the ground to show their respect.

Here we are...slaves: "We present ourselves to you as your slaves,"
"We are ready to be your slaves."

50.19	TEV	RSV
	But Joseph said to them, "Don't be afraid; I can't put myself in the place of God.	But Joseph said to them, "Fear not, for am I in the place of God?

Don't be afraid: if an object is required it should be "me": "Don't
be afraid of me." But it is Joseph and the whole situation that the
brothers fear.

I can't put myself in the place of God: this is the meaning of
the rhetorical question expecting a negative answer, "Can I take the
place of God?" (see RSV). In most languages a statement will carry the
message clearly, but if the rhetorical question is used, there should
be a strong indication that the answer is "No." Perhaps the translator
could use something like "Can I play God? Absolutely not!"

50.20	TEV	RSV
	You plotted evil against me, but God turned it into good, in order to preserve the lives of many people who are alive today because of what happened.	As for you, you meant evil against me; but God meant it for good, to bring it about that many people should be kept alive, as they are today.

plotted: "planned," "thought up," "decided to do."

turned it into good: a literal translation would be something
like "decided it for good," with the sense "made good come out of it."

[153]

50.21 TEV	RSV
You have nothing to fear. I will take care of you and your children." So he reassured them with kind words that touched their hearts.	So do not fear; I will provide for you and your little ones." Thus he reassured them and comforted them.

take care of: "provide (food) for."
reassured: the Hebrew word means "comfort," "console" someone who is grieving (see 37.35), but here the sense is "speak words that will take away the fears in the minds of the brothers."
with kind words that touched their hearts: literally "he spoke to them upon the heart," a Hebrew figure for speaking kindly and tenderly.

SECTION HEADING

The Death of Joseph (50.22-26): "Joseph Dies in Egypt."

50.22 TEV	RSV
Joseph continued to live in Egypt with his father's family; he was a hundred and ten years old when he died.	So Joseph dwelt in Egypt, he and his father's house; and Joseph lived a hundred and ten years.

his father's family: literally "his father's house" (RSV), but this has the sense of "all the descendants of his father," that is, his brothers and their children.

50.23 TEV	RSV
He lived to see Ephraim's children and grandchildren. He also lived to receive the children of Machir son of Manasseh into the family.	And Joseph saw Ephraim's children of the third generation; the children also of Machir son of Manasseh were born upon Joseph's knees.

lived to see: literally "he saw," but the whole point is that he lived long enough to see the children before he died.
grandchildren: this is the probable meaning of "third generation," but it could possibly mean "great grandchildren."
receive...into the family: literally "were born upon Joseph's knees" (RSV), but this is a figurative way of saying that Joseph formally received the children into the family. The details are not known, but the placing of a child on the knees of the head of the family was part of a ritual of reception or adoption.

50.24 TEV	RSV
He said to his brothers, "I am about to die, but God will	And Joseph said to his brothers, "I am about to die; but God will

certainly take care of you and lead you out of this land to the land he solemnly promised to Abraham, Isaac, and Jacob."	visit you, and bring you up out of this land to the land which he swore to Abraham, to Isaac, and to Jacob."

I am about to die: "I am dying."

take care of: here, in contrast to verse 21, the Hebrew verb is intensive and has the literal meaning of "visit," but it has the sense of "bless," "provide for," "protect," "care for."

solemnly promised: "vowed." See 22.16; 24.7; 26.3.

50.25   TEV   RSV

Then Joseph asked his people to make a vow. "Promise me," he said, "that when God leads you to that land, you will take my body with you."	Then Joseph took an oath of the sons of Israel, saying, "God will visit you, and you shall carry up my bones from here."

his people: literally "the sons of Israel" (RSV), a term which will from now on be frequently used for the Israelites, the descendants of Jacob.

make a vow: the same Hebrew word is used as of the solemn promise of God in verse 24.

God leads you to that land: literally "visits," as in verse 24, but here the blessing that is understood is that God will come and lead the Israelites out of Egypt and into the promised land, the land of Canaan.

my body: literally "my bones" (RSV), but since the body is to be embalmed, it may be more natural to use "body," "corpse."

50.26   TEV   RSV

So Joseph died in Egypt at the age of a hundred and ten. They embalmed his body and put it in a coffin.	So Joseph died, being a hundred and ten years old; and they embalmed him, and he was put in a coffin in Egypt.

died in Egypt: in Hebrew "in Egypt" comes at the end of the verse, but it should be taken with the whole verse, "So there in Egypt Joseph died...coffin."

EXODUS

THE NAME OF THE BOOK

The name "Exodus" comes from the Greek translation of the book and means "a going out," which refers to the departure of the people of Israel from their slavery in Egypt. The translator is advised to use a name that will suggest this exodus, perhaps "The Book of Departure," "Leaving Egypt," "Rescue from Egypt," or something like that.

INTRODUCTION

The name Exodus means "departure" and refers to the most important event in Israel's history, which is described in this book—the departure of the people of Israel from Egypt, where they had been slaves.

Above all, this book describes what God did as he liberated his enslaved people and formed them into a nation with hope for the future.

The central figure in the book is Moses, the man whom God chose to lead the people from Egypt.

CHAPTER 1

1.1-5: These verses give the names of Jacob's sons and the total number of his descendants who went to Egypt. (See Gen 46.8-27.)

SECTION HEADING

The Israelistes Are Treated Cruelly in Egypt (1.6-22): "The Egyptians Treat the Israelites Harshly."

1.6	TEV	RSV
	In the course of time Joseph, his brothers, and all the rest of that generation died,	Then Joseph died, and all his brothers, and all that generation.

In the course of time: the Hebrew has simply "And," but in English some other connection is needed to prevent the reader from concluding that the events of verse 6 follow immediately in time after those of verse 5. Something like "After some time" may be required in other languages.

the rest of that generation: literally "all that generation" (RSV). The reference is to all the descendants of Jacob and their families who traveled from Canaan to Egypt.

1.7 TEV	RSV
but their descendants, the Israelites, had many children and became so numerous and strong that Egypt was filled with them.	But the descendants of Israel were fruitful and increased greatly; they multiplied and grew exceedingly strong; so that the land was filled with them.

their descendants, the Israelites: literally "the sons of Israel," but the term no longer refers to the twelve sons of Jacob. It now refers to the descendants who are "the people of Israel." In Hebrew, "the sons of ___" is frequently used as the name for a tribe or a nation.

was filled with them: the people of Israel were to be found everywhere; there were very many of them.

1.8 TEV	RSV
Then, a new king, who knew nothing about Joseph, came to power in Egypt.	Now there arose a new king over Egypt, who did not know Joseph.

a new king: "another king," "another person as king of Egypt."
knew nothing about Joseph: literally "did not know Joseph," but from the context it is quite clear that the new king did not live during the time that Joseph was alive. The new king "had no knowledge of Joseph," that is, did not know the story of Joseph and what he had done for the Egyptians during the years of famine.

came to power: literally "arose" (RSV), but the meaning is nonliteral, "appeared," "came on the scene." One may translate "another man became king of Egypt."

1.9 TEV	RSV
He said to his people, "These Israelites are so numerous and strong that they are a threat to us.	And he said to his people, "Behold, the people of Israel are too many and too mighty for us.

his people: that is, the Egyptians, but the words would have been spoken to the king's officials. Note that the attention getter of the Hebrew, often translated "Behold" (RSV), has not been used in TEV. Languages will have different methods for introducing emphatic statements.

[157]

Israelites: "people of Israel."

are so numerous and strong: in Hebrew the two words have much the same meaning, "many," and one might translate, "there are so many of these people that...."

a threat to us: "danger to our nation." Although the Hebrew has only "too many and too strong for us" (see RSV), from the context it is clear that this is in reference to the possible threat to the security of the nation.

1.10 TEV	RSV
In the case of war they might join our enemies in order to fight against us, and might escape from^a the country. We must find some way to keep them from becoming even more numerous."	Come, let us deal shrewdly with them, lest they multiply, and, if war befall us, they join our enemies and fight against us and escape from the land."

^{a}escape from; or take control of.

In case of war: literally "If war happens (to us)" (see RSV). Note that TEV has rearranged the elements of the verse to fit English order better. Note also that this part of the verse explains the "threat" referred to in verse 9.

escape from: literally "go up from the land," which in all probability means escape, but in some Jewish sources it is understood as "rise up in revolt," that is, "take control of the land."

We must find some way: the Hebrew begins with another attention-getting word which is not easy to translate in English, "Give," "Come on," and TEV has included the idea in the structure of We must find some way. The Hebrew verb means something like "let us show ourselves wise"; TEV has translated by find some way. In some languages it may be possible to translate with something like "let us be wise enough to prevent them."

to keep them from: "to prevent them," which is the meaning involved in the Hebrew word often translated "lest" (RSV), that is, "in order that not."

1.11 TEV	RSV
So the Egyptians put slave drivers over them to crush their spirits with hard labor. The Israelites built the cities of Pithom and Rameses to serve as supply centers for the king.	Therefore they set taskmasters over them to afflict them with heavy burdens; and they built for Pharaoh store-cities, Pithom and Raamses.

the Egyptians: literally "they" (RSV), but it is often necessary in translation to replace pronouns with the person or thing to which the pronoun refers, in order to avoid misunderstanding.

slave drivers: literally "chiefs of compulsory labor," "bosses of slave labor." These are Egyptian bosses who direct the work of the Israelite slaves.

to crush their spirits: the Hebrew verb means "cause to bend down" in the sense of "humiliate," "force one to accept his dependent status," "oppress."

hard labor: "the work they are forced to do."

Pithom and Rameses: the exact location of these cities is not known, but they were probably in the eastern part of the Nile delta.

supply centers: "places where supplies are stored," "warehouse cities."

the king: literally "Pharaoh," but this is not a personal name; it is a title which means king, and TEV always uses king and never "Pharaoh."

1.12 TEV	RSV
But the more the Egyptians oppressed the Israelites, the more they increased in number and the farther they spread through the land. The Egyptians came to fear the Israelites	But the more they were oppressed, the more they multiplied and the more they spread abroad. And the Egyptians were in dread of the people of Israel.

oppressed: the Hebrew word is the same as that translated crush their spirits in verse 11.

spread through the land: literally "spread out," "break out," in the sense of having more and more children and establishing more and more homes across the land. They moved from their home in Goshen into other parts of Egypt.

fear: the Hebrew word has the sense of "feel a horror of," "feel a dread of," "be afraid of."

1.13-14 TEV	RSV
and made their lives miserable by forcing them into cruel slavery. They made them work on their building projects and in their fields, and they had no pity on them.	So they made the people of Israel serve with rigor, 14 and made their lives bitter with hard service, in mortar and brick, and in all kinds of work in the field; in all their work they made them serve with rigor.

The two verses are combined in TEV because elements of the two verses have been rearranged to fit better with English order.

made their lives miserable: literally "made their lives bitter" (RSV), that is, made the lives of the Israelites so difficult that it was almost more than they could bear.

cruel slavery: literally "caused them to serve as slaves with violence," that is, "used cruel force to make them work as slaves."

building projects: literally "mortar and brick" (RSV), but Hebrew often speaks of the individual items when referring to the total operation, in this case, building cities (see verse 11).

in their fields: that is, in plowing, planting, caring for, and reaping crops.

had no pity on them: this is an attempt to translate what seems to be meant in the Hebrew, which repeats in an emphatic way that the Israelites were forced "with violence" to do all their work.

1.15	TEV	RSV
	Then the king of Egypt spoke to Shiphrah and Puah, the two midwives who helped the Hebrew women.	Then the king of Egypt said to the Hebrew midwives, one of whom was named Shiphrah and the other Puah,

Shiphrah and Puah: not otherwise known, and it is not certain whether the names are Hebrew or Egyptian.

midwives who helped the Hebrew women: literally "Hebrew midwives," but commentators disagree as to whether these women were Egyptian or Hebrew. The word "Hebrew" is used for the people of Israel.

1.16	TEV	RSV
	"When you help the Hebrew women give birth," he said to them, "kill the baby if it is a boy; but if it is a girl, let it live."	"When you serve as midwife to the Hebrew women, and see them upon the birthstool, if it is a son, you shall kill him; but if it is a daughter, she shall live."

if it is a boy: the Hebrew has "and look at the two stones if it is a boy," but the meaning of the word translated "two stones" is uncertain. Some take it to refer to two stones on which the Hebrew women may have knelt as they gave birth (see RSV "birthstool"), while others take it to refer to the genitals of the baby, "look at the genitals to see if it is a boy." TEV has taken the latter view but has not translated the words specifically, assuming that every reader will know that the sex of the child would be determined by looking at its genitals.

1.17	TEV	RSV
	But the midwives were God-fearing and so did not obey the king; instead, they let the boys live.	But the midwives feared God, and did not do as the king of Egypt commanded them, but let the male children live.

God-fearing: literally "feared God" (RSV). This does not mean that they were afraid God would punish them, but rather that they worshiped and obeyed God. One might translate quite correctly, "worshiped God."

let the boys live: it is, of course, assumed that the girls were also allowed to live.

1.18   TEV

So the king sent for the midwives and asked them, "Why are
you doing this? Why are you
letting the boys live?"

                                        RSV

So the king of Egypt called the
midwives, and said to them, "Why
have you done this, and let the
male children live?"

  sent for: literally "called" (RSV), that is, sent word that they
should come to him.

1.19   TEV

 They answered, "The Hebrew
women are not like Egyptian
women; they give birth easily,
and their babies are born before
either of us gets there."

                                        RSV

The midwives said to Pharaoh, "Because the Hebrew women are not
like the Egyptian women; for they
are vigorous and are delivered
before the midwife comes to them."

  give birth easily: literally "are vigorous, lively," but the sense
is that they have no trouble in giving birth, and so give birth quickly.
  either of us: literally "the midwives," but Hebrew often uses a
third person construction when most languages require first person.
Here the midwives are the two who have been named.

1.20-21   TEV

Because the midwives were God-
fearing, God was good to them
and gave them families of their
own. And the Israelites continued
to increase and become strong.

                                        RSV

So God dealt well with the midwives; and the people multiplied
and grew very strong. 21 And because the midwives feared God he
gave them families.

  TEV has rearranged elements of these verses and combined verse
numbers in order to make the connection between elements clearer to
English readers. A similar rearrangement is likely to be needed in
other languages.
  good to them: "treated them kindly," "dealt favorably with them,"
"caused good things to happen to them."
  families: literally "houses," but the Hebrew word is frequently
used in the extended sense of families.
  increase and become strong: see verse 9.

1.22   TEV

Finally the king issued a command to all his people: "Take
every newborn Hebrew boy and
throw him into the Nile, but
let all the girls live."

                                        RSV

Then Pharaoh commanded all his
people, "Every son that is born
to the Hebrews[a] you shall cast
into the Nile, but you shall let
every daughter live."

[a]Sam Gk Tg: Heb lacks *to the
Hebrews*

all his people: "all the Egyptians."
Nile: the Nile river flows from south to north through the whole
of Egypt. See TEV map, "Egypt and Sinai."

C H A P T E R   2

SECTION HEADING

The Birth of Moses (2.1-10): "Moses Is Born."

2.1   TEV   RSV
   During this time a man from   Now a man from the house of
the tribe of Levi married a wom-   Levi went and took to wife a
an of his own tribe,   daughter of Levi.

During this time: this is one way to introduce the idea that the
birth of Moses took place during this time when boy babies were being
killed.
   tribe of Levi: literally "house of Levi" (RSV), but the reference
is to the descendants of Levi, and the normal word is "tribe."
   married: literally "went and took," but the verb "take" is frequently used in Hebrew with the sense of the English "marry."
   woman of his own tribe: literally "a daughter of Levi" (RSV), but
the word "daughter" is used for granddaughter, great-granddaughter, or
female descendant. An actual daughter of Levi would no longer be alive
(see 1.6).

2.2   TEV   RSV
and she bore him a son. When she   The woman conceived and bore a
saw what a fine baby he was, she   son; and when she saw that he
hid him for three months.   was a goodly child, she hid him
                                     three months.

she bore: literally "she became pregnant and bore" (see RSV). It
will depend largely on language usage whether or not one includes in
a translation the idea of conception.
   what a fine baby he was: "that he was a fine baby." The word "fine"
translates the literal "good," but this is not referring to how the
baby behaved. It has reference to the fact that the child was healthy
and well-formed.
   hid him: one assumes that the mother kept the child hid at home.

2.3   TEV   RSV
But when she could not hide him   And when she could hide him no
any longer, she took a basket   longer she took for him a bas-
made of reeds and covered it with   ket made of bulrushes, and daubed

tar to make it watertight. She put the baby in it and then placed it in the tall grass at the edge of the river.	it with bitumen and pitch; and she put the child in it and placed it among the reeds at the river's brink.

any longer: the child becomes more difficult to hide as he becomes older.

basket made of reeds: this would have been made of papyrus, a reedy plant that grows along the Nile, but one need not try to be too specific. Any type of reed or straw basket that is known in the culture should be satisfactory.

tar: literally "bitumen and pitch," but it is not necessary to find two words for this natural substance. See Genesis 6.14; 11.3.

watertight: "so that no water would leak into the basket."

tall grass: "reeds."

2.4 TEV	RSV
The baby's sister stood some distance away to see what would happen to him.	And his sister stood at a distance, to know what would be done to him.

the baby's sister: obviously an older sister, but her age is not known. See verse 7.

2.5 TEV	RSV
The king's daughter came down to the river to bathe, while her servants walked along the bank. Suddenly she noticed the basket in the tall grass and sent a slave girl to get it.	Now the daughter of Pharaoh came down to bathe at the river, and her maidens walked beside the river; she saw the basket among the reeds and sent her maid to fetch it.

The king's daughter: this is the term used by the Hebrew throughout this section. In English the term "princess" may be used for a king's daughter.

bathe: "take a bath in the river."

her servants: literally "her young women," probably referring to her court attendants.

noticed: "saw."

a slave girl: one of the slave girls who stayed with her to help her as she bathed.

2.6 TEV	RSV
The princess opened it and saw a baby boy. He was crying, and she felt sorry for him. "This is one of the Hebrew babies," she said.	When she opened it she saw the child; and lo, the babe was crying. She took pity on him and said, "This is one of the Hebrews' children."

[163]

princess: see verse 5.

opened it: although we are not told so in verse 3, the basket had been made with a cover that could be opened.

felt sorry for: "had compassion for," "was moved with pity for."

2.7	TEV	RSV
	Then his sister asked her, "Shall I go and call a Hebrew woman to nurse the baby for you?"	Then his sister said to Pharaoh's daughter, "Shall I go and call you a nurse from the Hebrew women to nurse the child for you?"

his sister asked: one must assume "came near the princess and asked."

nurse: "to feed at the breast," "to give milk to."

2.8	TEV	RSV
	"Please do," she answered. So the girl went and brought the baby's own mother.	And Pharaoh's daughter said to her, "Go." So the girl went and called the child's mother.

Please do: literally "Go" (RSV), but in Hebrew this is a proper way of saying, "Yes, please go and call her." In many languages, as in English, a literal translation would be impolite or improper and might be misunderstood.

2.9	TEV	RSV
	The princess told the woman, "Take this baby and nurse him for me, and I will pay you." So she took the baby and nursed him.	And Pharaoh's daughter said to her, "Take this child away, and nurse him for me, and I will give you your wages." So the woman took the child and nursed him.

the woman: the princess, of course, does not know that this is the child's mother.

I will pay you: literally "I will give you your wages" (RSV).

2.10	TEV	RSV
	Later, when the child was old enough, she took him to the king's daughter, who adopted him as her own son. She said to herself, "I pulled him out of the water, and so I name him Moses."[b]	And the child grew, and she brought him to Pharaoh's daughter, and he became her son; and she named him Moses,[b] for she said, "Because I drew him out[c] of the water."
	[b]MOSES: *This name sounds like the Hebrew for "pull out."*	[b]Heb *Mosheh* [c]Heb *mashah*

Later, when the child was old enough: this is clearly the sense of the literal "And the child grew" (RSV).

adopted him as her own son: literally "and he was to her as a son," but since this presupposes adoption, it may be simpler to state the fact in this way.

Moses: the Hebrew name sounds something like the Hebrew verb "pull out." The translator will have to provide a note for the reader, as TEV has done, in order for the reason for the choice of this name to be clear.

SECTION HEADING

Moses Escapes to Midian (2.11-25): "Moses Leaves Egypt and Goes to the Land of Midian."

2.11   TEV   RSV
When Moses had grown up, he   One day, when Moses had grown
went out to visit his people, the   up, he went out to his people and
Hebrews, and he saw how they were   looked on their burdens; and he
forced to do hard labor. He even   saw an Egyptian beating a Hebrew,
saw an Egyptian kill a Hebrew,   one of his people.
one of Moses' own people.

he went out: that is, he left the palace where he was living and went out to where the Hebrews were working.

to visit: the context makes clear that he is only making a temporary visit to the Hebrews.

forced to do hard labor: see 1.13-14.

kill: literally "striking" (with the fist or with a rock), and the word may be translated "beating"; but in verse 12 the same Hebrew word is used for "strike and kill," and that may well be the meaning here. It should be noted, however, that most translations understand the word in this verse to mean "beat."

2.12   TEV   RSV
Moses looked all around, and when   He looked this way and that, and
he saw that no one was watching,   seeing no one he killed the Egyp-
he killed the Egyptian and hid   tian and hid him in the sand.
his body in the sand.

looked all around: literally "turned this way and that."

saw that no one was watching: literally "saw that there was no one."

2.13   TEV   RSV
The next day he went back and saw   When he went out the next day,
two Hebrew men fighting. He said   behold, two Hebrews were strug-
to the one who was in the wrong,   gling together; and he said to
"Why are you beating up a fellow   the man that did the wrong, "Why
Hebrew?"   do you strike your fellow?"

[165]

went back: literally "went out," that is, to where the Hebrews were.

who was in the wrong: "who was doing wrong," "who was guilty."

2.14	TEV	RSV
	The man answered, "Who made you our ruler and judge? Are you going to kill me just as you killed that Egyptian?" Then Moses was afraid and said to himself, "People have found out what I have done."	He answered, "Who made you a prince and a judge over us? Do you mean to kill me as you killed the Egyptian?" Then Moses was afraid, and thought, "Surely the thing is known."

made you: "set you," "appointed you."

ruler: the Hebrew word is used for "chief," "prince," "ruler."

judge: "the one to decide our disputes."

said to himself: literally "said," but in the sense of "thought."

People have found out what I have done: literally "the thing (the fact that I have killed the Egyptian) has become known" (see RSV), but it may be simpler to express this in an active form.

2.15-16	TEV	RSV
	When the king heard about what had happened, he tried to have Moses killed, but Moses fled and went to live in the land of Midian.	When Pharaoh heard of it, he sought to kill Moses.
	One day, when Moses was sitting by a well, seven daughters of Jethro, the priest of Midian, came to draw water and fill the troughs for their father's sheep and goats.	But Moses fled from Pharaoh, and stayed in the land of Midian; and he sat down by a well. 16 Now the priest of Midian had seven daughters; and they came and drew water, and filled the troughs to water their father's flock.

heard about what had happened: literally "heard about this thing" (see verse 14).

tried to have Moses killed: literally "tried to kill Moses" (see RSV), but it is not likely that the king himself was trying to do the killing. Rather, he gave orders that Moses should be killed.

fled: literally "fled, ran away from the face (presence) of the king."

land of Midian: a territory east of the Gulf of Aqaba. See Genesis 37.26 and the TEV map, "Egypt and Sinai."

Jethro: the name is not given here in the Hebrew text and first occurs in 3.1, but see verse 18. TEV has chosen to identify him here at the first occurrence, as fitting English style better.

draw water: from the well.

troughs: "watering troughs," "containers from which the animals drank water."

sheep and goats: literally "flock" (RSV), but the flock would have been made up of sheep and goats.

[166]

2.17 TEV

But some shepherds drove Jethro's daughters away. Then Moses went to their rescue and watered their animals for them.

RSV

The shepherds came and drove them away; but Moses stood up and helped them, and watered their flock.

some shepherds: literally "The shepherds" (RSV), that is, "the men who were taking care of other flocks of sheep and goats."

went to their rescue: literally "stood up and helped" (RSV), but the Hebrew verb also has the meaning of "rescue," "save," from some difficulty. Here it is clear from the context that Moses resisted the shepherds and forced them to wait until he had watered the sheep for the seven women.

watered: "gave the animals water to drink."

2.18 TEV

When they returned to their father, he asked, "Why have you come back so early today?"

RSV

When they came to their father Reuel, he said, "How is it that you have come so soon today?"

their father: the Hebrew introduces here the name "Reuel" (see RSV); in fact, the father-in-law of Moses is known by both names, Jethro (3.10) and Reuel. For many readers it is very confusing to use two names for the same person; therefore TEV has chosen the more familiar name, Jethro, whenever a name is required. The translator is advised to follow the same procedure. If a name is required here, one should translate "their father, Jethro."

2.19 TEV

"An Egyptian rescued us from the shepherds," they answered, "and he even drew water for us and watered our animals."

RSV

They said, "An Egyptian delivered us out of the hand of the shepherds, and even drew water for us and watered the flock."

An Egyptian: the daughters did not know that Moses was not an Egyptian.

2.20 TEV

"Where is he?" he asked his daughters. "Why did you leave the man out there? Go and invite him to eat with us."

RSV

He said to his daughters, "And where is he? Why have you left the man? Call him, that he may eat bread."

invite him to eat with us: literally "Call him and he shall eat bread" (see RSV), but "bread" is used in the general sense of "food," and this is the way a polite invitation is issued.

[167]

	TEV	RSV
2.21	So Moses decided to live there, and Jethro gave him his daughter Zipporah in marriage,	And Moses was content to dwell with the man, and he gave Moses his daughter Zipporah.

decided: "agreed to," "was willing to."
to live there: literally "to live with the man" (see RSV), but this will mean "under the man's protection" and not that he lived in the same house.
gave...in marriage: the Hebrew has "gave," but it is clear in the context that the meaning is "gave Zipporah to Moses as his wife."

	TEV	RSV
2.22	who bore him a son. Moses said to himself, "I am a foreigner in this land, and so I name him Gershom."*c*	She bore a son, and he called his name Gershom; for he said, "I have been a sojourner*d* in a foreign land."

*c*GERSHOM: *This name sounds like the Hebrew for "foreigner."*   *d*Heb *ger*

Gershom: this is another play on words. The name sounds somewhat like the Hebrew word for "foreigner," and the translator should provide a note for the reader to explain this fact.

	TEV	RSV
2.23	Years later the king of Egypt died, but the Israelites were still groaning under their slavery and cried out for help. Their cry went up to God,	In the course of those many days the king of Egypt died. And the people of Israel groaned under their bondage, and cried out for help, and their cry under bondage came up to God.

Years later: literally "In those many days" (see RSV), but this formula can refer to years, and we know that Moses was in Midian many years.
went up to God: "was heard by God in heaven."

	TEV	RSV
2.24	who heard their groaning and remembered his covenant with Abraham, Isaac, and Jacob.	And God heard their groaning, and God remembered his covenant with Abraham, with Isaac, and with Jacob.

groaning: the Hebrew uses a different word from that used in verse 23, but the meaning is not essentially different; "cries of suffering."
his covenant: "the covenant he had made with." The word "covenant" means "agreement" (see Gen 6.18).

2.25   TEV   RSV

TEV	RSV
He saw the slavery of the Israel-ites and was concerned for them.*d*	And God saw the people of Israel, and God knew their condition.

*d*was concerned for them; *one an-cient translation* revealed him-self to them.

saw the slavery of the Israelites: literally "saw the sons of Israel" (see RSV), but one may safely assume that the point is not that God saw the people, but that he was aware of their condition, their slavery.

was concerned for them: the Hebrew is extremely difficult to translate, although in its barest form it would read "God knew," with-out any indication of what God knew. TEV has recognized the possibility that the Hebrew word "know" may also have the meaning of "care about," "be concerned about," and has supplied "them" as the object of God's concern. RSV understands "know" in the traditional way and supplies "their condition" as the object. Others, as the TEV marginal note shows, assume that the Greek translation has correctly preserved the meaning, and translate "he was made known to them," "revealed him-self to them." Others assume the sense to be "God considered what he should do" (see Gen 18.21). The translator must choose between the possibilities, and he may wish to add a footnote indicating other pos-sibilities, as TEV has done.

CHAPTER 3

SECTION HEADING

God Calls Moses (3.1-22): "God Calls Moses to Go to Egypt," "God Tells Moses to Go and Rescue His People."

3.1

TEV	RSV
One day while Moses was taking care of the sheep and goats of his father-in-law Jethro, the priest of Midian, he led the flock across the desert and came to Sinai, the holy mountain.	Now Moses was keeping the flock of his father-in-law, Jethro, the priest of Midian; and he led his flock to the west side of the wilderness, and came to Horeb, the mountain of God.

One day: the Hebrew has simply "And," but most languages will need some type of introductory expression for this new section.

across the desert: literally "behind the desert," but this would mean "to the other side of the desert." RSV has translated "to the west side," but this is doubtful.

Sinai: the Hebrew text has "Horeb" (RSV), as the mountain is re-ferred to by two names. Since, however, it is confusing for many readers to keep up with two names for the same place, TEV always uses the more familiar name <u>Sinai</u> wherever the mountain is referred to.

the holy <u>mountain</u>: literally "the mountain of God" (RSV), which will mean "the mountain on which God appears" and not "the mountain that belongs to God." In many languages "sacred mountain" or "holy mountain" will be best, where "holy" will mean "dedicated to God," "set apart for God's use."

3.2	TEV	RSV
	There the angel of the LORD appeared to him as a flame coming from the middle of a bush. Moses saw that the bush was on fire but that it was not burning up.	And the angel of the LORD appeared to him in a flame of fire out of the midst of a bush; and he looked, and lo, the bush was burning, yet it was not consumed.

the angel of the LORD: in many parts of the Old Testament "the angel of the LORD" is a kind of representation for God and cannot easily be distinguished from God himself. Often, as is the case in verse 4, when the angel of the LORD appears to a person, it is the LORD himself who continues the conversation.

appeared: "was seen," "became visible," "showed himself."

flame: literally "a flame of fire" (RSV).

bush: the Hebrew may refer to a particular kind of thorny bush, but it is probably wiser to use a general term.

Moses saw: literally "saw and behold," in other words, an emphatic, startled "looking" is involved, and the translator should seek some way to indicate to the reader the startling or noteworthy nature of the sight. Perhaps, "He saw that the bush was on fire, but was surprised that it was not burning up."

3.3	TEV	RSV
	"This is strange," he thought. "Why isn't the bush burning up? I will go closer and see."	And Moses said, "I will turn aside and see this great sight, why the bush is not burnt."

This is strange: note that TEV has inverted the order of elements in the verse. The Hebrew, "this great sight" (RSV), emphasizes how unusual this must have appeared to Moses.

I will go closer: literally "I will turn aside" (RSV), that is, from the path he is following, in order to go closer.

3.4	TEV	RSV
	When the LORD saw that Moses was coming closer, he called to him from the middle of the bush and said, "Moses! Moses!" He answered, "Yes, here I am."	When the LORD saw that he turned aside to see, God called to him out of the bush, "Moses, Moses!" And he said, "Here am I."

here I am: literally "Behold me," but this is the standard response when one is called (see Gen 22.1 and other examples in Genesis). One should translate with an expression that would be suitable for answering when one is addressed.

3.5 TEV	RSV
God said, "Do not come any closer. Take off your sandals, because you are standing on holy ground.	Then he said, "Do not come near; put off your shoes from your feet, for the place on which you are standing is holy ground."

Take off your sandals: literally "Take off your sandals from your feet" (see RSV), but language style should determine whether or not the whole is to be translated. Where sandals are not known, the ordinary word for footwear may be used.

holy ground: the Hebrew uses a word for "place" that may have the meaning of "sacred place," "place where God appears," and "holy ground" will have the meaning "ground set apart exclusively for God's use." See verse 1 and Genesis 28.11,16.

3.6 TEV	RSV
I am the God of your ancestors, the God of Abraham, Isaac, and Jacob." So Moses covered his face, because he was afraid to look at God.	And he said, "I am the God of your father, the God of Abraham, the God of Isaac, and the God of Jacob." And Moses hid his face, for he was afraid to look at God.

God of your ancestors: "God whom your ancestors worshiped," and who made his covenant with them. The Hebrew has "I am the God of your father" (RSV), which would literally mean a reference to the man named in 2.1. It is more likely, however, that the word is to be understood, as it frequently is, to mean "ancestor." The singular would then refer to Jacob, but the formula is used frequently of the ancestors, who are then named, and TEV has followed this approach and used a plural.

covered: literally "hid," but in the sense that he put a part of his robe or his hands over his face.

3.7 TEV	RSV
Then the LORD said, "I have seen how cruelly my people are being treated in Egypt; I have heard them cry out to be rescued from their slave drivers. I know all about their sufferings,	Then the LORD said, "I have seen the affliction of my people who are in Egypt, and have heard their cry because of their taskmasters; I know their sufferings,

I have seen: the Hebrew is intensive, "I have fully seen," "I know all about."

how cruelly my people are being treated: literally "the affliction of my people." The reference is to the plight of the people as recorded in 1.11-14.

[171]

cry out: see 2.23.
sufferings: "pain," "misery."

3.8   TEV   RSV

and so I have come down to rescue them from the Egyptians and to bring them out of Egypt to a spacious land, one which is rich and fertile and in which the Canaanites, the Hittites, the Amorites, the Perizzites, the Hivites, and the Jebusites now live.	and I have come down to deliver them out of the hand of the Egyptians, and to bring them up out of that land to a good and broad land, a land flowing with milk and honey, to the place of the Canaanites, the Hittites, the Amorites, the Perizzites, the Hivites, and the Jebusites.

come down: with "from heaven" being understood.

rescue: the Hebrew word has the meaning "take away," "pull out," "deliver" from some danger or difficulty.

from the Egyptians: literally "from the hand of the Egyptians" (RSV), but "hand" in Hebrew frequently expresses the idea of "power," "control." One might translate "rescue them from the power of the Egyptians," but in English the same meaning is conveyed by "rescue them from the Egyptians."

bring them out: literally "bring them up" (RSV), since in Hebrew, Egypt is thought of as "below" Canaan in the sense that Canaan is mountainous. Most languages are not as concerned about such a height difference in speaking of travel; they will follow the pattern of TEV of generally not taking it into account in translation.

spacious: literally "flowing with milk and honey" (RSV), but this is a set phrase that is frequently used to describe the land of Canaan. "Flowing with milk" means that the land is very good and that cattle grazing on the good grass will produce a lot of milk. "Flowing with honey" means that there are many trees and flowers from which bees can make honey. In most languages a literal translation will picture something like rivers of milk and honey, and it is probably best to speak of a good, fertile land that provides for all human needs.

the Canaanites...the Jebusites: these are the people of various tribes who were at this time living in the land of Canaan.

3.9   TEV   RSV

I have indeed heard the cry of my people, and I see how the Egyptians are oppressing them.	And now, behold, the cry of the people of Israel has come to me, and I have seen the oppression with which the Egyptians oppress them.

I have indeed heard: the Hebrew is emphatic, "And now behold the cry has come to me" (see RSV), but in English and in other languages one speaks of hearing a cry, rather than of a cry coming to one's ears. An emphatic form should be used that is suitable in the language (English indeed).

my people: literally "the sons of Israel," but the whole context underlines the idea that the people of Israel are God's people, and the Hebrew uses "my people" in verse 10.

3.10	TEV	RSV
	Now I am sending you to the king of Egypt so that you can lead my people out of his country."	Come, I will send you to Pharaoh that you may bring forth my people, the sons of Israel, out of Egypt."

Now: literally "Now go," but this is an emphatic introductory formula which may be translated differently in each language.

I am sending you: "I am telling you to go." It is possible to translate in the future, "I will send," but the present moment is in focus "I will send you now."

his country: literally "Egypt," but since "king of Egypt" is used, it is better in English to avoid the repetition of "Egypt."

3.11	TEV	RSV
	But Moses said to God, "I am nobody. How can I go to the king and bring the Israelites out of Egypt?"	But Moses said to God, "Who am I that I should go to Pharaoh, and bring the sons of Israel out of Egypt?"

I am nobody: literally "Who am I" (RSV), but this is a rhetorical question that expects the answer "Nobody." The question does not seek information but is a way of expressing emphatically that Moses feels he has no value. If the question is retained, many languages will have to provide an answer: "Who am I? I am nobody."

How can I: in some languages it will be best to change this rhetorical question to a statement, for example, "I cannot go...."

3.12	TEV	RSV
	God answered, "I will be with you, and when you bring the people out of Egypt, you will worship me on this mountain. That will be the proof that I have sent you."	He said, "But I will be with you; and this shall be the sign for you, that I have sent you: when you have brought forth the people out of Egypt, you shall serve God upon this mountain."

God answered: literally "And he said" (see RSV). But in order to avoid any misunderstanding, it is often necessary to supply the name of the person to whom the pronoun refers.

I will be with you: not only to accompany Moses, but to guide and help him. The "you" is singular, referring to Moses (see Gen 28.15).

you will worship me: the "you" is plural and refers to Moses and the people of Israel. Literally "serve God," but "serve" has the religious sense of "worship," "obey," "adore," and since God is speaking, it is necessary in most languages to shift to first person "me," since

God is speaking of himself and not of some other God. Note that TEV has changed the order of elements in the verse for better English style.

on this mountain: Mount Sinai (see verse 1).

proof: the Hebrew uses a word that means "sign" (RSV), that is, "what will show you something," "teach you something." Here the fact that the people will return to Sinai to worship God is said to be a proof, showing that God has sent Moses.

3.13	TEV	RSV
	But Moses replied, "When I go to the Israelites and say to them, 'The God of your ancestors sent me to you,' they will ask me, 'What is his name?' So what can I tell them?"	Then Moses said to God, "If I come to the people of Israel and say to them, 'The God of your fathers has sent me to you,' and they ask me, 'What is his name?' what shall I say to them?"

the God of your ancestors: the plural, "fathers," is used here (see verse 6).

name: the question about God's name includes also the question about his nature: "What is he like?" "What is his relationship to us?" If one knows the name of a person, one knows the nature and character of the person.

what can I tell them: "what answer can I give?" "how can I answer them?"

3.14	TEV	RSV
	God said, "I am who I am. You must tell them: 'The one who is called I AM^e has sent me to you.'	God said to Moses, "I AM WHO I AM."^e And he said, "Say this to the people of Israel, 'I AM has sent me to you.'"

^eI am who I am...I AM; *or* I will be who I will be...I WILL BE. *"I am" sounds like the Hebrew name Yahweh, traditionally transliterated as Jehovah. This name is represented in this translation by "the LORD" in capital letters, following a usage which is widespread in English versions.*

^eOr I AM WHAT I AM or I WILL BE WHAT I WILL BE

I am who I am: these words will need to be translated in the same way as the "name" of God in the last part of the verse, as is shown in the TEV note. In Hebrew the verb "to be" could have the meaning "I am," "I came to be," or "I will be." The answer is difficult to interpret, no matter which form is used, but there seems to be a message to Moses which says something like "I am God, and I will determine what kind of God I will be."

I AM: this is, of course, to be understood as a name, and there is no doubt that the Hebrew intended the reader to make the connection between I AM and the name LORD (Yahweh in Hebrew). See Genesis 2.4. The exact meaning is, however, much disputed. The most likely possibilities are "I am," or "I will be," but others argue that the meaning is "I create" or "I am the creator." Whichever form is chosen for the text, it will probably be necessary to have a footnote which includes some of the other possibilities, as TEV has done.

3.15 TEV	RSV
Tell the Israelites that I, the LORD, the God of their ancestors, the God of Abraham, Isaac, and Jacob, have sent you to them. This is my name forever; this is what all future generations are to call me.	God also said to Moses, "Say this to the people of Israel, 'The LORD,^{f} the God of your fathers, the God of Abraham, the God of Isaac, and the God of Jacob, has sent me to you': this is my name for ever, and thus I am to be remembered throughout all generations.
	^{f}The word LORD when spelled with capital letters, stands for the divine name, YHWH, which is here connected with the verb *hayah*, to be

my name forever: this name I AM (Yahweh), the LORD, is the personal name of God and always will be.
all future generations: literally "to generation, generation," but this is a Hebrew way of saying "generation after generation."

3.16 TEV	RSV
Go and gather the leaders of Israel together and tell them that I, the LORD, the God of their ancestors, the God of Abraham, Isaac, and Jacob, appeared to you. Tell them that I have come to them and have seen what the Egyptians are doing to them.	Go and gather the elders of Israel together, and say to them, 'The LORD, the God of your fathers, the God of Abraham, of Isaac, and of Jacob, has appeared to me, saying, "I have observed you and what has been done to you in Egypt;

the leaders: literally "the elders" (RSV), but in Hebrew culture the old men were considered to be the wise men, and therefore the natural leaders of the people of Israel.
I have come to them and have seen: the Hebrew uses an emphatic form of a verb that means "come and pay close attention to." In English and in many other languages this idea will be expressed with more than one verb: "come...and see," "visit...observe."

3.17 TEV	RSV
I have decided that I will bring	and I promise that I will bring

them out of Egypt, where they are being treated cruelly, and will take them to a rich and fertile land—the land of the Canaanites, the Hittites, the Amorites, the Perizzites, the Hivites, and the Jebusites.

you up out of the affliction of Egypt, to the land of the Canaanites, the Hittites, the Amorites, the Perizzites, the Hivites, and the Jebusites, a land flowing with milk and honey."'

I have decided: literally "I said," interpreted in the sense "I said to myself," "I resolved." RSV translates "I promise." For the rest of the verse see verse 8.

3.18   TEV

"My people will listen to what you say to them. Then you must go with the leaders of Israel to the king of Egypt and say to him, 'The LORD, the God of the Hebrews, has revealed himself to us. Now allow us to travel three days into the desert to offer sacrifices to the LORD, our God.'

                    RSV

And they will hearken to your voice; and you and the elders of Israel shall go to the king of Egypt and say to him, "The LORD, the God of the Hebrews, has met with us; and now, we pray you, let us go a three days' journey into the wilderness, that we may sacrifice to the LORD our God.'

My people: literally "They," but in most languages it will be necessary to identify the hearers. Note that in RSV "they" seems to refer to the people of Canaan, and this is not the meaning.

listen to what you say to them: literally "hear your voice" (see RSV), but in Hebrew the meaning is often the content of the "voice," that is, what is said.

revealed himself to us: the Hebrew uses a word that means something like "happened to," "make oneself available to," which may be translated "show himself to us." RSV translates "has met with us."

allow us: the Hebrew uses a polite form, "please let us."

travel three days: "make a journey of three days." This may be an expression used in a general way to indicate a considerable distance.

offer sacrifices: the Hebrew uses a general word, but it includes "burn animals as an offering."

3.19   TEV

I know that the king of Egypt will not let you go unless he is forced to do so.

                    RSV

I know that the king of Egypt will not let you go unless compelled by a mighty hand.*g*

*g*Gk Vg: Heb *no, not by a mighty hand*

unless he is forced to do so: the Hebrew, literally "and not with a mighty hand," is somewhat difficult to interpret, although there is no doubt that "with a mighty hand" means "with force," "be forced to

do something" (in this case, to release the people). It is possible
that the Hebrew "and not" is to be interpreted as "unless, except,"
but it is quite clear that this is the meaning of the early Greek
translation and what must be understood from the context.

3.20	TEV	RSV
But I will use my power and will punish Egypt by doing terrifying things there. After that he will let you go.	So I will stretch out my hand and smite Egypt with all the wonders which I will do in it; after that he will let you go.

I will use my power: this is what the literal "stretch out my
hand" (RSV) often means when spoken of God's action.
punish: literally "strike" (see RSV), but the Hebrew word is also
used for the "blows," that is, the "punishments," that God brings on
Egypt. See the description of the disasters that begins in 7.14.
terrifying things: the Hebrew word refers to what is "extraordi-
nary," "marvelous," "producing wonder and fear."

3.21	TEV	RSV
"I will make the Egyptians respect you so that when my people leave, they will not go empty-handed.	And I will give this people favor in the sight of the Egyptians; and when you go, you shall not go empty,

make the Egyptians respect you: the Hebrew expresses this idea by
using a figure, "I will give this people (the people of Israel) favor
in the eyes of the Egyptians" (see RSV); but most languages will express this directly: "the Egyptians will look with favor on (be favorably disposed toward) the Israelites." The meaning clearly is that
the Egyptians will have such a high regard and respect for the Israelites (caused by the fear of further punishment) that they will do all
they can to hasten their departure.
my people: literally "you" plural, but with the sense "all of you,
my people."
empty-handed: that is, "without taking anything with them."

3.22	TEV	RSV
Every Israelite woman will go to her Egyptian neighbors and to any Egyptian woman living in her house and will ask for clothing and for gold and silver jewelry. The Is-raelites will put these things on their sons and daughters and carry away the wealth of the Egyptians."	but each woman shall ask of her neighbor, and of her who sojourns in her house, jewelry of silver and of gold, and clothing, and you shall put them on your sons and on your daughters; thus you shall despoil the Egyptians."

will go...and will ask: although the Hebrew uses only the verb
"ask," in some languages it will be easier to make explicit that

[177]

"asking the neighbor" involves "going (to the neighbor's house) and asking."

any Egyptian woman: the Hebrew word refers to a foreigner who lives temporarily under the protection of a person. In this case the reference is probably to Egyptian women who are living and working in the homes of Israelites.

carry away: the Hebrew word means "carry away," "rescue," "plunder."

4.1-31: God gives Moses miraculous powers, and Moses returns to Egypt.

5.1—6.27: This section tells of the first appearance of Moses and Aaron before the king of Egypt, further oppression of the Israelites, and the family record of Moses and Aaron.

CHAPTER 6

SECTION HEADING

The LORD's Command to Moses and Aaron (6.28—7.7): "The LORD Commands Moses and Aaron to Go to the King of Egypt."

6.28

TEV	RSV
When the LORD spoke to Moses in the land of Egypt,	On the day when the LORD spoke to Moses in the land of Egypt,

When: literally "On the day when" (RSV), and the full form may be retained, but the term is often quite general in Hebrew.

6.29

TEV	RSV
he said, "I am the LORD. Tell the king of Egypt everything I tell you."	the LORD said to Moses, "I am the LORD; tell Pharaoh king of Egypt all that I say to you."

he said: the Hebrew repeats "and the LORD said to Moses" (see RSV). Whether or not this is retained will depend on the style of the receptor language.

6.30

TEV	RSV
But Moses answered, "You know that I am such a poor speaker; why should the king listen to me?"	But Moses said to the LORD, "Behold, I am of uncircumcised lips; how then shall Pharaoh listen to me?"

such a poor speaker: literally "a man of uncircumcised lips" (see RSV). In Hebrew the word "lips" is often used to refer to speech (as is "tongue," "mouth"), and that is clearly the case here. Also "uncircumcised" is applied to pagans and tends to take the general sense of "no good." To say "my lips are no good" is to say "I am not able to speak well," "I am a poor speaker."

why: in many languages the rhetorical question will need to be changed into a statement: "the king will not listen to me."

C H A P T E R   7

7.1

TEV	RSV
The LORD said, "I am going to make you like God to the king, and your brother Aaron will speak to him as your prophet.	And the LORD said to Moses, "See, I make you as God to Pharaoh; and Aaron your brother shall be your prophet.

I: the Hebrew uses an intensive particle, which some translations try to reproduce with "Behold" (RSV "See"). If the receptor language does not use this type of particle, the intensive nature of the statement may be conveyed in other ways, for example, "I want you to know this," "Listen to what I am saying." It is clear in the context that God is irritated with Moses' excuses for not obeying him.

like God...as your prophet: this is the use of a parallel example to describe how Aaron will speak for Moses. In many languages it will be necessary to make the parallel more explicit: "Your brother Aaron will be your spokesman; He will speak your message to the king, just as a prophet speaks the message of God to the people." The point of comparison is that just as God speaks to the prophet and the prophet speaks to the people, in the same way Moses will speak to Aaron and Aaron will speak to the king. There is certainly no thought that God is a poor speaker, like Moses.

7.2

TEV	RSV
Tell Aaron everything I command you, and he will tell the king to let the Israelites leave his country.	You shall speak all that I command you; and Aaron your brother shall tell Pharaoh to let the people of Israel go out of his land.

Tell Aaron: this is what the literal "You shall speak" means. Note that TEV has not repeated that Aaron is the brother of Moses (see verse 1). The style of the receptor language will determine whether or not this should be done.

7.3

TEV	RSV
But I will make the king stubborn, and he will not listen to you, no matter how many terrifying things I do in Egypt.	But I will harden Pharaoh's heart, and though I multiply my signs and wonders in the land of Egypt,

[179]

I will make the king stubborn: the Hebrew "I will harden the
heart" (see RSV) is a figure that means "cause to be stubborn," "cause
to refuse to listen," "cause not do what others want." In this verse
God causes the king to be stubborn.

and he will not listen to you: this explains "stubborn," and the
words are found in the Hebrew in verse 4 (see RSV).

terrifying things: the Hebrew uses two words that may be translated "signs and omens," but this will refer to "what shows God's
power." In this case the thought is of the plagues that God will bring
on Egypt.

7.4 TEV	RSV
Then I will bring severe punish-ment on Egypt and lead the tribes of my people out of the land.	Pharaoh will not listen to you; then I will lay my hand upon Egypt and bring forth my hosts, my people the sons of Israel, out of the land of Egypt by great acts of judgment.

Then: since he will not listen to you is used in verse 3, it is
not repeated here in TEV.

bring severe punishment: this translates the Hebrew "I will put
my hand on Egypt" and "with great judgments" (see RSV). In Hebrew "put
the hand on" is a figure for "punish," and "great judgments" refers to
"acts of punishment which are brought in judgment on Egypt."

the tribes of my people: the Hebrew has "my armies, my people,
the sons of Israel" (see RSV). TEV has chosen not to repeat "Israelites" (see verses 2,5) and has understood "armies" to refer to the
tribes of Israel rather than to literal armies.

7.5 TEV	RSV
The Egyptians will then know that I am the LORD, when I raise my hand against them and bring the Israelites out of their country."	And the Egyptians shall know that I am the LORD, when I stretch forth my hand upon Egypt and bring out the people of Israel from among them."

raise my hand against them: that is, "punish." In English, "raise
the hand against" can be used as a figure for "punish," while "put the
hand on" (verse 4) cannot. In some languages such an expression cannot
be used, and one will need to translate as in verse 4, "when I punish
them severely," "when I carry out my punishment on them."

7.6 TEV	RSV
Moses and Aaron did what the LORD commanded.	And Moses and Aaron did so; they did as the LORD commanded them.

did what the LORD commanded: the Hebrew has an element of repetition in the verse, and although repetition may give emphasis in

Hebrew, that is not always the case in other languages. Language style will determine whether it is retained.

7.7	TEV	RSV
	At the time when they spoke to the king, Moses was eighty years old, and Aaron was eighty-three.	Now Moses was eighty years old, and Aaron eighty-three years old, when they spoke to Pharaoh.

TEV has reversed the order of elements in the verse.

7.8—10.29: This section describes the miracles that the Lord did through Moses and the terrible disasters that were brought on Egypt; blood, frogs, gnats, flies, death of the animals, boils, hail, locusts, and darkness.

C H A P T E R   11

SECTION HEADING

Moses Announces the Death of the First-Born (11.1-10): "Moses Tells the King that Every First-Born Son Will Die."

11.1	TEV	RSV
	Then the LORD said to Moses, "I will send only one more punishment on the king of Egypt and his people. After that he will let you leave. In fact, he will drive all of you out of here.	The LORD said to Moses, "Yet one plague more I will bring upon Pharaoh and upon Egypt; afterwards he will let you go hence; when he lets you go, he will drive you away completely.

punishment: the Hebrew word, often translated "plague," means "a blow," "a stroke," as from a beating, and refers to the punishments that were brought on Egypt.
drive all of you out: the Hebrew verb means "throw out," "chase out," in the sense of forcing people to leave.

11.2	TEV	RSV
	Now speak to the people of Israel and tell all of them to ask their neighbors for gold and silver jewelry."	Speak now in the hearing of the people, that they ask, every man of his neighbor and every woman of her neighbor, jewelry of silver and of gold."

speak to the people: literally "speak in the ears of the people" (see RSV), but this figure does not mean "whisper," but rather "speak, and make sure that the people hear."

[181]

all of them: literally "every man and every woman."
ask their neighbors: this is discussed at 3.22. The reference is to Egyptian neighbors.

11.3	TEV	RSV

The LORD made the Egyptians respect the Israelites. Indeed, the officials and all the people considered Moses to be a very great man.	And the LORD gave the people favor in the sight of the Egyptians. Moreover, the man Moses was very great in the land of Egypt, in the sight of Pharaoh's servants and in the sight of the people.

made the Egyptians respect: this is discussed at 3.21.
very great man: this is to be understood in the sense, "a very important person."

11.4	TEV	RSV

Moses then said to the king, "The LORD says, 'At about midnight I will go through Egypt,	And Moses said, "Thus says the LORD: About midnight I will go forth in the midst of Egypt;

The LORD says: literally "This is what the LORD says" (see RSV), but the way the quotation is introduced will be determined by what is normal in the receptor language.
At about midnight: literally "About the middle of the night."

11.5	TEV	RSV

and every first-born son in Egypt will die, from the king's son, who is heir to the throne, to the son of the slave woman who grinds grain. The first-born of all the cattle will die also.	and all the first-born in the land of Egypt shall die, from the first-born of Pharaoh who sits upon his throne, even to the first-born of the maidservant who is behind the mill; and all the first-born of the cattle.

first-born son: it is clear in the Hebrew that only first-born males are to be killed.
who is heir to the throne: literally "who sits on his throne" (see RSV). In Hebrew, "to sit on the throne" means "to rule," "be king." TEV has taken this to refer to the son who would inherit the kingship if he were to live. Others assume that the reference is to the reigning king.
grinds grain: literally "who is behind (who uses) the hand mill" (see RSV). The "hand mill" consisted of two flat stones between which women ground grain into flour. TEV has expressed the function of the women using the hand mill, but in many cultures the hand grinding stone will be well known, and one might readily translate "the slave who turns (or, uses) the hand mill." Note that it is the woman, and not

her son, who turns the hand mill. This fact supports the view that it is the king, and not his son, who is described as sitting on the throne, since the two descriptions are parallel.

11.6 TEV	RSV
There will be loud crying all over Egypt, such as there has never been before or ever will be again.	And there shall be a great cry throughout all the land of Egypt, such as there has never been, nor ever shall be again.

loud crying: literally "a great cry" (RSV), but the thought is that the crying of many people would sound like one loud cry.

11.7 TEV	RSV
But not even a dog will bark at the Israelites or their animals. Then you will know that I, the LORD, make a distinction between the Egyptians and the Israelites.'"	But against any of the people of Israel, either man or beast, not a dog shall growl; that you may know that the LORD makes a distinction between the Egyptians and Israel.

not even a dog will bark: literally "a dog will not point his tongue," that is, "not even a dog will make a threatening move or a threatening sound." The point being made is that in contrast to the death and destruction among the Egyptians, there is complete calm among the people of Israel. In some languages it may be necessary to drop the figure of quiet dogs and say in direct language, "there will be complete calm and security.

make a distinction between: "deal with (or, treat) differently." The meaning clearly is that God will do one thing to the Egyptians, and something else for the people of Israel. In some languages the contrast will need to be made quite clear: "I will punish the Egyptians and bless the people of Israel."

11.8 TEV	RSV
Moses concluded by saying, "All your officials will come to me and bow down before me, and they will beg me to take all my people and go away. After that, I will leave." Then in great anger Moses left the king.	And all these your servants shall come down to me, and bow down to me, saying, 'Get you out, and all the people who follow you.' And after that I will go out." And he went out from Pharaoh in hot anger.

Moses concluded by saying: these words, not in the Hebrew, will need to be translated in some languages to make sure that the reader recognizes that a major break occurs in what Moses is saying. He has been speaking the LORD's message up to this point, and here he begins to speak for himself. Even though punctuation may show this, one should keep in mind that those who hear the translation read will not be aware of the punctuation marks.

[183]

your officials: literally "all these servants of yours" (see RSV), but the word "servant" is used, as it is frequently in Hebrew, for high government officials, who "serve" the king.

bow down before me: that is, to show respect.

beg me to take...away: note that TEV has changed direct discourse into indirect. The original form is a quotation of what the officials will say, "Leave with all the people who follow you." In many languages it is easier to change quotations of this type into indirect discourse in order to avoid a quotation within a quotation. How the information is conveyed must be determined by stylistic factors in the receptor language. Moses is making the point that God's punishment will be so great that the officials will do almost anything to get Moses and his people to leave, in order that no more punishments will come on them.

all my people: literally "people at my feet," in the sense that the people follow in the footsteps of Moses, that is, are "followers." One might translate "the people who follow me, who obey me."

11.9	TEV	RSV
	The LORD had said to Moses, "The king will continue to refuse to listen to you, in order that I may do more of my miracles in Egypt."	Then the LORD said to Moses, "Pharaoh will not listen to you; that my wonders may be multiplied in the land of Egypt."

had said: the Hebrew has simply "said" (RSV), and it may mean that the LORD spoke at this time. It should be noted, however, that verses 9 and 10 are a kind of summary and refer to what has already taken place.

will continue to refuse to listen: literally "will not hear" (see RSV), but the context shows that this is a continuing process and not an isolated incident.

in order that: the refusal of the king to listen provides the opportunity to do more miracles in punishing the Egyptians. TEV has understood this to refer to past miracles, as in verse 10.

11.10	TEV	RSV
	Moses and Aaron performed all these miracles before the king, but the LORD made him stubborn, and he would not let the Israelites leave his country.	Moses and Aaron did all these wonders before Pharaoh; and the LORD hardened Pharaoh's heart, and he did not let the people of Israel go out of his land.

all these miracles: the miracles of the punishments brought on the Egyptians, recorded in chapters 7 to 10.

C H A P T E R   12

12.1-20: These verses give the Lord's instructions to Moses regarding the Passover and the Festival of Unleavened Bread (bread made without yeast).

SECTION HEADING

The First Passover (12.21-28): "Moses and the People of Israel Celebrate the First Passover Festival."

12.21 TEV	RSV
Moses called for all the leaders of Israel and said to them, "Each of you is to choose a lamb or a young goat and kill it, so that your families can celebrate Passover.	Then Moses called all the elders of Israel, and said to them, "Select lambs for yourselves according to your families, and kill the passover lamb.

leaders: literally "old men," but they were considered to be wise and were accepted as the leaders. In the light of what follows one must assume that Moses spoke to the leaders, and the leaders then spoke to all the people of Israel. In some languages it will be necessary to make that clear.

Each of you: it is clear from the instructions that are given that the "you" refers to male heads of households, although it seems to be spoken only to the leaders.

a lamb or a young goat: the Hebrew word means "an animal from the flock" and could have been a sheep or a goat. In 12.5 it is specifically stated that a sheep or goat may be taken, but that the animal must be a one-year-old male.

families: it is clear that one animal was to be eaten by one family. It may be helpful to make this clear, for example, "take one animal for each family, so that you may celebrate...." Keep in mind that this festival was to be celebrated inside each house.

celebrate: "observe," "keep," "perform the ritual of," "carry out the instructions for."

Passover: the exact meaning of the Hebrew word is not known for certain, although it is used frequently as the name for the festival and the name for the animal that was killed and eaten. It would be possible simply to transliterate the Hebrew sounds, for example, "Pesach," as some languages do. But most translators will prefer to use a translation of the word, such as "Passover," which is based on the Hebrew verb used in verses 23 and 27. This verb seems to have the meaning "skip," "spare," "pass over," although the same verb elsewhere has the meaning of "limp," "be lame."

[185]

12.22 TEV	RSV
Take a sprig of hyssop, dip it in the bowl containing^j the animal's blood, and wipe the blood on the doorposts and the beam above the door of your house. Not one of you is to leave the house until morning.	Take a bunch of hyssop and dip it in the blood which is in the basin, and touch the lintel and the two doorposts with the blood which is in the basin; and none of you shall go out of the door of his house until the morning.

^j dip it in the bowl containing;
  or put it on the threshold
  covered with.

    sprig: "a bunch," a bundle of small branches made into a kind of brush. This could be used to sprinkle liquids on various objects.
    hyssop: a small bushy plant. If it is considered important to retain the name, one should translate with something like "a small bushy plant called hyssop." Note that the hyssop is to be used to smear blood on the posts and the beams above the doors.
    dip it in the bowl...blood: as the footnote in TEV shows, the meaning is uncertain. The Hebrew may be read literally as "dip it in the blood in the bowl" or as "dip it in the blood on the threshold." The first translation seems more likely, but the second possibility should probably be included in a note. The threshold is the doorsill, the bottom part of the doorway over which one steps when entering a house.
    leave the house: literally "go out the door" (see RSV), but the meaning is that once the blood is smeared on the posts, everyone should remain in the house.

12.23 TEV	RSV
When the LORD goes through Egypt to kill the Egyptians, he will see the blood on the beams and the doorposts and will not let the Angel of Death enter your houses and kill you.	For the LORD will pass through to slay the Egyptians; and when he sees the blood on the lintel and on the two doorposts, the LORD will pass over the door, and will not allow the destroyer to enter your houses to slay you.

    goes through Egypt: see 11.4.
    and will not let: literally "and will skip, or spare, or pass over the door and will not let." It may be helpful to retain the longer form. In some languages it may be helpful to rearrange elements; for example, "He will pass by the doors on which he sees the blood and will not let."
    Angel of Death: literally "the destruction" or "the destroyer" (RSV), but this seems to be understood in personal terms, and the destruction referred to is clearly the death of the first-born sons. A similar usage is found in the destroying angel of 2 Samuel 24.16. It is clear that the Angel of Death means "the angel that brings death."
    and kill you: the meaning is "kill your first-born sons."

12.24   TEV
You and your children must obey
these rules forever.

RSV
You shall observe this rite as
an ordinance for you and for
your sons for ever.

You and your children: literally "you and your sons" (RSV), but
the Hebrew often uses "sons" to indicate all descendants, and here it
is obvious that daughters are also expected to obey the rules. There
is some difficulty in translation in that clearly what is meant is
"your children, and their children, and their children, and so on
forever."

these rules: literally "this word as a rule (order)," but what is
meant are the details for celebrating the Passover, as given in verses
21-22.

12.25   TEV
When you enter the land that the
LORD has promised to give you,
you must perform this ritual.

RSV
And when you come to the land
which the LORD will give you,
as he has promised, you shall
keep this service.

has promised to give you: literally "will give to you," but this
is not just an expression of what will happen in the future. Rather,
it involves determination or promise.

perform this ritual: the Hebrew can be translated "keep this
service" (RSV), but the clear sense is "carry out the required actions
in celebrating the Passover Festival." The sense of "ritual" may be
translated by "act of worship."

12.26   TEV
When your children ask you, 'What
does this ritual mean?'

RSV
And when your children say to
you, 'What do you mean by this
service?'

your children: literally "your sons," but with the larger sense
(see verse 24).

What does this ritual mean?: literally "What is this service to
you (plural)?" The sense is "Why do you perform this ritual?"

12.27   TEV
you will answer, 'It is the sacrifice of Passover to honor the
LORD, because he passed over the
houses of the Israelites in
Egypt. He killed the Egyptians,
but spared us.'"
    The Israelites knelt down
and worshiped.

RSV
you shall say, 'It is the sacrifice of the LORD's passover,
for he passed over the houses
of the people of Israel in
Egypt, when he slew the Egyptians
but spared our houses.'" And the
people bowed their heads and
worshiped.

sacrifice: the Hebrew word means "killing," and in some languages it may be best to translate in this way, because the killing of the Passover animal is not like the normal sacrifices in which at least a part of the animal was burned up on an altar. Here there is no altar and no "offering" of the animal to God. The killing of the animal has a function different from that of the killing of an animal in the normal Hebrew sacrificial system.

Passover: the word has the sense of "Passover animal."

to honor the LORD: literally "to the LORD," "for the LORD." This could be interpreted as "killing the animal for the LORD," that is, so that he would skip the house that had blood at the door. It seems more likely, however, that "to the LORD" is used in a more general sense, "as a means of honoring the LORD," "to show our respect to the LORD."

because: the reason for observing the ritual each year is that at one time in the past the LORD passed over the houses of the Israelites.

passed over: the Hebrew verb means "be lame," "limp," but here it seems to have the meaning "skip over," "pass by."

spared us: literally "spared our houses" (RSV), but it is clear that "houses" does not refer to the building but to the people in the building. No one was killed in the houses of the Israelites. The Hebrew verb has the sense "save," "cause to escape," "rescue."

knelt down: the Hebrew verb means "bow down" or "kneel down" and is always understood as an act of worship and reverence.

worshiped: the Hebrew word also means "bow down" or "lie face down," and it has the sense of "worship." That is to say, the external act of bowing, kneeling, lying down, is used to convey the idea of reverence and obedience in the presence of the LORD.

12.28 TEV	RSV
Then they went and did what the LORD had commanded Moses and Aaron.	Then the people of Israel went and did so; as the LORD had commanded Moses and Aaron, so they did.

went and did: the Hebrew repeats the "did" to give emphasis. One might translate "did just as the LORD had commanded."

SECTION HEADING

The Death of the First-Born (12.29-36): "The Oldest Sons of the Egyptians Are Killed," "The LORD Kills the Oldest Sons."

12.29 TEV	RSV
At midnight the LORD killed all the first-born sons in Egypt, from the king's son, who was heir to the throne, to the son of the prisoner in the dungeon; all the first-born of the animals were also killed.	At midnight the LORD smote all the first-born in the land of Egypt, from the first-born of Pharaoh who sat on his throne to the first-born of the captive who was in the dungeon, and all the first-born of the cattle.

<u>midnight</u>: "the middle of the night," as in 11.4
<u>killed</u>: the Hebrew verb means "strike," "hit," but here it clearly means "kill." The verb is discussed at 2.11,12.
<u>heir to the throne</u>: this is discussed at 11.5.
<u>prisoner in the dungeon</u>: the person who has been captured and jailed in the most secure part of the prison. The meaning is that every first-born son, without exception, was killed.

12.30 TEV	RSV
That night, the king, his officials, and all the other Egyptians were awakened. There was loud crying throughout Egypt, because there was not one home in which there was not a dead son.	And Pharaoh rose up in the night, he, and all his servants, and all the Egyptians; and there was a great cry in Egypt, for there was not a house where one was not dead.

<u>not one home</u>: this means "not one Egyptian home." None of the Israelites was killed.

12.31 TEV	RSV
That same night the king sent for Moses and Aaron and said, "Get out, you and your Israelites! Leave my country; go and worship the LORD, as you asked.	And he summoned Moses and Aaron by night, and said, "Rise up, go forth from among my people, both you and the people of Israel; and go, serve the LORD, as you have said.

<u>Get out</u>: literally "Rise, go" (see RSV), but this is an emphatic Hebrew expression, "Get up and go," and almost has the sense of "leave immediately."
<u>Leave my country</u>: literally "go from among my people" (RSV), but the sense is that the Israelites should get out of the country.

12.32 TEV	RSV
Take your sheep, goats, and cattle, and leave. Also pray for a blessing on me."	Take your flocks and your herds, as you have said, and be gone; and bless me also!"

<u>pray for a blessing on me</u>: literally "bless me" (RSV), but the assumption is that Moses will pray to the LORD and ask him to bless (to be good to) the king of Egypt. One could translate "pray for me also."

12.33 TEV	RSV
The Egyptians urged the people to hurry and leave the country; they said, "We will all be dead if you don't leave."	And the Egyptians were urgent with the people, to send them out of the land in haste; for they said, "We are all dead men."

urged: the Hebrew verb has the sense of "exert strong pressure," but here obviously the pressure is that of words. The Egyptians said everything they could think of to hasten the departure of the Israelites.

the people: "the people of Israel."

We will all be dead if you don't leave: the Hebrew has only "We are all dead" (see RSV), but the meaning is clear: "As long as you stay here the LORD will continue to kill us, and if you don't leave soon all of us will be dead."

12.34 TEV	RSV
So the people filled their baking pans with unleavened dough, wrapped them in clothing, and carried them on their shoulders.	So the people took their dough before it was leavened, their kneading bowls being bound up in their mantles on their shoulders.

baking pans: the Hebrew word may also mean the pans or bowls in which the dough was mixed and kneaded.

unleavened dough: "bread dough made without yeast."

12.35 TEV	RSV
The Israelites had done as Moses had said, and had asked the Egyptians for gold and silver jewelry and for clothes.	The people of Israel had also done as Moses told them, for they had asked of the Egyptians jewelry of silver and of gold, and clothing;

Some of the ideas in this verse are discussed at 3.22.

12.36 TEV	RSV
The LORD made the Egyptians respect the people and give them what they asked for. In this way the Israelites carried away the wealth of the Egyptians.	and the LORD had given the people favor in the sight of the Egyptians, so that they let them have what they asked. Thus they despoiled the Egyptians.

Some of the ideas in this verse are discussed at 3.21-22.

SECTION HEADING

The Israelites Leave Egypt (12.37-42): "The People of Israel Leave."

12.37 TEV	RSV
The Israelites set out on foot from Rameses for Sukkoth.	And the people of Israel journeyed from Rameses to

There were about 600,000 men, not counting women and children.	Succoth, about six hundred thousand men on foot, besides women and children.

on foot: the people walked but may have used animals for carrying their possessions.

Rameses: see 1.11.

Sukkoth: the exact location is uncertain, but this is the first stopping place for the people of Israel as they fled eastward from Egypt. It is usually located almost directly east of Pithom. See TEV map, "Egypt and Sinai."

12.38 TEV	RSV
A large number of other people and many sheep, goats, and cattle also went with them.	A mixed multitude also went up with them, and very many cattle, both flocks and herds.

A large number of other people: the Hebrew, often translated "mixed multitude" (RSV), refers to a group of people of various nationalities who left Egypt with the people of Israel, even though they were not Israelites themselves.

12.39 TEV	RSV
They baked unleavened bread from the dough that they had brought out of Egypt, for they had been driven out of Egypt so suddenly that they did not have time to get their food ready or to prepare leavened dough.	And they baked unleavened cakes of the dough which they had brought out of Egypt, for it was not leavened, because they were thrust out of Egypt and could not tarry, neither had they prepared for themselves any provisions.

baked unleavened bread: at Sukkoth the people of Israel baked the dough made without yeast, the dough that they had brought with them (see 12.34).

12.40 TEV	RSV
The Israelites had lived in Egypt for 430 years.	The time that the people of Israel dwelt in Egypt was four hundred and thirty years.

430 years: the point from which the 430 years is calculated is not indicated, but one may assume that the point of reference is the time Jacob and his family enter Egypt (Gen 46.5-6).

12.41 TEV	RSV
On the day the 430 years ended, all the tribes of the LORD's	And at the end of four hundred and thirty years, on that very

people left Egypt.   day, all the hosts of the LORD
                                      went out from the land of Egypt.

On the day: the writer wishes to emphasize that exactly 430 years
have passed.
      the tribes of the LORD's people: literally "the army of the LORD"
(see RSV), but the words are probably to be understood as "tribes
organized like an army," and not as if the people were an actual army.

12.42	TEV	RSV
	It was a night when the LORD kept watch to bring them out of Egypt; this same night is dedicated to the LORD for all time to come as a night when the Israelites must keep watch.	It was a night of watching by the LORD, to bring them out of the land of Egypt; so this same night is a night of watching kept to the LORD by all the people of Israel throughout their generations.

kept watch...keep watch: the Hebrew uses the same Hebrew verb to
indicate that just as the LORD "kept watch" (here the word means "protect," "take care of," "guard"), so the Israelites must "keep watch"
(here the word has the meaning of "give careful attention to" as well
as "stay awake"). In many languages it will be difficult to retain this
wordplay, and in that case one should translate "the LORD protected
(took care of) them" and "the Israelites must faithfully observe the
rules of the Passover Festival." A footnote could then explain that in
Hebrew the same word is used for "protect" and "faithfully observe."
      this same night: the night of Passover, celebrated every year on
the 14th day of the month Nisan in the Jewish calendar.
      is dedicated to: "belongs to," "is set apart to worship."

12.43-51: Instructions are given about celebrating Passover.

CHAPTER   13

*13.1-19: First-born male Israelites are to be dedicated to the
LORD; the Festival of Unleavened Bread is described; and the LORD lets
the people out of Egypt.*

SECTION HEADING

The Pillar of Cloud and the Pillar of Fire (13.20-22): "The LORD
Leads the People of Israel with a Cloud and Fire."

13.20	TEV	RSV
	The Israelites left	And they moved on from Succoth,

Sukkoth and camped at Etham   and encamped at Etham, on the
on the edge of the desert.   edge of the wilderness.

Etham: a place located on the eastern border of Egypt, right at
the edge of the desert.

13.21   TEV   RSV
During the day the LORD went in   And the LORD went before them
front of them in a pillar of cloud   by day in a pillar of cloud to
to show them the way, and during   lead them along the way, and
the night he went in front of   by night in a pillar of fire
them in a pillar of fire to give   to give them light, that they
them light, so that they could   might travel by day and by
travel night and day.   night;

went in front of them: for the purpose of leading them.
pillar of cloud: "a cloud shaped like a tall column or pillar."
The Hebrew word for "pillar" is used for anything that stands up
straight like a post or a pole, and here the word refers only to the
shape of the cloud.
pillar of fire: "fire shaped like a tall column or pillar."

13.22   TEV   RSV
The pillar of cloud was always   the pillar of cloud by day
in front of the people during   and the pillar of fire by night
the day, and the pillar of fire   did not depart from before the
at night.   people.

The verse repeats part of verse 21, and in some languages the
repetition should be avoided by combining verses 21 and 22. This will
depend on the significance of repetition in the receptor language.

C H A P T E R   14

SECTION HEADING

Crossing the Red Sea (14.1-31): "The People of Israel Cross the
Red Sea."

14.1   TEV   RSV
Then the LORD said to Moses,   Then the LORD said to Moses,

The LORD speaks through Moses but continues to lead in the cloud
and fire.

14.2   TEV   RSV

TEV	RSV
"Tell the Israelites to turn back and camp in front of Pi Hahiroth, between Migdol and the Red Sea, near Baal Zephon.	"Tell the people of Israel to turn back and encamp in front of Pihahiroth, between Migdol and the sea, in front of Baal-zephon; you shall encamp over against it, by the sea.

turn back: "go back in the direction from which they came."

Pi Hahiroth...Migdol...Baal Zephon: none of these towns can be located with certainty, but they must be on the eastern edge of the Nile Delta. See the TEV map, "Egypt and Sinai."

the Red Sea: at this point the Hebrew only has "Sea," but it is more likely that an arm of the Red Sea is intended rather than the Mediterranean. When the Hebrew refers to this arm of the Red Sea, it calls it "the Sea of Reeds." It is known today as the "Gulf of Suez," and in ancient times it may have extended farther north than it does today.

14.3   TEV   RSV

TEV	RSV
The king will think that the Israelites are wandering around in the country and are closed in by the desert.	For Pharaoh will say of the people of Israel, 'They are entangled in the land; the wilderness has shut them in.'

will think: literally "will say," but this is frequently used in the sense "say to himself," "think."

wandering around in the country: that is, "have not yet been able to escape from the country of Egypt."

closed in by the desert: that is, "the desert has served as a barrier which they have not been able to cross, and they are still in the country."

14.4   TEV   RSV

TEV	RSV
I will make him stubborn, and he will pursue you, and my victory over the king and his army will bring me honor. Then the Egyptians will know that I am the LORD." The Israelites did as they were told.	And I will harden Pharaoh's heart, and he will pursue them and I will get glory over Pharaoh and all his host; and the Egyptians shall know that I am the LORD." And they did so.

make him stubborn: literally "harden his heart" (see RSV), as in 7.3, where the matter is discussed.

pursue: "chase after," "run after," "try to catch."

my victory...will bring me honor: literally "I will be honored because of the king of Egypt," but the clear meaning is that "the king will be led to try to catch you, I will overthrow his army, and this will bring me honor." It may be necessary to translate "he will pursue you, and when he does, I will destroy his army, and people will recognize how great I am" or "...how powerful I am." The Hebrew word often

has the sense that some group recognized the greatness, power, or
ability of some person, and then publicly praised that person for his
greatness, power, or ability. In fact it may need to be translated as
"people will praise me."

did as they were told: in some languages it may be necessary to
specify: "did what Moses told them and went back and camped near the
Red Sea."

14.5   TEV   RSV

    When the king of Egypt was   When the king of Egypt was
told that the people had escaped,   told that the people had fled,
he and his officials changed their   the mind of Pharaoh and his
minds and said, "What have we   servants was changed toward the
done? We have let the Israelites   people, and they said, "What is
excape, and we have lost them as   this we have done, that we have
our slaves!"   let Israel go from serving us?"

    was told: by his officials.
    the people: "the people of Israel."
    had escaped: "had run away" from their work as slaves. This should
not be translated in such a way as to indicate that they had actually
succeeded in leaving the country (see verse 3).
    changed their minds: literally "his heart was turned," but the
heart is thought of as the center of decision and not primarily of
feeling. The receptor language use regarding decision will determine
just how the idea of changing the mind is expressed.
    What have we done?: this rhetorical question will need to be
changed to a statement in many languages, for example, "this is a terrible thing we have done," "We have done the wrong thing."

14.6   TEV   RSV

The king got his war chariot and   So he made ready his chariot and
his army ready.   took his army with him,

    war chariot: a vehicle with two wheels that was pulled by horses
and used in battle. The king had his own chariot and probably a driver,
since Egyptian chariots usually carried more than one person.

14.7   TEV

He set out with all his chariots,   and took six hundred picked
including the six hundred finest,   chariots and all the other
commanded by their officers.   chariots of Egypt with officers
                                     over all of them.

    all his chariots: that is, "the chariots of the whole army,"
which included the regular chariots and the 600 special chariots.
    finest: we do not know why these are the finest, but probably
they are better constructed, or equipped with better weapons.

14.8	TEV	RSV

The LORD made the king stubborn, and he pursued the Israelites, who were leaving triumphantly.[l]

[l]triumphantly; *or* under the protection of the LORD.

And the LORD hardened the heart of Pharaoh king of Egypt and he pursued the people of Israel as they went forth defiantly.

triumphantly: the Hebrew has literally "with a high hand," and this may have the meaning "defiantly" (RSV), "triumphantly," "like conquerors," "showing that they are free." But it is also possible that "with a high hand" is to be understood of the LORD. In that case the meaning will be "while the LORD protected them with his mighty power." This is the reason why TEV has included a footnote, and the translator may find it wise to put one interpretation in the text and include the other possibility in a footnote.

14.9	TEV	RSV

The Egyptian army, with all the horses, chariots, and drivers, pursued them and caught up with them where they were camped by the Red Sea near Pi Hahiroth and Baal Zephon.

The Egyptians pursued them, all Pharaoh's horses and chariots and his horsemen and his army, and overtook them encamped at the sea, by Pihahiroth, in front of Baal-zephon.

the Red Sea: literally, "the sea," discussed at verse 2.

14.10	TEV	RSV

When the Israelites saw the king and his army marching against them, they were terrified and cried out to the LORD for help.

When Pharaoh drew near, the people of Israel lifted up their eyes, and behold, the Egyptians were marching after them; and they were in great fear. And the people of Israel cried out to the LORD;

saw: literally "lifted up their eyes and saw" (see RSV), but this means "they looked up and saw." A literal translation often produces an impossible meaning.

were terrified: "became terribly afraid."

cried out...for help: the Hebrew word means "call for help," and usually means with a loud voice.

14.11	TEV	RSV

They said to Moses, "Weren't there any graves in Egypt? Did you have to bring us out here in the desert to die? Look what you have done by bringing us out of Egypt!

and they said to Moses, "Is it because there are no graves in Egypt that you have taken us away to die in the wilderness? What have you done to us, in bringing us out of Egypt?

<u>Weren't there any graves in Egypt?</u>: the rhetorical question may need to be turned into a statement; for example, "There were plently of graves (places to be buried) in Egypt."

<u>Did you have to...?</u>: this rhetorical question may also be turned into a statement, for example, "There was no need for you to bring us out here in the desert to die." If both rhetorical questions are retained, it will often be necessary to supply their answers; for the first, "Of course there were!" and for the second, "Of course you didn't!" Style and language usage must determine which will best convey the correct message.

<u>Look what you have done</u>: In the Hebrew this is also a rhetorical question, "What have you done to us in bringing us out of Egypt?" But the answer that is presupposed is "You have destroyed us." Unless the question and answer pattern is normal in the receptor language, it will usually be better to shift to a statement. One could translate "You have destroyed us by bringing us out of Egypt."

14.12 TEV	RSV
Didn't we tell you before we left that this would happen? We told you to leave us alone and let us go on being slaves of the Egyptians. It would be better to be slaves there than to die here in the desert."	Is not this what we said to you in Egypt, 'Let us alone and let us serve the Egyptians'? For it would have been better for us to serve the Egyptians than to die in the wilderness."

<u>Didn't we tell you...?</u>: the expected answer to the rhetorical question is "Of course we did." In many languages a statement will be more meaningful: "We told you this would happen."

<u>We told you to</u>: TEV has shifted to indirect discourse rather than have a quotation within a quotation within a rhetorical question. This is normally much simpler and is recommended for most translations.

14.13 TEV	RSV
Moses answered, "Don't be afraid! Stand your ground, and you will see what the LORD will do to save you today; you will never see these Egyptians again.	And Moses said to the people, "Fear not, stand firm, and see the salvation of the LORD, which he will work for you today; for the Egyptians whom you see today, you shall never see again.

<u>Moses answered</u>: literally "Moses said to the people" (RSV), but English style requires a word like "answer" when the speaking is in response to what others have said. If the translation is to sound natural, the stylistic pattern of the receptor language will need to be respected.

<u>Stand your ground</u>: "stand firm" (RSV), "stay where you are."

<u>what the LORD will do to save you</u>: literally "the salvation of the LORD" (RSV), but this means "the activity of the LORD in saving you" and in most languages will have to be expressed in a verbal form.

[197]

This is made perfectly clear in the Hebrew by the addition "(salvation) which he will do for you" (see RSV).

14.14	TEV	RSV
	The LORD will fight for you, and all you have to do is keep still."	The LORD will fight for you, and you have only to be still."

fight for you: "fight against your enemies, so that you will not have to fight."

keep still: the Hebrew word has the primary meaning of "remain silent," but it also may include the sense of "remain inactive."

14.15	TEV	RSV
	The LORD said to Moses, "Why are you crying out for help? Tell the people to move forward.	The LORD said to Moses, "Why do you cry to me? Tell the people of Israel to go forward.

Why are you...?: this rhetorical question may need to be turned into a statement: "There is no need for you to cry out to me for help!"

move forward: not, of course, toward the advancing Egyptian army; they are to resume their march away from Egypt.

14.16	TEV	RSV
	Lift up your walking stick and hold it out over the sea. The water will divide, and the Israelites will be able to walk through the sea on dry ground.	Lift up your rod, and stretch out your hand over the sea and divide it, that the people of Israel may go on dry ground through the sea.

walking stick: "stick," "staff" used to make walking easier, particularly over rough ground.

hold it out: literally "hold out your hand" (see RSV), but the assumption is made that the walking stick is held in the hand he holds out; he does not hold the stick in one hand while raising an empty hand over the sea.

The water will divide: literally "split it," "cause it to divide," and one may prefer to translate this as part of the command, rather than connecting it with the result of the command, but this is primarily a matter of style.

14.17	TEV	RSV
	I will make the Egyptians so stubborn that they will go in after them, and I will gain honor by my victory over the king, his army, his chariots, and his drivers.	And I will harden the hearts of the Egyptians so that they shall go in after them, and I will get glory over Pharaoh and all his host, his chariots, and his horsemen.

make...stubborn: literally "harden the heart" (see RSV), but see 7.3; 14.4.

go in after them: "follow the people of Israel as they walk through the sea."

I will gain honor by my victory: this is the same Hebrew construction as in 14.4, where the details are explained. Here, the drowning of the Egyptians is not specifically stated but is assumed. The full logical sequence is "the Egyptians will follow the Israelites, I will bring the sea back on top of the Egyptians, and people will honor me for my victory over the Egyptians."

drivers: the Hebrew word may mean "riders," "people who ride on horses," but here there is reason to believe that the word refers, not to cavalry, but to the men who guided the horses that were pulling the chariots.

14.18 TEV	RSV
When I defeat them, the Egyptians will know that I am the LORD."	And the Egyptians shall know that I am the LORD, when I have gotten glory over Pharaoh, his chariots, and his horsemen."

When I defeat them: literally "when I have been glorified with the king of Egypt," but the underlying idea is the same as in verse 17, and the sense is "when I have won the victory over the king, and people praise me for it." The full form could be translated, but it would be repetitious, and the use of repetition in the receptor language should determine whether or not this is done.

14.19 TEV	RSV
The angel of God, who had been in front of the army of Israel, moved and went to the rear. The pillar of cloud also moved until it was	Then the angel of God who went before the host of Israel moved and went behind them; and the pillar of cloud moved from before them and stood behind them,

The angel of God: in 3.2 it is "the angel of the LORD" that appears to Moses at the burning bush. See the comments at 3.2.

army: the Hebrew word means "camp" and is used of an army camp and sometimes of the army itself. Here, however, one should not use a term that would indicate a group of armed men, as the word is probably intended only to indicate a large number of people. The difficulty with using a word like "camp" is that here the people of Israel are on the move and not in camp.

to the rear: that is, behind the Israelites and between them and the Egyptians, as is said also of the pillar of cloud.

14.20 TEV	RSV
between the Egyptians and the Israelites. The cloud made it	coming between the host of Egypt and the host of Israel. And there

dark for the Egyptians, but gave light to the people of Israel,^{m} and so the armies could not come near each other all night.

was the cloud and the darkness; and the night passed^p without one coming near the other all night.

^{m}*Probable text* The cloud...Israel; *Hebrew unclear.*

^{p}Gk: Heb *and it lit up the night*

the Egyptians: the Hebrew uses the word "camp," as in verse 19, "between the camp of the Egyptians and the camp of Israel," but this means the whole group of people.

The cloud...Israel: as the note in TEV indicates, this is one of those places where it is not really possible to know with any certainty what the Hebrew text means. This has led to many suggestions for changing the text. Note that the RSV "and the night passed" follows the Greek translation and not the Hebrew text, and this may be what was originally intended, but we can only guess. If this choice is made, the sense will be "the cloud made it dark earlier than usual, and this kept the Egyptians from attacking the Israelites." TEV, on the other hand, has adjusted the text to give the sense that the cloud made it night on one side and daytime on the other. The thought would then be that the people of Israel could move about in the light, while the Egyptians were in the dark and could not attack. Other possibilities are also open, as will be seen in the various translations and commentaries, but the translator is advised to choose one of the solutions and try to give some meaning in the translation. Honesty would require some kind of note to indicate the uncertainty of the translation.

14.21   TEV

Moses held out his hand over the sea, and the LORD drove the sea back with a strong east wind. It blew all night and turned the sea into dry land. The water was divided,

RSV

Then Moses stretched out his hand over the sea; and the LORD drove the sea back by a strong east wind all night, and made the sea dry land, and the waters were divided.

held out his hand: it is not stated here that he had his walking stick as in verse 16, but in some languages it may be necessary to assume that he had it in his hand.

with a strong east wind: "by sending a strong east wind," "by causing a strong wind to blow from the east."

14.22   TEV
and the Israelites went through the sea on dry ground, with walls of water on both sides.

RSV
And the people of Israel went into the midst of the sea on dry ground, the waters being a wall to them on their right hand and on their left.

on both sides: literally "on their right hand (side) and on their left."

14.23   TEV
The Egyptians pursued them and
went after them into the sea
with all their horses, chariots,
and drivers.

          See verse 17 for comments.

14.23   RSV
The Egyptians pursued, and went
in after them into the midst of
the sea, all Pharaoh's horses,
his chariots, and his horsemen.

14.24   TEV
Just before dawn the LORD looked
down from the pillar of fire and
cloud at the Egyptian army and
threw them into a panic.

14.24   RSV
And in the morning watch the
LORD in the pillar of fire and
of cloud looked down upon the
host of the Egyptians, and
discomfited the host of the
Egyptians,

     Just before dawn: literally "the morning watch," which would refer
to the last period of the night, approximately from 2 a.m. to 6 a.m.
     looked down: the Hebrew verb means "look down from a higher place
to a lower."
     threw them into a panic: the Hebrew word means "cause confusion,"
"create panic."

14.25   TEV
He made the wheels of their
chariots get stuck, so that they
moved with great difficulty. The
Egyptians said, "The LORD is
fighting for the Israelites
against us. Let's get out of
here!"

14.25   RSV
clogging[q] their chariot wheels
so that they drove heavily; and
the Egyptians said, "Let us flee
from before Israel; for the LORD
fights for them against the
Egyptians."

     [q]Or *binding*. Sam Gk Syr: Heb
     removing

     made the wheels...get stuck: the Hebrew has "removed the wheels,"
but several early translations have "bound the wheels," that is, by
causing them to mire down in the soft ground. This is probably what is
intended.
     against us: literally "against the Egyptians," but in most lan-
guages one does not refer to oneself in the third person.
     Let's get out of here!: literally "Let us flee from Israel."

14.26   TEV
     The LORD said to Moses,
"Hold out your hand over the
sea, and the water will come
back over the Egyptians and
their chariots and drivers."

14.26   RSV
     Then the LORD said to Moses,
"Stretch out your hand over the
sea, that the water may come
back upon the Egyptians, upon
their chariots, and upon their
horsemen."

Hold out your hand: see verse 21.

14.27   TEV

So Moses held out his hand over
the sea, and at daybreak the water
returned to its normal level. The
Egyptians tried to escape from
the water, but the LORD threw them
into the sea.

RSV

So Moses stretched forth his
hand over the sea, and the sea
returned to its wonted flow
when the morning appeared; and
the Egyptians fled into it, and
the LORD routed[r] the Egyptians
in the midst of the sea.

[r]Heb *shook off*

    at daybreak: literally "at the turning of the morning," referring
to the dawn.
    normal level: "as it was before."
    threw them into: the Hebrew means "shake off into," like shaking
drops of water off the hands.

14.28   TEV

The water returned and covered
the chariots, the drivers, and
all the Egyptian army that had
followed the Israelites into the
sea; not one of them was left.

RSV

The waters returned and covered
the chariots and the horsemen
and all the host[s] of Pharaoh
that had followed them into the
sea; not so much as one of them
remained.

[s]Gk Syr: Heb *to all the host*

    all the Egyptian army: although the Hebrew could be translated
"to" (as in the RSV margin), this is probably not the meaning. A literal translation might read "which belonged to the whole army," but
the sense is clearly that the whole army is covered by the water.

14.29   TEV

But the Israelites walked through
the sea on dry ground, with walls
of water on both sides.

RSV

But the people of Israel walked
on dry ground through the sea,
the waters being a wall to them
on their right hand and on their
left.

    on both sides: as in verse 22.

14.30   TEV

    On that day the LORD saved
the people of Israel from the
Egyptians, and the Israelites saw
them lying dead on the seashore.

RSV

    Thus the LORD saved Israel
that day from the hand of the
Egyptians; and Israel saw the
Egyptians dead upon the seashore.

from the Egyptians: literally "from the hand of the Egyptians" (RSV), with the meaning "from the control of, the power of, the Egyptians."

14.31 TEV	RSV
When the Israelites saw the great power with which the LORD had defeated the Egyptians, they stood in awe of the LORD; and they had faith in the LORD and in his servant Moses.	And Israel saw the great work which the LORD did against the Egyptians, and the people feared the LORD; and they believed in the LORD and in his servant Moses.

the great power: literally "the mighty hand," which could possibly refer to the act itself (RSV "great work"), but it is more likely that in Hebrew the meaning is "the great power with which" the act is accomplished.

had defeated: literally "did against" (RSV), but there can be no doubt that this refers to the destruction of the Egyptian army in the sea.

stood in awe of: the Hebrew word is often translated "fear," but the meaning is not "be frightened of"; it is rather "have respect for," "be reverent before." The sense is that the Israelites now really understand the power of the LORD, in contrast to the attitudes expressed in verses 11 and 12.

had faith in: the Hebrew word has the meaning of "believe," but this is more than mere mental agreement and includes "put one's trust in."

15.1-27: These verses describe the victory songs of Moses and Miriam and the story about bitter water.

C H A P T E R   16

SECTION HEADING

The Manna and the Quails (16.1-21): "The Lord Provides Food for the Israelites," "The Lord Gives the People Manna and Quails."

16.1 TEV	RSV
The whole Israelite community set out from Elim, and on the fifteenth day of the second month after they had left Egypt, they came to the desert of Sin, which is between Elim and Sinai.	They set out from Elim, and all the congregation of the people of Israel came to the wilderness of Sin, which is between Elim and Sinai, on the fifteenth day of the second month after they had departed from the land of Egypt.

The whole Israelite community: literally "all the assembly of the people of Israel" (see RSV).

Elim: the fourth stopping place after crossing the Red Sea.

desert of Sin: it is purely accidental that the Hebrew name "Sin" sounds in English like "sin," "evil." The name "Sin" seems to be related to "Sinai," but the name is not identical with the name used for the desert of Sinai mentioned in 19.1.

16.2	TEV	RSV
	There in the desert they all complained to Moses and Aaron	And the whole congregation of the people of Israel murmured against Moses and Aaron in the wilderness,

complained: the Hebrew word means "murmur," "grumble," "complain."

16.3	TEV	RSV
	and said to them, "We wish that the LORD had killed us in Egypt. There we could at least sit down and eat meat and as much other food as we wanted. But you have brought us out into this desert to starve us all to death."	and said to them, "Would that we had died by the hand of the LORD in the land of Egypt, when we sat by the fleshpots and ate bread to the full; for you have brought us out into this wilderness to kill this whole assembly with hunger."

We wish that: the Hebrew is literally "Who will give that...," and it is sometimes translated as "Would that" (RSV). But it is a Hebrew figure of speech that expresses a wish, in this case unfulfilled.

the LORD had killed us: literally "we had died by the hand (by the action) of the LORD" (RSV), but in many languages it is better to express the idea directly, as TEV has done.

sit down and eat meat: literally "sit around pots of meat" (see RSV), but what is meant is not that the people could just sit around the pots and watch the meat cook. This is a way of saying "we could sit and eat plenty of meat (that had been cooked in pots)."

as much other food as we wanted: literally "ate bread to the full" (RSV), meaning "ate as much as we wanted." "Bread" is used in Hebrew to refer to food in general, and here it seems clear that the reference is to all kinds of food and not just bread.

starve us all to death: literally "kill this whole assembly with hunger" (RSV), but "to kill with hunger" is better expressed in English as "(cause) to starve to death."

16.4	TEV	RSV
	The LORD said to Moses, "Now I am going to cause food to rain down from the sky for all of you. The people must go out every day	Then the LORD said to Moses, "Behold, I will rain bread from heaven for you; and the people shall go out and gather a day's

and gather enough for that day.
In this way I can test them to
find out if they will follow my
instructions.

portion every day, that I may
prove them, whether they will
walk in my law or not.

food: literally "bread" (RSV), but see verse 3, although here it
is quite possible that the literal "bread" should be retained.

cause...to rain: the Hebrew verb uses a form that means "cause
to."

from the sky: the Hebrew word can mean "the place where God lives
(heaven)," but also as here, "the sky."

enough for that day: this is what is meant by the literal "the
matter of a day in its day."

I can test them to find out: there is only one Hebrew verb, but
it has the sense "test to find out."

follow my instructions: literally "if they will walk in my law or
not" (see RSV), but "walk in" has the meaning "obey," "live by," "follow," and "my law" refers to the instructions about gathering the
manna (see verse 27) rather than the Law of Moses.

16.5   TEV   RSV
On the sixth day they are to   On the sixth day, when they
bring in twice as much as usual   prepare what they bring in, it
and prepare it."   will be twice as much as they
                                     gather daily."

they are to bring in: the Hebrew is not perfectly clear. But the
meaning seems to be that people will gather more on the sixth day, and
when they prepare it, they will find that there is exactly twice as
much as on normal days. It may be best to translate in some way as
this.

16.6   TEV   RSV
    So Moses and Aaron said to   So Moses and Aaron said to all
all the Israelites, "This evening   the people of Israel, "At evening
you will know that it was the   you shall know that it was the
LORD who brought you out of Egypt. LORD who brought you out of the
                                    land of Egypt,

you will know: that is, at that time they will see the miracle
that the LORD is going to perform in giving them food.

16.7   TEV   RSV
In the morning you will see the   and in the morning you shall see
dazzling light of the LORD's   the glory of the LORD, because
presence. He has heard your   he has heard your murmurings
complaints against him—yes,   against the LORD. For what are
against him, because we are   we, that you murmur against us?"
only carrying out his instruc-
tions."

the dazzling light of the LORD's presence: literally "the heaviness (the glory) of the LORD" (see RSV), but this refers to the bright light that shows that the LORD is present. See in particular the appearances at Mount Sinai (19.16-20).

we are only carrying out his instructions: literally "what are we that you should complain against us?" (see RSV), but it is clear that with this rhetorical question Moses is really affirming that he is nothing. If the people complain against him, they are really complaining against the LORD, because Moses is just carrying out the LORD's instructions.

16.8 TEV	RSV
Then Moses said, "It is the LORD who will give you meat to eat in the evening and as much bread as you want in the morning, because he has heard how much you have complained against him. When you complain against us, you are really complaining against the LORD."	And Moses said, "When the LORD gives you in the evening flesh to eat and in the morning bread to the full, because the LORD has heard your murmurings which you murmur against him— what are we? Your murmurings are not against us but against the LORD."

The verse is almost a repetition of what has just been said, although the words used are somewhat different. In languages in which such repetitions are a problem, it may be necessary to combine elements from verses 7 and 8.

16.9 TEV	RSV
Moses said to Aaron, "Tell the whole community to come and stand before the LORD, because he has heard their complaints."	And Moses said to Aaron, "Say to the whole congregation of the people of Israel, 'Come near before the LORD, for he has heard your murmurings.'"

come and stand before the LORD: literally "come near before the LORD," but this is a term used in Hebrew to mean "come and stand in the presence of the LORD." This usually meant in a holy place, such as the Tent of the LORD's Presence (see 25.8; 26.1).

16.10 TEV	RSV
As Aaron spoke to the whole community, they turned toward the desert, and suddenly the dazzling light of the LORD appeared in a cloud.	And as Aaron spoke to the whole congregation of the people of Israel, they looked toward the wilderness, and behold, the glory of the LORD appeared in the cloud.

dazzling light of the LORD: literally "the heaviness (the glory) of the LORD" (see verse 7).
in a cloud: or "in the cloud" (see 13.21).

16.11-12   TEV

The LORD said to Moses, 12 "I have heard the complaints of the Israelites. Tell them that at twilight they will have meat to eat, and in the morning they will have all the bread they want. Then they will know that I, the LORD, am their God."

RSV

And the LORD said to Moses, 12 "I have heard the murmurings of the people of Israel; say to them, 'At twilight you shall eat flesh, and in the morning you shall be filled with bread; then you shall know that I am the LORD your God.'"

meat: this is what the literal "flesh" (RSV) means in this context.

they will have all the bread they want: literally "be filled with bread" (RSV), but this literal translation seems very awkward in English, and it seems best to shift the emphasis.

16.13   TEV

In the evening a large flock of quails flew in, enough to cover the camp, and in the morning there was dew all around the camp.

RSV

In the evening quails came up and covered the camp; and in the morning dew lay round about the camp.

a large flock of quails: literally "quails" (RSV), but the context indicates that a large flock is involved. Quails are wild birds similar to small chickens. See *Fauna and Flora of the Bible*, pages 66-67.

flew in: literally "came up" (RSV), but the Hebrew verb is used in a general sense of "came," and it is obvious that they came by flying into the camp.

enough to cover the camp: the sense, of course, is not that the entire camp was hidden, but that there were so many birds that the ground in the camp was covered with them.

there was dew all around the camp: literally "there was a layer of dew around the camp," but the receptor language will need to use a word that is normally used for dew.

16.14   TEV

When the dew evaporated, there was something thin and flaky on the surface of the desert. It was as delicate as frost.

RSV

And when the dew had gone up, there was on the face of the wilderness a fine, flake-like thing, fine as hoarfrost on the ground.

evaporated: literally "went up," but English speaks of the disappearance of dew as evaporation, not movement.

thin: the Hebrew word means "thin," "fine," "not thick," or even "crushed," like dust.

flaky: "scale-like," but the Hebrew word occurs only here, and the precise meaning is not known. Perhaps the sense is "crisp." The older interpretation, "round," is probably not correct.

[207]

delicate: the Hebrew uses the same word as is translated "thin" above.

frost: "hoarfrost," "white frost," that is, frozen dew that covers everything with a white layer.

16.15 TEV	RSV
When the Israelites saw it, they didn't know what it was and asked each other, "What is it?"	When the people of Israel saw it, they said to one another, "What is it?"^w For they did not know what it was. And Moses
Moses said to them, "This is the food that the LORD has given you to eat.	said to them, "It is the bread which the LORD has given you to eat.

^wOr "It is manna." Heb man hu

What is it?: this seems to be what the Hebrew intends, although an unusual Hebrew form is used that ties the question more closely to the explanation of the name "manna." See verse 31 and the TEV note.

food: literally "bread," and since the manna was like bread, there may be good reason to translate as "bread," although the word is frequently used in a more general way.

16.16 TEV	RSV
The LORD has commanded that each of you is to gather as much of it as he needs, two quarts for each member of his household."	This is what the LORD has commanded: 'Gather of it, every man of you, as much as he can eat; you shall take an omer apiece, according to the number of the persons whom each of you has in his tent.'"

as he needs: literally "as he can eat."

two quarts: "two litres." Literally "an omer" (RSV), a Hebrew dry measure of approximately two quarts or two liters. There is no point in retaining the transliteration "omer," as this will have no meaning. The translator is advised to translate into the most commonly used unit of measure for grains and the like.

for each member of his household: literally "for each person according to the number of your people that each has in his tent" (see RSV). This does not refer to people physically present in a tent but to people who make up a family, that is, a man's dependents, including wives, children, and slaves.

16.17 TEV	RSV
The Israelites did this, some gathering more, others less.	And the people of Israel did so; they gathered, some more, some less.

did this: that is, gathered manna, but the measuring takes place when they get back to the tents after gathering it.

16.18 TEV	RSV
When they measured it, those who gathered much did not have too much, and those who gathered less did not have too little. Each had gathered just what he needed.	But when they measured it with an omer, he that gathered much had nothing over, and he that gathered little had no lack; each gathered according to what he could eat.

measured it: literally "measured it with an omer (measure)," and one could say "measured it with a quart measure," but in English the word "measured" presupposes that a measure is used.

16.19 TEV	RSV
Moses said to them "No one is to keep any of it for tomorrow."	And Moses said to them, "Let no man leave any of it till the morning."

for tomorrow: literally "until morning," but the point of wanting to keep it was that one would then not have to gather manna the next day, or that one was afraid there would be no manna the next day.

16.20 TEV	RSV
But some of them did not listen to Moses and saved part of it. The next morning it was full of worms and smelled rotten, and Moses was angry with them.	But they did not listen to Moses; some left part of it till the morning, and it bred worms and became foul; and Moses was angry with them.

was full of worms: that is, it had rotted, and worms were feeding on it.
smelled rotten: "stank," "had a bad smell."

16.21 TEV	RSV
Every morning each one gathered as much as he needed; and when the sun grew hot, what was left on the ground melted.	Morning by morning they gathered it, each as much as he could eat; but when the sun grew hot, it melted.

what was left on the ground: literally "it," but the context makes clear that what the people gathered did not melt, but only what had not been gathered and on which the sun shone.

16.22-36: These verses provide additional details about manna.

[209]

CHAPTER 17

SECTION HEADING

Water from the Rock (17.1-7): "Moses Provides Water by Striking a Rock."

17.1 TEV	RSV
The whole Israelite community left the desert of Sin, moving from one place to another at the command of the LORD. They camped at Rephidim, but there was no water there to drink.	All the congregation of the people of Israel moved on from the wilderness of Sin by stages, according to the commandment of the LORD, and camped at Rephidim; but there was no water for the people to drink.

community: the Hebrew word means "assembly," "gathering," but if no such word is available, particularly to describe a group that happens to be traveling, it may be necessary to translate "all the people of Israel."

the desert of Sin: see 16.1.

moving from one place to another: literally "by their camp-breaking," but the sense is that from time to time they broke camp and moved on to another camping place.

at the command of: literally "at the mouth of," but the meaning is that the Israelites moved on when the LORD told them to.

Rephidim: the exact location is not known, but the place is located between the desert of Sin and the desert of Sinai (19.1) in the Sinai Peninsula (see the TEV map, "Egypt and Sinai").

no water there to drink: literally "no water for the people to drink" (RSV).

17.2 TEV	RSV
They complained to Moses and said, "Give us water to drink."	Therefore the people found fault with Moses, and said, "Give us water to drink." And Moses said
Moses answered, "Why are you complaining? Why are you putting the LORD to the test?"	to them, "Why do you find fault with me? Why do you put the LORD to the proof?"

complained: "found fault with," "quarreled with," "reproached." The Hebrew verb means "dispute, quarrel (in public)," and is sometimes used for what we would describe as a "lawsuit," although clearly here the sense is that of public accusation rather than a legal trial.

complaining: literally "disputing with me." The Hebrew verb is the same as in the first part of the verse.

putting the LORD to the test: the Hebrew verb has the meaning "test or try someone or something to see if he or it is worth anything or has any value." Here the testing consists of doubting that the LORD is able to help them (see verse 7). If the idea of testing God proves difficult, one may find it necessary to translate "Why are you assuming that the LORD cannot help you? Why are you doubting that the LORD is powerful?" In some languages it will be easier to change the question to a statement: "You are doubting the LORD," "You are putting the LORD to the test," "You do not believe the LORD is with us."

17.3   TEV

But the people were very thirsty and continued to complain to Moses. They said, "Why did you bring us out of Egypt? To kill us and our children and our livestock with thirst?"

17.3   RSV

But the people thirsted there for water, and the people murmured against Moses, and said, "Why did you bring us up out of Egypt, to kill us and our children and our cattle with thirst?"

were very thirsty: literally "thirsted there for water" (RSV).

continued to complain: the Hebrew word is not the same as that in verse 2, but it has a similar meaning, "murmur," "grumble," "complain."

Why did you bring us out of Egypt?: the question may be changed to a statement: "You should not have brought us out of Egypt."

To kill us...thirst?: this question serves as a kind of continuation to the previous question, "Did you bring us out here to kill us?" It may be necessary to shift to a statement, "You brought us out here to kill us...."

with thirst: that is, "to make us so thirsty that we would die."

17.4   TEV

Moses prayed earnestly to the LORD and said, "What can I do with these people? They are almost ready to stone me."

17.4   RSV

So Moses cried to the LORD, "What shall I do with this people? They are almost ready to stone me."

prayed earnestly: literally "cried out loudly for help," but it is clear that this is a prayer.

What can I do with these people?: in some languages the question may be shifted to a statement, "I can do nothing with these people." The essential meaning is "I cannot govern or manage these people because they are hopeless; they will not accept my leadership."

stone me: "kill me by throwing large stones on me."

17.5   TEV

The LORD said to Moses, "Take some of the leaders of Israel with you, and go on ahead of the people. Take along the stick with which you struck the Nile.

17.5   RSV

And the LORD said to Moses, "Pass on before the people, taking with you some of the elders of Israel; and take in your hand the rod with which you struck the Nile, and go.

leaders: literally "elders," "old men," but it is not so much their age as their wisdom which is in focus.

the stick: this is the "walking stick" that Moses used to perform his miracles in Egypt (see 4.4; 7.15; etc.).

struck the Nile: that is, when Moses struck the Nile River and made it turn to blood (7.17,10).

17.6	TEV	RSV

TEV
I will stand before you on a rock at Mount Sinai. Strike the rock, and water will come out of it for the people to drink." Moses did so in the presence of the leaders of Israel.

RSV
Behold, I will stand before you there on the rock at Horeb; and you shall strike the rock, and water shall come out of it, that the people may drink." And Moses did so, in the sight of the elders of Israel.

Mount Sinai: the Hebrew has "Horeb," but the use of two names for the same place is difficult for many readers, and TEV has used the more familiar name whenever the less familiar occurs.

in the presence of: literally "before the eyes of," that is, all the leaders saw Moses do this.

17.7	TEV	RSV

TEV
The place was named Massah and Meribah,P because the Israelites complained and put the LORD to the test when they asked, "Is the LORD with us or not?"

PMASSAH...MERIBAH: *These names in Hebrew mean "testing" and "complaining."*

RSV
And he called the name of the place Massah^x and Meribah,^{y} because of the faultfinding of the children of Israel, and because they put the LORD to the proof by saying, "Is the LORD among us or not?"

^{x}That is *Proof*
^{y}That is *Contention*

was named: literally "he named" (see RSV), which would mean that Moses gave the names.

Massah: the Hebrew name is related to the verb translated "put to the test" (see verse 2), and a footnote will be needed to explain to the reader this play on words.

Meribah: the Hebrew name is related to the verb translated "complain" (see verse 2). The footnote should make sure that the reader sees the connection with verse 2 and the rest of this verse.

Is the LORD with us or not?: this is the direct question referred to in verse 2 as putting the LORD to the test.

17.8—18.27: The Israelites fight a war with the Amalekites, Jethro visits Moses, and Moses appoints judges to help him.

C H A P T E R   19

SECTION HEADING

The Israelites at Mount Sinai (19.1-25): "The LORD Speaks to the People at Mount Sinai."

19.1-2 TEV	RSV
The people of Israel left Rephidim, and on the first day of the third month after they had left Egypt they came to the desert of Sinai. There they set up camp at the foot of Mount Sinai,	On the third new moon after the people of Israel had gone forth out of the land of Egypt, on that day they came into the wilderness of Sinai. 2 And when they set out from Rephidim and came into the wilderness of Sinai, they encamped in the wilderness; and there Israel encamped before the mountain.

the first day of the third month: literally "On the third new moon (month)" (RSV). The Hebrew is not completely clear, but if the meaning in TEV is correct, the sense will be "two months and one day."
the desert of Sinai: the desert area surrounding Mount Sinai. Note how TEV has combined elements found in the two verses, in accord with English usage.

19.3 TEV	RSV
and Moses went up the mountain to meet with God. The LORD called to him from the mountain and told him to say to the Israelites, Jacob's descendants:	And Moses went up to God, and the LORD called to him out of the mountain, saying, "Thus you shall say to the house of Jacob, and tell the people of Israel:

went up the mountain to meet with God: literally "went up to God" (RSV), but the meaning is "went up the mountain to where God had come down on top of the mountain." A literal translation might leave the false impression that Moses went up to God in heaven.
Note: 19.3b-8 need not be included in a shorter Bible, as the same material will occur later.
from the mountain: if a translation would leave the false impression that God was speaking from within the mountain, it would be better to translate "from the top of the mountain."
told him to say to the Israelites: TEV has shifted to indirect discourse, but it may be better in some languages to retain direct discourse: "This is what you shall say to the people of Israel."
Jacob's descendants: literally "house of Jacob" (RSV), but with the meaning "Jacob's descendants," also called "Israelites" from Jacob's other name, "Israel."

[213]

19.4	TEV	RSV

"You saw what I, the LORD, did to the Egyptians and how I carried you as an eagle carries her young on her wings, and brought you here to me.

You have seen what I did to the Egyptians, and how I bore you on eagles' wings and brought you to myself.

did to the Egyptians: this refers to the punishment of the Egyptians and the exodus of the Israelites.

carried you as an eagle carries her young on her wings: literally "carried you on eagle's wings" (see RSV), but this is a figure of speech that compares God's care, concern, and leadership to the protecting care of an eagle for its young chicks that cannot yet fly. The eagle was supposed to carry its young on its back when danger was near. Comparisons such as this are difficult to translate, and various possibilities will be open, depending on the use of such figures in the receptor language. One might consider something like "I protected you, cared for you and brought you here. I took care of you and carried you (not literally, of course) as an eagle carries her young chicks." In some languages it may be necessary to drop the figure entirely; for example, "I took care of you, carried you carefully, and brought you safely here."

here to me: literally "to me," but it is quite clear that the "to me" refers to the location at Mount Sinai. God had been with the people at the Red Sea, but in another sense he brought them to him when he brought them to Mount Sinai.

19.5	TEV	RSV

Now, if you will obey me and keep my covenant, you will be my own people. The whole earth is mine, but you will be my chosen people,

Now therefore, if you will obey my voice and keep my covenant, you shall be my own possession among all peoples; for all the earth is mine,

Now: this is not so much a time word as a way of introducing a new thought. The receptor language usage will determine what will best introduce the new subject.

obey me: literally "obey my voice" (RSV), that is, "do what I tell you to do," "obey my commands."

covenant: "agreement." The Hebrew word is used particularly for an agreement between God and his people, in which God's promise to help the people is dependent upon the people's obedience to the laws that God gives them. One might translate "if you will keep your side (or, part) of the agreement I am making with you."

my covenant: it is the LORD's covenant in the sense that he is the originator of the agreement. He initiates the agreement (and to that extent it is one-sided), and the people are expected to obey his commands.

my own people...my chosen people: TEV uses these two expressions to translate Hebrew words which may be literally translated "my personal, valued possession." This means that the people of Israel will now belong completely to the LORD and that the LORD has chosen them from among the other nations. Where a single Hebrew word involves complex ideas, it is often better to use two or more words in the receptor language.

The whole earth is mine: the thought is that since the whole earth belongs to the LORD, he could have chosen any people he wished, but he chose the people of Israel.

19.6 TEV	RSV
a people dedicated to me alone, and you will serve me as priests."	and you shall be to me a kingdom of priests and a holy nation. These are the words which you shall speak to the children of Israel."

a people dedicated to me alone: literally "a holy nation" (RSV), but the word "holy" does not refer primarily to moral purity. Something is called "holy" in Hebrew when it belongs exclusively to God and is not used for any purpose other than that which God directs. One can translate with such words as "set apart completely for God's use," "dedicated to God," "belonging completely to God," "that God alone controls."

you will serve me as priests: literally "you shall be to me a kingdom of priests" (RSV). The point being made is that just as priests represent the people before God, so the nation of Israel (like a whole nation of priests) will represent the other nations before God.

In Hebrew the verse concludes with "These are the words that you shall speak to the people of Israel" (see RSV). This is, of course, a repetition of the words spoken in verse 3 in introducing the statement. In English and in other languages the repetition of the introductory formula, particularly after only a short statement, is very awkward stylistically. It is for this reason that TEV has dropped the repetition, although of course no content has been lost.

19.7 TEV	RSV
So Moses went down and called the leaders of the people together and told them everything that the LORD had commanded him.	So Moses came and called the elders of the people, and set before them all these words which the LORD had commanded him.

went down: the Hebrew has only "went," but it is clear in context that Moses had to go down the mountain in order to call the leaders.

leaders: literally "elders" (see 17.5).

told them: literally "set before their faces," but this, like the English "put before them," has the meaning of "spoke to them," "told them."

everything: literally "all these words" (RSV), but the Hebrew "words" also refers to commandments and instructions, which is what is meant here.

19.8 TEV	RSV
Then all the people answered together, "We will do everything that the LORD has said," and Moses reported this to the LORD.	And all the people answered together and said, "All that the LORD has spoken we will do." And Moses reported the words of the people to the LORD.

answered: "responded." The use of "answered" does not mean that Moses asked the people a question and they answered it. The meaning is that after hearing all the laws and commands, the people responded by saying that they would keep them. In some languages one may have to translate "When the people heard all the commands, they said...."
said: the reference is, of course, to what the LORD had commanded the people to do.
reported: literally "brought back," One may translate "went back up the mountain and told the LORD what the people had said."

19.9-15: These verses describe the instructions as to how the people should prepare to worship the LORD, and give the warning that they should not come up on the mountain.

SECTION HEADING

The LORD Comes Down on Mount Sinai (19.16-25).

19.16 TEV	RSV
On the morning of the third day there was thunder and lightning, a thick cloud appeared on the mountain, and a very loud trumpet blast was heard. All the people in the camp trembled with fear.	On the morning of the third day there were thunders and lightnings, and a thick cloud upon the mountain, and a very loud trumpet blast, so that all the people who were in the camp trembled.

On the morning of the third day: that is, after Moses had been with the LORD and come back to the camp. One might translate "Moses came down from the mountain and had been back in camp three days."
thunder and lightning: it should be made clear that these occur on the mountain and not in the camp.
thick cloud: "dark cloud," "heavy cloud." The cloud, thunder, and lightning are to be understood as symbols of the LORD's presence on the mountain.
a very loud trumpet blast: "a very loud sound made when a trumpet is blown." The trumpet was used as a warning signal but also as a call to assemble for worship.
was heard: it will often be preferable to translate "all the people heard."
trembled with fear: the Hebrew has only one word, but it is often used in the sense of "shaking from fear."

19.17   TEV
Moses led them out of the camp
to meet God, and they stood at
the foot of the mountain.

RSV
Then Moses brought the people
out of the camp to meet God;
and they took their stand at
the foot of the mountain.

to meet God: the meaning is the same as for Moses in verse 3. The
people are to come into the presence of God, but they must remain at
the foot of the mountain; they must not go into the full presence of
God as Moses does.

the foot of the mountain: "the lower part of the mountain," "the
bottom of the mountain."

19.18   TEV
All of Mount Sinai was covered
with smoke, because the LORD had
come down on it in fire. The smoke
went up like the smoke of a fur-
nance, and all the people trembled
violently.

RSV
And Mount Sinai was wrapped in
smoke, because the LORD descended
upon it in fire; and the smoke of
it went up like the smoke of a
kiln, and the whole mountain
quaked greatly.

had come down on it in fire: the LORD appears as a fire, and one
may have to translate "The LORD had appeared in the form of fire and
had come down on the mountain, which was now covered with smoke."

smoke of a furnace: the reference is to the smoke that boils up
violently from a very hot fire that is being blown with bellows, "like
smoke from a forge," "like smoke from a fire used to melt metal."

all the people trembled: or one may follow the translation "the
whole mountain trembled" (see RSV). The difficulty is that a few Hebrew
manuscripts and the Greek translation read "the people," while other
Hebrew manuscripts read "the mountain." It would be appropriate to
choose one of these and indicate the other possibility in a note.

19.19   TEV
The sound of the trumpet became
louder and louder. Moses spoke,
and God answered him with thunder.

RSV
And as the sound of the trumpet
grew louder and louder, Moses
spoke, and God answered him in
thunder.

Moses spoke: it would probably be better to use "Moses kept speaking," since Moses is responding to the sound of the trumpet.

with thunder: "in a voice that sounded like thunder." The meaning of the Hebrew is not quite certain. A word is used that means
"voice," but this word is also at times used for thunder (in the plural
in verse 16). The translator should probably interpret the word as
"thunder," but he may wish to include a note to indicate that it is
possible the meaning is "God answered in a voice."

[217]

19.20 TEV	RSV
The LORD came down on the top of Mount Sinai and called Moses to the top of the mountain. Moses went up	And the LORD came down upon Mount Sinai, to the top of the mountain; and the LORD called Moses to the top of the mountain, and Moses went up.

went up: that is, "went up to the top of the mountain."

19.21 TEV	RSV
and the LORD said to him, "Go down and warn the people not to cross the boundary to come and look at me; if they do, many of them will die.	And the LORD said to Moses, "Go down and warn the people, lest they break through to the LORD to gaze and many of them perish.

warn the people: "tell the people that they will be punished if they...."

cross the boundary: the Hebrew uses a verb that may be translated "break through." But here the people are warned not to break through the boundary set at the foot of the mountain; it was to keep them away from the presence of the LORD.

look at me: the Hebrew has only "look," but the context makes clear that it is looking at the LORD that is forbidden. There are frequent references in the Old Testament to the view that anyone who sees God must die.

19.22 TEV	RSV
Even the priests who come near me must purify themselves, or I will punish them."	And also let the priests who come near to the LORD consecrate themselves, lest the LORD break out upon them."

who come near me: the sentence is of a general nature and refers to the fact that before priests enter the Tent of the LORD's Presence or the Temple, they must make themselves ritually pure. If this last idea is difficult to express, one might consider a general formula: "take the necessary precautions and prepare themselves," "obey strict rules in preparing themselves."

I will punish them: literally "the LORD will break out against them." Note that third person "the LORD" has been changed to first person to accord with English usage. "Break out" has the force of punish, but if a specific form of punishment is required, one should use "kill."

19.23-24: Since these verses are essentially a repetition of the thought that the people must not cross the boundary, they need not be included in a series of Old Testament selections.

19.25   TEV   RSV
Moses then went down to the peo-   So Moses went down to the people
ple and told them what the LORD   and told them.
had said.

   went down: that is, "down from the top of the mountain to the
camp."

C H A P T E R   20

SECTION HEADING

   The Ten Commandments (20.1-17): "God Gives Moses the Ten Commandments." The Ten Commandments may be described as "The Ten Laws," "The
Ten Most Important Rules for Life," or even "The Ten Words (Sayings)."

20.1   TEV   RSV
   God spoke, and these were   And God spoke all these
his words: words, saying,

   and these were his words: literally "all these words, saying"
(RSV). The receptor language usage will determine how the discourse is
introduced.

20.2   TEV   RSV
"I am the LORD your God who   "I am the LORD your God, who
brought you out of Egypt, where   brought you out of the land of
you were slaves.   Egypt, out of the house of bond-
                                        age.

   brought you out: "caused you to leave," "made it possible for you
to leave."
   where you were slaves: literally "the house of servants (slaves)"
(see RSV), but this is a figure of speech which pictures Egypt as a
prison for slaves. It is normally simpler to describe the condition
of the Israelites, as TEV has done.

20.3   TEV   RSV
"Worship no god but me.   "You shall have no other
                                        gods before^f me.

                     ^{f}Or *besides*

   Worship no god but me: literally "There shall not be for you
other gods before me" (see RSV). It is clear, of course, that the
meaning of "There shall not be for you" is "You shall not worship."

[219]

There is some dispute among scholars about the exact meaning of the Hebrew words translated "before me," but the translator is advised to follow the interpretation "besides me," that is, no other god is to be worshiped. One might consider a translation such as "Worship no other god. Worship only me." The text does not deny the existence of other gods.

20.4	TEV	RSV
	"Do not make for yourselves images of anything in heaven or on earth or in the water under the earth.	"You shall not make for yourself a graven image, or any likeness of anything that is in heaven above, or that is in the earth beneath, or that is in the water under the earth;

for yourselves: this includes the idea, "for you to worship."

images: literally "an idol or any likeness" (see RSV). The meaning may be expressed by "Do not make any statue (that is, wood or metal figure) or draw any picture to worship." Strictly speaking it would have been the god represented by the statue (idol) or the picture (likeness) that would have been worshiped.

anything in heaven: this is probably intended to include God himself, as well as sun, moon, stars, birds. One might consider "Do not make and worship any likeness of me or anything else in heaven (or, the sky)...."

on earth: meaning, in particular, men and animals.

under the earth: this would refer to dragons, fish, and other sea creatures. "Water under the earth" will include the seas as well as the underground water, which the Hebrews understood as a great ocean beneath the earth.

20.5	TEV	RSV
	Do not bow down to any idol or worship it, because I am the LORD your God and I tolerate no rivals. I bring punishment on those who hate me and on their descendants down to the third and fourth generation.	you shall not bow down to them or serve them; for I the LORD your God am a jealous God, visiting the iniquity of the fathers upon the children to the third and fourth generation of those who hate me,

bow down to: that is, "in worship," "in reverence to."

worship: literally "serve." This verb means to serve God or other gods. It is frequently used to express the ideas of obedience and worship. One might translate "pray to."

I tolerate no rivals: the Hebrew verb is sometimes translated "jealous," but the English word includes elements that are not present in the Hebrew. What is meant is that God will not put up with other gods. One might even translate accurately with "I will not allow you to have other gods."

I bring punishment: the Hebrew is sometimes translated more or less literally as "visiting the evil upon" (see RSV). But the Hebrew word for "visit" means in this context "come to punish (for the evil done)" or "cause to suffer."

those who hate me: this is another way of speaking of those who abandon God and worship other gods. It is the action of turning against God that is central, as can be seen in the contrast between this word and "obeying" God in verse 6. One might even translate correctly with "hate me and disobey me" in contrast to love me and obey my laws in verse 6.

descendants...fourth generation: that is, the person, his children, his grandchildren, and his great-grandchildren.

20.6	TEV	RSV
	But I show my love to thousands of generations^t of those who love me and obey my laws.	but showing steadfast love to thousands of those who love me and keep my commandments.

^{t}thousands of generations; *or* thousands.

I show my love: the Hebrew word translated "love" refers to God's love and his faithfulness in keeping his promises. It is a difficult word to translate. Some suggestions that might be considered: "steadfast, unchanging love," "love and trustworthiness," "the kind of love that can always be depended upon." If an adequate word for love cannot be found, one might emphasize its other components, for example, "I will keep my promises," "I will bless." One might even consider "I will love and be good to" or "I will be loyal to."

thousands of generations: this is probably the meaning of the Hebrew. The LORD keeps his promises not only to the great-grandchildren, but to the great-great-grandchildren, and so on for a thousand generations. As the TEV note shows, however, it is possible to interpret the Hebrew as meaning that God shows his love to thousands of people. The number thousands may have the meaning, "more than can be counted," "numberless."

20.7	TEV	RSV
	"Do not use my name for evil purposes, for I, the LORD your God, will punish anyone who misuses my name.	"You shall not take the name of the LORD your God in vain; for the LORD will not hold him guiltless who takes his name in vain.

Do not use my name for evil purposes: literally "Do not take (speak) the name of the LORD your God in an idle (empty, useless) way" (see RSV). TEV has used the first person pronoun in accord with English usage, since God is speaking. But note that "I, the LORD your God" conveys the content. It is not easy to know exactly what this commandment means, but it is probable that it includes a rejection of using God's name in taking false oaths and of using God's name in magic practices. It is advisable in translation to find a general expression that will include these and other possible wrong uses of God's name, for example, "in an evil way," "in a way that is wrong." If, however, no such general expression is satisfactory, one should probably choose something like "Do not use my name to say something is true when it is really a lie."

misuses: this is an English way of repeating "uses my name for evil purposes," which the Hebrew repeats here (see RSV). If no satisfactory word is available to summarize the longer expression when it is repeated, one may repeat the full expression here, although the significance of repetition in the receptor language would need to be taken into account.

20.8	TEV	RSV
	"Observe the Sabbath and keep it holy.	"Remember the sabbath day, to keep it holy.

Observe: literally "Remember" (RSV), but the point is, of course, not simply to remember that the seventh day of the week is the Sabbath. Rather "Remember" has the sense of "Remember what you must do because it is a holy day," and this idea may be readily expressed by "observe" or "keep" the laws in regard to the Sabbath. One might translate "Do not forget to obey the laws concerning...."

Sabbath: this refers, of course, to Saturday, but the word means "day of rest." One might even translate "day when people must not work."

holy: the Hebrew word means "belongs completely to God," "is set apart for God's use." One might even translate, "You must remember that the day of rest belongs completely to God, and you must keep the laws that God has given you about it."

20.9	TEV	RSV
	You have six days in which to do your work,	Six days you shall labor, and do all your work;

You have six days in which to do your work: it is best to translate in some such way as this, as the Hebrew is not to be interpreted as a command to work six days. Rather, the idea is that six days are enough time for you to get your work done. The Hebrew uses two verbs, "labor (or, serve)" and "do your work," but no sharp distinction can be drawn between them; and it is often better to use a single verb in translation, unless the receptor language uses two words with much the same meaning.

20.10	TEV	RSV
	but the seventh day is a day of rest dedicated to me. On that day no one is to work—neither you, your children, your slaves, your animals, nor the foreigners who	but the seventh day is a sabbath to the LORD your God; in it you shall not do any work, you, or your son, or your daughter, your manservant, or your maidservant,

live in your country.   or your cattle, or the sojourner
                                         who is within your gates;

dedicated to me: literally "a sabbath to the LORD your God" (RSV).
But English requires a shift to the first person and includes what is
intended with "to," that is "dedicated to," "set aside for the use of."
    no one is to work: in English style this is easier than the literal
"you shall not work, you or your children..." (see RSV).
    your children: literally "your son, or your daughter" (RSV), but
this will apply to all the sons and daughters in a family.
    foreigners: the Hebrew word refers to foreign people who are tem-
porarily living in a country. One may translate "people from another
tribe (or, nation)."
    in your country: literally "within your gates" (RSV), but this
refers to city gates and has an extended sense which readily includes
the whole country, which may have to be translated as "tribe" in some
languages.

20.11   TEV   RSV
In six days I, the LORD, made the   for in six days the LORD made
earth, the sky, the seas, and   heaven and earth, the sea, and
everything in them, but on the   all that is in them, and rested
seventh day I rested. That is why   the seventh day; therefore the
I, the LORD, blessed the Sabbath   LORD blessed the sabbath day
and made it holy.   and hallowed it.

    I, the LORD: literally "the LORD" (RSV), but since the LORD is
speaking (see verse 2), it is more natural in English to use the first
person.
    rested: although the Hebrew word used here could have the sense
"rest after becoming tired," it is more likely that the word is to be
understood in a more general sense, "did not work."
    blessed: "said that it was good," "said that things would go well
for people who kept the Sabbath laws about not working."
    holy: see verse 8.

20.12   TEV   RSV
    "Respect your father and   "Honor your father and your
your mother, so that you may   mother, that your days may be
live a long time in the land   long in the land which the LORD
that I am giving you.   your God gives you.

    Respect: literally "Make heavy," in the sense of "Honor" (RSV),
"Show respect for," "Give honor to," "View with high regard," "Consider important."
    so that: in other words, "if you do, the result will be that...."
    the land that I am giving you: "the promised land," "the land of
Canaan." In some languages "land" will have to be translated "country,"
"portion of earth."

20.13   TEV   RSV
   "Do not commit murder.   "You shall not kill.

    Do not commit murder: the Hebrew verb is sometimes translated as
"kill," but there is good evidence that the word means "kill ille-
gally," "kill without the approval of the law or the community,"
"wrongfully take another person's life." In English, "murder" is
closer to the meaning than the more general "kill," although "murder"
has a component of "intention" that is not everywhere present in the
Hebrew verb. The difficulty in using the normal word for "kill" is
that this would seem to legislate against killing in war or the execution of a criminal, and this commandment does not appear to have that
sense.

20.14   TEV   RSV
   "Do not commit adultery.   "You shall not commit adul-
                                         tery.

    Do not commit adultery: in Hebrew the word translated "adultery"
has the meaning of "break the vow to be faithful to one's marriage
partner," "be unfaithful (sexually)," "to have sexual intercourse with
someone other than one's marriage partner." That is to say, the word
always involves violence to a marriage relationship, and not just un-
lawful sexual activity as such. In Hebrew thought a husband committed
adultery only when he had sexual relations with another man's wife,
while a wife committed adultery if she had sexual relations with anyone other than her husband. In languages without a general term it may
be possible to translate "Do not sleep with another man's wife (addressed to males), and do not sleep with another man (addressed to
females)."

20.15   TEV   RSV
   "Do not steal.   "You shall not steal.

    Do not steal: "Do not take as your own what belongs to someone
else," but it seems that all languages have words for stealing.

20.16   TEV   RSV
   "Do not accuse anyone   "You shall not bear false
falsely.   witness against your neighbor.

    Do not accuse anyone falsely: the word translated "accuse" means
"to testify," "to witness," at a trial. The sense then is "tell a lie
while being a witness against someone at a trial." The word "anyone"
translates a Hebrew word that is often translated "neighbor," but it
does not mean the person who lives next to you. Rather it means someone of the same community, that is, "a fellow Israelite," "a fellow
human being."

20.17   TEV   RSV
    "Do not desire another man's   "You shall not covet your
house; do not desire his wife, his   neighbor's house; you shall not
slaves, his cattle, his donkeys,   covet your neighbor's wife, or
or anything else that he owns."   his manservant, or his maidservant,
                                       or his ox, or his ass, or anything
                                       that is your neighbor's."

    desire: "desire and try to get," "long to have," "covet."
    another man's: "neighbor," as in verse 16.
    his slaves: literally "male slave and female slave."

SECTION HEADING

    The People's Fear (20.18-21): "The People of Israel Are Afraid of
the Presence of God."

20.18   TEV   RSV
    When the people heard the   Now when all the people per-
thunder and the trumpet blast   ceived the thunderings and the
and saw the lightning and the   lightnings and the sound of the
smoking mountain, they trembled   trumpet and the mountain smoking,
with fear and stood a long way   the people were afraid and trem-
off.   bled; and they stood afar off,

    heard...and saw: literally "saw," but English requires both words,
unless a general word (for example, "perceive," covering both seeing
and hearing) can be used. In most languages a trumpet blast cannot be
"seen."
    thunder...smoking: see 19.21.

20.19   TEV   RSV
They said to Moses, "If you speak   and said to Moses, "You speak
to us, we will listen; but we are   to us, and we will hear; but let
afraid that if God speaks to us,   not God speak to us, lest we
we will die."   die."

    we will die: in the minds of the people, hearing God speak seems
to be understood in the same way as seeing God (see 19.21).

20.20   TEV   RSV
    Moses replied, "Don't be   And Moses said to the people,
afraid; God has only come to   "Do not fear; for God has come
test you and make you keep on   to prove you, and that the fear
obeying him, so that you will   of him may be before your eyes,
not sin."   that you may not sin."

    to test you: the Hebrew verb is the same as that used in 17.2.

[225]

Here test will have the sense "find out if you are willing to believe him (or, trust him)."

keep on obeying him: literally "that the fear of him may be before your eyes" (RSV), where "fear" clearly has the sense of "obey" and does not mean "be afraid of," while "before your eyes" is a figurative way of describing what is always present. The clause thus means "so that obedience to the LORD is always present with you." However, it is more natural to express this idea by "so that you will continue to obey him."

20.21 TEV	RSV
But the people continued to stand a long way off, and only Moses went near the dark cloud where God was.	And the people stood afar off, while Moses drew near to the thick darkness where God was.

dark cloud: the Hebrew does not use the same word as in 19.16, but the meaning is much the same.

20.22—23.33: This section contains laws about many things that the LORD wanted the people of Israel to do, and ends with promises and instructions for the people.

C H A P T E R 24

SECTION HEADING

The Covenant Is Sealed (24.1-8): "The People Accept God's Agreement with Them," "The People Accept the Agreement God Made with Them."

24.1 TEV	RSV
The LORD said to Moses, "Come up the mountain to me, you and Aaron, Nadab, Abihu, and seventy of the leaders of Israel; and while you are still some distance away, bow down in worship.	And he said to Moses, "Come up to the LORD, you and Aaron, Nadab, and Abihu, and seventy of the elders of Israel, and worship afar off.

to me: literally "to the LORD," but English requires first person. One might translate "to the place where I am," "to the place where I, the LORD, am."

Nadab, Abihu: these are sons of Aaron (see 6.23).

leaders: literally "elders."

still some distance away: "before you get too close to me."

bow down in worship: the Hebrew verb means "bow down" to show respect, to worship.

24.2   TEV

You alone, and none of the others, are to come near me. The people are not even to come up the mountain."

          RSV

Moses alone shall come near to the LORD; but the others shall not come near, and the people shall not come up with him."

You: literally "Moses," but English requires second person.

24.3   TEV

Moses went and told the people all the LORD's commands and all the ordinances, and all the people answered together, "We will do everything that the LORD has said."

          RSV

Moses came and told the people all the words of the LORD and all the ordinances; and all the people answered with one voice, and said, "All the words which the LORD has spoken we will do."

commands...ordinances: the Hebrew uses two words, "words" and "commandments," but the Hebrew has a variety of ways of speaking of commandments, which may not be available in other languages. One might well translate "all that the LORD had commanded the people to do."

24.4   TEV

Moses wrote down all the LORD's commands. Early the next morning he built an altar at the foot of the mountain and set up twelve stones, one for each of the twelve tribes of Israel.

          RSV

And Moses wrote all the words of the LORD. And he rose early in the morning, and built an altar at the foot of the mountain, and twelve pillars, according to the twelve tribes of Israel.

commands: literally "words," that is, "what the LORD said," and this means his commands to the people.

he built: literally "he got up and built" (see RSV), but in English it is easier to leave unstated the fact that Moses had to get up from sleep in order to build the altar.

altar: a table or platform built of stone and used for burning animals as offerings to God.

stones: the Hebrew word means a stone (usually long) that has been set up as a memorial. One might translate "Moses set up twelve stones to remind the people of the twelve tribes of Israel."

24.5   TEV

Then he sent young men, and they burned sacrifices to the LORD and sacrificed some cattle as fellowship offerings.

          RSV

And he sent young men of the people of Israel, who offered burnt offerings and sacrificed peace offerings of oxen to the LORD.

young men: literally "young men of the sons (children) of Israel," but "of the sons of Israel" is obvious, and the statement is redundant, at least in English.

[227]

sacrifices: this refers to the sacrifices that were burnt up completely upon the altar. That is, after the animal had been skinned and cleaned, all its meat was burned up on the altar (see Lev 1). Where sacrifices are unknown, one may translate "gifts that are burned" or "animals that are burned as gifts."

fellowship offerings: in this offering, after the animal had been skinned and cleaned, a part of it was burned on the altar, but most of the meat was kept and eaten by the whole community as a sign that they belonged to one another and were the people of God (see Lev 3). If adequate terms are not found, it may be necessary to explain in a footnote that some sacrifices were burned completely on the altar, but that fellowship offerings were used as food for the community.

24.6 TEV	RSV
Moses took half of the blood of the animals and put it in bowls; and the other half he threw against the altar.	And Moses took half of the blood and put it in basins, and half of the blood he threw against the altar.

took: at the time when the animals were killed. In many languages it will be necessary to indicate when Moses took the blood, or even to reverse the order of verses 5 and 6 in order to show clearly the sequence of events: the animals are killed, their blood is taken, and then they are burned on the altar.

blood of the animals: if it is necessary to indicate which animals, one may assume that the blood came from both the animals killed for the whole burnt offering and those killed for the fellowship offering.

threw against the altar: the blood was thrown against the sides of the altar. One may assume that it was collected in a container and splashed against the sides of the altar.

24.7 TEV	RSV
Then he took the book of the covenant, in which the LORD's commands were written, and read it aloud to the people. They said, "We will obey the LORD and do everything that he has commanded."	Then he took the book of the covenant, and read it in the hearing of the people; and they said, "All that the LORD has spoken we will do, and we will be obedient."

book of the covenant: that is, the book containing the agreement that God is making with his people, and particularly the things he commands the people to do.

read it aloud: literally "read it in the ears of the people" (see RSV), that is, "read it so the people could hear it." "Moses read it and the people listened."

24.8 TEV	RSV
Then Moses took the blood in the bowls and threw it on the	And Moses took the blood and threw it upon the people, and

people. He said, "This is the
blood that seals the covenant
which the LORD made with you
when he gave all these commands."

said, "Behold the blood of the
covenant which the LORD has
made with you in accordance
with all these words."

blood that seals the covenant: literally "blood of the covenant"
(RSV), but the meaning is that the blood validates or guarantees· the
agreement. The underlying thought is that since the people have said
they would obey the LORD's commands, Moses throws the blood on them
as if to say, "This blood means that you are promising with your own
blood that you will keep the agreement." The people are really making
a strong promise: "If we don't keep the agreement, may our blood be
poured out like that of the animals which is thrown on us." One might
translate "This blood is a sign that you promise to keep the agreement
that the LORD has made with you."

*24.9—31.17: Moses stays on the mountain for forty days, while the
LORD tells him how to make all the things needed for worship, including
the LORD's Tent.*

C H A P T E R   31

31.18   TEV
    When God had finished speak-
ing to Moses on Mount Sinai, he
gave him the two stone tablets
on which God himself had written
the commandments.

                    RSV
    And he gave to Moses, when
he had made an end of speaking
with him upon Mount Sinai, the
two tables of the testimony,
tables of stone, written with
the finger of God.

    This verse is important in a set of selections that will include
chapter 32. One might introduce it with a section heading: "God Gives
Moses the Ten Commandments," "The Tablets with the Ten Commandments."
    stone tablets: "flat stones," "stone slabs" on which writing
could be engraved.
    on which God himself had written: literally "written by the finger
of God" (see RSV), which could mean that God used his finger to scratch
the stone to produce the writing, but which is probably intended to be
understood in a more general sense, "God wrote with his own hand."

C H A P T E R   32

SECTION HEADING

    The Gold Bull-Calf (32.1-35): "The People Worship a Gold Bull."

[229]

32.1 TEV	RSV
When the people saw that Moses had not come down from the mountain but was staying there a long time, they gathered around Aaron and said to him, "We do not know what has happened to this man Moses, who led us out of Egypt; so make us a god*f* to lead us." *f*a god; *or* some gods.	When the people saw that Moses delayed to come down from the mountain, the people gathered themselves together to Aaron, and said to him, "Up, make us gods, who shall go before us; as for this Moses, the man who brought us up out of the land of Egypt, we do not know what has become of him."

was staying there a long time: the reference is, of course, to the forty days Moses stays on the mountain (see 24.18).

this man Moses: literally "this Moses," but the words have a derogatory meaning, "this fellow Moses," "this unimportant man named Moses."

a god: the Hebrew word has a plural form with a plural verb, but it may be understood as a singular or a plural, as the note in TEV shows. Since only one bull was made, it seems wise to interpret the word as a singular, but it may be well to include a note indicating that the choice is not certain.

lead us: literally "walk before us," but this has the meaning "lead," "show us the way."

32.2 TEV	RSV
Aaron said to them, "Take off the gold earrings which your wives, your sons, and your daughters are wearing, and bring them to me."	And Aaron said to them, "Take off the rings of gold which are in the ears of your wives, your sons, and your daughters, and bring them to me."

gold earrings: literally "gold rings which are in the ears" (see RSV).

32.3 TEV	RSV
So all the people took off their gold earrings and brought them to Aaron.	So all the people took off the rings of gold which were in their ears, and brought them to Aaron.

all the people: this does not necessarily mean that the men also wore earrings, although since verse 2 indicates that male children wore earrings, it is not impossible. But nothing else in the Old Testament (not even Gen 35.4) indicates with any clarity that Israelite men wore earrings.

32.4 TEV	RSV
He took the earrings, melted them, poured the gold into a mold, and	And he received the gold at their hand, and fashioned it with a

made a gold bull-calf.

The people said, "Israel, this is our god, who led us out of Egypt!"

graving tool, and made a molten calf; and they said, "These are your gods, O Israel, who brought you up out of the land of Egypt!"

mold: the Hebrew is not at all clear, and there is great difficulty in interpreting the meaning of this part of the verse. Since it is, however, quite clear that the Hebrew word used to describe the gold bull refers to an image that has been made in a mold, TEV has emphasized this. But the Hebrew also has a word that means "stylus," a sharp writing instrument (see Isa 8.1), which is a possible reference to a tool used to shape metal. If this is to be included (it is not in TEV), one would have to assume that the melted gold was poured into a mold. Then, after it was hard, some type of tool was used to do the final shaping of the image. The translator should keep in mind the order of priority. It is most important to state clearly that Aaron made it. Of next importance is that he made it in a mold, and third, that he used some kind of instrument (whether for shaping, or perhaps for polishing, is not certain). Because of the uncertainty, TEV has preferred to omit the last element.

bull-calf: the Hebrew word means a young bull, but it does not necessarily mean an animal as young as a calf, which would be sexually immature. In fact, all that we know about these images would lead to the conclusion that this is a young, strong bull, now sexually mature. A translation such as "young bull" might best represent the meaning of the Hebrew. In some languages it may be necessary to translate "and made a figure of gold which looked like a young bull."

our god: or "our gods" (see verse 1).

32.5	TEV	RSV

Then Aaron built an altar in front of the gold bull and announced, "Tomorrow there will be a festival to honor the LORD."

When Aaron saw this, he built an altar before it; and Aaron made proclamation and said, "Tomorrow shall be a feast to the LORD."

announced: one may assume that Aaron stood near the altar, which was to be used the next day for the sacrifices.

a festival: "a religious festival," "a religious celebration." There was usually food but also dancing and singing at religious festivals.

to honor the LORD: literally "to the LORD" (RSV), that is, "dedicated to the LORD." Note that the making of the bull as a god is not interpreted by Aaron or the people as a rejection of the LORD. Probably the bull is thought of as somehow representing the LORD, perhaps as a symbol of fertility thought of as a gift from God.

32.6	TEV	RSV

Early the next morning they brought some animals to burn as

And they rose up early on the morrow, and offered burnt

sacrifices and others to eat as
fellowship offerings. The people
sat down to a feast, which turned
into an orgy of drinking and sex.

offerings and brought peace offerings; and the people sat down to
eat and drink, and rose up to
play.

sacrifices...fellowship offerings: see 24.5.

sat down to a feast...an orgy of drinking and sex: literally "sat
down to eat and drink and they got up to play" (see RSV), but the word
"drink" means "to drink wine," and the word "play" has more than one
meaning. It may mean "laugh," "joke," "play," "amuse oneself," but it
may also have a sexual meaning. The context indicates that the people
are not playing games, and verse 25 supports the view that an orgy is
involved. Perhaps one could express the idea with a translation like
"the people ate, and there was a lot of drinking, dancing, and sex";
but a form must be chosen that can be used in polite company to speak
of such an orgy.

32.7	TEV	RSV

The LORD said to Moses,
"Hurry and go back down, because
your people, whom you led out of
Egypt, have sinned and rejected
me.

And the LORD said to Moses,
"Go down; for your people, whom
you brought up out of the land
of Egypt, have corrupted themselves;

Hurry and go back down: literally "Go, descend," but the urgency
of the Hebrew may be readily expressed in English with Hurry.

your people: with the underlying meaning, "they are no longer my
people." One might retain something of the correct feeling with a
translation like "you led these people out of Egypt, and now they have
left me."

have sinned and rejected me: these two English verbs are an attempt to translate a single Hebrew verb which has a broad meaning of
"ruin," "spoil," "misuse," "act in a ruinous way." The context makes
clear that this involves the sin of turning from God to worship the
bull.

32.8	TEV	RSV

They have already left the way
that I commanded them to follow;
they have made a bull-calf out of
melted gold and have worshiped it
and offered sacrifices to it.
They are saying that this is their
god, who led them out of Egypt.

they have turned aside quickly
out of the way which I commanded
them; they have made for themselves a molten calf, and have
worshiped it and sacrificed to
it, and said, 'These are your
gods, O Israel, who brought you
up out of the land of Egypt!'"

the way: obedience to God's commands is frequently spoken of as
a path to follow. Here one might translate "They have not obeyed the
commands I gave them," if the imagery of a path as a way of life is
not possible in the receptor language.

this is their god: TEV has shifted to indirect discourse, but in many languages it may be more meaningful to retain the quotation, "This is your god (or, These are your gods) that brought you out of Egypt."

32.9 TEV	RSV
I know how stubborn these people are.	And the LORD said to Moses, "I have seen this people, and behold, it is a stiff-necked people;

I know: literally "I have seen...and behold" (RSV), but this is a way of speaking about coming to know.

stubborn: literally "stiff-necked" (RSV), but this is a figurative way of saying that the people are stubborn and rebellious, that they will not listen or obey. This can be expressed by a great variety of figurative expressions in many languages.

32.10 TEV	RSV
Now, don't try to stop me. I am angry with them, and I am going to destroy them. Then I will make you and your descendants into a great nation."	now therefore let me alone, that my wrath may burn hot against them and I may consume them; but of you I will make a great nation."

don't try to stop me: the Hebrew verb means "leave me alone," "don't interfere with my plan to destroy the people of Israel."

I am angry with them: in Hebrew the anger of the LORD is compared to a fire that will burn up the people. In a few languages this idea may be retained, but in most it will be necessary to drop the figure of fire and speak of the LORD's anger and destruction.

make you and your descendants: literally "make you," but of course this means that Moses will have many children and descendants, who will become a great nation.

32.11 TEV	RSV
But Moses pleaded with the LORD his God and said, "LORD, why should you be so angry with your people, whom you rescued from Egypt with great might and power?	But Moses besought the LORD his God, and said, "O LORD, why does thy wrath burn hot against thy people, whom thou hast brought forth out of the land of Egypt with great power and with a mighty hand?

pleaded with: the Hebrew uses an expression that means something like "make sweet (or, gentle) the face of," which is used in the sense of "appease, flatter," but here the meaning is "plead with," "try to change the mind of."

why should you be...?: this rhetorical question may need to be reformed into a statement, "you should not be...." Or in some languages a reply to the question will be necessary, "There is no reason for you to be so angry."

[233]

angry: the Hebrew uses a figure which compares anger to fire
(burning anger), but in many languages this figure will have to be
dropped or another figure used.

with great might and power: literally "with great power and a
mighty hand" (see RSV), but "hand" is a figurative term with the sense
of power in action. One might translate "by the great and powerful
things you did."

32.12	TEV	RSV
	Why should the Egyptians be able to say that you led your people out of Egypt, planning to kill them in the mountains and destroy them completely? Stop being angry; change your mind and do not bring this disaster on your people.	Why should the Egyptians say, 'With evil intent did he bring them forth, to slay them in the mountains, and to consume them from the face of the earth'? Turn from thy fierce wrath, and repent of this evil against thy people.

Why should the Egyptians be able to say: the thought is that if
God destroys his people, the Egyptians will be the real victors; they
will be able to say, "...." In many languages the rhetorical question
will not carry that message. It will be necessary to restructure, for
example, "If you kill your people, the Egyptians will really win the
victory. They will say..." or one could translate as a negative statement with direct discourse, "The Egyptians should not be able to say,
'The LORD led his people....'"

planning to kill them: literally "for evil," but the meaning is
that God brought his people out of Egypt for evil purposes, and those
evil purposes were to kill the Israelites.

destroy them completely: literally "eliminate them from the face
of the earth" (see RSV). This means "so that no trace of them will be
left," "so that memory of them will end," "so that not one of them is
left."

Stop being angry: literally "Turn from your fierce anger" (see
RSV), but this is a Hebrew figure of speech that in many languages
will have to be translated, "Don't be angry any longer."

change your mind: the Hebrew word is sometimes translated "re-
pent" (RSV), but in English that carries the meaning "turn away from
sin," which is not intended here. The Hebrew word is to be understood
in the sense "change your mind," "change your opinion," that is, "don't
do what you said you would do."

disaster: the Hebrew word is sometimes translated "evil" (RSV),
and it can have the meaning of "sin." But here the word refers to
God's plan to kill the people of Israel, and is the same word used
earlier in the verse. It is best to translate it by repeating this
element from the first part of the verse, if such repetition is acceptable in the receptor language. Or one could generalize, "this ca-
lamity," "this disaster," "this terrible punishment," if it is clear
to the readers that the word refers to the destruction of the Israelites. A verbal construction may be simpler: "Do not cause your people
to suffer in this way."

32.13 TEV	RSV
Remember your servants Abraham, Isaac, and Jacob. Remember the solemn promise you made to them to give them as many descendants as there are stars in the sky and to give their descendants all that land you promised would be their possession forever."	Remember Abraham, Isaac, and Israel, thy servants, to whom thou didst swear by thine own self, and didst say to them, 'I will multiply your descendants as the stars of heaven, and all this land that I have promised I will give to your descendants, and they shall inherit it for ever.'"

Remember: this is not to be understood as if God needed to be reminded of the existence of Abraham, Isaac, and Jacob. The thought is, rather, that Moses reminds God of how he had chosen them as his own people and made his promises to them. The Hebrew only uses one word for "Remember," but since the real meaning is "Remember the promises you made to Abraham, Isaac, and Jacob," TEV has found it stylistically easier to repeat the word.

the solemn promise: literally "to whom you swore (or, took an oath) by yourself, saying." What the Hebrew means is quite clear, although it is hard to express in other languages. Moses is reminding God, "You took an oath. You said, 'I take a vow that if I do not bless you, I will cease to exist. I promise....'" This is usually so difficult to express in other languages that it is often more accurate to translate the basic idea with "binding promise," "solemn promise," "promise that is sure and can never be changed," "promise that I myself will guarantee." In some languages one may use an expression as "You swore on your own blood (on your own name or head) and said...."

to give them: TEV has shifted to indirect discourse, but in many languages it may be easier to retain the direct quotation of the words God spoke.

32.14 TEV	RSV
So the LORD changed his mind and did not bring on his people the disaster he had threatened.	And the LORD repented of the evil which he thought to do to his people.

changed his mind: see verse 12.
disaster: see verse 12.

32.15 TEV	RSV
Moses went back down the mountain, carrying the two stone tablets with the commandments written on both sides.	And Moses turned, and went down from the mountain with the two tables of the testimony in his hands, tables that were written on both sides; on the one side and on the other were they written.

[235]

went back down the mountain: "started back down the mountain." Since Joshua appears in verse 17 as a companion of Moses as Moses descends toward the camp, it may be necessary to include something like "went back down the mountain (part way down the mountain) to where Joshua was waiting for him." The last mention of Joshua, Moses' helper, is found in 24.13, and one must assume that during the forty days Moses was on top of the mountain, Joshua was waiting for him on a lower part of the mountain, somewhere between the top and the camp.

written on both sides: an active form may be used, "on which God had written the commandments on the front and on the back." The Hebrew emphasizes this by repeating the statement. In many languages the repetition would detract from this point rather than emphasize it, and so the repetition will need to be dropped.

32.16 TEV	RSV
God himself had made the tablets and had engraved the commandments on them.	And the tables were the work of God, and the writing was the writing of God, graven upon the tables.

engraved: literally "the writing was the writing of God, engraved upon the tablets" (see RSV), that is, God had written the commandments by engraving the words on the stone.

32.17 TEV	RSV
Joshua heard the people shouting and said to Moses, "I hear the sound of battle in the camp."	When Joshua heard the noise of the people as they shouted, he said to Moses, "There is a noise of war in the camp."

Joshua: see 24.13. One must assume that Joshua met Moses half-way down the mountain.

battle: "war." The shouting sounds to Joshua as if the people are fighting.

32.18 TEV	RSV
Moses said, "That doesn't sound like a shout of victory or a cry of defeat; it's the sound of singing."	But he said, "It is not the sound of shouting for victory, or the sound of the cry of defeat, but the sound of singing that I hear."

shout...cry: this refers to the sounds that would be made by people celebrating a victory or mourning defeat by an enemy; for example, "people who shout when they are winning in war or people who are being defeated; it is the noise of people singing."

32.19 TEV	RSV
When Moses came close enough to the camp to see the bull-calf and to see the people dancing, he became furious. There at the foot of the mountain, he threw down the tablets he was carrying and broke them.	And as soon as he came near the camp and saw the calf and the dancing, Moses' anger burned hot, and he threw the tables out of his hands and broke them at the foot of the mountain.

became furious: literally "his anger burned hot" (see RSV), but in some languages the comparison of anger to heat will need to be dropped, and the idea of "very angry" will have to be expressed in nonfigurative language. See verse 11.

he was carrying: literally "from his hands" (see RSV).

and broke them: "and they broke."

32.20 TEV	RSV
He took the bull-calf which they had made, melted it, ground it into fine powder, and mixed it with water. Then he made the people of Israel drink it.	And he took the calf which they had made, and burnt it with fire, and ground it to powder, and scattered it upon the water, and made the people of Israel drink it.

melted it: literally "burned it in the fire" (see RSV). If the bull was made with a wooden core covered by gold plate, it would be possible to burn it. Otherwise, one must assume that the gold was melted into lumps.

ground it into fine powder: the method is not known, but one may assume that it was broken into small pieces and those were reduced to powder by the use of grinding stones. One might translate "ground it until it was like dust."

mixed it with water: literally "scattered it (sprinkled it) on the surface of the water," but the purpose must have been to mix the gold dust with the water so the people could be made to drink it. There may be a reference here to the practice described in Numbers 5.16-28, but this is not certain.

32.21 TEV	RSV
He said to Aaron, "What did these people do to you, that you have made them commit such a terrible sin?"	And Moses said to Aaron, "What did this people do to you that you have brought a great sin upon them?"

What did...to you: the rhetorical question assumes the answer "Nothing." One may need to translate "These people did nothing to harm you, you should not have made them sin." Or one may need to supply an answer to the question: "They did nothing to you."

made them commit such a terrible sin: literally "brought this great sin upon them" (see RSV), but the context is quite clear that

Aaron's action resulted in the people's sinning. The idea is not simply that Aaron sinned and the people suffered the consequences.

32.22 TEV	RSV
Aaron answered, "Don't be angry with me; you know how determined these people are to do evil.	And Aaron said, "Let not the anger of my lord burn hot; you know the people, that they are set on evil.

angry with me: it is quite clear in the context that Moses' anger is directed against Aaron first of all.

determined...to do evil: the Hebrew is a bit complicated but has the sense "that they are (always) for evil," that is, "inclined to do evil," "determined to do evil." One may translate "they have their thoughts on doing evil things," "they are always thinking of evil things."

32.23 TEV	RSV
They said to me, 'We don't know what has happened to this man Moses, who brought us out of Egypt; so make us a god to lead us.'	For they said to me, 'Make us gods, who shall go before us; as for this Moses, the man who brought us up out of the land of Egypt, we do not know what has become of him.'

See verse 1.

32.24 TEV	RSV
I asked them to bring me their gold ornaments, and those who had any took them off and gave them to me. I threw the ornaments into the fire and out came this bull-calf!"	And I said to them, 'Let any who have gold take it off'; so they gave it to me, and I threw it into the fire, and there came out this calf."

See verse 2.

ornaments: the Hebrew has simply "gold," but the reference is to the earrings of verse 2.

out came: in contrast to what is said in verse 4, Aaron is stating that the bull produced itself in the fire in an almost miraculous way. In many languages this element of miracle or surprise may need to be stated: "and suddenly it became a bull," "I looked and there was this bull."

32.25 TEV	RSV
Moses saw that Aaron had let the people get out of control and make fools of themselves in front of their enemies.	And when Moses saw that the people had broken loose (for Aaron had let them break loose, to their shame among their enemies),

out of control: the exact meaning of the Hebrew word is not known, but it probably has the sense of "break loose," "run loose," "be out of control."

make fools of themselves: the meaning of the Hebrew word is uncertain, but it seems to have the meaning of "derision," "whisper," "shame." The literal "to derision among their enemies" (see RSV) then seems to mean "they did what should have made them ashamed in front of their enemies," "they acted in such a way that their enemies derided them," "their enemies were glad that the people of Israel had acted so shamelessly."

32.26 TEV	RSV
So he stood at the gate of the camp and shouted, "Everyone who is on the LORD's side come over here!" So all the Levites gathered around him,	then Moses stood in the gate of the camp, and said, "Who is on the LORD's side? Come to me." And all the sons of Levi gathered themselves together to him.

gate: "entrance."
who is on the LORD's side: "who belongs to the LORD."
come over here: literally "(come) to me" (RSV), that is "come here where I am."
the Levites: literally "the sons of Levi" (RSV), but this means "the descendants of Levi," that is, the Levites.

32.27 TEV	RSV
and he said to them, "The LORD God of Israel commands every one of you to put on your sword and go through the camp from this gate to the other and kill your brothers, your friends, and your neighbors."	And he said to them, "Thus says the LORD God of Israel, 'Put every man his sword on his side, and go to and fro from gate to gate throughout the camp, and slay every man his brother, and every man his companion, and every man his neighbor.'"

The LORD God of Israel: "The LORD who is the God that Israel worships."
every one of you: the Hebrew expresses this in direct discourse, and in some languages it may be simpler to retain the quoted command.
put on your sword: where swords are not known or not worn fastened to a belt, one may translate "take your weapon," or one may name the particular weapon that would be used in war.
your neighbors: that is, "the people that you know."

32.28 TEV	RSV
The Levites obeyed, and killed about three thousand men that day.	And the sons of Levi did according to the word of Moses; and there fell of the people that day about three thousand men.

obeyed: literally "did what Moses commanded."

32.29 TEV	RSV
Moses said to the Levites, "Today you have consecrated yourselves*g* as priests in the service of the LORD by killing your sons and brothers, so the LORD has given you his blessing."	And Moses said, "Today you have ordained yourselves*8* for the service of the LORD, each one at the cost of his son and of his brother, that he may bestow a blessing upon you this day."
gSome ancient translations Today you have consecrated yourselves; *Hebrew* Consecrate yourselves today; *or* You have been consecrated today.	*8*Gk Vg See Tg: Heb *ordain yourselves*

you have consecrated yourselves: the Hebrew vowels (added to the text at a later time) make the verb read as a command, but some of the early translations read it as a past tense, as the note in TEV shows. The Hebrew is literally "fill your hands," but this is a technical expression which means "consecrate," "set aside as belonging to God," "present to God." Here the meaning is "you have set yourself apart as priests," "you have made yourself priests."

by killing: the Hebrew uses a form that seems to mean "at the cost of" (RSV), "in exchange for." But the sense is "because you did not spare," "because you killed."

his blessing: this consists in making the Levites priests. One may translate "has done something good for you."

32.30 TEV	RSV
The next day Moses said to the people, "You have committed a terrible sin. But now I will again go up the mountain to the LORD; perhaps I can obtain forgiveness for your sin."	On the morrow Moses said to the people, "You have sinned a great sin. And now I will go up to the LORD; perhaps I can make atonement for your sin."

perhaps: "it may be that," "it is possible that."

obtain forgiveness: the Hebrew word, which means "cover," is often translated "make atonement for" (RSV), but this puts the emphasis at the wrong place. The meaning is that sin is "covered" when the relationship is restored. This is usually expressed as "forgiveness." One might translate "perhaps I can get God to forgive your sin." As is clear from the following two verses, Moses' method of getting the people's sin "covered" is by praying that God will forgive them.

32.31 TEV	RSV
Moses then returned to the LORD and said, "These people have	So Moses returned to the LORD and said, "Alas, this people

| committed a terrible sin. They have made a god out of gold and worshiped it. | have sinned a great sin; they have made for themselves gods of gold. |

These people: the Hebrew introduces this statement by the use of a word that is difficult to translate in English. It is sometimes translated "Alas" (RSV), that is, an expression of sorrow or regret. Many languages will have similar introductory words. In a language like English, one might express the idea by translating "Moses...sighed in sorrow and said, 'These people....'"

32.32 TEV	RSV
Please forgive their sin; but if you won't, then remove my name from the book in which you have written the names of your people."	But now, if thou wilt forgive their sin—and if not, blot me, I pray thee, out of thy book which thou hast written."

Please forgive: the Hebrew uses a complicated, shortened structure, but this clearly expresses the meaning.

remove my name: that is, "erase," "move out," "draw a line through."

the book in which...your people: literally "your book in which you have written" (see RSV), but this refers to a book in which God writes the names of all those who belong to him. The thought may be compared to a ruler who keeps a list of his subjects and removes their names when they die. If this is not made clear, the reader may think of a book with commandments written in it (see 24.7) or something like that.

32.33 TEV	RSV
The LORD answered, "It is those who have sinned against me whose names I will remove from my book.	But the LORD said to Moses, "Whoever has sinned against me, him will I blot out of my book.

It is those who: that is, "I will remove the names of any people who."

whose names: literally "him" (RSV), but it is obviously the name of the person that will be removed from the book.

32.34 TEV	RSV
Now go, lead the people to the place I told you about. Remember that my angel will guide you, but the time is coming when I will punish these people for their sin."	But now go, lead the people to the place of which I have spoken to you; behold, my angel shall go before you. Nevertheless, in the day when I visit, I will visit their sin upon them."

the place: that is, the promised land.

[241]

my angel: in this part of the Old Testament, the angel of the LORD is essentially equal to the presence of the LORD himself (see 3.2,4).

32.35 TEV	RSV
So the LORD sent a disease on the people, because they had caused Aaron to make the gold bull-calf.	And the LORD sent a plague upon the people, because they made the calf which Aaron made.

a disease: the Hebrew says, "the LORD struck the people," but the verb is used for sending plagues or disasters (see 7.14—10.29). Here an epidemic disease is probably intended. "The LORD caused the people to be ill," "the LORD made the people suffer a bad illness."

they had caused Aaron to make: literally "they made the bull that Aaron made" (see RSV); what is in focus is that the people asked for a god and forced Aaron to make the bull.

CHAPTER   33

33.1-11: The LORD commands the people of Israel to leave Mount Sinai. From this point on the LORD speaks to Moses in the LORD's Tent, which the people take with them as they travel.

SECTION HEADING

The LORD Promises to Be with His People (33.12-23): "The LORD Promises to Help His People."

33.12 TEV	RSV
Moses said to the LORD, "It is true that you have told me to lead these people to that land, but you did not tell me whom you would send with me. You have said that you know me well and are pleased with me.	Moses said to the LORD, "See, thou sayest to me, 'Bring up this people'; but thou hast not let me know whom thou wilt send with me. Yet thou hast said, 'I know you by name, and you have also found favor in my sight.'

Moses said: in Hebrew the words are in direct discourse, and in some languages it will be necessary to retain them, rather than shift to indirect as TEV has done.

It is true: literally "See" (RSV), but in Hebrew this is frequently used as an introductory formula, and it will need to be adjusted to what is normal in the receptor language.

lead these people to that land: literally "bring up these people" (see RSV), with the sense "bring them out of Egypt and bring them to the land that I have promised." In many languages it will be necessary to make this explicit, "to lead these people from Egypt to the land you gave them."

tell me: literally "cause me to know."

send with me: that is, to help, to assist, or to guide Moses. There is some difficulty here. In verse 2, God has told Moses that he will send an angel to guide him, but Moses' plea here seems to be a request that the LORD himself go with him, as the following verses show.

know me well: literally "know you by name" (RSV), but in Hebrew this means much more than that he knows Moses' name; it means that the LORD is intimately acquainted with Moses and knows all about him. TEV has shifted to indirect discourse.

are pleased with me: literally "you have found favor in my sight" (RSV), but this is a Hebrew figure of speech which means "be pleased with." It may often be necessary to state this positively, "you have accepted me as yours," "I have pleased you."

33.13 TEV	RSV
Now if you are, tell me your plans, so that I may serve you and continue to please you. Remember also that you have chosen this nation to be your own."	Now therefore, I pray thee, if I have found favor in thy sight, show me now thy ways, that I may know thee and find favor in thy sight. Consider too that this nation is thy people."

Now: TEV has not included the special Hebrew form that is used in polite speech to make a request (RSV "I pray thee").

if you are: that is, "if you are pleased with me." The literal form is the same as in verse 12.

tell me your plans: literally "show me your ways" (see RSV), in the sense "let me know the paths you are going to follow," "let me know what you are going to do."

serve you: literally "know you" (see RSV), but this does not mean "know about you" or "be acquainted with you"; rather it has the sense "know what you want and what I should do."

continue to please: the literal form is the same as in verse 12.

Remember: literally "See," but this is used to call God back to acknowledge that these are his people and not Moses' people. One might translate "Admit," "Don't forget."

you have chosen: although these words do not occur in the Hebrew text, they are included in English to make clear what is really meant by the literal "this nation is your people" (see RSV).

33.14 TEV	RSV
The LORD said, "I will go with you, and I will give you victory."	And he said, "My presence will go with you, and I will give you rest."

I: literally "My face (my presence)." The idea may be expressed by some emphatic form, "I myself." In many languages it would sound very strange for a person to speak of himself by referring to his face, as the Hebrew does.

will give you victory: the Hebrew verb literally means something like "cause you to have quiet, or rest," but what is intended is that Israel will overthrow all enemies so that there will be peace, with no enemies left to attack them. One might translate "overthrow all your enemies," "make you victorious so that you can live in peace."

33.15	TEV	RSV
	Moses replied, "If you do not go with us, don't make us leave this place.	And he said to him, "If thy presence will not go with me, do not carry us up from here.

you: literally "your face (presence)," as in verse 14.
make us leave: literally "cause to go up" (see verse 12).

33.16	TEV	RSV
	How will anyone know that you are pleased with your people and with me if you do not go with us? Your presence with us will distinguish us from any other people on earth."	For how shall it be known that I have found favor in thy sight, I and thy people? Is it not in thy going with us, so that we are distinct, I and thy people, from all other people that are upon the face of the earth?"

How will anyone know: this is a rhetorical question that assumes an answer, "No one will be able to know." In many languages it will be simpler to change to a statement, "No one will know...if you do not go...." Or it may be necessary to reverse the elements, "Unless you go with us, no one will know...."

pleased: the same literal form as in verse 12.
Your presence with us: the use of a noun such as this is one way in English to repeat the idea of "your going with us." In some languages one would use "The fact that you are going with us."

distinguish us from: that is, "make us different from," "set us apart from," "show that we are different from."

any other people: literally "all people," but in English the singular is more emphatic here.

on earth: literally "on the face (surface) of the earth" (see RSV), but the idea of "surface" is redundant in English. People normally do not live beneath the earth's surface. The Hebrew is a kind of set phrase that simply means "on the earth," "on the whole earth."

33.17	TEV	RSV
	The LORD said to Moses, "I will do just as you have asked, because I know you very well and I am pleased with you."	And the LORD said to Moses, "This very thing that you have spoken I will do; for you have found favor in my sight, and I know you by name."

[244]

<u>know you very well...am pleased</u>: see verse 12.

33.18   TEV   RSV
    Then Moses requested, "Please,   Moses said, "I pray thee, show me
let me see the dazzling light of   thy glory."
your presence."

    <u>Please</u>: this translates the Hebrew polite form used to make a
request (see verse 13).
    <u>the dazzling light of your presence</u>: literally "your heaviness,"
but with the sense of splendor, magnificence, glory. The reference, of
course, is to God himself, and one might translate "let me see you in
all your glory." TEV has chosen to emphasize the dazzling light that
appears when the LORD is present.

33.19   TEV   RSV
    The LORD answered, "I will   And he said, "I will make all
make all my splendor pass before   my goodness pass before you,
you and in your presence I will   and will proclaim before you
pronounce my sacred name. I am   my name 'The LORD'; and I will
the LORD, and I show compassion   be gracious to whom I will be
and pity on those I choose.   gracious, and will show mercy on
                                      whom I will show mercy.

    <u>all my splendor</u>: literally "all my goodness" (RSV), but here
again this refers to the LORD himself and is another way of speaking
of his glory (see verse 22). The word "goodness" here is not to be
understood in a moral sense. It refers, rather, to what might be called
"beauty." One might translate "I will pass in front of you and show
you all my beauty (or, splendor)."
    <u>pronounce</u>: literally "call out before you," that is, "speak so
that you can hear it."
    <u>my sacred name</u>: the Hebrew uses the personal name "Yahweh" (see
3.14), reflected here in the translation "I am the LORD" (see the discussion in 3.14-15). One might translate "I will pronounce my own sacred
name, 'the LORD.'"
    <u>I show compassion...those I choose</u>: literally "I will have com-
passion on whom I will have compassion and I will have pity on whom
I will have pity" (see RSV). The sense is "I choose the ones on whom
I have pity (or, mercy)." Here the underlying meaning is "I reveal myself to whomever I wish, and I choose to reveal myself to you." If the
general expression cannot include this element, it may be necessary
to make it quite clear in the translation. The Hebrew terms for compassion and pity are closely related, and one may have to use a single
term in translation, "show love for" or "be kind to."

33.20   TEV   RSV
I will not let you see my face,   But," he said, "you cannot see
because no one can see me and   my face; for man shall not see
stay alive,   me and live."

[245]

I will not let you: literally "you cannot" (RSV), but with the sense "because I will not allow it to happen."

stay alive: "continue to live." The thought is that to look directly at God brings death to human beings. It may be necessary to translate "anyone who sees my face will die" or "if any person sees me he will die."

33.21 TEV	RSV
but here is a place beside me where you can stand on a rock.	And the LORD said, "Behold, there is a place by me where you shall stand upon the rock;

here is: the Hebrew uses an intensive form, often translated "Behold" (RSV), but it is more of an attention getter than anything else.

33.22 TEV	RSV
When the dazzling light of my presence passes by, I will put you in an opening in the rock and cover you with my hand until I have passed by.	and while my glory passes by I will put you in a cleft of the rock, and I will cover you with my hand until I have passed by;

the dazzling light of my presence: literally "my heaviness (my glory)" (see verse 18). In some languages one may have to say "When I pass by and show you my brightness, I will put you...."

I will put you: in many languages the order will need to be reversed: "I will put you...and then I will pass by."

opening: "split," "a cleft."

cover you with my hand: "hold my hand over your eyes."

33.23 TEV	RSV
Then I will take my hand away, and you will see my back but not my face."	then I will take away my hand, and you shall see my back; but my face shall not be seen."

but not my face: the Hebrew uses a passive, "my face will not be seen."

CHAPTER 34

SECTION HEADING

The Second Set of Stone Tablets (34.1-9): "Two Stone Tablets Are Again Made." "God Once Again Writes on the Stone Tablets."

34.1   TEV

The LORD said to Moses, "Cut two stone tablets like the first ones, and I will write on them the words that were on the first tablets, which you broke.

See 32.15-19.

34.1   RSV

The LORD said to Moses, "Cut two tables of stone like the first; and I will write upon the tables the words that were on the first tables, which you broke.

34.2   TEV

Get ready tomorrow morning, and come up Mount Sinai to meet me there at the top.

34.2   RSV

Be ready in the morning, and come up in the morning to Mount Sinai, and present yourself there to me on the top of the mountain.

to meet me there: literally "stand there before me."

34.3   TEV

No one is to come up with you; no one is to be seen on any part of the mountain; and no sheep or cattle are to graze at the foot of the mountain."

34.3   RSV

No man shall come up with you, and let no man be seen throughout all the mountain; let no flocks or herds feed before that mountain."

No one: the Hebrew "No man" (RSV) is used in a general sense to include women and children. Where an active form is required, one may translate "No one must be on any part of the mountain. Do not graze cattle or sheep on the bottom part of the mountain."

34.4   TEV

So Moses cut two more stone tablets, and early the next morning he carried them up Mount Sinai, just as the LORD had commanded.

34.4   RSV

So Moses cut two tables of stone like the first; and he rose early in the morning and went up on Mount Sinai, as the LORD had commanded him, and took in his hand two tables of stone.

early the next morning he carried: literally "he got up early in the morning and went...and took in his hand" (see RSV). In English some of these verbs need to be left unexpressed for stylistic reasons. This will also be true in some other languages, while others may require even more transitionals.

34.5   TEV

The LORD came down in a cloud, stood with him there, and pronounced his holy name, the LORD.^{h}

34.5   RSV

And the LORD descended in the cloud and stood with him there, and proclaimed the name of the LORD.

Exo 34.5

[h]THE LORD: *See 3.14, and Word List.*

    in a cloud: the sense may be "hidden by a cloud" or "wrapped in a cloud."

    pronounced: "said his holy name by saying, 'The LORD'" (see 33.19).

34.6 TEV	RSV
The LORD then passed in front of him and called out, "I, the LORD, am a God who is full of compassion and pity, who is not easily angered and who shows great love and faithfulness.	The LORD passed before him, and proclaimed, "The LORD, the LORD, a God merciful and gracious, slow to anger, and abounding in steadfast love and faithfulness,

    I, the LORD: literally "The LORD, the LORD" (RSV), but in English the idea is more readily expressed in the first person.

    not easily angered: literally "long of anger," "slow to get angry." In some languages there are idiomatic expressions for this idea, "with a cool heart" or "with cool insides."

    great love and faithfulness: the Hebrew uses two words that relate directly to the covenant relationship, with the sense "I am loyal and faithful, and I can be trusted." The point is that God can be trusted to do good and keep his promises to those who accept his covenant and obey him.

34.7 TEV	RSV
I keep my promise for thousands of generations[i] and forgive evil and sin; but I will not fail to punish children and grandchildren to the third and fourth generation for the sins of their parents."	keeping steadfast love for thousands, forgiving iniquity and transgression and sin, but who will by no means clear the guilty, visiting the iniquity of the fathers upon the children and the children's children, to the third and the fourth generation."
[i]thousands of generations; *or* thousands.	

    See 20.5-6.

    will not fail to punish: literally "will not consider innocent," "will not exempt from punishment." In some languages it may be necessary to say "will not allow people to escape punishment (or, suffering)."

34.8 TEV	RSV
Moses quickly bowed down to the ground and worshiped.	And Moses made haste to bow his head toward the earth, and worshiped.

    quickly bowed down: literally "hurried and bowed down."

34.9   TEV   RSV
He said, "Lord, if you really are   And he said, "If now I have found
pleased with me, I ask you to go   favor in thy sight, O Lord, let
with us. These people are stub-   the Lord, I pray thee, go in the
born, but forgive our evil and   midst of us, although it is a
our sin, and accept us as your   stiff-necked people; and pardon
own people."   our iniquity and our sin, and take
                                     us for thy inheritance."

    pleased: the literal form is the same as in 33.12.
    I ask you to go: the Hebrew uses a third person form that is bet-
ter expressed in the second person in English.
    with us: the Hebrew uses a word that is often translated "in the
midst of us," but the sense is "be very close to us" rather than simply
"in the center of our group."
    stubborn: literally "stiff-necked" (RSV).

    34.10-28: Once again God's people promise to keep the agreement
that he has made with them.

SECTION HEADING

    Moses Goes (Comes) Down from Mount Sinai (34.29-35): "The Light
on Moses' Face," "Moses' Appearance When He Came Down from the Mountain."

34.29   TEV   RSV
    When Moses went down from   When Moses came down from
Mount Sinai carrying the Ten Com-   Mount Sinai, with the two tables
mandments, his face was shining   of the testimony in his hand as
because he had been speaking with   he came down from the mountain,
the LORD; but he did not know it.   Moses did not know that the skin
                                     of his face shone because he had
                                     been talking with God.

    his face: literally "the skin of his face" (RSV), but in English
one normally includes the skin when speaking of the face.
    was shining: this is not reflection of normal light from an oily
face. The intent is to say that a strange or unusual light shone from
his face.
    because he had been speaking: the point is that Moses was in the
presence of the glory of the LORD (the dazzling light of the LORD's
presence), and his face continued to be illuminated by that light even
after he left the presence of the LORD.

34.30   TEV   RSV
Aaron and all the people looked   And when Aaron and all the people
at Moses and saw that his face   of Israel saw Moses, behold, the
was shining, and they were afraid   skin of his face shone, and they
to go near him.   were afraid to come near him.

afraid to go near him: this fear of what is holy is similar to the fear expressed at Mount Sinai (see 20.18-19). In some cases the meaning will not be clear unless one states the cause explicitly, for example, "because he had been with the LORD."

34.31	TEV	RSV
	But Moses called them, and Aaron and all the leaders of the community went to him, and Moses spoke with them.	But Moses called to them; and Aaron and all the leaders of the congregation returned to him, and Moses talked with them.

them: the first them refers to verse 30 and means "Aaron and all the people."
went to him: Moses is still apparently some distance from the people, but close enough for them to see that his face is shining.
them: the second them refers to "Aaron and all the leaders of the community."

34.32	TEV	RSV
	After that, all the people of Israel gathered around him, and Moses gave them all the laws that the LORD had given him on Mount Sinai.	And afterward all the people of Israel came near, and he gave them in commandment all that the LORD had spoken with him in Mount Sinai.

gave them all the laws: literally "he commanded them all that the LORD had said" (see RSV), with the sense that he passed on to the people all the laws that the LORD had commanded him to give them.

34.33	TEV	RSV
	When Moses had finished speaking with them, he covered his face with a veil.	And when Moses had finished speaking with them, he put a veil on his face;

a veil: the Hebrew word refers to a "covering" of some kind, a veil, or possibly a mask. Often one will translate "he covered his face with a cloth."

34.34	TEV	RSV
	Whenever Moses went into the Tent of the LORD's presence to speak to the LORD, he would take the veil off. When he came out, he would tell the people of Israel everything that he had been commanded to say.	but whenever Moses went in before the LORD to speak with him, he took the veil off, until he came out; and when he came out, and told the people of Israel what he was commanded,

Tent of the LORD's Presence: literally "before the LORD" (RSV), but this is a way of speaking of the Tent in which the LORD appeared (see 33.7-11). It may be translated "the Tent where the LORD was."

34.35 TEV	RSV
and they would see that his face was shining. Then he would put the veil back on until the next time he went to speak with the LORD.	the people of Israel saw the face of Moses, that the skin of Moses' face shone; and Moses would put the veil upon his face again, until he went in to speak with him.

went to speak: that is, went into the Tent of the LORD's Presence to speak with the LORD.

35.1—40.38: This section describes in detail how the Tent of the LORD's Presence was made. It was built according to the instructions that the LORD had given Moses on Mount Sinai. When the Tent was dedicated to the LORD, the cloud covered it to show that the LORD was there.

LEVITICUS

THE NAME OF THE BOOK

The name "Leviticus" comes from the Greek translation and refers to "The Book about Levitical Priests." The translator may wish to use something like "The Book about the Duties of Priests" or "The Book about Sacrifices."

INTRODUCTION

Leviticus contains regulations for worship and religious cere-monies in ancient Israel, and for the priests who were responsible for carrying out these instructions.

The main theme of the book is the holiness of God and the ways in which his people were to worship and live. Israel will keep itself holy and maintain its relationship with "the holy God of Israel" by faithful obedience to his commands.

Only one small part of the book is included in this selection of passages.

C H A P T E R   19

SECTION HEADING

Love Your Neighbor (19.11-18): "God Commands Love for One Another."

19.11 TEV	RSV
"Do not steal or cheat or lie.	"You shall not steal, nor deal falsely, nor lie to one another.

The LORD says, "Do not...": in this selection the words "The LORD says" will need to be introduced to make sure the reader understands that these commands come from God.

cheat: the Hebrew verb has the sense of "lie, deceive," but it is more than speaking a lie and almost has the sense "deal falsely" (RSV), "take advantage of." The Hebrew has literally "a man to his fellow," but this is the way of saying "to one another" (RSV). TEV has assumed that to put this in would be redundant or too wordy.

19.12	TEV	RSV
Do not make a promise in my name if you do not intend to keep it; that brings disgrace on my name. I am the LORD your God.	And you shall not swear by my name falsely, and so profane the name of your God: I am the LORD.

make a promise in my name: literally "make a vow (or, take an oath) in my name." This refers to the kind of promise in which one states "May God strike me dead if I do not do...." In some languages one may translate "make a promise by using my name" or "use my name when you make a promise."

if you do not intend to keep it: literally "in falsehood, deception," but "swear falsely" (see RSV) will have the sense of "make a promise when you do not intend to keep it."

brings disgrace on: literally "profanes" (see RSV), that is, "make no longer holy." The underlying sense is that if one swears or takes an oath in the name of God and does not keep it, people will say that God is not holy.

my name: literally "the name of your God" (RSV), but in English the first person is required. TEV has retained part of the phrase in the LORD your God.

19.13	TEV	RSV
"Do not take advantage of anyone or rob him. Do not hold back the wages of someone you have hired, not even for one night.	"You shall not oppress your neighbor or rob him. The wages of a hired servant shall not remain with you all night until the morning.

take advantage of: the Hebrew verb has the sense of "wrong someone," "extort something from someone."

one night: literally "until morning" (see RSV). The meaning is that the poor laborer needs to be paid in order that he may eat, and the employer should not even wait until the next morning to pay him.

19.14	TEV	RSV
Do not curse a deaf man or put something in front of a blind man so as to make him stumble over it. Obey me; I am the LORD your God.	You shall not curse the deaf or put a stumbling block before the blind, but you shall fear your God: I am the LORD.

deaf...blind: unprotected people are considered to be the special concern of the LORD.

Obey: literally "fear" (RSV), but the primary focus is not fear of punishment, but honor and respect for the LORD's character.

19.15 TEV	RSV
"Be honest and just when you make decisions in legal cases; do not show favoritism to the poor or fear the rich.	"You shall do no injustice in judgment; you shall not be partial to the poor or defer to the great, but in righteousness shall you judge your neighbor.

honest and just: in Hebrew the idea is expressed negatively, "You shall do no injustice" (RSV), and positively, "in righteousness shall you judge." The scene is a trial in a law court.

show favoritism to the poor: literally "lift up the face of the poor," which is a figure for showing partiality.

19.16 TEV	RSV
Do not spread lies about anyone, and when someone is on trial for his life, speak out if your testimony can help him. I am the LORD.	You shall not go up and down as a slanderer among your people, and you shall not stand forth against the life^g of your neighbor: I am the LORD.

^{g}Heb *blood*

spread lies: literally "walk as a slanderer" (see RSV), which has the sense of going around to destroy the good name of people.

someone is on trial...help him: this is an attempt to translate in a meaningful way a Hebrew expression that literally says "do not stand against the blood of your fellow" (see RSV). The situation presupposes a law court, and "blood" may be understood as life, but the meaning is not fully clear in Hebrew. The meaning, however, seems to be that when a fellow Israelite is on trial for his life, any person who can help should give testimony. It is also possible that the meaning is that a person should not bring any false accusation that could result in the death sentence.

19.17 TEV	RSV
"Do not bear a grudge against anyone, but settle your differences with him, so that you will not commit a sin because of him.^{h}	"You shall not hate your brother in your heart, but you shall reason with your neighbor, lest you bear sin because of him.

^{h}so...him; *or* so that you do not commit this sin against him.

bear a grudge: literally "hate in your heart" (see RSV), with the sense of a continued, deep-seated hatred.

settle your differences: the Hebrew verb may also be understood in the sense of "rebuke," "reprove," and the sense would then be: rebuke him so that you will not have a part in his sin.

so that...because of him: as the TEV footnote shows, the exact meaning of the Hebrew is not certain. A literal translation, "and you shall not lift up upon him (because of him?) sin," probably has the sense "become guilty of sin because of what he does."

19.18 TEV	RSV
Do not take revenge on anyone or continue to hate him, but love your neighbor as you love yourself. I am the LORD.	You shall not take vengeance or bear any grudge against the sons of your own people, but you shall love your neighbor as yourself; I am the LORD.

neighbor: the Hebrew word has the meaning "fellow," "friend," and probably refers to a fellow Israelite. Note that in the previous sentence the Hebrew has "the sons of your people," which means "any Israelite." Here, since the words are given wider application, it may be suitable to think of "fellow-man," that is, anyone.

NUMBERS

THE NAME OF THE BOOK

The name "Numbers" comes from the Latin translation of the Greek title and refers to the numbering of the people of Israel. The translator may wish to use a term that would refer to this numbering of the people, but it would also be possible to speak of "The Book of Wilderness Wanderings" or something similar.

INTRODUCTION

The book of Numbers tells the story of the people of Israel during nearly forty years of wandering, from the time they left Mount Sinai until they finally reached the eastern border of the land of Canaan. The name Numbers comes from the census (or numbering) of the people reported in the book, but only a few important incidents are included in this selection of passages.

CHAPTER   6

SECTION HEADING

The Priestly Blessing (6.22-27): "The Priests Bless the People," "The Words the Priests Use to Bless the People."

6.22	TEV	RSV
	The LORD commanded Moses	The LORD said to Moses,

The LORD commanded Moses: this follows a long series of commands God gives to Moses while the Israelites are still in the Sinai Desert.

[256]

6.23   TEV   RSV
to tell Aaron and his sons to   "Say to Aaron and his sons, Thus
use the following words in bless-   you shall bless the people of
ing the people of Israel: Israel: you shall say to them,

the following words: this is an English expression used to summarize what follows. The Hebrew has "saying this you shall bless...say
to them" (see RSV). The receptor language pattern for introducing
quotations should be used.

6.24   TEV   RSV
May the LORD bless you and   The LORD bless you and keep
take care of you;   you:

May the LORD: the blessing is a form of prayer, and this should
be made clear in translation. One might consider "I pray that."
bless you: "make it possible for you to prosper," "give you power
to be successful," "do what will be good for you."
take care of you: the Hebrew word means "guard," "keep" (RSV),
"protect," but it also has the wider sense of doing what is necessary
for one's well-being.

6.25   TEV   RSV
May the LORD be kind and   The LORD make his face to
gracious to you;   shine upon you, and be gracious
                                    to you:

be kind: literally "cause his face to shine upon you" (see RSV),
but this is a figurative expression in Hebrew that has the meaning
"deal kindly with," "treat kindly." In most languages a literal translation will not convey the correct meaning, although one might translate with something like "look upon you in a friendly way," if this can
include the meaning "and do something to help you."
gracious: the idea is not "be polite" but "show you his favor,"
"do what is good for you because of his grace," "show you his love and
concern."

6.26   TEV   RSV
May the LORD look on you with   The LORD lift up his counten-
favor and give you peace.   ance upon you, and give you peace.

look on you with favor: literally "lift up his face upon you" (see
RSV), which has a figurative sense of "show you his favor," "be favorable to you." This may be hard to translate in some languages, and
perhaps one will have to use something like "be very kind to you,"
"be like a close friend."
give you peace: the Hebrew word for "peace" includes such ideas
as "health," "wholeness," "prosperity," "salvation," and it may be
necessary to expand the translation if the word for "peace" in the

receptor language refers primarily to lack of war. One might translate, for example, "may the LORD give you happiness and prosperity," "may the LORD protect you and keep you well."

6.27	TEV	RSV
	And the LORD said, "If they pronounce my name as a blessing upon the people of Israel, I will bless them."	"So shall they put my name upon the people of Israel, and I will bless them."

pronounce my name as a blessing upon: literally "put my name upon" (RSV), but the use of the LORD's name in the blessing given in verses 24-26 is what is meant, and this needs to be made clear in the translation. One might translate "If they use my name when they bless...."

C H A P T E R   13

13.1-16: As the people of Israel traveled through the desert, they came near the land of Canaan. Moses chose twelve leaders and sent them into the land to find out what it was like. Among the twelve spies were Caleb and Joshua.

SECTION HEADING

The Spies (13.17-33): "Israelite Spies Enter Canaan," "Moses Sends Spies to the Land of Canaan."

13.17	TEV	RSV
	When Moses sent them out, he said to them, "Go north from here into the southern part of the land of Canaan and then on into the hill country.	Moses sent them to spy out the land of Canaan, and said to them, "Go up into the Negeb yonder, and go up into the hill country,

sent them out: literally "sent them to spy out the land of Canaan" (RSV), and it would be good to include this in a set of selections. The Hebrew word "spy" has the sense of "investigate," "see what is there"; it does not suggest modern concepts of spying in a secretive manner. "Explore" would give the right meaning.

Go north: the literal "Go up" (RSV) has the sense of Go north from where the Israelites are, that is, from an area south of the land of Canaan.

the southern part: the Hebrew uses the word "Negev" (RSV "Negeb"), which refers to the southern part of the land of Canaan. The word Negev is used in modern Israel for the same area.

the hill country: this refers to the mountain range running north and south through the land of Canaan.

13.18	TEV	RSV
	Find out what kind of country it is, how many people live there, and how strong they are.	and see what the land is, and whether the people who dwell in it are strong or weak, whether they are few or many,

Find out: literally "see" (RSV), but this is a Hebrew way of speaking of the whole process of obtaining information.

what kind of: in many languages it will be simpler to shift to direct questions; for example, "Find the answer to these questions: What kind of country is it?..." Direct questions could be used through verse 20.

strong: literally "strong or weak" (RSV). The reference is primarily to the military strength of the country. One might translate "Do they have a large army?"

13.19	TEV	RSV
	Find out whether the land is good or bad and whether the people live in open towns or in fortified cities.	and whether the land that they dwell in is good or bad, and whether the cities that they dwell in are camps or strongholds,

good or bad: the words may refer to whether the land is good for farming or not. But since this is clearly in focus in verse 20, the words may be taken in a more general sense, "a good place to live."

open towns or in fortified cities: the contrast is between cities with walls and towers, which can be used to defend them, and towns in the open country without walls and defenses. The latter, of course, would be more easily captured.

13.20	TEV	RSV
	Find out whether the soil is fertile and whether the land is wooded. And be sure to bring back some of the fruit that grows there." (It was the season when grapes were beginning to ripen.)	and whether the land is rich or poor, and whether there is wood in it or not. Be of good courage, and bring some of the fruit of the land." Now the time was the season of the first ripe grapes.

fertile: literally "fertile or lean (poor)," with the underlying question being "Does it produce good crops?" "Is it good for farming?"

wooded: literally "if there are trees or not."

be sure: the Hebrew uses a word that means "make yourself strong." It may have the sense of "be courageous," but TEV has taken it in a more general sense.

It was: as the round brackets (parentheses) show, this is a statement by the writer that interprets the story. It prepares the way for verse 23.

grapes: if grapes are not known, some descriptive phrase may be used, "sweet, juicy fruit called grapes." Or possibly a local substitute may be found, but this is usually not a happy solution, since grapes play an important role in Israelite agriculture.

13.21 TEV	RSV
So the men went north and explored the land from the wilderness of Zin in the south all the way to Rehob, near Hamath Pass in the north.	So they went up and spied out the land from the wilderness of Zin to Rehob, near the entrance of Hamath.

north...south: the readers of the Hebrew text knew where the wilderness of Zin (the extreme southern part of Canaan) and Rehob (on the northern border) were, and this information needs to be conveyed to modern readers.

Hamath Pass: literally "Lebo-hamath," which some translations transliterate, but the Hebrew may mean "entrance to Hamath" (see RSV), that is, "the pass (in the mountains) leading down to Hamath (on the Orontes River)."

13.22 TEV	RSV
They went first into the southern part of the land and came to Hebron, where the clans of Ahiman, Sheshai, and Talmai, the descendants of a race of giants called the Anakim, lived. (Hebron was founded seven years before Zoan in Egypt.)	They went up into the Negeb, and came to Hebron; and Ahiman, Sheshai, and Talmai, the descendants of Anak, were there. (Hebron was built seven years before Zoan in Egypt.)

Hebron: a city 30 kilometers (19 miles) south of Jerusalem.

the clans: the three names are not of individuals (although originally that may have been the case) but of clans or tribes of people.

race of giants: the Hebrew word "Anak" (plural "Anakim") is used for a tribe of early inhabitants of Canaan who are described as very tall, that is, giants. Hebrew readers would have known this, but it needs to be made clear for modern readers.

Zoan: the point is being made that, although Zoan is an ancient city, Hebron is even older. This is another statement by the writer which explains something in the text.

13.23 TEV	RSV
They came to Eshcol Valley, and there they cut off a branch which had one bunch of grapes on it so	And they came to the Valley of Eshcol, and cut down from there a branch with a single cluster

heavy that it took two men to
carry it on a pole between them.
They also brought back some pomegranates and figs.

of grapes, and they carried it
on a pole between two of them;
they brought also some pomegranates and figs.

Eschol Valley: this valley was near Hebron (see verse 24).
pomegranates and figs: if these fruits are not known, a descriptive phrase may be used. See Fauna and Flora of the Bible (published
by the United Bible Societies) for a description.

13.24   TEV
(That place was named Eschol*j*
Valley because of the bunch of
grapes the Israelites cut off
there.)

                RSV
That place was called the Valley
of Eshcol,*h* because of the cluster
which the men of Israel cut down
from there.

*j*ESHCOL: *This name in Hebrew means
"bunch of grapes."*

*h*That is *Cluster*

Eshcol Valley: in some languages it will be necessary to combine
this verse with verse 23. In any case a footnote will be needed to
tell the reader about the relation between "Eshcol" and "bunch of
grapes."

13.25   TEV
    After exploring the land for
forty days, the spies returned

                RSV
    At the end of forty days they
returned from spying out the land.

exploring: the same Hebrew verb is used as in verse 17, and
"explore" is probably closer to the correct meaning than "spy."

13.26   TEV
to Moses, Aaron, and the whole
community of Israel at Kadesh in
the wilderness of Paran. They
reported what they had seen and
showed them the fruit they had
brought.

                RSV
And they came to Moses and Aaron
and to all the congregation of
the people of Israel in the
wilderness of Paran, at Kadesh;
they brought back word to them
and to all the congregation,
and showed them the fruit of the
land.

community: the Hebrew word means "assembly," "gathering," and
refers to all the Israelites.
Kadesh: also known as Kadesh-Barnea, it is located in the Negev
near the border with Egypt.
wilderness of Paran: the area near Kadesh.
reported: literally "brought back word" (RSV), that is, "told
them."

[261]

13.27 TEV	RSV
They told Moses, "We explored the land and found it to be rich and fertile; and here is some of its fruit.	And they told him, "We came to the land to which you sent us; it flows with milk and honey, and this is its fruit.

the land: literally "the land to which you sent us" (RSV).
rich and fertile: literally "it flows with milk and honey" (RSV).
But this is a figurative expression which means "the land is good and
we can have many cattle that will give much milk, and there are many
flowers from which bees can make honey." It is probably better to use
some summary expression and not try to translate the figure literally,
since it will usually be misunderstood.
here is: that is, they showed Moses the fruit they had brought
back—grapes, pomegranates, and figs.

13.28 TEV	RSV
But the people who live there are powerful, and their cities are very large and well fortified. Even worse, we saw the descendants of the giants there.	Yet the people who dwell in the land are strong, and the cities are fortified and very large; and besides, we saw the descendants of Anak there.

powerful: "strong" (RSV). This probably refers to the strength
of their army rather than to individual physical strength.
well fortified: see verse 19.
descendants of the giants: literally "descendants of Anak" (see
verse 22).

13.29 TEV	RSV
Amalekites live in the southern part of the land; Hittites, Jebusites, and Amorites live in the hill country; and Canaanites live by the Mediterranean Sea and along the Jordan River."	The Amalekites dwell in the land of the Negeb; the Hittites, the Jebusites, and the Amorites dwell in the hill country; and the Canaanites dwell by the sea, and along the Jordan."

Amalekites: these are tribes of people considered to be the
original inhabitants of various sections of the land of Canaan.

13.30 TEV	RSV
Caleb silenced the people who were complaining against^k Moses, and said, "We should attack now and take the land; we are strong enough to conquer it."	But Caleb quieted the people before Moses, and said, "Let us go up at once, and occupy it; for we are well able to overcome it."

^{k}complaining against; or gathered
around.

silenced: "hushed," "caused to stop talking," "made be still."

complaining against: the Hebrew has one word, "toward," "against," which probably is intended to convey the meaning "opposed to," and the TEV text has extended the sense to complaining against. Others take the word in a more neutral sense, as in the TEV note, gathered around.

attack: the Hebrew uses an intensive form "go up" (RSV), and this has the sense of "make war," attack.

take: the Hebrew verb means "take possession of," "drive out someone else and take possession of."

conquer it: the Hebrew uses an intensive form, "be victorious," conquer.

13.31   TEV   RSV

But the men who had gone with Caleb said, "No, we are not strong enough to attack them; the people there are more powerful than we are."

Then the men who had gone up with him said, "We are not able to go up against the people; for they are stronger than we."

not strong enough: literally "not able" (RSV).
attack: the same Hebrew verb as in verse 30.
more powerful: the same Hebrew verb as in verse 28.

13.32   TEV   RSV

So they spread a false report among the Israelites about the land they had explored. They said, "That land doesn't even produce enough to feed the people who live there. Everyone we saw was very tall,

So they brought to the people of Israel an evil report of the land which they had spied out, saying, "The land, through which we have gone to spy it out, is a land that devours its inhabitants; and all the people that we saw in it are men of great stature.

a false report: the Hebrew word means "a false statement," that is, "they told lies."

doesn't even produce enough to feed: literally "eats," "devours" (RSV), but the sense is "It is a poor land, and since there is not enough to eat, the people are all dying, just as if the land itself were eating them up."

13.33   TEV   RSV

and we even saw giants there, the descendants of Anak. We felt as small as grasshoppers, and that is how we must have looked to them."

And there we saw the Nephilim (the sons of Anak, who come from the Nephilim); and we seemed to ourselves like grasshoppers, and so we seemed to them."

giants: the Hebrew refers to a race of giants. For most readers
the Hebrew word "Nephilim" (RSV) will have no meaning, and it is much
better to translate the word as giants.

descendants of Anak: see verse 22.

We felt: literally "We were in our eyes," that is, "We considered
ourselves to be," "We thought of ourselves as."

grasshoppers: the Hebrew word refers to a type of locust.

and that is how we must have looked to them: literally "and so
we were in their eyes," that is, "that is how they considered us,"
"that is what they saw when they looked at us." But this is only the
view of the spies as to what they assumed the inhabitants of Canaan
thought of them.

C H A P T E R   14

SECTION HEADING

The People Complain (14.1-10): "The People Are Afraid," "The
People Want to Return to Egypt."

14.1   TEV   RSV
    All night long the people   Then all the congregation
cried out in distress.   raised a loud cry; and the people
                                       wept that night.

    cried out in distress: the Hebrew is a bit complicated, "they
lifted up...and gave their voices and cried," but it is clear that
this is a Hebrew way of speaking of the intensity of the people's
crying. One might translate "wept and wailed," "cried bitterly."

14.2   TEV   RSV
They complained against Moses   And all the people of Israel
and Aaron, and said, "It would   murmured against Moses and
have been better to die in Egypt   Aaron; the whole congregation
or even here in the wilderness!   said to them, "Would that we
                                       had died in the land of Egypt!
                                       Or would that we had died in
                                       this wilderness!

    complained against: the Hebrew verb is sometimes translated
"murmur" (see RSV), but it refers to what might be called "grumbling,"
that is, the kind of talking which accuses someone else of being responsible for these unfortunate circumstances.

    It would have been better: literally "We wish that," but with the
sense that they would have preferred to die in Egypt rather than endure
what is now going to happen to them. They believe they will be killed
by the giants in the land of Canaan.

or even here: literally "or we wish that we would die here."

14.3 TEV	RSV
Why is the LORD taking us into that land? We will be killed in battle, and our wives and children will be captured. Wouldn't it be better to go back to Egypt?"	Why does the LORD bring us into this land, to fall by the sword? Our wives and our little ones will become a prey; would it not be better for us to go back to Egypt?"

Why: if the question form presents difficulties, one might translate "The reason the LORD is taking us to that land is that he wants to kill us...."

be killed in battle: literally "to fall by the sword" (RSV), that is, "to be killed by the sword," but that is a way of speaking of what happened during a war.

children: the Hebrew uses a word which could refer to the weak and helpless. But it is, of course, primarily the children that are intended, although the Hebrew word could include feeble or sick adults.

be captured: the Hebrew word means something like "war booty," but here, of course, it refers to the possibility that wives and children will be carried away captives as part of the spoils of war.

Wouldn't it be: if the rhetorical question (expecting the answer, "Yes, it would") is difficult, one may shift to a statement, "It would be much better if we went back to Egypt."

14.4 TEV	RSV
So they said to one another, "Let's choose a leader and go back to Egypt!"	And they said to one another, "Let us choose a captain, and go back to Egypt."

leader: the Hebrew word means "head," that is, "someone to guide and direct us."

14.5 TEV	RSV
Then Moses and Aaron bowed to the ground in front of all the people.	Then Moses and Aaron fell on their faces before all the assembly of the congregation of the people of Israel.

bowed to the ground: literally "fell on their faces" (RSV), but a literal translation might mean that they stumbled and hurt themselves. The figure means "bowed down with their faces toward the ground," which is a sign of worship, prayer, submission. The translator must be careful to show that they are prostrate on the ground, not bowing from the waist.

14.6	TEV	RSV

TEV: And Joshua son of Nun and Caleb son of Jephunneh, two of the spies, tore their clothes in sorrow

RSV: And Joshua the son of Nun and Caleb the son of Jephunneh, who were among those who had spied out the land, rent their clothes,

tore their clothes in sorrow: the tearing of one's clothes was a symbol of great inner feeling, of sorrow (as here) or of repentance. People tore their clothes to show that they were sorrowful.

14.7	TEV	RSV

TEV: and said to the people, "The land we explored is an excellent land.

RSV: and said to all the congregation of the people of Israel, "The land, which we passed through to spy it out, is an exceedingly good land.

explored: literally "passed through to explore it" (see RSV). See 13.17.

excellent: the Hebrew uses repetition to make the intensive "very, very good."

14.8	TEV	RSV

TEV: If the LORD is pleased with us, he will take us there and give us that rich and fertile land.

RSV: If the LORD delights in us, he will bring us into this land and give it to us, a land which flows with milk and honey.

is pleased with us: but the assumed meaning underlying the form is "If we do what pleases the LORD," and one may translate in that way. rich and fertile: see 13.27.

14.9	TEV	RSV

TEV: Do not rebel against the LORD and don't be afraid of the people who live there. We will conquer them easily. The LORD is with us and has defeated the gods who protected them; so don't be afraid."

RSV: Only, do not rebel against the LORD; and do not fear the people of the land, for they are bread for us; their protection is removed from them, and the LORD is with us; do not fear them."

rebel against: "turn your backs on," "refuse to obey," "reject as your God."

people who live there: literally "people of the land" (RSV).

We will conquer them easily: literally "they are our bread" (see RSV), but this is a figure, "We will eat them up (in the sense of destroy, overthrow) as easily as one eats up bread." This figure will not normally be understood in a literal translation, and it is usually

better to express the meaning, "It will be child's play to win the victory over them," "We will overthrow them with no difficulty at all."
    is with us: that is, "will protect us and take care of us."
    has defeated the gods who protected them: literally "their shade has left them," but this is a Hebrew figure that understands "shade" to mean "protection," and particularly the protection given by the gods. When this "protection" is no longer there, the meaning is that the gods themselves have been defeated. A literal translation will not be understood, and the translator must provide this information for his readers.

14.10	TEV	RSV
	The whole community was threatening to stone them to death, but suddenly the people saw the dazzling light of the LORD's presence appear over the Tent.	But all the congregation said to stone them with stones. Then the glory of the LORD appeared at the tent of meeting to all the people of Israel.

threatening: literally "saying," that is, "saying to one another and making plans."
    stone them to death: literally "stone them with stones" (RSV), but with the meaning, "put them to death by throwing stones on them."
    suddenly: literally "and," but the Hebrew "and" is used for all kinds of connections, and here the context makes it clear that this is a sudden intervention from God. In fact, it would be possible to begin the new section with this part of verse 10 rather than at the beginning of verse 11.
    the dazzling light of the LORD's presence: literally "the heaviness (glory) of the LORD" (see Exo 33.18).

SECTION HEADING

    Moses Prays for the People (14.11-25): "Moses Asks God to Forgive the People."

14.11	TEV	RSV
	The LORD said to Moses, "How much longer will these people reject me? How much longer will they refuse to trust in me, even though I have performed so many miracles among them?	And the LORD said to Moses, "How long will this people despise me? And how long will they not believe in me, in spite of all the signs which I have wrought among them?

reject me: the Hebrew word means reject, "disdain," "despise" (RSV), "treat with disrespect."
    refuse to trust in me: literally "will not trust me." The Hebrew has the sense "will not accept me as someone who can be trusted."
    miracles: the Hebrew word "signs" (RSV) refers to the miracles God does which show his greatness and power, for example, the miracles which God worked in Egypt.

[267]

14.12   TEV
I will send an epidemic and destroy them, but I will make you
the father of a nation that is
larger and more powerful than
they are!"

               RSV
I will strike them with the
pestilence and disinherit them,
and I will make of you a nation
greater and mightier than they."

     epidemic: that is, "a terrible disease." The Hebrew word refers
to a plague, particularly the bubonic plague.
     destroy them: the Hebrew word means "disinherit" (RSV), "take
property from." It is frequently used in the sense of "drive someone
from his land," but here TEV understands the meaning to be "make them
no longer my people," that is, destroy them.

14.13   TEV
     But Moses said to the LORD,
"You brought these people out of
Egypt by your power. When the
Egyptians hear what you have done
to your people,

               RSV
     But Moses said to the LORD,
"Then the Egyptians will hear
of it, for thou didst bring up
this people in thy might from
among them,

     You brought: reversing the order of the elements in Hebrew makes
the logical connections with verse 14 clearer in English, and this may
be true for other languages.
     hear what you have done to your people: literally "hear (of it)"
(RSV), but the context makes clear that what the Egyptians will hear
is that God has destroyed his people (see verse 12).

14.14   TEV
they will tell it to the people
who live in this land. These
people have already heard that
you, LORD, are with us, that you
appear in plain sight when your
cloud stops over us, and that you
go before us in a pillar of cloud
by day and a pillar of fire by
night.

               RSV
and they will tell the inhabitants of this land. They have heard
that thou, O LORD, are in the
midst of this people; for thou,
O LORD, art seen face to face,
and thy cloud stands over them
and thou goest before them, in
a pillar of cloud by day and in
a pillar of fire by night.

     people who live in this land: the meaning is not perfectly clear
in Hebrew, but this seems to refer to the people of the land of Canaan.
     with us: literally "in the midst of this people" (RSV), but the
"people" now referred to are the people of Israel. The point is not
that God is in the center, but that God guides and helps his people.
     in plain sight: literally "eye to eye," but this does not mean
that God is seen face to face (see RSV). See Exodus 33.20,23. It means,
rather, that the form in which God appears (here, the cloud) is plainly
visible.

14.15 TEV	RSV
Now if you kill all your people, the nations who have heard of your fame will say	Now if thou dost kill this people as one man, then the nations who have heard thy fame will say,

all your people: literally "this people as one man" (RSV), that is, "the people of Israel will all die as completely as if one man were put to death."

14.16 TEV	RSV
that you killed your people in the wilderness because you were not able to bring them into the land you promised to give them.	'Because the LORD was not able to bring this people into the land which he swore to give to them, therefore he has slain them in the wilderness.'

you killed: the Hebrew uses third person, "the LORD" (RSV), but since the LORD is being addressed, English requires second person.

promised: literally "took an oath," "swore" (RSV), "vowed," but one may translate "solemnly promised," "promised by making a vow."

14.17 TEV	RSV
So now, LORD, I pray, show us your power and do what you promised when you said,	And now, I pray thee, let the power of the LORD be great as thou hast promised, saying,

LORD: TEV has used the second person form instead of the third person, to meet the requirements of English structure.

promised: the Hebrew word means "said," but it carries essentially the same meaning as "say firmly," "promise."

14.18 TEV	RSV
'I, the LORD, am not easily angered, and I show great love and faithfulness and forgive sin and rebellion. Yet I will not fail to punish children and grandchildren to the third and fourth generation for the sins of their parents.'	'The LORD is slow to anger, and abounding in steadfast love, forgiving iniquity and transgression, but he will by no means clear the guilty, visiting the iniquity of fathers upon children, upon the third and upon the fourth generation.'

I, the LORD: literally "The LORD" (RSV), but the first person is required in English structure.

not easily angered: see Exodus 34.6.

show great love and faithfulness: see Exodus 34.6-7.

14.19 TEV	RSV
And now, LORD, according to the greatness of your unchanging	Pardon the iniquity of this people, I pray thee, according

love, forgive, I pray, the sin
of these people, just as you
have forgiven them ever since
they left Egypt."

to the greatness of thy steadfast love, and according as
thou hast forgiven this people,
from Egypt even until now."

according to: the idea is clear: "just as your love is great, so
let your forgiveness be great," "because you love very much, forgive
very much."

unchanging love: see Exodus 20.6; 34.6.

forgive: two Hebrew words are used, but both have the sense of
"pardon," forgive, and no clear distinction in meaning can be drawn
between them.

14.20   TEV   RSV
    The LORD answered, "I will   Then the LORD said, "I have
forgive them, as you have asked.   pardoned, according to your word;

I will forgive: although the Hebrew verb may be translated in the
past, "I have forgiven," the reference is clearly not to some past
time but to the present or immediate future. The form of the Hebrew
verb emphasizes the completeness of the forgiveness rather than past
tense.

14.21   TEV   RSV
But I promise that as surely as   but truly, as I live, and as
I live and as surely as my pres-   all the earth shall be filled
ence fills the earth,   with the glory of the LORD,

as surely as: this is a form of oath-taking that may be difficult
to reproduce in many languages. The point of the structure is as follows: "just as it is certain that I am alive and just as it is certain
that my glory is everywhere, so you can be absolutely certain that
I will...."

my presence: literally "my heaviness (my glory)," but this is also
a way of speaking of God's presence; God is everywhere.

14.22   TEV   RSV
none of these people will live   none of the men who have seen
to enter that land. They have   my glory and my signs which
seen the dazzling light of my   I wrought in Egypt and in the
presence and the miracles that   wilderness, and yet have put me
I performed in Egypt and in the   to the proof these ten times
wilderness, but they have tried   and have not hearkened to my
my patience over and over again   voice,
and have refused to obey me.

none of these people: the verse gives the content of the promise
that is introduced in verse 21.

live to enter that land: in Hebrew this does not come until verse

23 ("will not see the land," "will not go into it"), but English structure does not readily accept such long sentences as the Hebrew uses. It will be better in many languages to break the thought into shorter sentences, as the TEV has done.

tried my patience: literally "put me to the test," but here the sense will be "have tested me to see how far they could go with me," "almost went so far that I was ready to destroy them." See Exodus 17.1-7; Numbers 20.1-13.

over and over again: literally "these ten times" (RSV), but this is a general expression for a large number of times.

have refused to obey me: literally "did not listen to my voice" (see RSV), but this is a way of speaking of what God commands and of the people's refusal to obey him.

14.23 TEV	RSV
They will never enter the land which I promised to their ancestors. None of those who have rejected me will ever enter it.	shall see the land which I swore to give to their fathers; and none of those who despised me shall see it.

never enter: literally "never see" (see RSV), but "see" does not mean "see from a distance" (as, for example, Moses did), but means "enter into and see."

I promised: "I made a solemn promise," "I took an oath."

ancestors: literally "fathers" (RSV), but the reference is to people of long ago, Abraham, Isaac, and Jacob, that is, to their ancestors.

rejected: the Hebrew word is the same as that used in verse 11.

14.24 TEV	RSV
But because my servant Caleb has a different attitude and has remained loyal to me, I will bring him into the land which he explored, and his descendants will possess the land	But my servant Caleb, because he has a different spirit and has followed me fully, I will bring into the land into which he went, and his descendants shall possess it.

my servant: the Hebrew word is used frequently in the Old Testament of those who "serve" God, that is, those who obey God and do what God wants them to do.

has a different attitude: literally "a different spirit is with him" (see RSV), but the Hebrew word "spirit" is frequently used in the sense of "temper," "mind," "disposition," "way of looking at things."

remained loyal to me: literally "followed after me" (see RSV), but this is a figure which means "remain loyal," "be fully committed to me," "belong completely to me."

possess: the Hebrew verb is the same one used in verse 12. Here it is used with the meaning "take possession," "make one's own," although the sense of driving others out is in the background.

[271]

14.25   TEV   RSV
in whose valleys the Amalekites   Now, since the Amalekites and
and Canaanites now live. Turn   the Canaanites dwell in the
back tomorrow and go into the   valleys, turn tomorrow and set
wilderness in the direction of   out for the wilderness by the
the Gulf of Aqaba."   way to the Red Sea."

     valleys: the people live in the valleys, which are more fertile
than the hills around them.
     the Amalekites and the Canaanites: see verse 29.
     Turn back: "turn around and start back."
     Gulf of Aqaba: literally "the Sea of Reeds" or "the Red Sea"
(RSV), but the Hebrew is applied both to the Sea which the Israelites
crossed at the Exodus and to the Gulf of Aqaba east of the Sinai Peninsula. See the map in TEV, "Egypt and Sinai." The people are commanded
to turn back south toward Eziongeber on the Gulf of Aqaba.

                    C H A P T E R   20

SECTION HEADING

     Events at Kadesh (20.1-13): "Moses Strikes the Rock to Provide
Water for the People." See also Exodus 17.1-7.

20.1   TEV   RSV
     In the first month the whole   And the people of Israel,
community of Israel came to the   the whole congregation, came into
wilderness of Zin and camped at   the wilderness of Zin in the first
Kadesh. There Miriam died and was   month, and the people stayed in
buried.   Kadesh; and Miriam died there,
                                         and was buried there.

     the first month: there is no information as to the year, but these
events must have occurred near the end of the forty years of wilderness
wandering.
     wilderness of Zin: see 13.21.
     Kadesh: see 13.26.
     Miriam: the sister of Moses and Aaron.

20.2   TEV   RSV
     There was no water where they   Now there was no water for
camped, so the people gathered   the congregation; and they as-
around Moses and Aaron   sembled themselves together
                                         against Moses and against Aaron.

     no water where they camped: literally "no water for the assembly"

(see RSV), but it is clearer to the reader to indicate that there was
no water available where they were.

gathered around: "assembled where Moses and Aaron were."

20.3	TEV	RSV
	and complained: "It would have been better if we had died in front of the LORD's Tent along with our fellow Israelites.	And the people contended with Moses, and said, "Would that we had died when our brethren died before the LORD!

complained: the Hebrew verb is one used for stating a case in a
law court or for quarreling.

It would have been better: the Hebrew expresses a wish that is
unfilled, "We wish that we had...."

in front of the LORD's Tent: literally "before the LORD" (RSV),
but this expression is used to speak of being present at a holy place,
and here the reference is to the Tent of the LORD's Presence, referred
to in 16.16-34.

our fellow Israelites: literally "our brothers" (see RSV), but
the term is used in Hebrew in a general, broad way of one who belongs
to the same community. The people referred to are those killed in
chapter 16. In a series of selections in which chapter 16 is not
included, it may be necessary to translate "along with Korah and his
followers," or the information could be included in a footnote.

20.4	TEV	RSV
	Why have you brought us out into this wilderness? Just so that we can die here with our animals?	Why have you brought the assembly of the LORD into this wilderness, that we should die here, both we and our cattle?

Why...?: this is a rhetorical question, and one might translate
"You brought us out here...to kill us."

us: literally "the assembly of the LORD" (RSV), but in English
it is not normal to refer to oneself in the third person in this way.
If it is felt necessary to retain the words, one might translate "Why
have you brought us out...? We are the assembly of the LORD's people."

20.5	TEV	RSV
	Why did you bring us out of Egypt into this miserable place where nothing will grow? There's no grain, no figs, no grapes, no pomegranates. There is not even any water to drink!"	And why have you made us come up out of Egypt, to bring us to this evil place? It is no place for grain, or figs, or vines, or pomegranates; and there is no water to drink."

Why: this is a rhetorical question that could be translated "You
brought us...."

this miserable place: literally "this bad place" (see RSV), but the Hebrew word is used of many kinds of badness, not just evil in a moral sense. The place is "bad" because nothing will grow there.

20.6	TEV	RSV
	Moses and Aaron moved away from the people and stood at the entrance of the Tent. They bowed down with their faces to the ground, and the dazzling light of the LORD's presence appeared to them.	Then Moses and Aaron went from the presence of the assembly to the door of the tent of meeting, and fell on their faces. And the glory of the LORD appeared to them,

the Tent: the Tent of the LORD's Presence, which was thought of as the place for meeting the LORD.

bowed down...ground: literally "fell on their faces" (RSV), but this refers to a deliberate act of worship and not an accidental fall (see 14.5).

the dazzling light of the LORD's presence: literally "the heaviness (the glory) of the LORD."

20.7-8	TEV	RSV
	The LORD said to Moses, 8 "Take the stick that is in front of the Covenant Box, and then you and Aaron assemble the whole community. There in front of them all speak to that rock over there, and water will gush out of it. In this way you will bring water out of the rock for the people, for them and their animals to drink."	and the LORD said to Moses, 8 "Take the rod, and assemble the congregation, you and Aaron your brother, and tell the rock before their eyes to yield its water; so you shall bring water out of the rock for them; so you shall give drink to the congregation and their cattle."

the stick that is in front of the Covenant Box: literally "the walking stick" (see RSV), but the reader needs to know that it is the one that had been placed in front of the Covenant Box (see 17.10).

in front of them all: literally "before their eyes" (RSV), in the sense, "where all of them can see you."

speak to: the verb is plural; both Moses and Aaron are asked to speak to the rock and tell it to bring forth water. There is no command to strike the rock with the stick, and one may assume that the stick was to be held by Moses.

that rock over there: literally "the rock" (RSV), but it is clear in the Hebrew that a specific rock is thought of. It is possible that the Hebrew intends to say "the rock in front of the people," but this seems less likely than that rock.

water will gush out of it: literally "it will give its water," but the form will need to be one that is normal in the receptor language.

you: in the last part of the verse the singular is used, referring to Moses.

bring water out: "cause water to go out."
animals: the Hebrew uses a general term that applies to all kinds
of domestic animals such as sheep, cows, donkeys.

20.9 TEV	RSV
Moses went and got the stick, as the LORD had commanded.	And Moses took the rod from before the LORD, as he commanded him.

went and got: literally "took the stick from before the LORD" (see
verse 8).

20.10 TEV	RSV
He and Aaron assembled the whole community in front of the rock, and Moses said, "Listen, you rebels! Do we have to get water out of this rock for you?"	And Moses and Aaron gathered the assembly together before the rock, and he said to them, "Hear now, you rebels; shall we bring forth water for you out of this rock?"

Moses: literally "he" (RSV), but it is clear that the reference
is to Moses.
rebels: "obstinate people," "disobedient people."
Do we have to get: literally "shall we" (RSV), but it is clear
that the words are used in a sarcastic way, and the translator will
need to find a way to express the sarcasm. If the question presents
a problem, perhaps one could translate "You are so disobedient to God
that you force us to get water from this rock."

20.11 TEV	RSV
Then Moses raised the stick and struck the rock twice with it, and a great stream of water gushed out, and all the people and animals drank.	And Moses lifted up his hand and struck the rock with his rod twice; and water came forth abundantly, and the congregation drank, and their cattle.

raised the stick: literally "raised his hand" (see RSV), but in
the context it is clear that the hand held the stick.
a great stream of water: literally "much water, a great amount
of water."

20.12 TEV	RSV
But the LORD reprimanded Moses and Aaron. He said, "Because you did not have enough faith to acknowledge my holy power before the people of Israel, you will not lead them	And the LORD said to Moses and Aaron, "Because you did not believe in me, to sanctify me in the eyes of the people of Israel, therefore you shall not bring this assembly into the

into the land that I promised   land which I have given them."
to give them."

reprimanded: literally "said" (RSV), but the context makes clear that what the LORD says is a rebuke, and in English it is normal style to include this element in the verb of saying.

Because: this part of the verse is difficult to translate because it is not clear what Moses did or failed to do that showed he did not have faith. Is it that he struck the rock instead of speaking to it? Is it that anger or doubt are involved in the expressions in verse 10? It is not possible to decide, particularly since other explanations are given in Psalms 106.32-33 and Deuteronomy 1.37; 3.26; 4.21. This means that care must be taken to translate in such a way that possibilities are not eliminated by the form of the translation.

you did not have enough faith: the "you" is plural. The verb has the meaning "believe in me" (RSV), "put your trust in me."

acknowledge my holy power before the people: literally "make me holy in the eyes of the sons of Israel" (see RSV), but "to make God holy" must have the sense "act in such a way that the people recognize that God is holy." The reference is not clearly identified, but it must be to something that Moses did or failed to do which made it difficult for the people to see the holy power of God. The word holy has the sense of "set apart," "different from the ordinary things of life."

lead: literally "cause to go in," that is, be the one who brings the people into the land.

20.13	TEV	RSV
	This happened at Meribah,^O where the people of Israel complained against the LORD and where he showed them that he is holy.	These are the waters of Meribah,^l where the people of Israel contended with the LORD, and he showed himself holy among them.

^OMERIBAH: *This name in Hebrew means "complaining."*

^lThat is *Contention*

This happened at Meribah: literally "These are the waters of Meribah" (RSV), but the sense is 'Moses brought forth the water at Meribah." A note will be needed to explain the play on words. The name Meribah is from the same root as the verbs in verse 3, and in this verse, complained and the form of the note should fit the word chosen in translation, "quarreling," "complaining," "striving," "contending."

showed them that he is holy: the same word is used as in verse 12.

C H A P T E R   21

SECTION HEADING

The Snake Made of Bronze (21.4-9): 'Moses Sets Up a Metal Snake," "The People Are Bitten by Poisonous Snakes."

21.4 TEV	RSV
The Israelites left Mount Hor by the road that leads to the Gulf of Aqaba, in order to go around the territory of Edom. But on the way the people lost their patience	From Mount Hor they set out by the way to the Red Sea, to go around the land of Edom; and the people became impatient on the way.

Mount Hor: this is the next stop after Kadesh, and it is described as being at the border of the territory of Edom (20.22-23), south and east of the Dead Sea.

the road that leads to the Gulf of Aqaba: literally "the road of (that leads to) the Red Sea." It is clear that the term "Red Sea" does not here refer to the body of water crossed at the Exodus from Egypt, but to the nearest body of water which bore the name, known today as the Gulf of Aqaba. It was the road from Canaan to Eziongeber.

Edom: see 20.14-20 for the refusal of the King of Edom to let the people of Israel pass through his territory.

lost their patience: the Hebrew uses a figurative expression that might be translated "their tempers became short," that is, "they became angry easily."

21.5 TEV	RSV
and spoke against God and Moses. They complained, "Why did you bring us out of Egypt to die in this desert, where there is no food or water? We can't stand any more of this miserable food!"	And the people spoke against God and against Moses, "Why have you brought us up out of Egypt to die in the wilderness? For there is no food and no water, and we loathe this worthless food."

spoke against: "criticized," "complained against."

complained: the Hebrew does not have a verb here, but English requires some verb to introduce the quotation, and complained carries on the content of spoke against.

Why: the rhetorical question may need to be transformed into a statement, "You brought us...to die. There is no food or water here."

We can't stand any more: "We detest," "We despise," "We are disgusted with."

this miserable food: the Hebrew word seems to mean "starvation ration," "terrible food," "worthless food" (RSV). The people are now tired of manna and quails. See Exodus 16.

21.6 TEV	RSV
Then the LORD sent poisonous snakes among the people, and many Israelites were bitten and died.	Then the LORD sent fiery serpents among the people, and they bit the people, so that many people of Israel died.

poisonous snakes: literally "fiery (burning) snakes" (see RSV),

[277]

but the sense seems to be that the bite of the snakes produced a burning sensation, and from the context it is clear that they are poisonous snakes.

were bitten and died: literally "they (the snakes) bit the people, and many died."

21.7	TEV	RSV
	The people came to Moses and said, "We sinned when we spoke against the LORD and against you. Now pray to the LORD to take these snakes away." So Moses prayed for the people.	And the people came to Moses, and said, "We have sinned, for we have spoken against the LORD and against you; pray to the LORD, that he take away the serpents from us." So Moses prayed for the people.

take...away: literally "cause to go away," "get rid of," "remove."

21.8	TEV	RSV
	Then the LORD told Moses to make a metal snake and put it on a pole, so that anyone who was bitten could look at it and be healed.	And the LORD said to Moses, "Make a fiery serpent, and set it on a pole; and every one who is bitten, when he sees it, shall live."

metal snake: the Hebrew uses a form of "burning" (see verse 6), but the context makes it clear that a metal snake is intended.

look at it and be healed: literally "shall see it and shall live," but "live" here means to be healed from the bite of the poisonous snake and live instead of die from its bite.

21.9	TEV	RSV
	So Moses made a bronze snake and put it on a pole. Anyone who had been bitten would look at the bronze snake and be healed.	So Moses made a bronze serpent, and set it on a pole; and if a serpent bit any man, he would look at the bronze serpent and live.

look at: the Hebrew verb, different from the verb in verse 8, means "gaze at," "look directly at."

be healed: the Hebrew verb is the same as that in verse 8.

CHAPTER   27

SECTION HEADING

Joshua Is Chosen as Successor to Moses (27.12-23): "The LORD Chooses Joshua as Moses' Successor," "Joshua Becomes the Leader of Israel."

27.12	TEV	RSV

The LORD said to Moses, "Go up the Abarim Mountains and look out over the land that I am giving to the Israelites.

The LORD said to Moses, "Go up into this mountain of Abarim, and see the land which I have given to the people of Israel.

the Abarim Mountains: a mountain range east of the Dead Sea and the Jordan River. Mount Nebo (Deut 34.1) is the main peak of the range. The Hebrew has "this mountain" (RSV), that is, "the mountain near at hand," "...that can be seen" from where the Israelites are camped.

I am giving: the Hebrew is the same as that translated I promised to give them in 20.12.

27.13	TEV	RSV

After you have seen it, you will die, as your brother Aaron did,

And when you have seen it, you also shall be gathered to your people, as your brother Aaron was gathered,

you will die: the Hebrew uses a figurative expression, "you will be gathered to your people" (see RSV), which means die, although it may be translated with an expression such as "go to the grave," "be buried."

your brother Aaron did: Aaron died on Mount Hor (see 20.22-29).

27.14	TEV	RSV

because both of you rebelled against my command in the wilderness of Zin. When the whole community complained against me at Meribah, you refused to acknowledge my holy power before them." (Meribah is the spring at Kadesh in the wilderness of Zin.)

because you rebelled against my word in the wilderness of Zin during the strife of the congregation, to sanctify me at the waters before their eyes." (These are the waters of Meribah of Kadesh in the wilderness of Zin.)

rebelled against my command: the Hebrew verb means "refuse to obey," "be disobedient" (see 20.12).

When the whole community complained against me: the Hebrew "the strife of the congregation" (RSV) is simply a brief way of referring to the complaining of the people (see 20.2-6), and the meaning needs to be made clear to the reader.

Meribah: see 20.13.

you refused to acknowledge: there is a bit of complication in the Hebrew, but it is essentially equivalent to what is in 20.12, and the translation here should follow what was done there.

27.15	TEV	RSV

Moses prayed,

Moses said to the LORD,

<u>prayed</u>: the Hebrew has "said" (RSV), but what follows is a prayer.

27.16	TEV	RSV
	"LORD God, source of all life, appoint, I pray, a man who can lead the people	"Let the LORD, the God of the spirits of all flesh, appoint a man over the congregation,

<u>God, source of all life</u>: literally "God of the spirits of all flesh" (RSV). But "all flesh" is a Hebrew way of speaking of all living things or of all mankind, and the Hebrew word for "spirits" refers to the breath, the symbol of life (see Gen 2.7). The reference is entirely to physical life and says nothing about "spiritual" life. The whole point is that God is the creator of all living beings. He is the source of all life.

<u>appoint</u>: the Hebrew word has the sense "find someone and name him (or, make him)" the leader.

<u>I pray</u>: these words are not explicitly in the Hebrew, but it is clear from the context that Moses is not giving a command to the LORD but praying to him.

<u>a man who can lead</u>: literally "a man over" (RSV), but this has the sense of "be in charge," <u>lead</u>.

27.17	TEV	RSV
	and can command them in battle, so that your community will not be like sheep without a shepherd."	who shall go out before them and come in before them, who shall lead them out and bring them in; that the congregation of the LORD may not be as sheep which have no shepherd."

<u>command them in battle</u>: literally "go out before them and come in before them, who shall lead them out and bring them in" (RSV). This Hebrew figure is sometimes used for leadership in ordinary affairs, but the context makes it clear that the primary focus is on leadership in war.

<u>like sheep without a shepherd</u>: the people without a leader can be easily attacked and destroyed, and if the comparison with sheep does not convey this idea, it may be necessary to drop the comparison and make a straightforward statement.

27.18	TEV	RSV
	The LORD said to Moses, "Take Joshua son of Nun, a capable man, and place your hands on his head.	And the LORD said to Moses, "Take Joshua the son of Nun, a man in whom is the spirit, and lay your hand upon him;

<u>capable man</u>: literally "a man with spirit in him" (see RSV). The Hebrew word for "spirit" is the same one used in verse 16, but here with reference to God-given ability or competence. The word is used

a number of times in the Old Testament to describe what we might call "natural ability," but which the Hebrew sees as a gift of God, just as surely as breath is a gift from him.

place your hands on his head: literally "lay your hand upon him" (RSV), but the verb is used in a technical sense, and "place hand(s) upon" has the meaning "consecrate," "set apart for some special use." If "lay hands upon" does not carry some of this technical meaning in the receptor language, it may be necessary to translate "put your hands upon him (or, upon his head) to show that he is set apart for this task," that is, to lead the people of Israel.

27.19   TEV   RSV
Have him stand in front of Elea-   cause him to stand before Eleazar the priest and the whole com-   zar the priest and all the con-
munity, and there before them all   gregation, and you shall com-
proclaim him as your successor.   mission him in their sight.

Eleazar: Aaron's successor as priest (see 20.25-27).
proclaim him as your successor: the Hebrew verb has the sense of "appoint," although it is not the same verb as in verse 15. One might translate "make him the leader of the people."

27.20   TEV   RSV
Give him some of your own author-   You shall invest him with some
ity, so that the whole community   of your authority, that all the
of Israel will obey him.   congregation of the people of
                                      Israel may obey.

authority: the Hebrew word is difficult to translate, but it refers to the power, splendor, majesty, and position that God had given to Moses as the leader of the people. Some of this special favor was to be given to Joshua.

27.21   TEV   RSV
He will depend on Eleazar the   And he shall stand before Elea-
priest, who will learn my will   zar the priest, who shall inquire
by using the Urim and Thummin.ᶠ   for him by the judgment of the
In this way Eleazar will direct   Urim before the LORD; at his word
Joshua and the whole community   they shall go out, and at his
of Israel in all their affairs."   word they shall come in, both he
                                      and all the people of Israel with
ᶠURIM AND THUMMIM: Two objects   him, the whole congregation."
used by the priest to determine
God's will; it is not known
precisely how they were used.

He will depend on: literally "He will stand before" (see RSV). The reference here is not to the rite of ordination but to the ongoing relationship between Joshua and Eleazar. The point is that although

God spoke directly to Moses, from this moment on he would speak to
Joshua through the priest. That is, from time to time Joshua will need
to come to the priest to find out what God wants him to do.

who will learn my will: literally "he will ask" (see RSV), but
the whole point is that Eleazar the priest will ask the LORD for the
answer to the question about what should be done. He will determine
what God wants done. This is expressed by the Hebrew "before the LORD"
(RSV).

by using the Urim and Thummim: literally "by the judgment of the
Urim" (RSV), but since the usual term contains both names, it seems
wise to use both in translation. The term "by the judgment of" has the
meaning "by the decision of." That is, the Urim and Thummim were used
to determine what God's decision was in answer to the questions stated.
As the footnote in TEV shows, the exact form of these objects and how
they were used is not known. What is known is that they were some type
of lots (perhaps dice, stones, bones, or discs) that were kept in a
pouch and thrown. The way the lots fell (whether in a certain order or
position, or with a certain side up) was used to answer yes or no to
the question posed to the divinity. The Hebrews believed that the way
the lots fell was not the result of chance but was guided by God himself. The translator will need to prepare a footnote to help his readers
understand what is involved here.

Eleazar will direct Joshua: the point being made is that the LORD
will direct the lots for Eleazar to read, Eleazar will direct Joshua,
and Joshua will direct the people. This is what is meant by the literal
"at his word they shall go out and at his word they shall come in, he
(Joshua) and all the people of Israel with him and the whole congregation" (see RSV).

27.22 TEV	RSV
Moses did as the LORD had command-ed him. He had Joshua stand before Eleazar the priest and the whole community.	And Moses did as the LORD com-manded him; he took Joshua and caused him to stand before Elea-zar the priest and the whole con-gregation,

had Joshua stand: literally "took Joshua and caused him to stand"
(RSV).

27.23 TEV	RSV
As the LORD had commanded, Moses put his hands on Joshua's head and proclaimed him as his suc-cessor.	and he laid his hands upon him, and commissioned him as the LORD directed through Moses.

Moses put his hands on Joshua's head: the Hebrew is essentially
the same as in verse 18, except that "hands" is in the plural here.
The Hebrew verb does not have a subject expressed, but in light of
verse 18 and the context, it is clear that it was Moses and not Eleazar
who put hands on Joshua's head.

DEUTERONOMY

THE NAME OF THE BOOK

The name "Deuteronomy" comes from the Greek translation and refers to "A Repetition of the Law," or more accurately to a "copy of the Law" (see 17.18). Since, however, the book is really a farewell address by Moses, it may be more appropriate to use a title which would suggest this; perhaps, "The Book of the Final Words of Moses."

INTRODUCTION

The book of Deuteronomy is organized as a series of addresses given by Moses to the people of Israel in the land of Moab, where they had stopped at the end of the long wilderness journey and were about to enter and occupy Canaan.

The great theme of the book is that God has saved and blessed his chosen people, whom he loves; so his people are to remember this, and love and obey him, so that they may have life and continued blessing. In the book Moses recounts many of the incidents that occurred in the period of wandering, but only some of Moses' admonitions to the people of Israel have been included in this set of selections.

CHAPTER 4

SECTION HEADING

Moses Urges Israel to Be Obedient (4.1-14): "Moses Tells the People to Obey God's Law."

4.1

TEV

Then Moses said to the people, "Obey all the laws that I am teaching you, and you will live and occupy the land which the

RSV

"And now, O Israel, give heed to the statutes and the ordinances which I teach you, and do them; that you may live, and go

[283]

LORD, the God of your ancestors, is giving you.	in and take possession of the land which the LORD, the God of your fathers, gives you.

Then Moses said to the people: these words are not in the Hebrew text. But since we are here dealing with long sections of discourse, it is necessary in English and in many other languages to make clear who the speaker is. This is particularly needed here after the lengthy summary of historical events in chapters 1—3.

Obey: the English word "obey" covers the meaning of two Hebrew words, "hear...and do" (see RSV).

all the laws: the Hebrew uses two words, often translated statutes" and "ordinances" (RSV), but no sharp distinction in meaning can be maintained. In many languages it will not make sense to try to find two words for laws. Often in Deuteronomy a single word may be used where the Hebrew may have two, three, or four words for laws.

I am teaching you: the Hebrew verb does not have the sense of "repeating to you so that you can memorize," but rather "instructing you," "telling you."

and you will live: note that the English structure Obey...and you will live is really a conditional idea, "If you obey...you will live." But the meaning is essentially the same, and the form chosen will depend on how such ideas are best expressed in the receptor language.

occupy: literally "go in and take possession of" (RSV).

4.2 TEV	RSV
Do not add anything to what I command you, and do not take anything away. Obey the commands of the LORD your God that I have given you.	You shall not add to the word which I command you, nor take from it; that you may keep the commandments of the LORD your God which I command you.

Do not add anything to: "Do not make any additional laws."

do not take anything away: "do not remove any of the laws from those that are to be obeyed." The law that God gave at Mount Sinai cannot be changed.

Obey: literally "to keep," but in English a command carries the meaning more clearly, and of course "keep" is used in the sense of "obey," "do what the law commands."

4.3 TEV	RSV
You yourselves saw what the LORD did at Mount Peor. He destroyed everyone who worshiped Baal there,	Your eyes have seen what the LORD did at Baal-peor; for the LORD your God destroyed from among you all the men who followed the Baal of Peor;

You yourselves saw: literally "Your eyes saw" (see RSV), but this is a Hebrew way of speaking of personal involvement.

Mount Peor: this refers to the story told in Numbers 25.1-5. Peor is a mountain in Moab, and the name "Baal-Peor" derives from that incident. For most readers it will be helpful to identify the location as a mountain.

everyone: the Hebrew has "every man...from among you" (see RSV), that is, every Israelite.

worshiped: literally "walked after," but this is a Hebrew figure ("go after," "follow") to indicate service to and worship of the god.

Baal: literally "the Baal of Peor," that is, the Baal who was worshiped at Peor. Baal (which means "Lord") was a Canaanite god responsible for the fertility of people, animals, and the land.

4.4	TEV	RSV
	but those of you who were faithful to the LORD your God are still alive today.	but you who held fast to the LORD your God are all alive this day.

were faithful to the LORD: literally "held on to," but the meaning is clearly "continued to worship," "remained faithful to."

4.5	TEV	RSV
	"I have taught you all the laws, as the LORD my God told me to do. Obey them in the land that you are about to invade and occupy.	Behold, I have taught you statutes and ordinances, as the LORD my God commanded me, that you should do them in the land which you are entering to take possession of it.

all the laws: see verse 1.
invade and occupy: literally "enter to take possession of" (see RSV).

4.6	TEV	RSV
	Obey them faithfully, and this will show the people of other nations how wise you are. When they hear of all these laws, they will say 'What wisdom and understanding this great nation has!'	Keep them and do them; for that will be your wisdom and your understanding in the sight of the peoples, who, when they hear all these statutes, will say, 'Surely this great nation is a wise and understanding people.'

Obey them faithfully: literally "Keep them and do them" (RSV), but in English this type of repetition of synonyms is less natural than the use of verb and adverb as in TEV. One might translate "Be faithful in keeping them."

this will show...how wise you are: the Hebrew construction is awkward in a literal translation, "this will be your wisdom and understanding in the eyes of the nations" (see RSV), and it is better to restructure into a more natural form in most languages. Note that TEV has used wise to cover the meaning of two Hebrew words, although both are translated in the last part of the verse.

4.7	TEV	RSV

"No other nation, no matter how great, has a god who is so near when they need him as the LORD our God is to us. He answers us whenever we call for help.

For what great nation is there that has a god so near to it as the LORD our God is to us, whenever we call upon him?

No other nation: the Hebrew uses a rhetorical question (see RSV) which assumes the answer, "No nation has a god so near." It is simpler in most languages to use a direct statement.

near: although the meaning of the word is "close at hand" in location, the primary focus is on the fact that God is able to help immediately when he is needed.

answers: the meaning is not just that God replies verbally, but that he comes to help and gives what is asked for.

4.8	TEV	RSV

No other nation, no matter how great, has laws so just as those that I have taught you today.

And what great nation is there, that has statutes and ordinances so righteous as all this law which I set before you this day?

No other nation: a rhetorical question (see RSV) has been changed into a statement.

just: "righteous," "fair," "nondiscriminatory."

I have taught: literally "I am giving before you" (see RSV); the sense is "instruct," "teach."

4.9	TEV	RSV

Be on your guard! Make certain that you do not forget, as long as you live, what you have seen with your own eyes. Tell your children and your grandchildren

"Only take heed, and keep your soul diligently, lest you forget the things which your eyes have seen, and lest they depart from your heart all the days of your life; make them known to your children and your children's children—

Be on your guard: the Hebrew may be translated literally "Above all be on guard to yourself and guard your life exceedingly," but this is a Hebrew figure for "Watch out," "Be careful," "Take care."

do not forget: this combines in English two expressions in Hebrew that mean the same thing, "so that you not forget" and "so that they not leave your heart" (see RSV). In some languages repetitions of this kind are possible, but they are not acceptable in many other languages.

as long as you live: this is what the expression "all the days of your life" (RSV) means.

4.10 TEV	RSV
about the day you stood in the presence of the LORD your God at Mount Sinai,^{x} when he said to me, 'Assemble the people. I want them to hear what I have to say, so that they will learn to obey me as long as they live and so that they will teach their children to do the same.'	how on the day that you stood before the LORD your God at Horeb, the LORD said to me, 'Gather the people to me, that I may let them hear my words, so that they may learn to fear me all the days that they live upon the earth, and that they may teach their children so.'

^{x}Sinai; *or* Horeb.

Mount Sinai: literally "Horeb," but the same place is intended, and in many languages it is confusing if the reader has to remember that "Sinai" and "Horeb" are the same. He is likely to think that because two names are used, two places are intended. It is wiser to use the most familiar term throughout the translation, as TEV has done.

obey: literally "fear" (RSV), but the Hebrew word does not here primarily mean "be afraid of"; rather it has the sense of "stand in awe of," "have respect for," and then by extension "worship," obey.

4.11 TEV	RSV
"Tell your children how you went and stood at the foot of the mountain which was covered with thick clouds of dark smoke and fire blazing up to the sky.	And you came near and stood at the foot of the mountain, while the mountain burned with fire to the heart of heaven, wrapped in darkness, cloud, and gloom.

Tell your children how: these words do not occur in the Hebrew. But it seems clear that this and the following verses are a continuation of the instruction to the children referred to in verse 10 and not merely a continuation of the historical summary in chapters 1—3.

covered with thick clouds of dark smoke: the Hebrew is compressed, "darkness, clouds, and gloom (darkness)" (see RSV), but the meaning is probably that the mountaintop is covered with clouds of dark smoke. In any case the translator should try to describe the scene in terms that will be meaningful to the reader.

fire blazing up to the sky: literally "the mountain was burning with fire up to the heart of heaven" (see RSV). If this is thought of as a volcanic eruption, it would be possible in many languages to speak of the mountain burning, but the description may mean that God appeared in the form of fire, without the assumption that the mountain itself was on fire. The expression "up to the heart of heaven" is certainly unusual, but it seems to mean "as high as the sky."

4.12 TEV	RSV
Tell them how the LORD spoke to you from the fire, how you heard him speaking but did not see him in any form at all.	Then the LORD spoke to you out of the midst of the fire; you heard the sound of words, but saw no form; there was only a voice.

Tell them how: this is not in the Hebrew (see verse 11).

heard him speaking: this expresses in English the meaning of the Hebrew "you heard the voice (sound) of words...only a voice (sound)."

did not see him in any form at all: literally "did not see a form" (see RSV), but what is being said is that the people did not see God, they only heard him. It is not being stated that they couldn't see anything; they would have seen, for example, the slope of the mountain. The Hebrew adds "except a voice" (RSV "there was only a voice"), which TEV omits, since the idea is included earlier in the verse.

4.13 TEV	RSV
He told you what you must do to keep the covenant he made with you—you must obey the Ten Commandments, which he wrote on two stone tablets.	And he declared to you his covenant, which he commanded you to perform, that is, the ten commandments;*b* and he wrote them upon two tables of stone.

*b*Heb *words*

He told you what you must do to keep the covenant he made with you: this expresses in straightforward English what the Hebrew means with "he declared to you and his covenant which he commanded you to do" (see RSV).

Ten Commandments: literally "ten words," but the Hebrew "word" is used for a statement, here a commandment.

two stone tablets: see Exodus 31.18; 34.1-4.

4.14 TEV	RSV
The LORD told me to teach you all the laws that you are to obey in the land that you are about to invade and occupy.	And the LORD commanded me at that time to teach you statutes and ordinances, that you might do them in the land which you are going over to possess.

told me: literally "commanded me at that time" (RSV).

all the laws: see 4.1.

that you are to obey: literally "that you should do them" (see RSV).

invade: literally "cross over," but the sense is "cross the Jordan River and enter."

SECTION HEADING

Warning against Idolatry (4.15-24): "Moses Warns the People not to Worship Idols."

4.15	TEV	RSV

TEV: "When the LORD spoke to you from the fire on Mount Sinai, you did not see any form. For your own good, then, make certain

RSV: "Therefore take good heed to yourselves. Since you saw no form on the day that the LORD spoke to you at Horeb out of the midst of the fire,

When the LORD...: TEV has rearranged the elements of the verse for a more logical connection in English.

For your own good, then, make certain: literally "guard exceedingly your soul (life)," with the sense "be very careful about yourselves" (see RSV), "take care for your own good to make certain." Since the warning refers to verse 16, TEV has placed the words at the end of verse 15. Note that RSV inserts "beware" in verse 16 to make the connection.

4.16	TEV	RSV

TEV: that you do not sin by making for yourselves an idol in any form at all—whether man or woman,

RSV: beware lest you act corruptly by making a graven image for yourselves, in the form of any figure, the likeness of male or female,

sin: the Hebrew word means "act in a destructive way," but the sense is "destroy your relationship with God," sin.

for yourselves: that is, "for you to worship."

an idol in any form at all: literally "an idol, a representation of any idol, an image." The meaning of this piling up of words can best be expressed in most languages by "any kind of idol at all," since the exact significance of each of the four Hebrew words cannot be determined with accuracy, and most languages will not have precise parallels to these four words.

man or woman: literally "male or female," but the focus in this verse is on idols in human form.

4.17	TEV	RSV

TEV: animal or bird,

RSV: the likeness of any beast that is on the earth, the likeness of any winged bird that flies in the air,

animal or bird: literally "the image of any animal which is on the earth, the image of any bird with wings which flies in the sky" (see RSV), but in English a literal translation would sound awkward and redundant. It is understood that animals are on earth and birds fly in the air (that is what the literal "sky" means here).

4.18	TEV	RSV

TEV: reptile or fish.

RSV: the likeness of anything that

creeps on the ground, the likeness
of any fish that is in the water
under the earth.

reptile: literally "the image of anything creeping on earth" (see
RSV). Although this will include snakes and other reptiles, it will
also include many kinds of small animals. See Genesis 1.24.
fish: literally "the image of any fish which is in the water under
the earth" (see RSV). But it may be assumed that fish live in water,
and the expression "water under the earth" is a Hebrew way of describing seas, lakes, and other bodies of water, all of which are thought
to be connected with the large body of water beneath the earth (see
Gen 1.9-10). It is not necessary to introduce all this information
into the translation, since this is simply the Hebrew way of speaking
of fish, and that is all that is in focus.

4.19 TEV	RSV
Do not be tempted to worship and serve what you see in the sky— the sun, the moon, and the stars. The LORD your God has given these to all other peoples for them to worship.	And beware lest you lift up your eyes to heaven, and when you see the sun and the moon and the stars, all the host of heaven, you be drawn away and worship them and serve them, things which the LORD your God has allotted to all the peoples under the whole heaven.

Do not be tempted to worship and serve: this expresses in English
what is meant by the literal "so that you will not lift up your eyes
(look at)...and see...and be led astray and worship them and serve
them" (see RSV).
in the sky: the Hebrew uses the same word for "heaven" (RSV) and
"sky."
the stars: literally "the stars, all the army of the skies" (see
RSV), but the descriptive phrase is a poetic way of speaking of the
stars. In many languages, to speak of the stars as the army of the
skies would make little sense without an extensive explanation. The
entire focus at this point is on the stars, and so TEV has chosen not
to include the poetic description.
has given these: the Hebrew verb means "give a share to," "divide,"
"assign."
all other peoples: literally "all the peoples under the whole
heaven" (RSV), that is, all the people on earth. But English needs to
say "other people" in order to make clear that the Israelites are not
included.
for them to worship: these words are not in the Hebrew, but the
context makes clear that this is what is meant.

4.20 TEV	RSV
But you are the people he rescued	But the LORD has taken you, and

from Egypt, that blazing furnace.	brought you forth out of the
He brought you out to make you his	iron furnace, out of Egypt, to
own people, as you are today.	be a people of his own posses-
	sion, as at this day.

you are the people: this is the emphasis that the Hebrew text makes, "and you (emphatic) the LORD took."

rescued: this one English verb carries the meaning of the Hebrew "took...and brought out" (see RSV).

that blazing furnace: the literal "furnace of iron" (see RSV) does not mean a furnace made of iron but a furnace hot enough to smelt iron, that is, a very hot furnace or forge. Egypt was a place of testing and torment for the people of Israel, as severe as a hot fire that melts iron. If such a figure cannot be readily translated, one may translate the idea with something like "that place of terrible suffering."

his own people: literally "people of possession" (see RSV), that is, a people that belonged to God alone and that could not be taken from him. The figure is that of property which is owned. God "owns" his people just as a man owns property—they belong to him.

as you are today: literally "as this day" (see RSV), but the reference is to the fact that the rescue from Egypt made the Israelites God's people, and now, almost forty years later, they still belong to him.

4.21 TEV	RSV
Because of you the LORD your God	Furthermore the LORD was angry
was angry with me and solemnly	with me on your account, and he
declared that I would not cross	swore that I should not cross
the Jordan River to enter the	the Jordan, and that I should
fertile land which he is giving	not enter the good land which
you.	the LORD your God gives you for
	an inheritance.

Because of you: this refers to the incident at Meribah (see Num 20.12).

solemnly declared: literally "took an oath," "vowed," "swore" (RSV).

fertile land: literally "good land" (RSV), but it is probably the ability to grow good crops thad led to the description "good."

is giving you: literally "is giving you as a possession." The same word is used in verse 20 about God's people. Here it means that they will own the land God is giving them. In English this is obvious, and the use of "give as a possession" would sound awkward.

4.22 TEV	RSV
I will die in this land and never	For I must die in this land,
cross the river, but you are	I must not go over the Jordan;
about to go across and occupy	but you shall go over and take
that fertile land.	possession of that good land.

[291]

occupy that fertile land: "take possession of that good land" (see verse 21).

4.23   **TEV**   **RSV**

TEV	RSV
Be certain that you do not forget the covenant that the LORD your God made with you. Obey his command not to make yourselves any kind of idol,	Take heed to yourselves, lest you forget the covenant of the LORD your God, which he made with you, and make a graven image in the form of anything which the LORD your God has forbidden you.

Be certain: literally 'Watch yourself," that is, "Take care," "Watch your step."

Obey his command: these words are not specifically in the Hebrew, but this is what is meant by the literal "so that you do not forget... and make." The command is part of the covenant agreement and is expressed literally by "anything which the LORD your God has commanded you" (RSV "forbidden you").

any kind of idol: see verse 16. Two of the Hebrew words for idol are used here.

4.24   **TEV**   **RSV**

TEV	RSV
because the LORD your God is like a flaming fire; he tolerates no rivals.	For the LORD your God is a devouring fire, a jealous God.

like a flaming fire: literally "is a devouring fire" (RSV), but in many languages it is easier to express this figure of speech with a comparison. The Hebrew word "devouring," "eating," is often used to describe a fire that burns things up and destroys them.

tolerates no rivals: the Hebrew, often translated "a jealous God" (RSV), is difficult to translate. The word does not have the sense of "fearful of being replaced," which the English "jealous" might convey. Rather, the sense is "will not put up with any rivals," that is, "will not let Israel worship other gods."

C H A P T E R   6

SECTION HEADING

The Great Commandment (6.1-9): "The Commandment to Love God."

6.1   **TEV**   **RSV**

TEV	RSV
"These are all the laws that the LORD your God commanded me to	"Now this is the commandment, the statutes and the ordinances

teach you. Obey them in the land that you are about to enter and occupy.	which the LORD your God commanded me to teach you, that you may do them in the land to which you are going over, to possess it;

These: this refers back to chapter 5, and particularly to the Ten Commandments.

all the laws: see 4.1.

Obey them: literally "that you should do them" (see RSV), which has the sense of a command.

enter: literally "cross over to there," that is, "cross the Jordan River to enter."

6.2 TEV	RSV
As long as you live, you and your descendants are to honor the LORD your God and obey all his laws that I am giving you, so that you may live in that land a long time.	that you may fear the LORD your God, you and your son and your son's son, by keeping all his statutes and his commandments, which I command you, all the days of your life; and that your days may be prolonged.

As long as you live: literally "all the days of your life" (RSV). The order of elements in the verse has been rearranged in TEV.

you and your descendants: literally "you and your son and your son's son" (RSV), but the reference is clearly to all the descendants.

honor: literally "fear" (RSV), but not in the sense of "be afraid of"; rather, "stand in awe of," "worship," "serve," "have reverence for."

live in that land a long time: literally "extend your days" (see RSV), which of course means "live a long time." In light of 5.16 and other parallels, the reference is probably to long life in the promised land.

6.3 TEV	RSV
Listen to them, people of Israel, and obey them! Then all will go well with you, and you will become a mighty nation and live in that rich and fertile land, just as the LORD, the God of our ancestors, has promised.	Hear therefore, O Israel, and be careful to do them; that it may go well with you, and that you may multiply greatly, as the LORD, the God of your fathers, has promised you, in a land flowing with milk and honey.

become a mighty nation: literally "increase very much," that is, "have many children and become a great nation."

rich and fertile land: literally "a land flowing with milk and honey." See Exodus 3.8.

6.4   TEV   RSV
    "Israel, remember this! The   "Hear, O Israel: The LORD
LORD—and the LORD alone—is our   our God is one LORD;*e*
God.*f*

*f*The LORD...is our God; *or* The   *e*Or *the* LORD *our God, the* LORD
  LORD, our God, is the only God;   *is one*
  or The LORD our God is one.   Or *the* LORD *is our God, the* LORD
                                is one
                                Or *the* LORD *is our God, the* LORD
                                alone

    remember this: literally "Hear" (RSV), but the Hebrew word is used
as an emphatic introduction and means more than "listen."
    The LORD—and the LORD alone—is our God: literally "The LORD our
God LORD one (or, alone)," but there is considerable discussion about
what this means. The translations indicated in the TEV text and note
are all possible, but the emphasis certainly falls on the LORD's
uniqueness. There is no other God like the LORD (see Exo 15.11). The
LORD is the one and only God that Israel is to worship. Since the statement is practical and not merely theoretical, it would be helpful if
the translation could emphasize "the God we worship," our God, as TEV
has tried to do.

6.5   TEV   RSV
Love the LORD your God with all   and you shall love the LORD your
your heart, with all your soul,   God with all your heart, and with
and with all your strength.   all your soul, and with all your
                                    might.

    Love: the traditional translation, "you shall love" (RSV), should
be understood as a command and not just a statement about the future.
The verb is often difficult to translate. It is obvious that the model
from which a term can be chosen is not sexual love or friendship, but
family love, with a heavy emphasis on the idea of loyalty.
    with all your heart: in Hebrew thought, the heart is not primarily
the seat of the emotions but the seat of will. If we were to translate
accurately in English, we would probably have to translate "love the
LORD with your whole mind," that is to say, "love the LORD with all
your thoughts and your will."
    with all your soul: the word translated "soul" does not refer to
some hidden inner part of man. Rather it is the Hebrew word that is
used for "life," the life principle. The same word is used in Genesis
3.7 to speak of man as a living being. In many languages, as in English, a correct translation might be "love God with your whole life"
or "love God with your whole being."
    with all your strength: the Hebrew word is a general word for
"power," "might." The sense, of course, is that all one's energies are
to be devoted to loving God.

6.6   TEV   RSV

Never forget these commands that   And these words which I command
I am giving you today.   you this day shall be upon your
                                    heart;

Never forget: literally "shall be upon your heart" (RSV), but
"heart" has the sense of "mind" (see verse 5), and the meaning is
"continue to remember."

6.7   TEV   RSV

Teach them to your children. Re-   and you shall teach them dili-
peat them when you are at home   gently to your children, and
and when you are away, when you   shall talk of them when you sit
are resting and when you are   in your house, and when you walk
working.   by the way, and when you lie
                                    down, and when you rise.

Teach them: the Hebrew verb means "repeat," "say again and again,"
and has the sense of "teach," "cause to learn," "help memorize."
Repeat: the Hebrew has "talk of them" (RSV), which is a command
to discuss the commands.
when you are at home: this expresses in a more natural way what
is really meant by the literal "sit in your house."
when you are away: literally "when you walk in the path," but the
real meaning is to be seen in contrast with the preceding statement,
that is, "when you are traveling and away from home."
when you are resting: this is the general meaning of the literal
"when you are lying down."
when you are working: literally "when you get up," but the real
meaning is to be seen in the contrast with the previous line, "when you
get up and go to work."

6.8   TEV   RSV

Tie them on your arms and wear   And you shall bind them as a
them on your foreheads as a   sign upon your hand, and they
reminder.   shall be as frontlets between
                                    your eyes.

Tie them on your arms: the Hebrew word often translated "hand"
also means "forearm." The Hebrew has "as a sign" (RSV), that is, "something to remind you," and TEV has combined this with the next line.
This may have been intended as a literal admonition, but whether it
was or not, this was later taken literally and is the origin of phylacteries, small boxes which were tied to the forearm and forehead
and which contained scripture verses.
wear them on your foreheads as a reminder: literally "they shall
be as *totaphoth* between your eyes," but "between the eyes" is a Hebrew
way of speaking of the forehead. The meaning of the Hebrew *totaphoth*
is uncertain. It may have the specific sense, "phylacteries," or it
may have a more general meaning of "symbol," "sign," "reminder." TEV
has assumed this second sense.

[295]

6.9   TEV   RSV
Write them on the doorposts of   And you shall write them on the
your houses and on your gates.   doorposts of your house and on
                                     your gates.

    doorposts: the posts or sides of the door frames.
    gates: these would be the gates of the town and not of the individ-
ual house.

SECTION HEADING

    Warning against Disobedience (6.10-15): "Moses Warns the People
Not to Disobey the LORD."

6.10   TEV   RSV
    "Just as the LORD your God   "And when the LORD your God
promised your ancestors, Abraham,   brings you into the land which
Isaac, and Jacob, he will give you   he swore to your fathers, to
a land with large and prosperous   Abraham, to Isaac, and to Jacob,
cities which you did not build.   to give you, with great and
                                     goodly cities, which you did
                                     not build,

    Just as: TEV has reversed elements of the verse to make the con-
nection with what follows clearer.
    he will give you: literally "he will cause you to go in" "he will
bring you in."
    with large and prosperous cities: this is what is intended by the
Hebrew, "big and good cities." The promise is that when they arrive in
the land, they will find cities already built.

6.11   TEV   RSV
The houses will be full of good   and houses full of all good
things which you did not put in   things, which you did not fill,
them, and there will be wells that   and cisterns hewn out, which
you did not dig, and vineyards and   you did not hew, and vineyards
olive orchards that you did not   and olive trees, which you did
plant. When the LORD brings you   not plant, and when you eat and
into this land and you have all   are full,
you want to eat,

    good things: such as food, clothing, furniture.
    wells: literally "cisterns dug out," that is, holes dug in the
ground for collecting and storing rain water.
    When the LORD brings you into this land: these words are found in
the Hebrew in verse 10, but TEV transfers the words here to make it
clear that the eating occurs after the people enter the land of Canaan.
In some languages this will need to be stated.

6.12   TEV   RSV

TEV	RSV
make certain that you do not forget the LORD who rescued you from Egypt, where you were slaves.	then take heed lest you forget the LORD, who brought you out of the land of Egypt, out of the house of bondage.

make certain that you do not: literally "guard yourself so that you do not."

where you were slaves: literally "house of slaves," but this is a figurative and derogatory way of referring to Egypt ("slave quarters"), where the Israelites had been slaves.

6.13   TEV   RSV

TEV	RSV
Honor the LORD your God, worship only him, and make your promises in his name alone.	You shall fear the LORD your God; you shall serve him, and swear by his name.

Honor: literally "fear" (RSV).

make your promises: literally "take a vow," "swear" (RSV), "make a solemn promise."

6.14   TEV   RSV

TEV	RSV
Do not worship other gods, any of the gods of the peoples around you.	You shall not go after other gods, of the gods of the peoples who are round about you;

worship: literally "go after" (RSV), a figure often used for "follow, worship, serve" other gods.

6.15   TEV   RSV

TEV	RSV
If you do worship other gods, the LORD's anger will come against you like fire and will destroy you completely, because the LORD your God, who is present with you, tolerates no rivals.	for the LORD your God in the midst of you is a jealous God; lest the anger of the LORD your God be kindled against you, and he destroy you from off the face of the earth.

If you do: TEV has reversed the order of elements in the verse, since the "lest" (meaning "in order that not") refers to verse 14 and not to the first part of 15. The thought is "Do not worship other gods so that God will not be angry." In many languages the idea can be represented more readily with a conditional sentence, as TEV has done.

come against you like fire: the Hebrew verb means "become hot" and is a figurative way of speaking. TEV has tried to carry this idea by the comparison with fire.

completely: literally "from upon the face of the earth" (see RSV), that is, no trace of them will be left upon the surface of the earth (anywhere on earth).

tolerates no rivals: see 4.24.

C H A P T E R   18

SECTION HEADING

The Promise to Send a Prophet (18.14-22): "Moses Promises that the Lord Will Send Prophets to the People."

18.14 TEV	RSV
Then Moses said, "In the land you are about to occupy, people follow the advice of those who practice divination and look for omens, but the LORD your God does not allow you to do this.	For these nations, which you are about to dispossess, give heed to soothsayers and to diviners; but as for you, the LORD your God has not allowed you so to do.

Then Moses said: the words are not in the Hebrew, but the speaker needs to be named, particularly at the beginning of new sections.

In the land you are about to occupy: literally "these nations which you are dispossessing" (see RSV), that is, you will drive out the people who now occupy the land and take their land as your own.

follow the advice of: literally "hear," but in the sense of "listen to," "give heed to" (RSV), "pay attention to."

those who practice divination: the Hebrew verb has the meaning "cause something to make an appearance," and particularly to cause spirits or ghosts of dead people to appear. The word then is used in the general sense of "practice magic" of any kind.

look for omens: the Hebrew word refers to people who practice divination by consulting lots which have been cast.

18.15 TEV	RSV
Instead, he will send you a prophet like me from among your own people, and you are to obey him.P	"The LORD your God will raise up for you a prophet like me from among you, from your brethren—him you shall heed—

Pa prophet...him; or prophets... them.

send: literally "raise up" (RSV), in the sense of cause to appear, make present, which is more readily expressed in English by send.

a prophet like me: the Hebrew word is singular, but the context makes clear that the thought is of a series of prophets appearing one after the other. This is particularly clear in verses 20 and 21. As the TEV note shows, this idea may be expressed more clearly if the plural is used. This verse is cited in the New Testament with the singular (Acts 3.22; 7.37), but that fact should not be allowed to hide the meaning here.

from among your own people: literally "from among you, from your brothers" (see RSV), but that means from among the people of Israel.

[298]

18.16   TEV   RSV
   "On the day that you were   just as you desired of the LORD
gathered at Mount Sinai, you   your God at Horeb on the day of
begged not to hear the LORD speak   the assembly, when you said, 'Let
again or to see his fiery presence me not hear again the voice of the
any more, because you were afraid   LORD my God, or see this great
you would die.   fire any more, lest I die.'

   Mount Sinai: the Hebrew text has Horeb, but see 4.10.
   begged not to hear: TEV has shifted to indirect discourse, while
the Hebrew uses direct discourse in the first person singular. Receptor
language usage should determine which form will express the meaning
more readily.
   his fiery presence: literally "this great fire" (RSV), but the
reference is, of course, to the fire on the mountain that showed the
presence of the LORD.

18.17   TEV   RSV
So the LORD said to me, 'They have   And the LORD said to me, 'They
made a wise request.   have rightly said all that they
                                     have spoken.

   They have made a wise request: this expresses the sense of the
literal "They said well what they said." The RSV "all" is not in the
standard Hebrew text and is probably not original.

18.18   TEV   RSV
I will send them a prophet like   I will raise up for them a
you from among their own people;   prophet like you from among
I will tell him what to say, and   their brethren; and I will put
he^q will tell the people every-   my words in his mouth, and he
thing I command.   shall speak to them all that
                                     I command him.

^{q}a prophet...him...he; or prophets
  ...them...they.

   a prophet: see verse 15.
   I will tell him what to say: this is the meaning of the literal
"I will give (place) words in his mouth" (see RSV).

18.19   TEV   RSV
He will speak in my name, and I^r And whoever will not give heed
will punish anyone who refuses to   to my words which he shall speak
obey him.   in my name, I myself will require
                                     it of him.

^{r}He will speak...and I; or When a
 prophet speaks in my name, I.

   speak in my name: that is, speak as my representative, and the

[299]

meaning is essentially the same as "say what I tell him to say."

    I will punish: literally "I will demand (it) from him" (see RSV), which has the sense "I will hold him accountable"; that is, "I will make him pay the penalty," and the underlying meaning is I will punish him.

18.20 TEV	RSV
But if any prophet dares to speak a message in my name when I did not command him to do so, he must die for it, and so must any prophet who speaks in the name of other gods.'	But the prophet who presumes to speak a word in my name which I have not commanded him to speak, or who speaks in the name of other gods, that same prophet shall die.'

    if any prophet: the conditional sentence, as in TEV, is often an easier structure than the relative clause (RSV "the prophet who..."), but this will depend upon the receptor language.

    dares: "is so bold, insolent, arrogant," that is, "acts without considering the situation or the consequences."

18.21 TEV	RSV
"You may wonder how you can tell when a prophet's message does not come from the LORD.	And if you say in your heart, 'How may we know the word which the LORD has not spoken?'—

    You may wonder: literally "if you say in your heart" (RSV), that is, if you think...(then I will answer). The answer is, of course, given in verse 22. The English You may wonder has the meaning "If you should ask yourself."

18.22 TEV	RSV
If a prophet speaks in the name of the LORD and what he says does not come true, then it is not the LORD's message. That prophet has spoken on his own authority, and you are not to fear him.	when a prophet speaks in the name of the LORD, if the word does not come to pass or come true, that is a word which the LORD has not spoken; the prophet has spoken it presumptuously, you need not be afraid of him.

    it is not the LORD's message: literally "that is a word which the LORD did not speak" (see RSV), but "word" is frequently used to speak of a whole discourse, everything that is said.

    on his own authority: literally "arrogantly," "presumptuously" (RSV), and the Hebrew word is related to the verb translated dares in verse 20. The point is that such a prophet has no regard for the consequences and speaks his own message, rather than the message of God.

    you are not to fear him: it is also possible to understand "you are not to fear what he says."

C H A P T E R   30

SECTION HEADING

Conditions for Restoration and Blessing (30.1-20): "You Must Choose Whether You Will Have Curses or Blessings."

30.1 TEV	RSV
"I have now given you a choice between a blessing and a curse. When all these things have happened to you, and you are living among the nations where the LORD your God has scattered you, you will remember the choice I gave you.	"And when all these things come upon you, the blessing and the curse, which I have set before you, and you call them to mind among all the nations where the LORD your God has driven you,

I have now given you: this refers to chapter 29, where disasters and punishment are promised if the people refuse to keep the covenant which the LORD is making with them. At the same time chapter 30 really continues the warnings and the promises. The first sentence in TEV expresses the idea of the literal "the blessings and the curses which I have set before you." TEV has restructured in order to avoid the complicated structure of the Hebrew. Note, for example, that RSV has a single sentence running through verse 3. It is up to the people to decide whether they will receive blessings (if they keep the covenant) or curses (if they break the covenant).

has scattered: the Hebrew verb has the meaning of "scatter," "disperse," and is used here in a figurative way to speak of being taken in captivity into distant lands.

remember: literally "bring back to your heart," but the "heart" is where thinking takes place, and the sense is "call to mind, recall."

30.2 TEV	RSV
If you and your descendants will turn back to the LORD and with all your heart obey his commands that I am giving you today,	and return to the LORD your God, you and your children, and obey his voice in all that I command you this day, with all your heart and with all your soul;

with all your heart: literally "with all your heart (mind) and with all your soul (life)" (see RSV).

30.3 TEV	RSV
then the LORD your God will have mercy on you. He will bring you back from the nations where he	then the LORD your God will restore your fortunes, and have compassion upon you, and he will

[301]

has scattered you, and he will
make you prosperous again.

gather you again from all the
peoples where the LORD your God
has scattered you.

have mercy on: the Hebrew verb has the meaning "show love for,"
"have compassion on."

bring you back: literally "gather" (RSV), in contrast to "scatter"
in verse 1. TEV has reversed elements and placed the return as prior in
time to the prosperity.

make you prosperous again: the meaning of the Hebrew is not clear.
It can mean "bring back from captivity," "bring about a restoration,"
"change one's condition or fortune from bad to good." TEV has interpreted in this last way, but "prosperous" needs to be understood in a
larger sense than financial prosperity—"to prosper, to be well off, to
be in favorable circumstances."

30.4 TEV	RSV
Even if you are scattered to the farthest corners of the earth, the LORD your God will gather you together and bring you back,	If your outcasts are in the uttermost parts of heaven, from there the LORD your God will gather you, and from there he will fetch you;

the farthest corners of the earth: literally "at the end (or, edge)
of heaven (or, the sky)," but the thought is of that distant point where
earth and sky meet.

bring you back: literally "take you from there," but with the same
sense as bring you back.

30.5 TEV	RSV
so that you may again take pos-session of the land where your ancestors once lived. And he will make you more prosperous and more numerous than your ancestors ever were.	and the LORD your God will bring you into the land which your fathers possessed, that you may possess it; and he will make you more prosperous and numerous than your fathers.

make you more prosperous: the Hebrew verb here means "make things
go well for you," "cause you to have things good," but the sense is
the same as for the verb "prosper" in verse 3.

30.6 TEV	RSV
The LORD your God will give you and your descendants obedient hearts, so that you will love him with all your heart, and you will continue to live in that land.	And the LORD your God will circumcise your heart and the heart of your offspring, so that you will love the LORD your God with all your heart and with all your soul, that you may live.

will give...obedient hearts: literally "will circumcise (your) heart(s)" (RSV), which is a figure. Just as physical circumcision was the sign that the male belonged to the people of God, a spiritual "circumcision of the heart" will make you truly one of the people of God. In many languages this figure cannot be readily retained, and it may be necessary to do as TEV has done: drop the figure and state the meaning directly. One must not forget that "heart" refers to what in English might be referred to as the mind.

with all your heart: see verse 2.

and you will continue to live in that land: literally "so that you may live" (see RSV), but this has the sense "continue to live," and the focus is upon life in the promised land, although in that land is not in the Hebrew text at this point.

30.7 TEV	RSV
He will turn all these curses against your enemies, who hated you and oppressed you,	And the LORD your God will put all these curses upon your foes and enemies who persecuted you.

turn...against: literally "give (or, place)...upon," but the context indicates that the curses are taken from the obedient people of Israel and placed on their enemies.

who hated you and oppressed you: literally "and those hating you who persecuted (or, pursued) you," but in English it is simpler to restructure as TEV has done. The Hebrew verb for "oppressed (persecuted)" means to chase after with the intent of harming.

30.8 TEV	RSV
and you will again obey him and keep all his commands that I am giving you today.	And you shall again obey the voice of the LORD, and keep all his commandments which I command you this day.

obey him: literally "hear the voice of the LORD," but this means to do what he says to do.

30.9 TEV	RSV
The LORD will make you prosperous in all that you do; you will have many children and a lot of livestock, and your fields will produce abundant crops. He will be as glad to make you prosperous as he was to make your ancestors prosperous,	The LORD your God will make you abundantly prosperous in all the work of your hand, in the fruit of your body, and in the fruit of your cattle, and in the fruit of your ground; for the LORD will again take delight in prospering you, as he took delight in your fathers,

make you prosperous: the Hebrew verb means "cause you to have more than enough," that is, so that there is plenty left over. Although it is not the same verb used in verses 3 and 5, the meaning is much the same.

all that you do: literally "all the work of your hand" (see RSV), that is, "all that your hand does," but this is a Hebrew figure for all that you do.

have many children: literally "in the fruit of your womb" (see RSV), which is a figurative way of speaking of having many children.

a lot of livestock: literally "in the fruit of your cattle" (see RSV), which is also figurative.

fields...abundant crops: literally "the fruit of your ground" (see RSV), which applies not only to fruit but to grain, olives, and all kinds of produce.

He will be as glad: the Hebrew has "the LORD will again take delight in" (RSV), and it may be helpful to translate "He will again be as glad."

30.10 TEV	RSV
but you will have to obey him and keep all his laws that are written in this book of his teachings. You will have to turn to him with all your heart.	if you obey the voice of the LORD your God, to keep his commandments and his statutes which are written in this book of the law, if you turn to the LORD your God with all your heart and with all your soul.

but you will have to: the Hebrew uses a conditional ("if," "when"), but this makes a complicated sentence in English. TEV has used an expression that means "(if you want this to happen) you will have to."

30.11 TEV	RSV
"The command that I am giving you today is not too difficult or beyond your reach.	"For this commandment which I command you this day is not too hard for you, neither is it far off.

beyond your reach: literally "far off" (RSV), but in the sense of "unattainable," "impossible to do."

30.12 TEV	RSV
It is not up in the sky. You do not have to ask, 'Who will go up and bring it down for us, so that we can hear it and obey it?'	It is not in heaven, that you should say, 'Who will go up for us to heaven, and bring it to us, that we may hear it and do it?'

sky: in Hebrew the same word is used for sky and heaven, but here the physical location is in focus rather than the dwelling place of God.

30.13   TEV
Nor is it on the other side of
the ocean. You do not have to
ask, 'Who will go across the
ocean and bring it to us, so
that we may hear it and obey it?'

RSV
Neither is it beyond the sea,
that you should say, 'Who will
go over the sea for us, and
bring it to us, that we may
hear it and do it?'

the ocean: the primary reference may be to the Mediterranean Sea,
but other seas and oceans were known.

30.14   TEV
No, it is here with you. You
know it and can quote it, so
now obey it.

RSV
But the word is very near you;
it is in your mouth and in your
heart, so that you can do it.

You know it: literally "in your mouth" (RSV), with the sense "You
are able to speak it."
can quote it: literally "in your heart" (RSV), that is, "in your
mind," "you have memorized it."

30.15   TEV
"Today I am giving you a
choice between good and evil,
between life and death.

RSV
"See, I have set before you
this day life and good, death
and evil.

good and evil: TEV has rearranged the elements to accord with
English patterns of indicating choice. The words refer to the choice
between blessings and curses announced in verse 1.

30.16   TEV
If you obey the commands of the
LORD your God,² which I give you
today, if you love him, obey him,
and keep all his laws, then you
will prosper and become a nation
of many people. The LORD your
God will bless you in the land
that you are about to occupy.

²One ancient translation If you
obey the commands of the LORD
your God; Hebrew does not have
these words.

RSV
If you obey the commandments
of the LORD your God^c which
I command you this day, by
loving the LORD your God, by
walking in his ways, and by
keeping his commandments and
his statutes and his ordinances,
then you shall live and multiply,
and the LORD your God will bless
you in the land which you are
entering to take possession of it.

^{c}Gk: Heb lacks If you obey the
commandments of the LORD your
God

If...your God: as the TEV note shows, these words are not in the
standard Hebrew text, but there is good reason to believe that it was
part of the original Hebrew text and that it was accidentally omitted.

[305]

obey him: literally "walk in his ways" (see RSV), that is, "do what he wants you to do."

all his laws: this summarizes three Hebrew words (RSV "commandments...statutes...ordinances") which refer to laws. It is not necessary to find three words that mean much the same thing.

prosper: literally "live" (RSV), but with the sense of continue to live and enjoy life.

become a nation of many people: literally "become many," but the thought is of the nation as a whole.

30.17 TEV	RSV
But if you disobey and refuse to listen, and are led away to worship other gods,	But if your heart turns away, and you will not hear, but are drawn away to worship other gods and serve them,

you disobey: literally "your heart turns away" (RSV), with the sense of turning the mind against God, that is, rebelling, disobeying.

30.18 TEV	RSV
you will be destroyed—I warn you here and now. You will not live long in that land across the Jordan that you are about to occupy.	I declare to you this day, that you shall perish; you shall not live long in the land which you are going over the Jordan to enter and possess.

I warn you here and now: literally "I declare to you this day" (RSV), but this is a device to intensify the seriousness of the statement, and languages will differ in the way they do this.

30.19 TEV	RSV
I am now giving you the choice between life and death, between God's blessing and God's curse, and I call heaven and earth to witness the choice you make. Choose life.	I call heaven and earth to witness against you this day, that I have set before you life and death, blessing and curse; therefore choose life, that you and your descendants may live,

I am now giving you the choice: see verses 1 and 15.

I call heaven and earth to witness: the idea of calling someone to be a witness in a legal situation is here extended, and heaven and earth are thought of in personal terms. If such personifications are not possible in the receptor language, one may need to find a way of saying something like, "What I am telling you is so important that if heaven and earth could speak, they would speak for me to remind you of the choice they heard you make." The Hebrew adds "that you and your descendants may live" (RSV). TEV omits these words because the same idea is found in this and the following verse.

30.20 TEV	RSV
Love the LORD your God, obey him and be faithful to him, and then you and your descendants will live long in the land that he promised to give your ancestors, Abraham, Isaac, and Jacob."	loving the LORD your God, obeying his voice, and cleaving to him; for that means life to you and length of days, that you may dwell in the land which the LORD swore to your fathers, to Abraham, to Isaac, and to Jacob, to give them."

be faithful: literally "cling to," "hold to," but this has the sense "maintain allegiance to."

then you...will live long: literally "that will be life and length of days" (see RSV), which is a Hebrew way of speaking of living a long time.

CHAPTER 32

SECTION HEADING

Moses' Final Instructions (32.45-52): "Moses Is Told He Is About to Die," "Moses Prepares for Death."

32.45 TEV	RSV
When Moses had finished giving God's teachings to the people,	And when Moses had finished speaking all these words to all Israel,

God's teachings: literally "all these words" (RSV), referring to the teachings that God had commanded him to give to the people of Israel.

32.46 TEV	RSV
he said, "Be sure to obey all these commands that I have given you today. Repeat them to your children, so that they may faithfully obey all of God's teachings.	he said to them, "Lay to heart all the words which I enjoin upon you this day, that you may command them to your children, that they may be careful to do all the words of this law.

Be sure to obey: literally "Set to your heart," but this has the sense of remember them and do them. RSV "Lay to heart" has a similar meaning.

faithfully obey: literally "to take care to do," "guard yourself so that you do."

32.47 TEV	RSV
These teachings are not empty words; they are your very life. Obey them and you will live long in that land across the Jordan that you are about to occupy."	For it is no trifle for you, but it is your life, and thereby you shall live long in the land which you are going over the Jordan to possess."

These teachings: that is what is meant by the literal "this."
empty words: "words with no meaning."
they are your very life: that is, "your life depends on whether or not you obey them."
Obey them and: that is, "If you obey them...."

32.48 TEV	RSV
That same day the LORD said to Moses,	And the LORD said to Moses that very day,

That same day: that is, the day he finished giving God's teachings to the people.

32.49 TEV	RSV
"Go to the Abarim Mountains in the land of Moab opposite the city of Jericho; climb Mount Nebo and look at the land of Canaan that I am about to give the people of Israel.	"Ascend this mountain of the Abarim, Mount Nebo, which is in the land of Moab, opposite Jericho; and view the land of Canaan, which I give to the people of Israel for a possession;

the Abarim Mountains: this refers to the mountain range east of the Dead Sea and the Jordan Valley.
Mount Nebo: this is one of the highest mountains in the Abarim range, and TEV tries to make this clear.

32.50 TEV	RSV
You will die on that mountain as your brother Aaron died on Mount Hor,	and die on the mountain which you ascend, and be gathered to your people, as Aaron your brother died in Mount Hor and was gathered to his people;

die: literally "die...and be gathered to your people" (RSV), which is a figurative way of speaking of death, with the sense of entering the grave or the world of the dead.
Mount Hor: a mountain on the border of Edom, where Aaron died, according to Numbers 20.22; 21.4; 33.37.

32.51 TEV	RSV
because both of you were unfaithful	because you broke faith with me

to me in the presence of the people
of Israel. When you were at the
waters of Meribah, near the town
of Kadesh in the wilderness of
Zin, you dishonored me in the
presence of the people.

in the midst of the people of
Israel at the waters of Meribath-
kadesh, in the wilderness of Zin;
because you did not revere me as
holy in the midst of the people
of Israel.

unfaithful: see Numbers 27.12-14 for a discussion of translation
and other problems in this verse.

32.52 TEV	RSV
You will look at the land from a distance, but you will not enter the land that I am giving the people of Israel."	For you shall see the land before you; but you shall not go there, into the land which I give to the people of Israel."

will not enter: literally "will not go there."

CHAPTER 34

SECTION HEADING

The Death of Moses (34.1-12): "Moses Dies."

34.1 TEV	RSV
Moses went up from the plains of Moab to Mount Nebo, to the top of Mount Pisgah east of Jericho, and there the LORD showed him the whole land: the territory of Gilead as far north as the town of Dan;	And Moses went up from the plains of Moab to Mount Nebo, to the top of Pisgah, which is opposite Jericho. And the LORD showed him all the land, Gilead as far as Dan,

Mount Pisgah: see 32.49. Although it is not certain, Pisgah may
be a prominent peak on Mount Nebo, which is in the Abarim range of
mountains.

34.2 TEV	RSV
the entire territory of Naphtali; the territories of Ephraim and Manasseh; the territory of Judah as far west as the Mediterranean Sea;	all Naphtali, the land of Ephraim and Manasseh, all the land of Judah as far as the western sea,

Mediterranean Sea: this is the meaning of the literal "western
sea." For the location of the territories in this and the next verse,

one should consult a map such as "Division of Canaan" in TEV.

34.3   TEV   RSV
the southern part of Judah; and   the Negeb, and the Plain, that
the plain that reaches from Zoar   is, the valley of Jericho the
to Jericho, the city of palm   city of palm trees, as far as
trees.   Zoar.

     the southern part of Judah: that is, the Negev (RSV "Negeb").
     Zoar: the location is not known, but it must have been a city near
the Dead Sea.

34.4   TEV   RSV
Then the LORD said to Moses,   And the LORD said to him, "This
"This is the land that I prom-   is the land of which I swore
ised Abraham, Isaac, and Jacob   to Abraham, to Isaac, and to
I would give to their descend-   Jacob, 'I will give it to your
ants. I have let you see it, but   descendants.' I have let you
I will not let you go there."   see it with your eyes, but you
                                       shall not go over there."

     See 32.52.

34.5   TEV   RSV
     So Moses, the LORD's servant,   So Moses the servant of the
died there in the land of Moab, as   LORD died there in the land of
the LORD had said he would.   Moab, according to the word of
                                       the LORD,

     the LORD's servant: the term is used in a way that means something
more than "one who worships the LORD." The sense is almost "the LORD's
chosen one," "the intimate friend of the LORD."

34.6   TEV   RSV
The LORD buried him in a valley   and he buried him in the valley
in Moab, opposite the town of   in the land of Moab opposite
Bethpeor, but to this day no   Beth-peor; but no man knows
one knows the exact place of   the place of his burial to this
his burial.   day.

     Bethpeor: the location of the town is not known, but it must be
in Moab, a few miles from Mount Nebo.

34.7   TEV   RSV
Moses was a hundred and twenty   Moses was a hundred and twenty
years old when he died; he was   years old when he died; his
as strong as ever, and his eye-   eye was not dim, nor his natural
sight was still good.   force abated.

he was as strong as ever: literally "his vitality (or, vigor) of life had not slipped away," that is, he had not lost his strength.

34.8   TEV   RSV
The people of Israel mourned for   And the people of Israel wept
him for thirty days in the plains   for Moses in the plains of Moab
of Moab.   thirty days; then the days of
                                        weeping and mourning for Moses
                                        were ended.

mourned for: the Hebrew has "wept for" (RSV) and "the weeping of the ceremony of mourning for." That is to say, we are dealing with personal sorrow and a formal period of mourning, which TEV has summarized in this way.

34.9   TEV   RSV
    Joshua son of Nun was filled   And Joshua the son of Nun
with wisdom, because Moses had ap-   was full of the spirit of wisdom,
pointed him to be his successor.   for Moses had laid his hands upon
The people of Israel obeyed Joshua   him; so the people of Israel
and kept the commands that the   obeyed him, and did as the LORD
LORD had given them through Moses.   had commanded Moses.

filled with wisdom: literally "full of the spirit of wisdom" (RSV). Here "spirit" has reference to ability or capacity and is left implicit in TEV. The Hebrew word for "spirit, wind, breath" has a large number of meanings, including human attitudes and abilities.
    appointed him to be his successor: literally "placed his hands upon him" (see RSV), but this should be understood as a technical figure for appointing or ordaining. The overall thought is that some of the wisdom of Moses is transmitted to Joshua through this act of appointment.

34.10   TEV   RSV
    There has never been a proph-   And there has not arisen a proph-
et in Israel like Moses; the LORD   et since in Israel like Moses,
spoke with him face-to-face.   whom the LORD knew face to face,

like Moses: see 18.18, but Moses is seen as the most important prophet with whom the LORD spoke directly.
    spoke: literally "knew" (RSV), but the point is that the LORD was intimately associated with Moses and spoke directly to him.

34.11   TEV   RSV
No other prophet has ever done   none like him for all the signs
miracles and wonders like those   and the wonders which the LORD
that the LORD sent Moses to   sent him to do in the land of
perform against the king of   Egypt, to Pharaoh and to all

[311]

Deut 34.11

| Egypt, his officials, and the entire country. | his servants and to all his land, |

miracles and wonders: the two Hebrew words refer to the miracles performed in Egypt that showed God's power, and mean much the same thing. It is not necessary to find two words to use in speaking of these miracles.

34.12 TEV	RSV
No other prophet has been able to do the great and terrifying things that Moses did in the sight of all Israel.	and for all the mighty power and all the great and terrible deeds which Moses wrought in the sight of all Israel.

No other prophet has been able: TEV repeats this thought from verse 11, in order to make a separate sentence of verse 12 for the sake of clarity. Often in translation the repetition of a thought will make the meaning clearer for the reader.

the great and terrifying things: literally "all the mighty hand (power) and all the great (things that cause) fear," which refers to the miracles that Moses performed during the period of forty years in the desert.

Selected Bibliography

Childs, Brevard S. 1974. The Book of Exodus (The Old Testament Library). Philadelphia: Westminster.

> One of the best commentaries on any Old Testament book, but not easy to use. The Hebrew is transliterated, and much attention is given to literary and theological problems, but the careful reader will find much help with detailed problems.

Craigie, P. C. 1976. The Book of Deuteronomy (The New International Commentary). Grand Rapids: Eerdmans.

> A helpful introduction followed by comments on individual verses. Many of the questions translators raise are answered, although often quite briefly.

Hyatt, J. P. 1971. Exodus (New Century Bible). London: Oliphants.

> Usually helpful notes on details of the text that may prove troublesome for translators. A knowledge of Hebrew is not presupposed.

Orlinsky, Harry M., editor. 1969. Notes on the New Translation of the Torah. Philadelphia: The Jewish Publication Society of America.

> Helpful notes on details of the text, particularly those accepted in the New Jewish version of the Torah. Knowledge of Hebrew is helpful, but not required.

Rylaarsdam, J. Coert. 1952. The Book of Exodus (The Interpreter's Bible, Volume 1). New York: Abingdon.

> Brief but helpful notes provide more insight about general meaning than about details of interpretation.

Bibliography

Snaith, N. H. 1967. Leviticus and Numbers (The Century Bible, New Edition). London: Nelson.

Many helpful comments on individual words and ancient practices. No knowledge of Hebrew is required.

Speiser, E. A. 1964. Genesis (The Anchor Bible). Garden City, New York: Doubleday.

Contains a good introduction, an independent and rather literal translation, and helpful notes and comments. Does not require a knowledge of Hebrew.

Von Rad, Gerhard. 1961. Genesis: A Commentary (The Old Testament Library). Translated by John H. Marks. Philadelphia: Westminster.

Uses the RSV as its basic text, and no knowledge of Hebrew is required. More help is provided in grasping the general meaning than in understanding details of interpretation.

Glossary

This glossary contains terms which are technical from an exegetical or a linguistic viewpoint. Other terms not defined here may be referred to in a Bible dictionary.

active, active form, active voice. See voice.

command. See imperative.

condition is that which shows the circumstance under which something may be true. In English, a conditional phrase or clause is usually introduced by "if."

conjunctions are words which serve as connectors between words, phrases, clauses, and sentences. "And," "but," "if," "because," etc., are typical conjunctions in English.

connecting link. See connective.

connective is a word or phrase which connects other words, phrases, clauses, etc. See conjunctions.

construction. See structure.

context is that which precedes and/or follows any part of a discourse. For example, the context of a word or phrase in Scripture would be the other words and phrases associated with it in the sentence, paragraph, section, and even the entire book in which it occurs. The context of a term often affects its meaning, so that a word does not mean exactly the same thing in one context that it does in another.

culture is the sum total of the ways of living built up by the people living in a certain geographic area. A culture is passed on from one generation to another, but undergoes development or gradual change.

descriptive is said of a word or phrase which characterizes or describes another term.

direct address, direct discourse. See discourse.

Glossary

discourse is the connected and continuous communication of thought by
  means of language, whether spoken or written. The way in which the
  elements of a discourse are arranged is called discourse structure.
  Direct discourse is the reproduction of the actual words of one
  person quoted and included in the discourse of another person; for
  example, "He declared, '*I will have nothing to do with this man.*'"
  Indirect discourse is the reporting of the words of one person
  within the discourse of another person, but in an altered grammatical
  form rather than as an exact quotation; for example, "He said
  he would have nothing to do with that man."

dynamic equivalence is a type of translation in which the message of
  the original text is so conveyed in the receptor language that the
  response of the receptors is (or, can be) essentially like that of
  the original receptors, or that the receptors can in large measure
  comprehend the response of the original receptors, if, as in certain
  instances, the differences between the two cultures are extremely
  great. See also formal equivalence.

emphasis (emphatic) is the special importance given to an element in a
  discourse, sometimes indicated by the choice of words or by position
  in the sentence. For example, in "Never will I eat pork again,"
  "Never" is given emphasis by placing it at the beginning of the
  sentence.

explicit refers to information which is expressed in the words of a
  discourse. This is in contrast to implicit information. See implicit

figure, figure of speech, or figurative expression involves the use of
  words in other than their literal or ordinary sense, in order to
  bring out some aspect of meaning by means of comparison or asso-
  ciation; for example, "raindrops dancing on the street," or "his
  speech was like thunder."

formal equivalence is a type of translation in which the features of
  form in the source text have been more or less mechanically
  reproduced in the receptor language.

idiom or idiomatic expression is a combination of terms whose meanings
  cannot be understood by adding up the meanings of the parts. "To
  hang one's head," "to have a green thumb," and "behind the eight-
  ball" are English idioms. Idioms almost always lose their meaning
  or convey a wrong meaning when translated from one language to
  another.

imagery. See figure.

imperative refers to forms of a verb which indicate commands or requests.
  In "Go and do likewise," the verbs "go" and "do" are imperatives.
  In most languages, imperatives are confined to the grammatical
  second person; but some languages have corresponding forms for the

[316]

first and third persons. These are usually expressed in English by the use of "may" or "let"; for example, "May we not have to beg!" "Let them work harder!"

implicit (imply, implied) refers to information that is not formally represented in a discourse, since it is assumed that it is already known to the receptor, or evident from the meaning of the words in question. For example, the phrase "the other son" carries with it the implicit information that there is a son in addition to the one mentioned. This is in contrast to explicit information, which is expressly stated in a discourse. See explicit.

indirect discourse. See discourse.

intensive refers to increased emphasis or force in any expression, as when "very" occurs in the phrase "very active," or "highly" in the phrase "highly competitive."

interjections are exclamatory words or phrases, invariable in form, usually used to express emotion. "Hey!" "Oh!" and "Indeed!" are examples of interjections.

literal means the ordinary or primary meaning of a term or expression, in contrast with a figurative meaning. A literal translation is one which represents the exact words and word order of the source language; such a translation frequently is unnatural or awkward in the receptor language.

manuscripts are books, documents, letters, etc., written by hand. Thousands of manuscript copies of various Old and New Testament books still exist but none of the original manuscripts.

noun is a word that names a person, place, thing, idea, etc., and often serves to specify a subject or topic of a discourse.

parallel, parallelism, generally refers to some similarity in the content and/or form of a construction; for example, "The man was blind, and he could not see." The structures that correspond to each other in the two statements are said to be parallel.

particle is a small word whose grammatical form does not change. In English the most common particles are prepositions and conjunctions.

passive, passive form, passive voice. See voice.

person, as a grammatical term, refers to the speaker, the person spoken to, or the person or thing spoken about. First person is the person(s) speaking ("I," "me," "my," "mine," "we," "us," "our," "ours"). Second person is the person(s) or thing(s) spoken to ("thou," "thee," "thy," "thine," "ye," "you," "your," "yours"). Third person is the person(s) or thing(s) spoken about ("he," "she," "it," "his," "her," "them," "their," etc.). The examples here

[317]

given are all pronouns, but in many languages the verb forms
have affixes which indicate first, second, or third person and
also indicate whether they are <u>singular</u> or <u>plural</u>.

<u>personification</u> is a reference to an inanimate object or an abstract
idea as though it were personal and/or animate; as in "Wisdom is
calling out," referring to wisdom as if it were a person.

<u>phrase</u> is a grammatical construction of two or more words, but less than
a complete clause or a sentence. A phrase is usually given a name
according to its function in a sentence, such as "noun phrase,"
"verb phrase," "prepositional phrase," etc.

<u>plural</u> refers to the form of a word which indicates more than one. See
<u>singular</u>.

<u>possessive</u> refers to a grammatical relationship in which one noun or
pronoun is said to "possess" another ("John's car," "his son,"
"their destruction"). See also <u>possessive pronouns</u> under <u>pronouns</u>.

<u>pronouns</u> are words which are used in place of nouns, such as "he," "him,"
"his," "she," "we," "them," "who," "which," "this," "these," etc.
<u>Possessive pronouns</u> are pronouns such as "my," "our," "your,"
"his," etc., which indicate possession.

<u>prose</u> is the ordinary form of spoken or written language, without the
special forms and structure of meter and rhythm which are characteristic of poetry.

<u>qualifier</u> is a term which limits the meaning of another term.

<u>receptor</u> is the person(s) receiving a message. The <u>receptor language</u> is
the language into which a translation is made. For example, in a
translation from Hebrew into German, Hebrew is the source language
and German is the receptor language. The <u>receptor culture</u> is the
culture of the people for whom a translation is made, especially
when it differs radically from the culture of the people for whom
the original message was written. See <u>culture</u>.

<u>redundant</u> refers to anything which is entirely predictable from the
context.

<u>relative clause</u> is a dependent clause which qualifies the object to
which it refers. In "the man whom you saw," the clause "whom you
saw" is relative because it relates to and qualifies "man."

<u>restructure</u> is to reconstruct or rearrange. See <u>structure</u>.

<u>rhetorical</u> refers to forms of speech which are employed to highlight or
make more attractive some aspect of a discourse. A <u>rhetorical
question</u>, for example, is not designed to elicit an answer but to
make an emphatic statement.

sarcasm (sarcastic) is an ironical and frequently contemptuous manner of
    discourse in which what is said is intended to express its opposite;
    for example, "That was a wise thing to do!" when intended to convey
    the meaning, "That was a stupid thing to do!"

sentence is a grammatical construction composed of one or more clauses
    and capable of standing alone.

singular refers to the form of a word which indicates one thing or
    person, in contrast to plural, which indicates more than one. See
    plural.

structure is the systematic arrangement of the elements of language,
    including the ways in which words combine into phrases, phrases
    into clauses, and clauses into sentences. Because this process may
    be compared to the building of a house or a bridge, such words as
    structure and construction are used in reference to it. To separate
    and rearrange the various components of a sentence or other unit of
    discourse in the translation process is to restructure it.

style is a particular or a characteristic manner in discourse. Each
    language has certain distinctive stylistic features which cannot be
    reproduced literally in another language. Within any language,
    certain groups of speakers may have their characteristic discourse
    styles, and among individual speakers and writers, each has his
    own style.

subject is one of the major divisions of a clause, the other being the
    predicate. Typically the subject is a noun phrase. It should not be
    confused with semantic "agent."

symbol is a form, whether linguistic or nonlinguistic, which is arbitrar-
    ily and conventionally associated with a particular meaning. For
    example, the word "cross" is a linguistic symbol, referring to a
    particular object. Similarly, within the Christian tradition, the
    cross as an object is a symbol for the death of Jesus.

synonyms are words which are different in form but similar in meaning,
    as "boy" and "lad." Expressions which have essentially the same
    meaning are said to be synonymous. No two words are completely
    synonymous.

textual refers to the various Greek and Hebrew manuscripts of the
    Scriptures. Textual problems arise when it is difficult to
    reconcile or to account for conflicting forms of the same text in
    two or more manuscripts. See also manuscripts.

transitionals are words or phrases which mark the connections between
    related events. Some typical transitionals are "next," "then,"
    "later," "after this," "when he arrived."

Glossary

transliteration is representing in the receptor language the approximate
    sounds or letters of words occurring in the source language, rather
    than translating their meaning; for example, "Amen" from the Hebrew
    or the title "Christ" from the Greek.

verbs are a grammatical class of words which express existence, action,
    or occurrence, as "be," "become," "run," "think," etc.

voice in grammar is the relation of the action expressed by a verb to
    the participants in the action. In English and many other languages
    the active voice indicates that the subject performs the action
    ("John hit the man"), while the passive voice indicates that the
    subject is being acted upon ("the man was hit").

vowels were not originally included in the Hebrew system of writing;
    they were added later as marks associated with the consonants.

wordplay (play on words) in a discourse is the use of the similarity in
    the sounds of two words to produce a special effect.

Index

This index includes concepts, key words, and terms for which the Guide contains a discussion useful for translators.